International
Perspectives on
Homelessness

Recent Titles in
Contributions in Sociology

International Perspectives on Homelessness

Edited by
VALERIE POLAKOW
and
CINDY GUILLEAN

Contributions in Sociology, Number 135

GREENWOOD PRESS
Westport, Connecticut • London

Library of Congress Cataloging-in-Publication Data

International perspectives on homelessness / edited by Valerie Polakow and Cindy Guillean.
     p. cm—(Contributions in sociology, no. 135 ISSN 0084–9278)
   Includes bibliographical references and index.
   ISBN 0–313–30855–1 (alk. paper)
   1. Homelessness. 2. Homelessness—Cross-cultural studies. I. Polakow, Valerie. II.
Guillean, Cindy. III. Series.
HV4493.H654   2001
362.5—dc21   00–049090

British Library Cataloguing in Publication Data is available.

Library of Congress Catalog Card Number: 00–049090
ISBN: 0–313–30855–1
ISSN: 0084–9278

First published in 2001

Greenwood Press, 88 Post Road West, Westport, CT 06881
An imprint of Greenwood Publishing Group, Inc.
www.greenwood.com

Printed in the United States of America

The paper used in this book complies with the
Permanent Paper Standard issued by the National
Information Standards Organization (Z39.48–1984).

10 9 8 7 6 5 4 3 2 1

Contents

Introduction

VALERIE POLAKOW AND CINDY GUILLEAN

What is the meaning of homelessness at the dawn of the twenty-first century? What are the subtle but all-encompassing differences between placelessness and homelessness; between those who live *in* the streets and those *of* the streets? What are the discourses that states use to construct homelessness—a behavioral pathology and asocial lifestyle or a structural outcome of inequality, poverty, and shrinking or deficient social policies? What does the prevalence of homelessness amid affluence and growing globalization of markets tell us about social citizenship rights in different regions of the world—in countries with long-established democracies as well as those that have recently experienced major transformations in their political and economic structures? These are some of the compelling questions that the authors of this international volume explore, as they seek to illuminate the causes of homelessness and develop both a critique of existing national policies as well as recommendations for change.

International Perspectives on Homelessness spans four distinct regions of the globe—Europe, Australia, the Americas, and Africa—and includes eleven countries. The organization of the volume is structured to reflect the scope and magnitude of global homelessness. By beginning with an analysis of homelessness in some of the wealthiest democracies in Europe, Australia, and the United States—where resources are abundant and the impact of global capitalism on domestic infrastructures is increasingly apparent—the reader is invited to consider the consequences of neoliberal market policies in affluent countries, before shifting to an analysis of such impacts on countries in Latin America and Africa which face a confluence of additional political challenges.

Each author in this volume documents the conditions of homelessness within the context of globalization, national political agendas, national housing policies, and domestic infrastructures that shape the realities of homelessness, poverty, and social exclusion. While the problem of homelessness persists across diverse regions of the world, the damaging impact on individuals—children, women, and men—presents a unique face in each of the countries represented, so that each chapter unravels the particular threads of a national policy that, to greatly varying degrees, denies or ignores the fundamental rights of its own citizens and residents.

The first chapter of the volume begins with a comprehensive introduction to "the changing face of homelessness" that has taken place across Europe, and frames the sociopolitical context for homelessness in the countries of the fifteen-member European Union. The Nordic countries, generally regarded as the most progressive in terms of universal social policies and social citizenship rights, are critically examined in terms of national discourses and shrinking social policies. Social rights and housing policies in Sweden are analyzed in relation to the public imaging of homeless people and the power relations that reproduce homelessness. In Denmark, social policy is analyzed as a discursive practice that legitimizes declining social supports in the current welfare state, a discourse that focuses on the social-psychological characteristics of the homeless population and not on structural causes of exclusion and marginalization. Germany, despite great wealth and a "success story" of good overall housing provisions, has left many homeless people living in poverty and socially marginalized. Access barriers, cuts in the social sector, and declining public housing supports and interventions erode housing provisions for vulnerable groups, including homeless children and women fleeing from domestic violence. The author argues that for homelessness to be reduced significantly, the state must adhere to urgent social responsibilities involving prevention and action. The case of Greece is presented as an example of a Southern European country with no statutory obligation to provide social housing, where homelessness has been recognized as a social problem only since the 1990s. Previously family solidarity and family safety nets filled the gaps left by deficient social welfare provisions. Homelessness in England, examined through the prism of a social exclusion framework, points to a shrinking social housing supply with restricted access, as rising income inequality, market-driven resource restrictions, welfare policy changes, isolation, and marginalization increase the vulnerability to homelessness.

From Europe, the focus shifts to Australia, where the dispossession of aboriginal peoples continues to contest European policy perspectives. Lack of housing, poverty, and citizen rights are analyzed where homelessness is viewed as a growing social, economic, and human rights problem requiring committed government action, public support, and genuine empowerment of the homeless. The Americas, including the United States, Argentina, and Brazil, presents diverse and disturbing realities. In the United States, vast income inequalities, persistent family and child poverty, minimum-wage no-benefit unstable jobs, and a declining supply of affordable housing all form the backdrop of Draconian welfare policy changes and benefit cuts resulting in a rising tide of homelessness in the new, "de-welfared" state. Homelessness and alternative housing policies are examined in Argentina, with a particular focus on the urban expulsion of low-income people as the city becomes a center for transnational investments and globalized markets. A working model of a grassroots housing organization is presented as an alternative, self-management housing solution. Brazil, recently returned to democracy, is examined in terms of the impact of social policies on homelessness. The rights of the excluded and questions about whether the poor are merely "paper citizens" are discussed in the context of neoliberal policies, with a particular focus on violence against street children.

The volume concludes with two chapters that map the terrain of shelter and homelessness in two African countries: Kenya and South Africa. Housing policies and practices in postcolonial Kenya are analyzed, key homeless constituencies are discussed, and their lived realities are portrayed: urban squatters, the rural landless, street children, single mothers, disabled and HIV-AIDS victims, and displaced persons and refugees fleeing from war, famine, and ethnic violence. In postapartheid South Africa, the political significance of housing is examined, and the lack of fit between the form in which housing is delivered and the actual "on the ground" housing needs of poor families is explored. Housing policies and shelter needs are graphically depicted through ethnographic cases of diverse African households.

Homelessness is a fundamental existential dislocation, or, as Toni Morrison tells us, it is to exist "on the hem of life" . . . where "there is no place to go . . . the end of something, an irrevocable, physical fact, defining and complementing our metaphysical condition" (Morrison 1970, 18). The geography of placelessness and the meaning of home and the right to housing are urgent postmodern realities. The complex conditions, causes, and forms of international homelessness presented by the expert authors of this volume raise vital policy and practice issues and recommendations. We hope that this book challenges the reader to further discussion, understanding, and action.

NOTE

The editors would like to thank Chris Tee Weixelman for her help in preparing the tables and the Index for this volume.

REFERENCE

Morrison, T. 1970. *The Bluest Eye*. New York: Pocket Books.

EUROPE

The Changing Face of Homelessness in Europe

DRAGANA AVRAMOV

HOUSING THE POOR IN EUROPE

This chapter identifies the difficulties and obstacles that poor and disadvantaged groups in Europe have in accessing and maintaining adequate housing and discusses the impact of housing policies on social exclusion and segregation. Similarities and differences in West and East European countries are identified on the basis of the data from the EUROSTAT Household Panel Study and national statistical offices. In the first part, the impact of housing affordability, availability and security on the quality of life of low-income citizens is documented. In the second part, the socially vulnerable groups and areas of policy action in advanced welfare systems are identified and analyzed.

IDENTIFICATION OF THE PROBLEM: AFFORDABILITY, SUPPLY AND SECURITY OF TENURE

Difficulties that low-income people encounter in accessing and maintaining a dwelling are associated with high costs for rent, maintenance, water, fuel and power, charges which leave them with a low disposable income for other basic needs. High costs, amplified by the mismatch between the demand that exceeds the supply of affordable standard quality housing, keep people in poverty—particularly the elderly, single-person households, one-income families, and single parents—and prove to be a serious obstacle for young adults and socially disadvantaged groups who try to access their first independent dwellings.

Disproportionately high housing costs, inadequate housing conditions of socially disadvantaged households, and problem housing estates generate living conditions that are not compatible with human dignity, but conducive to material deprivation, conflict within families, vandalism and crime in local communities, loosening of social bonds, and detachment from mainstream social values and norms. For the minority of people with multiple personal problems, social exclusion may result in housing exclusion in its extreme form—homelessness.

THE COST OF HOUSING AS A BASIC NEED

In the majority of advanced market economies housing costs account for the second largest share of consumption in an average household. Housing as a basic need engulfs on average 22% of the family budget, while food takes up 23%. Expenditures on food generally comprise the most important household budget item in Southern European countries, followed immediately by housing-related costs (gross rent, fuel, electricity, and construction). In the northern countries, housing tends to be the biggest expenditure for an average household. Over the past two decades the overall trend has been an increase in the share of housing costs, and a rise in prices has been sharper than for other basic needs (EUROSTAT 1996a).

Low-income people, particularly lone parent families, single persons, and the elderly, find not only that housing is the largest expenditure, but also that they are obliged to spend proportionately more on housing than more affluent people. For example, in Italy the lowest income households spend as much as 26 percent of their income on housing, while the highest income groups spend only 16 percent. In Belgium, families and single people who have no work-related income but are living on welfare benefits may have to spend as much as one-half of their income on rented accommodation in old housing in run-down neighborhoods (Avramov 1995a). In market economies, retired people spend proportionally more on housing-related costs than any other socioeconomic group.

In countries in transition to market economies, rents and housing-related costs (traditionally kept low in planned economies) are on the rise. Two basic needs, food and housing, swallow half of household incomes, as they do in other European countries. However, in transition countries, food is a much more important household budget item than housing. In Hungary, for example, food accounts for 34 percent of the average budget, and housing for 14 percent (Hungarian Central Statistical Office 1996).

While costs for food and housing increased in transition countries in all income categories, the proportion of household resources spent on food and housing by those belonging to the lowest income category are considerably higher than in highest income households. The total expenditure for these two basic needs stands at 54 percent for the lowest income groups and at 38 percent for the affluent in Hungary (Hungarian Central Statistical Office 1996).

The deregulation of the state-owned housing sector and an emerging housing market have been associated with massive sales of housing to sitting tenants at conditions more favorable than on the free market. Simultaneously, with the privatization of the public housing stock, there has been a rise in housing-related costs, namely fuel, electricity, water, and communal charges, which have affected all socioeconomic categories. Between 1989 and 1994, housing costs increased from 10 percent to 14 percent of expenditures in an average Hungarian household (Avramov 1995b).

In most transition countries, a large part of the state-owned housing stock was in bad condition. After it was sold to sitting tenants at below-market prices, an adequate maintenance system was not established. Hence, in recent years, there have been difficulties with maintenance and further deterioration of the formerly stateowned multiapartment buildings that are now joint property of the owners of individual flats. Even under quasi-market conditions, some of the poorest households in formerly state-owned housing could not make use of the right to buy. They now occupy the tiny residual part of social housing the ownership of which was transferred to the local authorities. With the sharp decline in the supply of newly constructed social housing, access to housing for low-income people wanting to set up their first independent household has become particularly costly.

As a basic need, housing represents permanent costs, and these leave little or no place for substitution. The standard of living and quality of life of people are largely determined by housing conditions and the disposable income left after making housing payments. For the less affluent, the impact of rising housing costs is twofold: they are confined to substandard, often overcrowded, housing, and after paying housing-related costs, they do not have enough to meet other basic needs. High rents keep many in forced cohabitation in crammed apartments in old housing with poor amenities. Lower income families and single persons dependent on market rents are forced to make serious savings on food, health care, medication, child care, transportation, communication, education, household amenities, clothing, and leisure.

After paying housing costs, socially disadvantaged groups, particularly the elderly, single people, lone parents, the unemployed, and the disabled, may find themselves isolated from family and friends because they cannot afford communication and transportation costs. This isolation may lead to the weakening of social ties, detachment from others, and loneliness. High housing costs may prevent families from moving out of dilapidated housing estates and crime-ridden neighborhoods in which children and adolescents are exposed to the world of drugs, prostitution, and major criminal activity which suck youth into the world of street counterculture. High housing costs may keep estranged couples and young adults in forced cohabitation, leading to high stress levels and even domestic violence. Lack of affordable housing may keep young adults in forced cohabitation with their parents prolonging the state of "sociological child-hood" and postponing the formation of new households and families. High housing costs and lack of community care for individuals with mental disabilities, personality disorders, or substance abuse problems may be conducive to homelessness.

In addition to problems with personal accommodation, including shortage of space, leaky roof, damp or rot, and a lack of basic amenities and adequate heating facilities, one major concern of European citizens is vandalism or neighborhood crime. The most widespread problem with accommodation in the United Kingdom is insecurity in household environments. As many as three of every ten households in the United Kingdom experience problems with their accommodation as a result of neighborhood vandalism or crime (EUROSTAT 1998a).

HOUSING SUPPLY

In the majority of advanced market economies, there is no physical shortage of housing units on the general housing market. Structure of the housing stock in terms of dwelling size, quality, and equipment clearly shows marked improvements in housing conditions in Northern, Western, and Southern Europe in recent decades. Housing statistics that report on the quantity and quality of the housing stock indicate no crude shortage of dwellings and a shift toward an emphasis on the quality and growth of the owner-occupied sector (European Commission 1998a).

While at the national level the number of dwellings exceeds by far the number of households in almost all advanced market economies,[1] at the subnational level, in all countries, there are regions with a high concentration of secondary residences, vacant rural dwellings, and empty apartments and regions—particularly urban—with varying degrees of housing shortage on the market. There is a generalized shortage of affordable rented housing of decent quality and reasonable security of tenure. The problems of accessing housing in advanced market economies occur primarily for the poor who have too little income to afford the standard quality housing available on the market.

Furthermore, there is also a mismatch between the structure of the housing stock and household dynamics. The housing market adapted swiftly to households wanting large, high-quality housing. It did not address the need for small, moderate-price housing for an ever-growing number of one-person households. The housing market is not tailored to meet the housing needs of single young adults and the single elderly who may be in need of supported housing. In Belgium, Denmark, Germany, France, and the Netherlands, for example, on the average, three of every ten households consist of one person, but only one of every ten dwellings consists of one or two rooms.[2] Young adults under the age of 30 who establish an independent household spend proportionately more on

Figure 1.1
Owner-Occupied, Social and Private Rented Sectors, 1990 (percentage of the total housing stock)

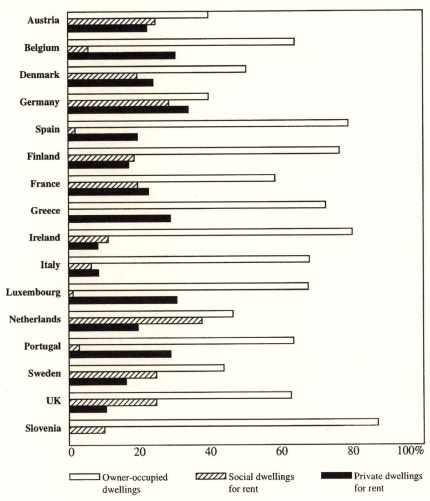

Source: Avramov 1998; data for Slovenia: Duffy 1998.

rent than average households. In Belgium, for example, single young people spend one-third of their budget on rent, while other types of households use less than one-fourth of the household income on rent.

In many European countries, particularly in Southern and Eastern Europe, low-income families are especially vulnerable to overcrowding. In Portugal, Italy, and Greece, one of every four households is living in overcrowded conditions with more than one person per room. As a rule, in Northern and

Western Europe, the proportion of households living in overcrowded conditions stands below 10 percent. In the Netherlands, only one of every 100 households occupies an overcrowded dwelling. Although the magnitude of the phenomenon varies significantly from one country to another, income level and employment status are the key variables of vulnerability everywhere. On the average, in the 15 European Union countries, 21 percent of the unemployed and 16 percent of low-income households experience overcrowding (EUROSTAT 1998a).

In planned economies there has traditionally been a severe shortage of housing, and overcrowding in urban dwellings is still widespread. It is estimated that in Poland there is a shortage of two million dwellings. The inadequate supply in times of planned economies is exacerbated by a sharp reduction in house building in the 1990s throughout Eastern and Central Europe. In Poland, by 1995, housing construction had fallen to one-third of its rate in the late 1980s. In Moldova, in the early 1990s, house building was reduced by 70 percent (Duffy 1998).

Access to Home Ownership

Two average incomes or one high income from stable employment are necessary to realize home ownership under standard market conditions. Most European citizens are able to fulfill this requirement at some stage in their lives. The percentage of owner-occupiers has been increasing throughout Europe in recent decades. In Western Europe the proportion of owner-occupied dwellings ranges between 38 percent in Germany, at the lower end of the scale, and 80 percent in Ireland, at the upper end (see Figure 1.1). In some transition countries, in which public housing was sold at below-market prices, home ownership has become more widespread than in advanced market economies. In Slovenia, for example, nine of every ten households own the dwelling they occupy.

A significant proportion of the unemployed, people with casual work, the quasi-employed and underemployed, single persons, and one-parent families, however, are not able to secure sufficient resources to buy or provide the necessary guarantees to access loans or mortgages. The disadvantaged are dependent on the rental market rather than on the general housing market. For some people rented accommodation is a transitional choice or a temporary necessity; others may depend all their lives on the rental market, be it social or private.

HOUSING OPTIONS OF POOR AND DISADVANTAGED GROUPS

Opportunities for the poor and disadvantaged groups to access and maintain a stable residence in standard quality accommodation are largely determined by the supply of rented housing and income supplements to cover rent and housing-related costs. Access to publicly funded housing with protected rents and access to housing benefits for tenants in private-rented housing play a pivotal role in

Table 1.1
Households Receiving Housing Allowance (percentage of total households)

	1980	1985	1990	1995
Denmark	12.7	15.2	18.5	22.0
France	10.5	21.7	21.3	26.7
Netherlands	8.0	13.0	16.0	14.1
Finland	15.8	13.7	12.6	18.1
United Kingdom	16.0	22.0	17.0	20.0

Source: Avramov 1996, on the basis of data from European Commission.

making housing affordable. The regulatory framework for private rented housing, particularly protection of tenants from excessive rent increases, unwarranted notices to quit, and evictions is among the most important of housing policy instruments.

Conditions on the private housing market do not adjust spontaneously to the needs of weak competitors, those who have low incomes, or other social disadvantages. They are modified by state intervention in the housing domain. Indeed, in the European advanced market economies, policies and measures to facilitate access to housing form a standard instrument of social protection. The level of financial commitment and types of state intervention in the housing system vary according to specific policy measures and target groups. Policies are translated into measures of indirect subsidies to first-time home buyers—by means of advantageous interest rates and tax relief, and tax abatement for the construction of rented accommodation—and direct investments into social rented housing, rent allowances, subsidies, housing improvement, and urban renewal grants. These measures are either targeted specifically at low-income households and other vulnerable groups such as the disabled, elderly, immigrants, refugees and ethnic minorities, or at groups identified as vulnerable and who are granted preferential access to various forms of housing assistance.

Forms of state involvement in the housing sector, as well as the amount of public resources invested, vary remarkably. They are reflected *inter alia* in differences in the ownership structure of the housing stock (see Figure 1.1) and in numbers of tenants receiving housing allowances (see Table 1.1). As a rule, countries in which state involvement is high have a large stock of social rented housing and a generalized system of income replacements and housing benefits.

Housing Allowance

Housing allowance is the most effective means of lowering housing costs for low- and middle-income households and facilitating access to housing for new households. The vast majority of households receiving a housing allowance in Denmark, France, or Finland live in rented accommodations. In some countries this allowance can be granted irrespective of family composition and type of tenure. In Finland, for example, students are also eligible for housing allowance, and indeed they account for 20 percent of allowance recipients.

Since the early 1980s, a growing proportion of households receive housing allowances. However, the increase in number of recipients was frequently associated with the decline in the real value of the allowance. In many countries the housing allowance did not follow an increase in rent—particularly in private-rented accommodation—or in utility costs.

Housing allowance, subsidy, and housing improvement grants for low-income households, disabled persons, the elderly, foreign residents, refugees, and ethnic minorities are built into the social legislation of several market economies. However, as a rule, some social rights, including housing benefits, are discretionary. The social legislation includes sets of principles and rules of procedure for protection of economically weak groups. But social welfare assistance laws leave much room for interpretation. The temporary decrease in the number of households receiving housing allowance in the early 1990s in the United Kingdom, France, and Finland—where recession, deterioration of the labor market, and slowdown of household consumption occurred like elsewhere in Europe—does not reflect a decline in the number of needy households but a decline in the state provision to the needy (Table 1.1).

Level of benefits may vary greatly within the same normative system in one country due to the differences in the criteria used by local authorities to assess needs. A survey of 100 welfare services in Sweden showed a high degree of variation in the way they estimated the degree of need and determined the level of entitlements of their clients. Many European countries, particularly in Eastern, Central and Southern Europe, have not yet introduced a generalized system of housing allowance, or such benefits are granted to a negligible proportion of the needy.

Social-Rented Housing

The social goal of publicly funded, non-profit, or limited-profit housing is to assist lower income groups to access and maintain affordable accommodation. Many European countries (e.g., Belgium, France, Germany, and Finland) have determined income ceilings which exclude people from accessing social housing if they are considered able enough to enter other housing sectors.

There are, however, exceptions—some Nordic countries, the Netherlands, the UK, and Ireland do not apply a system of income threshold to measure inclusion and exclusion from social housing. In some countries, social housing is established as a universal service of public interest. In order to avoid social segregation in Sweden, Denmark, and Norway, for example, access to publicly funded housing is not reserved for specific target groups, and there is no income ceiling for access. However, all these countries have specific social priority criteria or reserve quotas of dwellings which local authorities, other representatives of governments, or housing associations can allocate to households in poverty or in difficulty. The universal function of social-rented housing is thus combined with some priority, be it statutory or discretional, given to specific vulnerable groups such as the homeless, disabled, low-income households, single parents, divorced people, large families, the aged, immigrants, ethnic groups, and minorities.

The composition of social landlords varies among countries, as does the ownership and control of publicly funded or co-funded housing. Landlords can be governments, local authorities, public corporations, or housing associations, and ownership and control can be public, semi-public, or private. However, social landlords share the same goal: to promote access to housing for low- and medium-income groups. All are limited-profit or non-profit organizations. The allocation system varies considerably among European countries: it depends on whether or not income ceilings determine access to social housing, and it varies according to group targeting, terms of preferential treatment, and methods used to guarantee priority allocation to those identified as socially disadvantaged or in difficulty.

However, one generalization can be made: regardless of policy rhetoric about the aims of social housing, it is ultimately the relationship between the size of the public-rented housing stock and the proportion of households in housing need which reveals whether social housing performs the function of an open public service, whether it is a marginal sector serving the meritorious poor and some disadvantaged groups, or whether it is providing residual housing for problem groups.

Netherlands is the country with the largest publicly funded housing for rent— the social sector accounts for 36 percent of the housing stock (see Figure 1.1). In Germany, the UK, Sweden, and Austria, one in four dwellings are social housing rentals. Only in the minority of advanced market economies does the supply of publicly funded housing with protected rents stand at below 10 percent of total housing stock. Belgium and Luxembourg are the two Western European countries with the smallest supply of social rented housing. Southern European countries, for example Spain, Portugal, and Italy, have traditionally had a marginal publicly funded housing sector. Greece stands out as the only market economy with a nonexistent social-rental housing stock. In these countries, fiscal benefits and advantageous loans targeted at first-time homebuyers are the main or even sole form of state allocation of resources.

The size of the public rental housing stock, system of allocation of social housing, and mobility of tenants determine whether there is a social mix in publicly funded housing or a concentration of socially disadvantaged tenants. It may be said that in the Netherlands almost "everybody" has passed through public housing at some stage in his or her life. There is a wide consensus that the sector provides an open public service. As a rule, tenants in social-rented housing are not stigmatized. By contrast, when social housing is reduced to residual housing estates earmarked for disadvantaged groups, it may become part of the problem rather than a solution to social exclusion. Tenants may be stigmatized and segregated simply by living in social housing that shelters the unemployed, non-earner groups, and difficult tenants.

In recent years, the trend in some countries has been a rise of income ceiling required to access social housing, although there was no substantial increase in the size of the social housing stock. The effect of the enlargement of the number of eligible households is that the allocation system tended to push individuals with multiple problems out of the system of standard housing protection towards crisis intervention and provision of accommodation in emergency shelters for homeless people.

When there is a shortage of social housing, it is difficult to pursue a policy of balanced composition of tenants and reach two goals: housing those who are most needy and achieving a social mix. In many countries there is a high concentration of "ultra social" tenants in lower-quality, old social housing estates while new, better-quality social housing is allocated to medium-income households. Even though there may be clear legal or administrative guidelines for registration on waiting lists and social priority criteria for the selection of applicants, the system may be tilted in favor of those seen by providers as more meritorious or who pose a lesser financial risk for social landlords. The cost of protected rents and the risk of unpaid rent are disincentives for providers to allocate housing to "ultra social" tenants. A survey in Belgium has shown that only one-third of social dwellings are allocated in accordance with the adopted social criteria.

In all countries in transition to market economies, housing privatization of the formerly state-owned housing stock has changed the ownership structure in the 1990s substantially. In several countries housing privatization started prior to the transition to market economies, but it is only in recent years that the process was remarkably accelerated. It is also in recent years that the "right to buy" legislation has affected the ownership structure in large urban areas.

The privatization of housing started in Hungary in the late 1980s and it was more widespread in the countryside. By the mid-1990s, almost half of the housing stock was passed into private ownership, and the fastest privatization occurred in urban areas. In Budapest, the share of publicly owned housing fell from 50 percent to 17 percent of the housing stock over the recent four-year period. Dwellings were sold under special terms at prices and loan conditions more favorable than on the market—sales price per one square meter was one quarter of the estimated market price. As a result, by 1995 the share of the housing stock owned by the local authorities in Hungary had fallen to 6 percent. In Lithuania, less than 5 percent of housing remains in the public sector.

This marginal housing stock, owned by the local authorities, to which protected rents are applied is expected to serve as social housing for the disadvantaged. The stock available to the poor that can be allocated on social grounds has become minimal in most transition countries and is considerably below levels maintained in most Northern and Western European countries. A generalization may be made regarding social-rented housing in transition economies:

it has become residual housing, which as a rule, provides poor quality, poorly equipped, and badly maintained housing for the severely deprived tenants.

Although it may be concluded that in many European countries it is becoming increasingly difficult for new households to access social housing of standard quality, it may be said that the security of sitting tenants is high. Once tenants move into publicly funded housing, they enjoy a high degree of protection—as a rule they benefit from stable public assistance through protected rents or housing allowances and have a high security of tenure. Housing inclusion of the less fortunate, who may be on waiting lists for social housing for years or who are socially disqualified from public support, depends on the private-rented market.

Private-Rented Housing

Groups served by the private-rented sector are socially very heterogeneous. The market tends to polarize: on the one hand there is an abundant offer of high-quality, spacious, expensive private lettings, and on the other a scarce supply of standard quality affordable housing is for rent. Groups served by the top segment of the private rental market are "footloose," more advantaged people who, due to a lifestyle choice, do not want to buy and are not interested in the long-term security of tenancy contracts. In the lower segment are young people in training or in their first employment (who are eventually expected to save enough money to become home buyers), and on the bottom are individuals or families too poor to access home ownership and too marginalized to obtain access to social housing.

In many European countries like Germany, France, the Netherlands, or Denmark, the overwhelming majority of young households live in rented accommodations. In Germany eight of every ten households in which the reference person is below the age of 30 are renting (EUROSTAT 1998a). In recent years young adults are becoming increasingly more dependent on their parents to help them acquire their first independent housing. In Germany two of every ten young households receive financial help from relatives or friends.

Difficulties which young people encounter throughout Europe in accessing a stable job imply that, for many, private lettings are a necessary temporary solution. In the face of insecurity in the labor market, young people seem to be more cautious and tend to postpone making long-term financial commitments associated with a mortgage or housing loan. First, independent housing is increasingly rented. In Finland in 1991, three of every ten people who formed a new household were first-time home buyers, and by 1995, only two of ten ventured into purchasing their first accommodation (Hannikainen and Kärkkäinen 1998).

Young adults are dependent on the rental market more than any other age group. They are most affected by a shortage of medium-cost rental dwellings and more particularly of small housing units. It is this part of the housing market that traditionally serves young people in early stages of independence and family formation. Young households starting a family experience difficulties in the private rental market not only because of high rents but also because private landlords often discriminate against families with small children. For private landlords, children are frequently seen as a hazard—they make noise, can disturb neighbors, and spoil property.

There is a general shortage of single-occupancy rooms for the unemployed and those with casual or low-paying jobs. There is a widespread shortage of housing for students. In Sweden, a country with a generous housing policy, there is a shortage of student housing in 13 of 30 university towns (Sahlin 1998).

People living on unemployment or welfare benefits find themselves competing for private lettings in the substandard segment of the housing market. The poor and socially marginalized cannot access good quality housing: their housing options are scarce, and housing security low. In many advanced market economies, and in all transition countries, there is a shortage of low- and medium-price lettings, and housing allowance is either too low to cover the cost of rent in private rented dwellings or is not granted to tenants in the private sector. Under conditions of high demand for rental accommodation, private landlords tend to give preference to short-term tenancies, which enables them to increase rents every time a contract expires. Those tenants who have low social mobility are at a clear disadvantage and find themselves under permanent housing stress.

In transition economies, the private-rented sector is barely emerging. It is small and under new, largely unregulated market conditions; it supplies accommodation mainly for the better-off transient population.

THE REGULATORY FRAMEWORK: RENT CONTROL AND SECURITY OF TENANTS IN PRIVATE-RENTED HOUSING

In all countries, but particularly in those in which the rental sector consists predominantly of private lettings (see Figure 1.2), regulations regarding rent control and protection of tenants from arbitrary notice to quit are an important part of the housing protection system. Emphasis on legislation, encouraged by financial incentives, is the main instrument to address the interests of both tenants in private-rented accommodation and landlords. Routes to balanced protection of tenants and landlords differ sharply among European countries. The debate about rent control and security of tenure is often addressed in terms of advocacy for no public regulation, on the one hand, and calls for heavy regulation on the other hand. In fact, in European advanced market economies, just as there are rules and regulations in the labor market, there is no "free" unregulated housing market either. However, the regulatory framework of private-rented housing varies considerably: control may be set for one or more areas but not for all; may be targeted at specific types of lettings in terms of age, surface, or quality; and may be foreseen as a transitional rather than long-term measure. What is regulated depends on the specific situation in each country and the mainstream values and norms regarding public policy. Measures change

Figure 1.2
Rental Dwellings: Private and Other (percentage of total rental stock), 1990

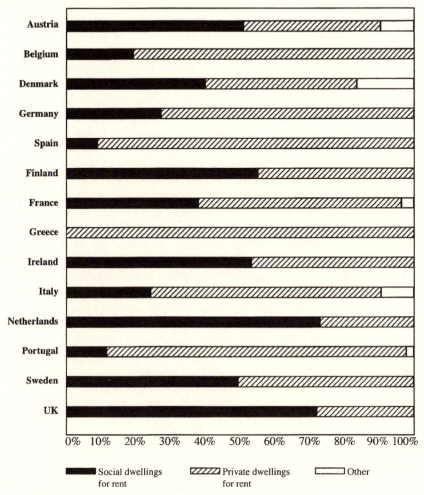

Source: Avramov 1998, on the basis of data from European Commission.

over time to address the changing face of social vulnerability and to pursue innovative, more effective approaches to public involvement in assisting weak competitors in the housing market.

Private-Sector Rent Control

Over the past three decades, experience has shown that too much interference of governments in the private-rental sector affects the housing supply. Strong rent control, which protects tenants to the detriment of landlords' interests, may induce low profitability, which in turn results in lower production. Owners who come into possession of an extra dwelling, through inheritance or marriage, may feel insufficiently legally protected and may be reticent to put their vacant property on the rental market. The ultimate losers in such a system are young adults who want to form a family or establish an independent household but cannot access rental accommodations. Those seeking a first-time tenancy find themselves excluded from private-rented accommodations because the legal system and administrative practice are targeted at preserving the *status quo* for sitting tenants rather than increasing supply.

By the early 1990s rent freeze and life-long tenancy in the private-rental sector, once used as instruments of social policy, had been abandoned in most European countries. Private-sector rent control has declined throughout Europe since the 1960s; however, some form of rent regulation in private-rented housing is implemented in many countries (e.g., Austria, Belgium, Denmark, Spain, France, Luxembourg, the Netherlands, Portugal, and Sweden) (Avramov 1996).

In several countries protective rents are applied only to a part of the private-rental stock, and control is usually limited to older buildings. In Luxembourg, rent control applies to buildings constructed before 1944, while only a few houses constructed after World War II are subject to such regulation. In Austria, a form of rent control implemented through a guiding figure scheme implies that tenants can take legal steps if landlords overcharge. But cheap, old flats are vanishing from the market. By 1994, the segment of the private housing market to which rent control applies in the lowest quality category D housing in Austria had fallen to 3 percent of the housing stock. In Denmark, municipalities can opt for housing regulations which set criteria for reasonable rent. In buildings completed after 1992, however, rents may be freely negotiated (Avramov 1996).

In Germany, France, and the Netherlands there is no rent control, but the system reserves some regulatory power. Neighborhood comparison and quality criteria are typical indicators used to ensure reasonable rent levels. In Belgium and the United Kingdom there is free determination of rent in private-rented housing. While there is no rent ceiling or reasonable rent for a new tenant in these two countries, there are restrictions regarding rent increases during a tenancy contract.

Duration of Rental Contract: Notices to Quit and Evictions

There has been a general tendency toward an increase of landlords' rights to opt for short-term contracts. However, many countries aim at longer-term protection of tenants from frequent rent increases by means of fixed-term tenancies. For example, in Belgium the formula for tenancy contracts in private lettings determined by the legislature is 3 + 6 + 9 years. This means that the standard duration of tenancy in private lettings is initially set at three years. If the contract is not cancelled by the tenant or landlord with a regular notice to quit, the tenure is automatically extended for another six years. After this period the automatic extension of tenancy contracts is for another nine years. In practice, however, half of the rental agreements are made for one or two years, or else there is no written contract. The problems that tenants encounter in Belgium, as in several other countries, are not lack of good laws but their weak negotiating position due to a shortage of affordable lettings and lack of an effective system of public control to ensure that landlords comply with the existing legislation.

In advanced market economies, owners and landlords cannot evict a tenant if they find another willing to pay more. A landlord can terminate a tenancy by a regular notice to quit based on terms foreseen in the rental agreement and in the tenancy law or may seek an extraordinary termination if a tenant does not meet his obligations. Legally defined reasons for termination of tenancies include: end of contract, demolition or refurbishing, owner's need for personal use of a dwelling, arrears of rent, tenant's unacceptable behavior, or use of an apartment contrary to terms of the tenancy agreement. Termination of regular tenancies requires a period of notice varying between two months and a year, depending on the duration of a tenancy. Extraordinary termination of tenancy due to a tenant's violation of contractual terms such as default of payment, disturbance of domestic peace, or misuse of the apartment does not require a period of notice. It does, however, entail juridical procedure of eviction that may last as long as one year.

A significant number of tenants accumulates arrears with rent and utility bills. In Greece, four of every ten households were in arrears with their rent payment. In countries for which data are available from the European Household Panel Survey,[3] it is the unemployed (19%), single parents (18%), and couples with children (15%) who are particularly likely to accumulate arrears with housing payments. "The problem increases with the number of children, e.g. 9% of couples with one dependent child, 13% with two and 21% with three or more dependent children" (EUROSTAT 1998a, 204) were in arrears with rent and utility bills in 1994.

Measures to avoid evictions based on tenants' default of payment are implemented in many countries. The legal framework of preventive action includes a broad range of social assistance to tenants threatened by loss of a home. Measures range from assumption of rent arrears and counselling to transitional measures such as stay of eviction or postponement of enforcement of court orders to evict.

In many transition countries, the private-rental market is largely an uncharted territory. Reasonable rent control, effective regulation of the duration of tenancy contracts, guarantees against unwarranted notice to quit, housing allowance for needy tenants in private-rented accommodations, and public involvement in the private-rented sector are still to be addressed in the legal system and administrative practice.

THE CHANGING FACE OF SOCIAL VULNERABILITY

The housing options of low-income groups had narrowed by the turn of the twentieth century in many European countries as a consequence of one or more processes which affected the affordability of dwellings available on the market, namely, the disengagement of governments in the provision of social housing,[4] massive sales of social housing to sitting tenants, declining rent control in the private sector, upgrading of old inner-city private dwellings which, when refurbished, become unaffordable to low-income tenants,[5] a decrease in the real value of housing allowance and other cash transfers, and an increase in rent and housing-related costs.

Poverty may be identified as the single largest obstacle for people to overcome in obtaining standard quality housing, and it is the key factor in housing deprivation. However, recent years have brought about the changing face of housing vulnerability. This poses new challenges for the identification and implementation of measures complementary to general social, housing, and welfare protection. Vulnerable groups do not seem to differ between advanced market economies and countries in transition to market economies (Avramov 1995a; Duffy 1998). What differs is the size of risk groups, the number of people for whom risks of severe deprivation materialize, the degree of legal and social protection, and the level of public support the needy may expect to receive. As a rule, when the population in need of affordable, standard quality housing and income replacement is large, the level of public support for those perceived as less meritorious or belonging to out-groups is lower, and they may be subjected to overt discrimination.

The problems commonly found in Europe regarding affordability and access to standard quality housing affect, in particular, elderly, low-income households living in old housing; young people in transition to first employment and independent housing; single parents; one-earner, low-income families; unemployed and nonworker groups; immigrants and refugees; and groups with specific needs for accommodation and social support services, such as substance abusers, battered women, disabled, and marginalized homeless people.

Retired persons are most likely to be at risk of poverty, particularly elderly persons living alone. Widows make up one of the poorest groups, and elderly tenants who do not own a home particularly have housing problems. As a rule, elderly home owners are overrepresented in poor-quality housing which needs urgent repairs, even though their dwellings, which used to house families, may be spacious and underoccupied. The burden of housing costs is exacerbated by high utility bills because old houses are frequently humid and have poor insulation and inadequate, often expensive, electric heating. In order to remain in independent housing and preserve a degree of autonomy, elderly individuals and couples may need special housing adaptations which are costly, or supported housing which frequently is not available. The predominance of single women among the very old (over age 80) implies that those with a small pension insufficient to cover repair expenses, house improvements, and care at home, particularly if they are living in the countryside or in problem neighborhoods, may be constrained to bad housing, insufficient care at home, isolation, and loss of social contacts.

For young adults below age 30, education is taking longer, and there is a longer transition between education and work. These young people are postponing starting a family, delaying their departure from parental households, and, when they form an independent household, increasingly depend on parents and family members for financial support. Whether single, a couple, or a family, young households tend to begin by renting a dwelling. Thus, the supply of rented accommodation and the regulatory mechanisms applied in private rented housing have repercussions not only for the quality of life and stress level of youth in transition to adulthood but also for long-term demographic trends. The temporary vulnerability of young people who, owing to unemployment, quasi-employment, job insecurity, or low incomes, cannot access independent housing and of those struggling with mortgage repayments or market rents is often expressed as frustration. It is transposed at the societal level, inter alia, through persistence of below-replacement fertility which contributes to accelerated population aging.

Single parents, the majority of whom are lone mothers, and their children are more exposed to material deprivation than other families. They depend on rental accommodation more than others. In many countries lone mothers have preferential access to social housing, but the slowdown in construction of new, publicly funded housing and the increase in the incidence of divorce and out-of-wedlock births have resulted in the prolongation of waiting time for social housing. Households headed by women may be on waiting lists for publicly funded housing for years. In the meantime, they depend on expensive private rented accommodation, which is not family friendly.

One-income unskilled-labor families and the unemployed and nonworker groups are particularly exposed to forced cohabitation in stressed families in which tensions have built up over years of living in overcrowded, substandard housing and being segregated in degraded housing estates. These living conditions may contribute to an increased incidence in domestic violence. Social stress translates into family tensions and conflicts and intergroup competition for scarce housing resources which may be conducive to social and ethnic intolerance, conflict, and riots.

The integration of immigrants is largely determined by the housing provisions. The low status of and discrimination against some immigrant groups, particularly those of non-European origin, in society and labor markets is aggravated by the lack of provisions and efficient legal protection in the housing market. First-time tenancy in private-rented accommodations may be particularly problematic because of unemployment, low income, insufficient knowledge of the language, physical appearance, and a lack of knowledge of the housing market. The uncertainty of their status makes asylum seekers and illegal immigrants extremely vulnerable. Social integration and the improvement of housing conditions for immigrants is a complex process because household structures often differ from those of natives. Low-income, large immigrant households with several children have housing needs which are not met by the standard housing market. The housing supply and the policy of allocation of publicly funded housing influence relations between the native population and immigrants. Difficult access to standard quality housing, segregation in asylum or reception centers or isolated housing estates, and high competition on the lower end of private rented housing between low-income local population and immigrants all give rise to social tension and conflict, as well as the formation of ethnic neighborhoods. "Urban islands" or "dual cities" are among the most common problems related to housing, city environments, and social integration of immigrants.

Homeless people form the smallest, albeit the most visible, part of the population who encounter obstacles in accessing affordable housing, general welfare protection, and care. The composition of the homeless population varies among countries and over time. It is generally known that people who become homeless have a combination of two or more handicaps and have experienced multiple severely stressful life experiences. Troubles in the family, dropping out of school, poor educational qualifications, casual income or no work-related earnings, a history of mental health problems, disabilities or personality disorders, alcohol and drug abuse, experiences of institutionalization (psychiatric hospitalization, jail, orphanage, foster care), chronic illness, sexual abuse, and domestic violence constitute a web of handicaps and traumatic events which may be conducive to homelessness. As a rule, homeless people lack the resources, opportunity, and ability to make use of social institutions. Their exclusion is associated with social stigmatization and isolation, low self-esteem, the feeling of not belonging, and never having been given a chance to be included in the society. Research shows that homelessness cannot be reduced solely to the housing dimension since the provision of accommodation, as a rule, needs to be combined with varying degrees of care.

In Europe women account for a small minority of the marginalized homeless population. However, substance abuse, especially the increase in the use of designer drugs among adolescents and young adults, is causing an increase in the number of women in need of crisis accommodation and care. Battered women who leave abusive partners—under dramatic conditions and often with children—are increasingly turning to emergency reception centers. While some argue that these women need assistance as homeless people, many reception centers, experts working in the field, and public authorities warn that most women who end up in emergency shelters are in need of supported accommodation only until their primary problem is addressed. Much of the provision in shelters for homeless people is not determined by the needs of battered and abused women or girls and women substance abusers.

SOCIAL RISKS AND CRISIS INTERVENTION

A major policy challenge at the turn of the twentieth century in Europe is the development of effective crisis intervention measures complementary to well-established general social, housing, and welfare protection.

The risk concept is important for understanding social and housing exclusion. Risk situations are affecting more people owing to the employment crisis and new welfare policy trends. Vulnerability factors are multiplying because of the growing duration of risk situations and the loosening of social bonds. Better understanding of the requirements for effective social inclusion can be achieved by addressing the coping strategies of people living under severe housing stress in dilapidated housing estates, in crime-ridden neighborhoods, in conflict-burdened households and overcrowded apartments, and of people overburdened by housing costs.

Understanding the role and functioning of family and informal networks of socially vulnerable people can facilitate the targeting of measures and benefits to reinforce the existing networks, rather than continuing to channel more and more resources and services into sheltering and assisting people once they fall through personal safety nets.

All the policies for fighting poverty and ensuring social protection are important, but they are not sufficient as is shown by the actual existence of home-lessness even in systems with widespread general protection. People with multiple problems fall out of the system of standard social and welfare protection, and complementary services for crisis intervention are needed for the homeless who have multiple, fast-changing problems (Koch-Nielsen 1999).

Our research shows that homeless people are, as a rule, poor, but this does not mean that we can automatically regard as identical those paths in and out of poverty and various situations of social exclusion with the paths into and out of homelessness. Homelessness as a specific form of extreme social exclusion and social detachment of individuals cannot be understood and tackled effectively from the perspective of generic debates about unmet housing needs, unemployment, and material deprivation which ultimately and inevitably lead to homelessness.

Homelessness can best be understood as the outcome of the social process of exclusion during which latently present risks materialize progressively. The process can be described and analyzed through the identification of risk factors, risk groups, and ways in which risks develop into visible handicaps for particular individuals belonging to risk groups. The social condition of homelessness may be described in terms of the living conditions, individual handicaps, and behavioral patterns of homeless people. While the focus on living conditions of homeless people is useful for the identification of specific needs and services for those who are homeless at a given point in time, it provides a weak foundation for making comprehensive preventive policies. In order to develop informed policies, we need to look at the living conditions and strategies of people at risk of social and housing exclusion who are protected from homelessness through welfare policies and family networks. This social context of standard protection can help us to understand the living conditions and social relations of homeless people whom the system has failed to protect.

LESSONS LEARNED ABOUT HOMELESSNESS

Risks of homelessness cut through three levels of causality: social structures, family networks, and personal fragility. They form a complex system of interactive causes and consequences. Though it may be said that poverty is the underlying risk factor of housing deprivation, it is an underlying cause but not a sufficient cause of homelessness. In the lives of people suffering from economic hardship, deprivation in terms of scarce financial, cultural, and social resources implies much more than housing stress and housing exclusion.

The housing dimension of deprivation is characterized by the absence of a personal, permanent, adequate dwelling.[6] Difficulties and obstacles in accessing and maintaining a home can be used as indicators of deprivation. A social condition of homelessness can thus be defined through the social mechanisms, processes, and handicaps that generate it: "Homelessness is the absence of a personal, permanent, adequate dwelling. Homeless people are those who are unable to access a personal, permanent, adequate dwelling or to maintain it due to financial constraints and other social barriers, and those people who are incapable of leading a fully independent life and need care and support in order to access and maintain such a dwelling" (Avramov 1999a, 13).

The first step toward understanding homelessness is the acknowledgment of the complexity of the paths into homelessness. The second analytical step entails separating or breaking the complex deterministic system into its component parts and regrouping it into meaningful systems—the indicators, explanatory variables, and causes of homelessness. In a simplified way, it may be said that the *decomposition* of this complex reality is necessary in order to analyze, measure, and connect the variables; *reconstruction* is necessary in order to interpret, assess prospects for the future, and explain *why* and *how* things happen the way they do.

Research about homelessness has made sufficient progress so that we can make informed assumptions about macro or structural causes, meso or intermediate causes, and micro or proximate causes (often referred to as personal causes) as components of the deterministic system. The terms structural, intermediate, and proximate indicate homelessness at different levels of causation and are not independent variables of homelessness. Combination of and feedback among background, intermediate, and personal factors cause homelessness. In earlier research I have identified several components of the three levels of causation which are specific to the housing dimension of social exclusion. They are relevant for the accumulation and organization of research findings and the connection and interpretation of the phenomena of housing exclusion and homelessness.

The key structural factors of housing exclusion may be identified as lack of affordable housing, lack of adequate social protection, lack of adequate assistance and care for individuals with mental disabilities or personality disorders, and juridical and social segregation of particular individuals or classes of individuals.

The way these macro social factors operate may be summarized in the following way: Lack of affordable housing entails severe competition at the bottom level of the rental market. Individuals who have social, physical, or mental disabilities are weak competitors at risk of being excluded from the regular housing market. Lack of adequate social protection of people who do not have enough income to live in a way compatible with human dignity ghettoizes people in severely substandard housing and run-down neighborhoods. Lack of community-based mental health care for individuals suffering from mental and personality disorders is one key determinant of homelessness for those belonging to this risk group. People who do not need to be institutionalized but need care and support in order to be able to live in independent housing are at risk of becoming homeless if they are not assisted by the community. Legislation that restricts movement, access to land, or housing for particular groups or classes of individuals (e.g., travelers and Gypsies, ethnic minorities, nonnationals, migrants, ex-offenders, and mentally or physically handicapped persons) is one key structural cause of homelessness. Even when legislation does not sanction segregation, the social practice may still operate as a strong factor in housing exclusion. Research shows that particular ethnic groups, individuals who cannot produce a secure employment record, and those with visible physical or mental disabilities are discriminated against in the private rental market.

The missing link in housing exclusion and homelessness research remains the identification and analysis of intermediate causes and a better understanding of ways in which they operate. While we can advance hypotheses about the importance of structures and functions of family, friends, informal networks, neighborhoods, peer groups, street gangs, and other subcultural groups, we still know little about the ways in which they operate. There is no reliable research that could highlight how networks may be preventing or exacerbating housing exclusion and homelessness.

The proximate, or personal, causes of homelessness are a set of factors associated with the personal histories and the personality features of individuals and may be conducive to social isolation and homelessness. Proximate causes of dislocation from regular housing may be identified as history of inadequate institutions (orphanages, succession of youth care institutions and foster families, mental hospitals, and prisons), troubles in the family, domestic violence, dropping out of school, substance abuse, and mental disability or personality disorder.

When risks materialize they may result in temporary living conditions that exacerbate fragility and produce new proximate causes. Sleeping rough, in an emergency shelter, squatting, and becoming estranged from family may be associated with minor criminal activity and identification with the street counterculture. If social intervention does not occur in these initial phases in the process of detachment, the condition of homelessness may lead to prostitution, major criminal activity, heavy substance abuse, and severe mental disability.

The experience of life on the street and in emergency shelters, where individuals encounter abuse, crime, and self-abuse, may become a determinant of long-term or lifelong rupture of social ties and detachment from the values of the mainstream culture.

In a somewhat simplified way, it may be said that the identification of structural factors which tell us how the society is organized helps us to identify the general risk factors of homelessness. The identification of intermediate level causes, through which background factors operate, tells us which specific population subgroups are most exposed to risks of homelessness. The micro, or personal, causes help us to perceive which particular individuals in a specific society are running the highest risk of homelessness.

The notion of risks implies a possibility, threat, hazard, chance of loss, or peril. It can be measured as the probability of an event's occurring. The size and the composition of groups for whom risks materialize and who find themselves homeless depends ultimately on the effectiveness of the system of family and social protection. In all societies only a small proportion of individuals belonging to groups at risk of homelessness fall through all of the existing social safety nets. Some of those who become homeless are able to develop personal coping strategies and build their own paths out of homelessness. Some are effectively assisted by the public authorities. Others just drift and rely on daily survival. A universal rule for every exposure to deprivation and hazard which affects those belonging to the risk groups and those who actually become homeless is: the longer the struggle, the higher the casualties (Avramov 1997).

The organization and function of society, in particular its social services, illustrate how risks materialize or how they are buffered in different European countries. Although there is a general shortage of affordable housing, the unemployment rate is high, and the divorce rates are among the highest in Europe, there are almost no homeless families in Finland. Those families who find themselves homeless are accommodated in temporary apartments for a few weeks before they are provided with permanent accommodation. In 1996 a total of 360 households composed of two or more persons (many of them Ingrian returnees to Finland awaiting permanent accommodation) were reported to have been temporarily homeless (Hannikainen and Kärkkäinen 1998). In the United Kingdom, by contrast, the overwhelming majority of some 150,000 households officially registered as homeless and in priority need of housing are families (Avramov 1995a). They may find themselves on waiting lists for housing for several years.

SOME INDICATORS OF THE MAGNITUDE OF RISK
GROUPS AND PEOPLE FOR WHOM RISKS MATERIALIZE

In terms of bad housing conditions, it can be estimated that in the European Union, out of its total population of 374 million inhabitants, at least 15 million people live in substandard or overcrowded dwellings, and 2.4 million people live in unconventional dwellings, which are mobile, semipermanent, or not built for human habitation.[7]

In terms of housing insecurity and housing stress in the 15 European Union countries, it may be estimated that 1.6 million people are under eviction procedures, and 400,000 people are evicted each year (Avramov 1996). EURO-STAT reports that 5 percent of home owners with an existing loan or mortgage were in arrears with their payments during the previous 12 months (in 1994) and that 8 percent of tenants were in arrears with their rent payment (1998b, 204).

It may be estimated that 1.8 million people in Europe pass each year through services for homeless people or other social emergency reception centers, and 1.1 million people may be dependent for their accommodation on public services, voluntary organizations, or charities on a daily basis.

The above conditions may overlap, and therefore it is not possible to add any of the given numbers in order to estimate the prevalence of housing exclusion. The above figures may be considered only as a preliminary indicator of the housing dimension of deprivation in the most prosperous European countries.

The currently available data for the estimates about the sheltered homeless in the 15 EU countries (see Table 1.2) are collected by service providers and statutory authorities for administration purposes. Typically, service providers count each entry into a particular shelter; however, the sum of entries does not correspond to the number of people assisted. Service providers document the turnover in services but do not report on the number of multiple users—those who have entered a particular shelter two, five, or fifty times. Even when services keep records that enable them to separate the number of homeless people from the turnover of clients in shelters which they run, they have no way of knowing how many times over the course of a year the same person has been accepted in shelters run by other organizations in the same town or in other cities or regions.

Difficulties in estimating the prevalence of homelessness may be summarized as follows. Targeted primary research of homelessness is rare at the national level and nonexistent at the European level. Surveys of the homeless population have typically focused on single problem areas, covered a small sample, are limited geographically to one locality, and provide only patchwork data. Homelessness as a human condition and housing exclusion as a social process still remain underresearched phenomena in the academic community. Due to lack of reliable empirical data, the estimates of the prevalence of housing exclusion and identification of needs of the homeless population often have to be based on data gathered for the purpose of administration of services and for fund-raising.

Table 1.2
Average Annual Number of People Who May Have Been Dependent on Services for the Homeless in the European Union in the Early 1990s

Country	On an average day or on day of a survey	Over the course of a year
Austria	6,100	8,400
Belgium	4,000	5,500
Denmark	2,947	4,000
Germany	490,700	876,450
Finland	4,000	5,500
France	250,000	346,000
Greece	5,500	7,700
Ireland	2,667	3,700
Italy	56,000	78,000
Luxembourg	194	200
Netherlands	7,000	12,000
Portugal	3,000	4,000
Spain	8,000	11,000
Sweden	9,903	14,000
UK	283,000	460,000

Source: Avramov 1995a, 1996.

In the overwhelming majority of EU member states, researchers are not able to undertake primary research on a nationally representative sample nor do they have much choice in the selection of available data sources. Therefore, all attempts to compare data on homelessness at the European level must take into account the different nature of sources and acknowledge that data from research and nonresearch sources have a different degree of accuracy (Avramov 1999a).

In proposing the figures in Table 1.2 as indicators of the magnitude of risk groups and the prevalence of homelessness, these arguments are not resolved. But in estimating the prevalence of homelessness some of the key limitations are addressed. An attempt has been made to minimize the effect of double counting service users as well as undercounting homeless persons.

The changes that occurred in the size of the homeless population in the second half of the 1990s can be documented only for a few European countries. Information from service providers and local authorities is provided on an annual basis only in Belgium, Finland, Luxembourg, and the United Kingdom. Data which come from different sources in each of these countries document the homelessness of different groups. Figures are not comparable across countries, but they document changes over time in a particular country. In Finland the number of homeless people has been declining continuously since 1987 (from 17,110 to 9,600 in 1996). In Sweden local social authorities identified 11,000 homeless clients; in 1993, social authorities and service providers had identified 9,903 clients. In Belgium the turnover of clients in shelters for homeless people has slightly declined between 1993 and 1995 (from 23,937 to 22,325). In the United Kingdom, after reaching the peak level of 144,780 in 1991, acceptances of homeless households for housing by the local authorities have slowly but steadily been declining. In 1994 the number of households accepted for housing under the statutory right of priority groups of homeless people stood at 122,660. In Germany many West German towns are reporting that the number of people in temporary accommodation for the homeless is declining. North Rhine Westphalia, the state which records the number of homeless people provided accommodation by the municipalities on yearly basis, has registered a decrease in homelessness in two consecutive years (June 1995 and June 1996). It also seems that in many municipalities across Germany chances of homeless people being supplied with regular permanent housing have improved in most recent years. These indicators are used as the basis for an assertion that homelessness is declining in Germany (Busch-Geertsema 1999). Information for these six countries seems to indicate that the number of homeless people has been decreasing in the mid-1990s.

The only country for which we can document an increase in the number of homeless users of services is Luxembourg. In Luxembourg the number of people sheltered in various institutions increased from 194 in 1994 to 343 in 1996. There were 5 homeless people per 10,000 inhabitants in 1994, and the number rose to 8 homeless per 10,000 population in 1996. Since the number of people affected by homelessness in Luxembourg is very small and the period of observation covers only three consecutive years, it is not possible to draw meaningful conclusions about trends in the prevalence of homelessness.

Before an attempt is made to explain why and how, under conditions of growing risks of homelessness in the mid-1990s, the number of people who have become homeless seems to have declined in a number of countries, several underresearched issues must be considered.

In the case of Finland, it may be reasonable to assume that a decrease of the number of homeless people is a targeted achievement of a comprehensive policy developed and implemented since 1987 with the aim of eradicating homelessness. The policy measure did not achieve its ultimate aim but managed to reduce by half the number of homeless people in less than 10 years. For other countries, a similar hypothesis may be a less realistic framework for an explanation of recent figures. Several more feasible hypotheses may need to be tested in order to explain changes in the number of registered homeless persons.

We know that in the 1990s services are increasingly oriented toward reintegration. In addition to emergency and transitional accommodation, a growing number are providing individual or group therapy, reconstitution of social networks, and professional training. They are providing the type of assistance and care that takes time. This means that people who enter these services stay in them longer. This in turn may imply that the turnover of clients is declining, namely, the number of multiple users of services over the course of a year is decreasing. Those who would have rotated between emergency night shelters in which a stay is limited to two or three months would have been counted as homeless every time they entered a new shelter. In innovative, more personalized services, which address the multiple needs of their clients, people stay longer, and an increasing number of people find paths out of homelessness. Thus a decrease in the number of people registered in shelters may be partly due to a lower turnover of clients and partly to successful reintegration of homeless people into permanent housing.

Declining numbers of homeless people registered by the local authorities may be merely an indicator of a lower rate of acceptance of people on waiting lists for housing. For example, in the United Kingdom research may be needed to determine whether the interpretations of the Code of Guidance, under which local authorities identify priority homeless groups, has become more discriminatory in the mid-1990s—a decrease in the number of households accepted for housing does not necessarily mean that the number of homeless people has decreased. It may merely mean that there has been a decreased supply of housing for homeless people or that homeless people have been discouraged from applying for council housing.

A comprehensive research study of the dynamics of homelessness would need to look at the time lag between the onset of risks, the growth in the number of people exposed to risks, the duration of the exposure to risks of individuals belonging to risk groups, the targeting of risk-reducing policies, and the manifestation of homelessness as the last stage of the process of accumulation of handicaps and extreme social exclusion.

No such research is currently being implemented at the European level. For the time being, the figures published by the service providers and statutory authorities, which seem to indicate lower levels of registered homelessness in several European countries, are being interpreted according to the convictions and convenience of individuals and interest groups.

SOCIAL STRATIFICATION OF HOMELESS PEOPLE

One conclusion that may be drawn on the basis of the present level of knowledge about homelessness is that people who find themselves homeless and who turn to reception centers for accommodation have very different backgrounds. It has often been said that homeless people are not a homogeneous group. What is usually meant by a nonuniformity of parts composing the homeless population is that homeless people experience a diversity of problems before and during their transition to homelessness. The concept of heterogeneity often implies, however, that homeless people are an unstructured aggregate. What, in fact, we perceive is a heterogeneity of backgrounds and a multiplicity of handicaps which are translated into a social stratification of homelessness. Homeless people are stratified according to the complexity of their problems and the type of public assistance and care they receive. At the top of the homeless pyramid are those people who are in housing need because they are recently arrived immigrants (e.g., *ausiedlers* in Germany, Ingrians in Finland, or expatriates from Pontos in Greece) or indebted evicted families. At the bottom are HIV-positive drug addicts sleeping rough and illegal immigrants.

Research seems to indicate that services for homeless people reproduce this social stratification. The preliminary research results in France (Marpsat and Firdion 1996) show that there is a segmentation of services and that better equipped services may be choosing better or easier clients. It is generally known that services set criteria for the admission of particular homeless subgroups. What needs to be researched is whether the stratification of services implies that the system itself becomes a framework for the marginalization and segregation of particular (difficult) homeless groups. The better quality services take in the less marginalized homeless—large dormitories take in the residual homeless, those with multiple problems. Even in Denmark, a country which may be considered as a forerunner in individualized approaches to assistance and care of vulnerable groups, large institutions have not ceased to exist. They are not staffed (Borner 1996). Instead, they exist in parallel to new small, staff-intensive establishments which care for particular groups, such as battered women.

Research results from a survey about the prevalence of psychiatric morbidity among homeless adults in the United Kingdom (Gill, Meltzer and Hinds 1996) show how the prevalence of neurotic and psychotic psychopathology varies according to the housing situation of homeless people. Residents of hostels, tenants of private sector leased accommodation, residents of night shelters, and people sleeping rough exhibit different psychiatric morbidity patterns. Severe living conditions no doubt may aggravate symptoms of psychopathology, but the indicators of psychiatric morbidity paired with information about the type of accommodation provided to homeless people reflect also how the services operate in selecting their clients.

Information from a variety of sources seems to indicate that those homeless people who have multiple problems associated with poverty, personality disorders, and substance abuse and who need labor and cost-intensive assistance and care are marginalized in large, depersonalized dormitories or left to fend for themselves.

Youngsters tend to stay away from shelters for homeless people (Avramov

1998). They gather in public places usually around train stations, and they tend to keep away from institutions and public authorities. Young people are usually contacted by street services which provide assistance to heterogeneous groups ranging from prostitutes and drug addicts to runaway kids. Young people are mainly clients of drifter teams and other street services, and they gather in groups which bond around the street counterculture.

RESPONSES TO SOCIAL EMERGENCY

Responses to crisis situations, which may be associated with the need for temporary accommodation, are frequently marked by the lack of clarity about the order of magnitude of the population in need and the provision of care and services without examining whether these are actually determined by client needs. Some groups in need of emergency assistance may not receive sufficient protection and public attention because they are less visible, or other groups may have better organized lobbyists who exercise greater pressure on behalf of their clients. A few highly publicized cases of neediness are interpreted as generalized trends. Or all those who turn to services for crisis intervention may be labeled as homeless. The lack of understanding of the social processes that generate housing and social exclusion are often translated into inadequate services.

We know that the number of services for crisis intervention is increasing at an unprecedented pace in many European countries. There are doubts that they may be operating as revolving doors for disadvantaged groups. They may be providing more care than the clients need or wish to receive. In many countries there is a fragmentation of services, competition between service providers, and a lack of cooperation between specialized services. Crisis intervention is highly costly and not sufficiently need based, and the success rates in terms of outputs and outcomes are generally unknown. This void needs to be filled by methodologically sound evaluations of policies and services by means of policy impact studies and performance measurements of services from the point of view of providers, other institutions, and users.

Under current conditions, an exchange of information at the international level needs to go a step farther than just taking stock of "good," "best," or "innovative" practice only on the basis of what policies and providers intend to achieve. Criteria for the measurement of success or innovation are usually set by providers, and outputs and outcomes remain beyond the critical analysis of performance from the point of view of other institutions and clients. Making an inventory of measures or projects without an evaluation of whether they actually work, how many disadvantaged people they actually reach, and how much they cost is not of much use for the translation of proposals into a realistic plan of action.

The unfeasibility of crisis intervention provided by public and voluntary organizations as a solution to housing deprivation may be illustrated by the huge cost for the public and the lack of convincing evidence about its effectiveness. "Because of their high personnel costs, voluntary organizations' hostels which offer assistance by social workers are often extremely expensive" warns Busch-Geertsema (1999, 478). The costs per day per person of temporary accommodation of homeless people in major German cities are between 40 and 70 Euros according to Busch-Geertsema. If extrapolated at the European level, the cost to the public of sheltering some 1.1 million people by the organizations working with homeless people, assuming that the standard of service delivery is comparable to German levels, which is clearly not the case in many countries, could range per day between 44 million and 77 million Euros.

The changing face of vulnerability imposes a need to redefine public responsibilities and community actions and to make providers more accountable. In the majority of European countries, there is no evidence that a shift of responsibility for the provision of accommodation, be it permanent or transitional, toward housing associations, voluntary groups, and charities is more effective and efficient than the provisions made by statutory authorities. More and more public resources are being channeled toward emergency provisions which include temporary accommodation. This is often done without examining whether these provisions are actually determined by client needs. There is evidence that services for homeless people are increasingly becoming a market-driven subsector which may be (re)producing clients.

The domain of service provision is a policy twilight zone. It is necessary to address the deadlock of the mainstream debate about services and new partnerships which is based more on ideologies than on sound knowledge. The debate about innovative models which are (presumably) transferable, although we do not know whether they actually work and how much they actually cost, has not contributed much to tackling homelessness or social exclusion.

CONCLUSIONS AND POLICY IMPLICATIONS

In the European Union countries, the minimum standards of housing adequacy are considerably higher than they are in most other parts of the world. Housing exclusion in Europe, like poverty, is measured against the standard of living of the majority of the population. The material dimension of social exclusion constitutes poverty in terms of insufficient financial resources available to an individual or a household to reach the minimum standard of living and quality of life that is considered to be normal for a given country. The distributional aspect of social exclusion implies that we are looking at the income disparities for a given country and not at the "absolute" minimum level of subsistence or the "survival basket." In systems with weaker social and housing protection, the standards of minimum quality of housing are, as a rule, lower. For example, a mobile home is not considered adequate housing in most European Union countries. The statutory obligation of public authorities to provide adequate housing to badly housed people is also considerably higher, especially in the Nordic countries.

Several European Union countries, including Finland, Sweden, and Denmark, have devised effective instruments to promote access to housing for the poor and disadvantaged groups and to tackle housing segregation and discrimination. Some countries, for example the United Kingdom and Belgium, have been abdicating public responsibility for badly housed people and those in need of housing over the past two decades or so, and they have been delegating the role of housing providers to the invisible hand of the housing market or voluntary organizations and charities. Several countries, particularly in Eastern and Central Europe, have yet to address, in a comprehensive way, the key areas of social and legal protection of poor and disadvantaged tenants. The changing face of social risk and the emergence of new vulnerable groups pose challenges for public policy and social emergency throughout Europe.

The European experience shows that policies to promote access to housing for the poor and disadvantaged groups must focus on making standard-quality housing affordable and secure. Since the affordability of housing is determined by the income level, burden of rent and utility costs, and disposable income left after the payment of housing, an advancement in the improvement of the standard of living requires measures that will cut across several areas of public policy, namely economy, employment, income, consumption, demography, social protection, and welfare.

Areas of policy action and instruments inherent to housing policies include an increase in the level of supply of social and private rented accommodation in order to meet the level of need and enhance housing options; the provision of a housing allowance to decrease the disproportionate burden of rent and utilities for the poor, disadvantaged groups, and people in difficulty; the improvement of the legislative framework and administrative practice to protect tenants in private rented accommodation from unwarranted notice to quit and eviction and to prevent discrimination of disadvantaged groups in the rental market; the dissemination of information about rights and entitlements regarding access to housing and public support for the improvement of housing conditions of the needy; and area-based policies to promote the regeneration of environment, the improvement of public spaces, and the eradication of vandalism and crime in the area.

Borderline housing, welfare, health care, and reintegration policies include crisis intervention to provide transitional accommodation and support to people with multiple problems. Areas of policy action include intervention at all levels of governance: international, national, and local.

Dealing with current problems related to unmet housing needs and difficulties, which low-income people and disadvantaged groups have in maintaining a dwelling through palliate measures, is an indispensable step forward in promoting social integration and improving the quality of life of European citizens. But in the long run it may be necessary to rethink the philosophy underlying several interrelated areas of public policy, namely work, housing, and demography.

On the one hand, new trends in the labor market require mobility of workers, and our societies are increasingly attaching high value to "foot loose" people who are willing to follow employment opportunities. Global processes in the economy imply that people are expected to change professions and places of work during their careers. On the other hand, governments are increasingly focusing their housing policies on promoting home ownership. The meaning of *home* has become almost exclusively tied to the concept of *ownership*. A rift is widening between work policies and access to housing policies. Work and workers are expected to be flexible—housing keeps people anchored. The majority of homeowners in Europe are repaying loans and mortgages which tie them down for several decades.

When there is a shortage of affordable rented housing of decent quality and size, many households, especially new families, find themselves in a no-choice situation: in order not to be penalized by excessively high rents and the lack of family-friendly rentals, people have to buy. Adjustments in the housing market are lagging behind demographic changes and new household dynamics. The housing needs of people change over the family's life cycle—they vary according to age, household size and composition, phase in family building or dissolution, level of income, specific-care needs, and changing norms, values, and expectations in the main domains of human activity.

In order to promote integrated labor, social, and housing policies, authorities may need to consider giving more incentive or even preferential treatment to rented housing and tenants. Diversification of housing options in rented accommodation could facilitate the mobility of people in terms of geographic movement and would be better suited to meet fast-changing needs associated with new family and household dynamics, population aging, and changes in income level over the lifetime of individuals.

Comparative overviews of policy choices and administrative practice in various European countries indicate that strong political will and the commitment of material and nonmaterial resources are the keys to effective prevention of housing exclusion (Avramov 1995a, 1996). In advanced welfare states, the policy choices translated into practice show that antipoverty and social integration measures are more effective when income protection is accompanied by a comprehensive system of housing supply and housing subsidies, benefits, and allowances. The Nordic countries, Denmark, Finland, and Sweden, have been successful in progressively removing obstacles to housing for low-income groups. They also implement a generous system of income transfers which enable people to maintain a home. Over the past ten years or so, they have all managed to contain the effects of the structural causes of housing deprivation and to reduce homelessness.

In countries which have focused their antipoverty measures on welfare transfers and emergency assistance for the homeless, but have pursued the policy of

disengagement from the public funding of permanent housing for socially vulnerable groups, large-scale homelessness persists. Indeed, in many countries, the
lack of adequate housing assistance to low-income groups has been a serious
stumbling point in the system of social protection. Lack of a right to the minimum subsistence means and the market-oriented housing policy which does not
foresee efficient safety nets for the poor are increasing risks of poverty and
housing stress in Southern European countries as well as in countries in transition to market economies. In Southern Europe, in the absence of effective
public policies and measures, family support has been the most effective (and
often the only) buffer against homelessness. Family solidarity has traditionally
played a significant role in preventing homelessness of adults with no income.
However, the changing family structures and culture are eroding the functional
basis of traditional family support. Transition to market economies in Eastern
and Central Europe has not been accompanied by effective social protection and
welfare and housing assistance to those who are too young or too old, too weak,
or too slow to profit from the new economic opportunities.

No single European country has yet developed a fully integrated system of
social protection to deal effectively, efficiently, and quickly with all types of
social emergencies and crisis situations. However, the policies that have best
addressed homelessness are mulitfaceted (as opposed to monofaceted), integrated (versus segmented), long term (versus short term), preventive (versus
curative), and structural (versus individual), and they include participation of
the homeless (versus imposed by public authorities). While it may be said that
services for emergency intervention are needed to assist people in need of shelter
who have multiple, albeit, fast-changing problems, they prove to be efficient
instruments of reintegration only providing that there is a continuation between
general social and welfare protection and crisis intervention (Avramov 1999a).

The Nordic countries, which can be held up as an example of the best practice
in integrated policy approach to homelessness, show that tackling difficulties
associated with homelessness requires coordination between both preventive and
responsive measures and a well thought-out approach to services. In the late
1990s, models of best practice are those schemes that extend services far beyond
temporary emergency assistance. They acknowledge that homelessness is not
only a housing condition. They operate under the assumption that housing the
homeless is indispensable but that it is not a sufficient tool for social reintegration of homeless people. They provide for people in need of housing and social
support, and their aim is to resettle homeless people into independent housing
and to provide sufficient support and care so that they are able to stay in individual housing. Depending on the set of specific needs of individuals, the integrated approach implies that, in addition to personal housing (as opposed to
placement in institutions), formerly homeless people may expect to receive individual guidance, counseling on how to manage their financial resources, guidance in reconstituting family and social ties, professional training, access to
protected employment, and psychological and medical support. This approach

questions the validity and usefulness of the assumption that all homeless people can, ought to, or will be integrated in the standard labor market.

REFERENCES

Ascher, F., ed. 1995. *Le logement en question, l'habitat dans les annés quatre-vingt-dix: Continuité et ruptures.* Paris: Editions de l'Aube.

Avramov, D. 1995a. *Homelessness in the European Union, Social and Legal Context of Housing Exclusion in the 1990s.* Brussels: Feantsa.

———. 1995b. *Housing Exclusion in Central and Eastern Europe.* Brussels: Feantsa.

———. 1996. *The Invisible Hand of the Housing Market.* Brussels: Feantsa.

———. 1997. *Report on Housing and Homelessness.* Project Human Dignity and Social Exclusion. Strasbourg: Council of Europe.

———. ed. 1998. *Youth Homelessness in the European Union.* Brussels: Feantsa.

———. ed. 1999a. *Coping with Homelessness: Issues to Be Tackled and Best Practices in Europe.* Aldershot, Brookfield USA, Singapore, Sydney: Ashgate Publishing.

———. 1999b. *Access to Housing for Disadvantaged Groups in the Council of Europe Member States.* Project Human Dignity and Social Exclusion. Strasbourg: Council of Europe.

Berthold, M. Hrsg. 1997. *Wege aus dem Ghetto . . . In der Krise des Sozialstaates muss sich die Wohnungslosenhilfe neu orientieren.* Bielefeld: Dokumentation der Bundestagung 1997 der BAG Wohnungslosenhilfe e. V. Materialien zur Wohnungslosenhilfe.

Borner, T. 1996. *Youth Homelessness in Denmark.* Brussels: Feantsa.

Busch-Geertsema, V. 1999. "Temporary Accommodation for Homeless People in Germany with Special Focus on the Provision for Immigrants and Asylum Seekers." In *Coping with Homelessness: Issues to Be Tackled and Best Practices in Europe,* ed. D. Avramov, 454–486. Aldershot, Brookfield USA, Singapore, Sydney: Ashgate Publishing.

Castel, R. 1995. *Les métamorposes de la Question Sociale en Europe.* Paris: Fayard.

Conseil National de l'Information Statistique. 1996. *Pour une meilleure connaissance statistique des sans-abri et de l'exclusion du logement,* no. 20. Paris: Conseil National de l'Information Statistique.

Council of Europe. 1992. *The European Social Charter.* Strasbourg: Council of Europe.

Department of Environment. 1993. *English House Condition Survey.* London: Her Majesty's Stationary Office.

Duffy, K. 1998. *Opportunity and Risk, Trends of Social Exclusion in Europe, Project on Human Dignity and Social Exclusion (HDSE).* Strasbourg: Council of Europe.

Environment and Urbanization. 1996. "Evictions," (6)1.

Esping-Andersen, G., ed. 1996. *Welfare States in Transition: National Adaptations in Global Economies.* London: Sage.

European Commission. 1993. *The Role of Housing in the Building of a Social Europe.* Proceedings of the Conference held in Brussels, Directorate General Employment, Industrial Relations and Social Affairs, Brussels.

———. 1994. *A Legal Analysis of the Impact of EC Legislation on the Housing Sector.* Brussels: Directorate General Employment, Industrial Relations and Social Affairs.

————. 1998a. *Social Protection in Europe 1997 Report.* Luxembourg: Directorate General Employment, Industrial Relations and Social Affairs, Office for Official Publications of the European Communities.

————. 1998b. *Housing Statistics in the European Union 1998.* Brussels: Employment and Social Affairs, Social Security and Social Integration, Unit V/E.2.

European Parliament. 1997. *Housing Policy in the EU Member States.* Luxembourg: Directorate General for Research, Social Affairs Series, W-14.

EUROSTAT. 1996a. *Social Portrait of Europe.* Luxembourg: Office of Official Publications of the European Communities.

————. 1996b. *Population, Households and Dwellings in Europe.* 1990/91 Censuses, Luxembourg: Office of Official Publications of the European Communities.

————. 1998a. *Social Portrait of Europe.* Luxembourg: Office of Official Publications of the European Communities.

————. 1998b. *Population and Social Conditions: Eurostat Databases.* Luxembourg: Office of Official Publications of the European Communities.

Gill, B., H. Meltzer, and K. Hinds. 1996. *The Prevalence of Psychotic Morbidity among Homeless Adults.* Bulletin no. 1. London: Office of Population Censuses and Surveys.

Guidicini, P., G. Pieretti, and M. Bergamaschi. 1997. *Gli esclusi dal territorio.* Milan: Franco Angeli.

Hannikainen, K., and S-L. Kärkkäinen. 1998. "Homelessness among Young People in Finland: Measures to Prevent It and Foreseeable Risks." In *Youth Homelessness in the European Union,* ed. D. Avramov. Brussels: Feantsa.

Haut Comité pour le Logement des Personnes Défavorisées. 1997. *Lever les obstacles au logement des personnes défavorisées.* 4éme rapport. Paris: Juillet.

Heddy, J. 1991. *Housing for Young People.* A Survey of the Situation in Selected EC Countries. Paris: Union Nationale des Foyers et Services pour Jeunes Travailleurs.

Hungarian Central Statistical Office. 1996. *Social Portrait of Hungary.* Budapest: KSH (Hungarian Central Statistical Office).

————. 1998. *Hungary 1997, Report on Major Processes in the Society and Economy.* Budapest: KSH (Hungarian Central Statistical Office).

Koch-Nielsen, I. 1999. "Conclusions and Policy Implications: Values and Policies in Relation to Homelessness." In *Coping with Homelessness: Issues to Be Tackled and Best Practices in Europe,* ed. D. Avramov, 397–404. Aldershot, Brookfield USA, Singapore, Sydney: Ashgate Publishing.

L'observatoire Européen du Logement Social, Comité Européen de Coordination del'Habitat Social (CECODHAS). 1994. *Le logement social dans l'Union européenne: Quelles politiques publiques à l'horizon 2000?* Paris: L'observatoire Européen du Logement Social.

Marpsat, M., and J-M. Firdion. 1996. *The Homeless in Paris.* Presentation at the EUROHOME Workshop 1, ICCR, 11–13 July, Vienna.

MISSOC. 1996. *Social Protection in the Member States of the Union.* European Commission, Directorate General Employment, Industrial Relations and Social Affairs. Luxembourg: Office for Official Publications of the European Communities.

Negri, N. C. Saraceno. 1996. *Le politiche contro la povertà in Italia.* Bologna: Il Mulino.

Nochlezhka. 1994. *Petersburg in the Early 90's, Crazy, Cold, Cruel . . .* Saint Petersburg, Russia: Charitable Foundation Nochlezhka.

Paugam, S., ed. 1996. *L'exclusion, l'état des savoir.* Paris: La Découverte.

Ridder, G., ed. 1997. *Les nouvelles frontières de l'intervention sociale.* Paris: L'Harmattan.

Room, G., ed. 1995. *Beyond the Threshold, the Measurement and Analysis of Social Exclusion.* Bristol, UK: Policy Press.

Sahlin, I. 1998. "Swedish Responses to Youth Housing Situation: General Exclusion and Special Assistance." In *Youth Homelessness in the European Union*, ed. D. Avramov. Brussels: Feantsa.

Sen, A. 1992. *Inequalities Re-examined.* Cambridge, MA.: Harvard University Press.

UNCHS—Habitat. 1996. *An Urbanising World. A Global Report on Human Settlements 1996.* Oxford: Oxford University Press.

United Nations. 1992. *The Right to Adequate Housing*, by Sachar R. for the Commission on Human Rights, E/CN 4/Sub.2:1992/15. New York: United Nations.

Vranken, J., et al. 1997. *Armoede en Sociale Uitsluiting.* Jaarboek 1997, Leuven: Amersfoot/Acco.

NOTES

This chapter is based on research undertaken by the author for the Council of Europe on Access to Housing for Disadvantaged Groups in the Council of Europe Member States and the DEMULOG project Houses for Low Income People, funded by the European Community, DG Research.

1. An exception is Germany where there is an excess of 1.4 million private households over the number of dwellings.

2. This does not imply that all single persons want to live in one- or two-room apartments. Those who can afford large dwellings will continue to occupy them as is shown by the housing conditions of the wealthy elderly (EUROSTAT 1996a). However, there is ample evidence that the demand for small apartments exceeds the supply in many European countries (Avramov 1998).

3. Belgium, Denmark, Germany, Greece, Spain, France, Ireland, Italy, Luxembourg, Portugal, the Netherlands, and the United Kingdom.

4. Only in Ireland and Germany has a renewed priority been given to investment in social housing in the 1990s (European Parliament 1997).

5. This should not be misinterpreted to imply that there is a need to maintain substandard housing for the poor and disadvantaged groups. It is an indicator of the need to accompany urban renewal and improvement of standards of housing quality with housing allowance so that low-income and disadvantaged groups can access standard quality accommodation.

6. Concepts such as personal, private, and adequate have been extensively defined by the United Nations (see, for example, 1992).

7. For an explanation about the estimations presented in this chapter, see Avramov 1995a, 1996. Sufficient information on housing conditions and emergency accommodation are available only for the 15 European Union countries—Belgium, Denmark, Germany, Greece, Spain, France, Ireland, Italy, Luxembourg, Netherlands, Austria, Portugal, Finland, Sweden, and the United Kingdom—not for all (40 or so depending on how one counts) European countries.

2

Homelessness in Sweden: An Avoidable Problem

INGRID SAHLIN

INTRODUCTION

There is an obvious risk that attention, information, policies, and even research oriented to a specific problem may contribute to its acceptance. Discussions about scope, causes, development, and solutions sometimes overshadow the simple question of why the problem exists at all. Sweden is a rather wealthy country with comparatively well-developed social security and equality, and it is indeed reasonable to ask why there are any homeless people at all in this country.[1] Homelessness is an avoidable problem, and it is caused by partly unintended, partly quite deliberate consequences of policies that are chosen and could be changed. Historical traditions, social and housing rights and policies, the public image of the homelessness problem, and the policies implemented to solve it all contribute to an explanation of Swedish homelessness. At the same time each is interrelated with the others in a self-reinforcing circle that yields and reproduces homelessness. This is, of course, not to deny the obvious fact that homelessness is ultimately produced by the housing market and the power relation it implies.

The concept of homelessness may be split up into at least two dimensions: lack of physical shelter and lack of control over one's living space. Those who have neither physical shelter nor control over a private space, such as people sleeping rough or circulating between shelters and acquaintances, will here be called *literally homeless*. However, good housing standards cannot completely outweigh the lack of control, or vice versa. In other words, an individual may be homeless despite a temporary stay in a castle, or despite having full control over a dwelling that does not give shelter against the elements. Housing quality, in turn, has at least two aspects: standards (e.g., bath, toilet, heating) and size. What is considered "normal" housing quality for a certain household varies, of course, over time and between countries. The dimension of control may be split into tenure security—the right to remain in the home—on the one hand, and the right to privacy and self-determination, on the other hand. Both of these aspects are culturally relative, and the latter aspect highlights, in addition, the distinction between individuals and households. Historically, the degree of privacy and self-determination has been small for women, children, and servants living in their masters' households. Before the twentieth century, it was unusual for single persons to have their own homes, but now 40 percent of Swedish households consist of only one person (Statistics Sweden, 1990 Census).

Accordingly, the meaning of individual or family homelessness is related to what is considered normal in a certain context. Furthermore, the extent to which the lack of a home is considered a problem by the society depends on the significance of the home in the sociocultural context. Where homelessness is perceived as a public problem, this recognition tends to alternate between two distinct perspectives—one that focuses on the supply and allocation of housing, and another that stresses the homeless individuals and their deficiencies. Recent changes in Swedish discourse and policies regarding homelessness may be summarized as a shift in emphasis from the first to the second of these perspectives (Sahlin 1992).

Even if there are, so far, no convincing indications of any dramatic increase of literal homelessness or substandard housing in the 1990s, homelessness in terms of lack of control is growing.[2] This tendency is related to the contemporary public discourse that focuses on individual deficiencies as the prime cause of homelessness. Hence, the favored solution is to control the homeless, which implies reduced security of tenure and impaired privacy. This composite of discourse, strategy, and consequences is intimately related to the fact that responsibility for solving the homelessness problem was, in the early 1990s, transferred from the housing authorities to the social authorities at both national and local levels.

HISTORICAL BACKGROUND

In the nineteenth century, homelessness was distinguished neither legally nor socially from unemployment. In national and local policies, two categories of poor people were considered problematic: vagrants and individuals "without defense." These people often had nowhere to live, but the crucial point was their unemployment. This implied that they did not belong to any household and hence, they were to a certain degree beyond control. The term "without defense" originally referred to people who could be enrolled in the army just because their labor was not needed at home. However, the concept and its legal implications prevailed long after the military draft system had changed, since they urged people to seek employment and stay with their masters, who in turn were responsible for their subsistence when they became ill or old (Lext 1968, 186ff.). People without defense were instead monitored and supervised by local authorities, which could command them to do work and forbid them to leave the community.

The traditional meaning of "vagrants" covers people staying in parishes other than the ones to which they belonged. Vagrancy was a crime per se, and strangers were, in addition, often suspected of committing other crimes like theft, unpermitted begging, and arson. As part of the liberalization of the labor market, people who could prove they were looking for work or had money for their supply were, from 1885 on, allowed to move between communities. Thereafter, the mobility and homelessness aspects were gradually detached from the vagrancy concept, which became associated only with asocial lifestyles, such as gambling, drinking, and idleness. The new "stationary vagrants" typically lived in urban hostels but could also have homes of their own (SOU 1962, 22, 107ff.). Among women, the law was applied primarily to those who were prostituted, whether they were homeless or not (SOU 1962, 22, 120, 202).

The 1847 Poor Law obliged the community to supply for the local poor, but this demand was balanced by the paupers' duties to the poverty boards. Disobedient paupers could be sentenced to the same kind of treatment as that given to people without defense. By the end of the nineteenth century, a considerable share of the poor relief was supplied through poorhouses, which fitted well into the contradictory endeavor of caring for and controlling the poor.[3] These institutions were justified as a way of rationalizing assistance, including making use of the paupers' labor force, but were also intended to deter poor parish members from asking for public assistance. In addition, they were regarded as a space for moral education, work training, and control of poor people's behavior and reproduction (see, e.g., CSA 1907). This was partly accomplished through rules of behavior and supervision. Dislocations to other rooms and roommates and ultimately eviction from the poorhouse were among the available sanctions (Sahlin 1996).

Industrialization, deregulation of the labor market, and urbanization in the decades around the turn of the century fortified the detachment of housing from employment. Municipalities hesitated to get involved in housing and claimed that it was the responsibility of employers and, to some extent, of philanthropic associations to supply permanent housing (Johansson 1962). However, when cities were overcrowded by migrants looking for work, and even "decent working class families" (Johansson 1962, 518) were found in destitute conditions, the authorities opened public localities to serve as temporary emergency shelters. At the beginning of the twentieth century, homelessness among poor, single men was also discovered to be a social problem and subjected to a series of investigations and political discussions (Swärd 1998, 56ff.).

Since the late nineteenth century, charity organizations and reform movements have argued that those who were simply poor, like old people with no relatives to take care of them, should be distinguished and physically separated from the asocial poor, who needed training and correction (CSA 1907, 127, 131ff.). In the first decades of the twentieth century, a differentiated legislation enabled and encouraged authorities to incarcerate and treat alcoholics, "negligent family suppliers," vagrants, and orphans in separate institutions. Subsequently, the poorhouses were increasingly inhabited by old poor, and after the pension reform in the 1930s and the emergence of social housing for families with children, most poorhouses were closed, or renamed "homes for the elderly."

In the early 1920s, Stockholm City built a number of rental flats to alleviate the housing need. At about the same time rents were regulated, and the first public housing agencies for the allocation of vacant flats were established (Johansson 1962, 529 ff.). Nevertheless, homelessness and the need for emergency shelters prevailed. A new, comprehensive housing policy, introduced in the 1930s, was implemented in the subsequent decades of continuing growth of wealth and welfare. It was decided that housing supply was a responsibility of the municipalities with financial support from the central government. An increasing part of the local housing stock was built, owned, and run by municipality housing companies, while local housing authorities mediated state loans and allocated vacant flats according to need and waiting time. Pensioners and low-income families received housing contributions. The rights of tenants versus their landlords were gradually reinforced during this period. Local and state authorities controlled the planning, building, and, to some extent, the allocation of housing. People with special needs for housing were given priority in the municipalities' housing queues and achieved full tenancy rights when they were assigned flats. Rents were regulated at first, but since the 1970s they have been settled through collective negotiations on the "use value" of the flat.[4] In the 1960s, there was a considerable shortage of housing, which hit poor, single men especially hard. However, through the construction of a great number of new homes—the so-called Million Program—the housing shortage was resolved in the mid-1970s and homelessness diminished.

In the 1980s, however, a number of problems in the housing market contributed to a turn in discourse and policy. Due to a surplus of housing, municipality housing companies suffered economically from high vacancy rates, which in turn stimulated a segregation process. A great number of newly built, owner-occupied, single-family houses in the late 1970s had drained the rental areas of two-parent families and middle-class tenants. Some of the rental housing projects became problem-ridden, disreputable, residential blocks characterized by empty flats, vandalism, and poor maintenance. A growing share of their tenants was made up of welfare-dependent people and immigrants or migrants from other regions. The municipality housing companies' response was to blame "noisy neighbors" for their projects' disrepute, and they lobbied for increased independence from the governing bodies regarding choice of tenants and evictions policies. Their "border control" was sharpened, and they demanded the transfer of their "social responsibility" to the local social authorities (see Sahlin 1996).

Eviction rates almost doubled between 1988 and 1993 (Flyghed and Stenberg 1993: 17). In the first four years of the 1990s, 27,000 households were threatened by eviction each year, and about 7,000 of them were actually evicted (NBHW 1998, 85). Since then, the number has decreased slightly. Nevertheless, in the period from 1994 to 1996, 17,381 households were evicted, the great majority on the grounds of rent arrears (NBHW 1998, 87). Since the late 1980s, social authorities have become increasingly involved in housing for tenants who have been rejected by landlords because of previous evictions, recorded rent arrears, or lack of regular income.

Homelessness policies in the last 150 years have fluctuated between two different discourses and practices. In the nineteenth century, the central and local state cared less about housing the poor than controlling them. Vagrants and people without defense were considered dangerous to society and in need of control and discipline. Their asocial lifestyle was thought to be the main problem and the cause of their homelessness. From the 1940s to the mid-1980s, the predominant policy was to increase access to affordable housing through planning for its supply and rationing. Since then a reorientation has taken place, starting with the landlords' notion of noisy neighbors, which retained features of the old vagrancy discourse. The landlords' view coincided with the shifts in housing and social policies, which began in the 1980s and were fully implemented in the 1990s, directly affecting homelessness.

POLICIES AND RIGHTS

In the last two decades, Swedish social and housing policies have gone through fundamental changes and reductions. This development reflects a broader ideological shift and a restructuring of the Swedish welfare model, the public economy, and politics.

Shrinking Social Policy

After World War II, Sweden gained an international reputation for its comprehensive welfare policy directed toward a comparatively high degree of social and economic equality. However, recent shifts in policies have changed this image. Tax reform measures passed in 1990 widened the income gap and increased rents, and adjustment to various European Union treaties entailed reducing public expenditures and abandoning the full-employment policy. Concurrently, an economic depression in the early 1990s and measures to reduce budget deficits led to a series of additional decisions which impoverished a considerable part of the population. Unemployment rates grew in the first half of the 1990s from around 1 to 2 percent to 10 percent, and reached 20 percent for young people. As the demand for social security grew dramatically, individual social benefits were cut stepwise, and eligibility criteria were sharpened (see, e.g., SOU 2000, 3, for an overview).

Almost all the components of the general welfare system were depreciated in the 1990s, in most cases, without being principally contested. This holds for the state guarantee for maintenance contributions from parents who are not living with their children, general child allowances, and means-tested housing contributions for low-income households. In addition, fees for social services like child day care and elderly care have increased. The net income gap has widened, and especially young people and single parents have suffered considerably from changes in the public sector (Statistics Sweden 1999a).

According to the sixth paragraph in the Social Service Act, valid since 1982, individuals who cannot satisfy their needs themselves or in other ways have a right, under certain conditions, to assistance from the local social authority for their subsistence and in other respects of their lives. This clause was, in the 1980s, interpreted quite generously as a right to a minimum income for those who had no resources and no other means of support. In principle, people dependent on social welfare were also entitled to contributions to their actual net rent. In the 1990s, however, due to the economic crisis, increasing numbers of people in need, and ideological changes, Swedish legislation and its interpretation have changed. The monthly amount of money regarded "necessary for a decent living" was reduced in most municipalities,[5] and currently contributions to housing costs are only accepted if they are "reasonable," that is "what local low-income households normally can afford" (SOSF 1998, 11:6), which is taken to mean a "normal" rent for a large-enough flat, regardless of the actual housing costs.

In principle, the Swedish system of social welfare would prevent people from becoming homeless because of poverty, since assistance is paid for rent and general living costs. Nevertheless, problems arise for those who are stuck with high-rent dwellings and cannot find any cheaper residence, those who are already homeless or need to break away from their families, and those who have rent arrears. The willingness of the local social authorities to contribute to their clients' rent debts was remarkably reduced in the beginning of the 1990s (Flyghed 1995, 111; NBHW and NBHBP 1994). Consequently, they have been less prone to prevent evictions. This tendency may, in turn, be related to the fact that the authorities now have other and cheaper options to preclude literal homelessness (Sahlin 1996).

In the cities, a few religious organizations—the City Mission and the Salvation Army—offer cheap or free meals and run shelters, but these groups are paid by the local social authorities. In Sweden there are no charities or private funds to help support people in need of assistance for their housing costs or rent debts.

Declining Housing Policy

From the 1940s to the late 1980s, Swedish housing policy has had some stable features. These were, primarily, general housing subventions for building and renovating houses, regardless of ownership and tenure; means-tested housing allowances to families with children and to pensioners, regardless of type of tenure; and a fairly big stock of public housing[6] owned by municipality housing companies and eligible for all kinds of tenants. Another cornerstone of this housing policy was a degree of local public control over allocation of building sites, newly built flats, and public housing. In the years from 1981 to 1993, municipalities could also control the allocation of private rental flats, if necessary, to counteract segregation and homelessness.[7] In the beginning of the 1990s, more than half of the municipalities ran public housing agencies which allocated flats according to waiting time and needs, where homelessness, overcrowding, and family split ups were among the criteria for precedence in the housing queue (Sahlin 1993).

As a result of the neoliberal system shift in the beginning of the 1990s,[8] including "deregulation" and reduced subsidies, the scope and importance of housing policy have been dramatically reduced. Very few new homes (except in special housing) have been built since the early 1990s, and government subsidies to housing are in fact being converted into a net return stemming from estate taxes. Rents grew with 50 percent at fixed prices from 1986 to 1997 (Turner 1999, 147), and they often exceeded costs for other types of tenure (Lind 1999, 179). Decreasing housing allowances (SOU 1996, 156), a widening income gap (SOU 1995, 104; Statistics Sweden 1999a, 101), and the fact that public housing is to a much greater extent allocated through the market add to the conclusion that low-income renters in general have become the ultimate victims of the system shift (Bergenstråhle 1999; Turner 1999).

During the 1990s, the economic situation worsened for families with children and young people (Statistics Sweden 1999, 101).[9] In 1995 young, single-person households paid an average of between 40 and 45 percent of their net income in rent (Turner 1999, 152). Persistently high vacancy rates in the 1990s[10] reflect the fact that many people cannot afford to rent vacant flats, but also that landlords prefer empty flats to tenants who appear "risky" to them.[11]

In 1991 a right-wing government, determined to start a system shift to the right by dismantling the housing policy, closed the government's Housing Department. At the same time, allocation of housing was deregulated, as was the obligation of municipalities to plan for their inhabitants' housing supply (Government Bill 1992/93, 242). Within the previous system, municipalities could condition their recommendations of state loans for building and rebuilding, and new houses, which were not included in the local housing plan, were refused state subventions. Furthermore, it was a common prerequisite that newly built flats should be allocated through the public housing queue. Without subsidies and the right of veto, municipalities lost their bargaining position in relation to landlords. The Social Democratic government, in power since 1995, has not, despite a present economic boom, restored the housing policy but has, rather, reinforced its dismantling (see SOU 1996, 156; Palme 1999).

Since the economic crisis of the mid-1990s, many municipalities have ceased to use their municipality housing companies as tools for a local, socially oriented housing policy, although this is still legally possible. They try instead to extract an economic return from their shares in the companies or even realize its capital resources by selling them to private for-profit companies. In 1998 homeless people could get precedence in housing queues in only 6 percent of the municipalities, and in 2000 only 5 percent still had public housing agencies (NBHBP 1998, 61; NBHBP 2000, 26).

Deficient Housing Rights

The Swedish constitution stipulates a right to housing and a right to work, but there is no corresponding specific legislation according to which homeless individuals, in general, can claim a right to housing. Nevertheless, some categories of people have an explicit right to some kinds of housing; this is described below as "rights to housing." Housing rights also include the right to keep a home, which is usually called "tenants' rights," as well as economic assistance to pay rents or rent arrears, which was discussed above in connection with rights to welfare.

Rights to Housing

The Social Service Act states an explicit right to housing only for those who, because of age or disabilities, need "special housing," for instance, physically disabled individuals who want flats that are adjusted for wheelchairs. Since the adoption of the Law on Support and Services in 1994, social, mental, and physical dysfunctions should be ranked equal in this respect, but the law has been implemented only to a small degree for these additional groups (NBHW 1998). Homeless people who are not disabled have no enforceable right to housing of any kind but can only refer to their general right to assistance; neither do people with dysfunctions have any right to "normal" housing (Sahlin 1999; NBHW 1998).

On the other hand, according to the third paragraph in the Social Service Act, municipalities are obliged to give emergency help to people within their borders who are suffering. This is mostly interpreted to mean that nobody should have to sleep rough but is entitled to, at the least, a bed for the night in a shelter or a cheap hotel. As soon as the immediate problem is solved and contact with the social authorities is established, however, subsequent conditions may be added, for instance, the client's sobriety and active job seeking. If individuals fail to live up to such demands, they may be refused even temporary shelter the next night.

Social authorities sometimes interpret the right to assistance according to the sixth paragraph of the Social Service Act to include a right to housing for families with dependent children but fail to convince landlords to accept them as tenants. However, many local social authorities still succeed in helping homeless families get priority in public landlords' housing queues or, at least, they offer them a subleased flat on the secondary housing market.

Tenants' Rights

Before the 1930s, many landlords were simultaneously the tenants' employers, and households risked eviction when tenants lost their jobs or were involved in strikes. Since then, however, tenants' rights have developed. According to the Tenants' Law, the landlord cannot evict the tenant household, if there is an ordinary rent contract, as long as tenants pay their rent on time and do not destroy the dwelling or cause trouble for their environment. Rents cannot be raised except through collective negotiations with the Tenants' Association. When landlords want to evict a tenant, they have to go to court where possible extra conditions in an individual contract will have no force. This is the meaning of "tenure security." Landlords are also somewhat protected against rent losses by the rule that tenants must give three months' notice before they can terminate the contract.

As soon as tenants break the fundamental rules in the contract, they are evictable. Rents are paid monthly in advance, and if they have not been paid within a week after the due date, or if they are repeatedly paid a few days too late, there are legal grounds for eviction. In the first case, tenancy may be regained if the rent debt is paid within another two weeks. Tenants also risk eviction if they disturb their neighbors. In 1993 a new clause was included in the Tenants' Act, stating that the landlord is obliged to stop ongoing disturbances by tenants by warning them and reporting them to the local social authorities for possible measures. If neighbor complaints continue, landlords are supposed to give the tenant notice to move. In serious cases, which according to the bill often refer to people with mental disorders or substance abuse problems who are "incapable of independent living," this can be done without awaiting any court procedure, even if the nuisance has ceased (Government Bill 1992/93, 115).[12]

Eviction records and registered debts are public in Sweden. Most landlords reject housing applicants with recorded rent debts or previous evictions.

In conclusion, the social and economic safety net has been weakened at the same time as housing costs have increased. Housing rights have been strengthened for only a minority of disabled individuals, but rather reduced for most tenants. There are more gaps and holes, which in crisis situations, may result in homelessness.

HOMELESSNESS AS A PUBLIC PROBLEM: SCOPE AND IMAGE

In the 1980s, the National Board of Housing, Building and Planning (NBHBP) regularly analyzed the municipalities' housing queues to assess the need for housing. In 1991 there were 100,000 waiting individuals who were homeless, excluding those who lived in their parents' homes, and including 5,000 people living in institutions (NBHBP 1991, 24ff., 33). According to a survey taken of local social authorities in 1990, about 11,000 clients were homeless in the sense that they were not guaranteed housing the following month (Sahlin 1993, 62f.). The gap between these figures tells something about how the choice of informants affects the count of homeless people.

Client Counting

Homeless people in Sweden are not counted on a regular basis anymore, and the public housing agencies are currently too few in number to give an accurate representation of need in the country. Some cities have repeatedly mapped homeless clients, known by local social authorities, but they differ regarding definitions and informants, and while some count those who are homeless on a certain day, others include all who were homeless at some point during the last year. However, they do not show any univocal trend for the country. The city of Stockholm has concluded that its number of homeless clients has remained about 3,000 in 1993, 1996 and 1999 (Ågren et al. 1997; *Svenska Dagbladet*, May 12, 1999). In the city of Malmö, on the other hand, the number has grown with 60 percent between 1993 and 1999, when it was 1,004 (municipal documents). Malmö includes tenants on the secondary housing market, which Stockholm in most cases does not.

In the early 1990s, at the central level, responsibility for homelessness issues was transferred from the NBHBP to the National Board of Health and Social Welfare (NBHW) before the 1993 counting of the homeless. On the basis of a nationwide survey of local social and criminal authorities, treatment institutions, voluntary associations, and other social agencies, NBHW concluded that there were about 9,900 homeless individuals in the country during a certain week in 1993, which corresponds to a little more than 11 individuals per 10,000 inhabitants. Responses were checked for double counts, but missing cases were not analyzed (NBHW 1993). The survey was repeated in April 1999. The number of homeless people now amounted to only 8,440, but comparison with the 1993 figures is not recommended because the definition was more narrow in 1999, while the circuit of informants was wider (NBHW 2000, 6).

These counts suffer from several limitations. One is that they include only those homeless people who report themselves as such to social authorities. Since the social authorities cannot offer normal housing, homeless people who are not their clients for other reasons, such as social welfare or substance abuse, will not be counted. The same holds true for clients who have been rejected by the social authorities because they did not meet the conditions for housing assistance. Furthermore, people who temporarily rent homes from the authorities are in most cases excluded since they do have some kind of rented flat for the moment,[13] as do people who are temporarily doubling up with families or friends.

An asocial lifestyle as cause and characteristic of homelessness is implied not only in the choice of respondents, but also in the questionnaire (1993 as well as 1999), which does not cover housing access but includes questions about needed care and treatment, disabilities and disorders, and "predominant type of substance abuse during the last month" (NBHW 1999c).

In 1993, 17 percent of the reported homeless clients were women (NBHW 1993b). This proportion has risen to 21 percent in 1999 (NBHW 2000, 48). Among the recorded homeless women in the last survey, 59 percent were reported to be drug or alcohol abusers, while 41 percent were regarded to have mental problems (NBHW 2000, 41). Homeless people without additional problems of this kind have hardly any reason to contact the social authorities. The under-representation of women in surveys of homeless people may reflect a general tendency among social workers and landlords to be more sensitive to the housing needs of women, at least if they have children. Nevertheless, among all counted women (1,772 individuals), 43 percent had children younger than 18. Probably the great majority of these children lived with their fathers or were in foster care, since 36 children were reported to be homeless (ibid., 37).

To sum up, there is so far no valid information on the development of Swedish homelessness in terms of housing qualities or literal homelessness, nor on the absolute numbers, besides regarding the clients of social agencies. However, the number of clients who were temporarily housed by the authorities in training flats, transitional flats, and category houses without normal tenancy rights increased nine times between 1973 and 1990, and grew further with 54 percent in the following decade. If these tenants are included as homeless, the number has definitely grown in the past decades (Sahlin 1996, 196; NBHBP 2000, 29).

The Public Image

Each year before Christmas, the City Mission of Stockholm and the Salvation Army market their activities in order to promote contributions from the public to their shelters. Their advertisements include photos of stereotypical drinkers and outsiders, and the texts indicate—or sometimes frankly propose—that homeless women are prostitutes, and that homeless men are mentally ill and substance abusers. Such images have contributed to reluctance among people with nowhere to live to call themselves homeless and to their feelings of shame when they are so labeled. Nevertheless, the image that is put forward in these campaigns fits in well with the message of the NBHW, namely, that homeless people are not like the rest of us but have chosen decisively asocial lifestyles.

Authorities at municipal and state levels also put forward the asocial lifestyle account of homelessness. This is obvious in the conclusions of the 1993 mapping of homelessness and in local measures against it. The report recommends more surveys of people without housing and budget counseling for those who cannot pay the rent. For those who are "incapable of independent living," the suggestions are for more cooperation between local social authorities and landlords,[14] reinforced follow-up visits in training flats, and more "low-threshold" institutions. Local social authorities are also encouraged to establish more small-scale one-gender shelters and specific units for homeless people who are mentally ill (NBHW and NBHBP 1994, 12ff.).

In its directives to a Commission for New Forms of Support for the Homeless, settled two days before Christmas Eve in 1998, the government declared that social responsibility for the homeless lies ultimately with local social authorities. The government would contribute 60 million Swedish kronor for improved support for the homeless, including forms of housing suitable for different categories of the homeless and improved cooperation with "voluntary associations, criminal justice, and health authorities" (Government Directives 1998, 56). There is no indication that new forms of housing allocation will be explored, or that landlord policies of eviction and rejection or restrictive tendencies within social welfare will be reviewed (Government Directives 1998, 56).

In an analysis of the prevalent discourse on homeless women among service providers, Sahlin and Thörn (2000) found the following features to be common and central to current public understanding of female homelessness:

Homeless women are perceived as *hidden* in a dual sense. They are invisible in the environment and in services dominated by men, and they conceal themselves from the society in general and authorities specifically; this implies a relatively vast hidden statistic. They are also said to be *repressed and exploited by men* who abuse them physically at home and exploit them sexually when they are homeless. They are further regarded as having *more severe problems* than men do, because they are more injured by homelessness while at the same time they avoid services and authorities. Hence, they are expected to need more treatment and a longer time to recover once they are "discovered." Finally, they are considered to have *special needs*, for example, protection from men, which has motivated a growing share of institutions and shelters for women only (Sahlin and Thörn 2000, 35f.).

In short, the image of the homeless as people with asocial lifestyles is promoted in concert by the government, local social authorities, and charity organizations. This image is reinforced by the current kind of surveys that primarily map asocial lifestyles among homeless clients with recorded social problems and then make general claims about homeless people's problems.

CONTEMPORARY HOMELESSNESS POLICIES

In place of the abandoned housing policy, a homelessness policy has emerged in Sweden, governed by a social work approach and inspired by the belief that homeless people need control and support. While their impact on housing allocation has diminished, the local social authorities have been assigned increased responsibility for homeless people and for misbehaving tenants. Both of these groups are in the legislation and the authority discourse subsumed under the label "incapable of independent living" (Government Bill 1992/93, 115), which has become a key concept in the new homelessness discourse (Sahlin 1998b). This development lies behind the reopening of night shelters in the last decade, as well as the establishment of various kinds of supported, training, or transitional housing organized and run by—or at least monitored by—local social authorities.

The Secondary Housing Market

In the late 1980s, a new discourse of homelessness evolved, focusing on lifestyles as the site for causes and solutions. This was the result of a convergence of several tendencies. First, public landlords fought for increased discretion in the selection of tenants and for escape from the responsibility for households that were regarded as "disturbing" or risky rent payers, and second, local social authorities were looking for new and cheaper forms to control and support their clients. When municipality housing companies excluded more tenants, they invited local social authorities as intermediate landlords for clients who would not otherwise be accepted. By viewing (potentially) homeless clients as incapable of independent living, the landlord role could be assimilated into social work discourse and practice. However, just like the old poorhouse a century ago, once this subleasing system was established, it was also used by social authorities as a means of monitoring and influencing their clients. Desire for housing and fear of eviction became tools for convincing clients to agree to and comply with work plans aimed at an altered lifestyle.

As a consequence, new forms of "social housing" for the homeless have emerged during the last decade: category houses, group homes, transitional flats, training flats, and so on in dwellings that local social authorities rent and sublease to homeless clients. These homes are let with special contracts, characterized by the absence of tenure security and by special rules and conditions such as sobriety, work participation, and prohibitions against pets and night guests. Tenants are supervised by social workers, who often keep an extra key for possible surprise home visits, and they risk being evicted immediately (without notice and without any court procedure) if they break the special rules. The tenants are selected from among homeless clients, in principle according to need, but, in practice, those with the best prospects are prioritized. Homeless families with children are rarely referred to shelters and hotels except in emergency situations but get access to the secondary housing market, primarily to the "highest steps" on the staircase, that is to ordinary flats integrated in residential areas. This is due to the strong conviction among local social authorities that children's homes should be as "normal" as possible, regardless of their parents' problems (Sahlin 1996).

According to a nationwide survey conducted in 1990, 8,600 flats were sublet to clients by local social authorities with special contracts (Sahlin 1993). Since then, at least the three biggest cities have increased their number considerably without having reduced literal homelessness (Sahlin 1998a). The *manifest* functions of this "secondary housing market" are to provide temporary housing, on the one hand, and to train homeless clients in "independent living" in order to reintegrate them into the regular housing market, on the other (Sahlin 1998a).

There is no proof, however, that this system does indeed help homeless people reenter the regular housing market.[15] On the contrary, tenants are frequently locked into the secondary housing market or thrown back from it to the grey area of lodging with acquaintances and staying in institutions or night shelters. The *latent* functions are probably better fulfilled, namely, to relieve other land-lords from the social responsibility for tenants whom they think may be unreliable as neighbors or rent payers, and thereby to legitimize exclusion from the housing market, and to extend the local social authorities' mastery and control over their clients (Sahlin 1996).

When local social authorities control a diverse stock of transitional, training, and category housing, they tend to organize it as a "staircase of transition," reflecting the idea that clients with difficulties living independently could gradually learn to do so (Sahlin 1998a). Various kinds of dwellings and leases are hierarchically arranged from a bottom step of deficient standards and minimal or absent tenants' control, such as in night shelters; rooms in group housing or small flats in category houses for alcoholics or drug addicts; training flats with increased standards and privacy; ordinary "transitional" flats, although with special restrictions of tenure; and finally one's own flat with a regular contract. The intention is that clients in the course of training, and through support and sanctions, will change their lifestyles and gradually move up the staircase of transition until they eventually become capable of independent living and are hence accepted in the regular housing market (Sahlin 1998a).

In Sweden there is a growing conception that homeless women experience and cope with homelessness in ways differing from men. One consequence of this view is the emergence of shelters and institutions targeting homeless women. Just as the men, they are subjected to surveillance and prohibitions regarding drugs, pets, and the like, but in addition, they are not allowed to accept male visitors. Consequently, homeless couples cannot stay together in shelters, institutions, or transitional flats but are forced to split up. The underlying idea is that women's problems are the same as those of men, but with "dependence on men" as an additional deficit. Therefore, women are supposed to need training in performing their gender role in a right way. Furthermore, the selection practice among institutions and services for homeless women excludes many of them. Most emergency centers for battered women fleeing from their homes reject women who abuse drugs or alcohol or have psychiatric problems. These conditions, complemented by the fact that women seem to have better access than men to ordinary housing, the "highest" steps in the staircase of transition, and to temporary lodging with relatives, contribute to the fact that the number of homeless women in shelters remains comparatively low, while their share of the secondary housing market is greater. Among all clients who received assistance in the form of housing by local social authorities in 1998, one-third were women (Sahlin and Thörn 2000; NBHW 1999c).

The secondary housing market has two pitfalls that are not yet fully recognized by social authorities. First, the original landlords are often quite happy with the reduced security of tenure, special rules of behavior, and the management assistance they get from social workers. There are simply no incentives for them to offer regular contracts, once these have been abolished, and they can mostly reject tenants on the same grounds as previously, so that the highest step is beyond reach even if tenants have proven capable of independent living (Sahlin 1998a). Despite high vacancy rates, public landlords have tightened their criteria for accepting tenants in the 1990s and often require them to have stable positions in the labor market and no recorded debts (Flyghed 1995, 113). Second, using a home or a chance to better housing as a reward for good behavior implies its opposite, namely, that eviction or transferral to lower steps in the staircase are utilized as sanctions for misbehavior. This, in turn, requires a last resort. Today, night shelters are filled with people who have stumbled and fallen in the staircase of transition or who are not even trusted to take the first step on it. According to a longitudinal case study, social workers regard these excluded clients as not only incapable of independent living, but also incapable of reform (Sahlin 1998b; see also Juhila 1992).[16]

Neo-Institutions Called Special Housing

A phenomenon, akin to the secondary housing market and relevant for homelessness in a broader sense, is the increasing number of "special housing" now substituting for total institutions for people with mental, social, or physical dysfunctions. They are mostly arranged as "group housing," in which residents have single rooms or small flats and share some common space, and where there is support or caring personnel available. Sometimes group housing results from nominal and economic changes of care institutions: former patients/clients are charged rents for their rooms and fees for services, which may be quite similar to what they used to be. Sometimes the tenants do not even have single rooms,[17] and in addition, the security of tenure is often very weak. Residents sublease their homes from the local social authorities and may, for instance, be dislocated to another room or housing unit if some other client is assessed to be in greater need. Still, they are precluded, economically and formally, from having their own homes outside the institution. Consequently, this kind of group housing creates a hybrid between normal housing and institutions.

The total number of flats or rooms in regulated special housing was, in 1998, assessed to be 149,200, of which the great majority targeted elderly, senile, or frail people. However, about 16,000 were established according to the Law on Support and Services for disabled persons. Among these, around 12,000 were inhabited by people with learning disabilities, and the remaining 4,000 were suffering from chronic mental illness (Sahlin 1999, 33; NBHW 1998, 80). National statistics do not register types of tenure, rents, or similar aspects of special housing. Special housing differs from the secondary housing market in that it is partly funded by the government and therefore somewhat regulated, and in that it does not aim at transition into the regular housing market. Still there is some overlap.

Among the various disabled target groups, it seems as though people with learning disabilities are the winners for two reasons. Their alternative would be rather small institutions or nursing homes, not ordinary flats for independent living. In addition, these groups have more often succeeded in obtaining regular contracts, a relative degree of self-determination in their homes, and self-contained apartments, which are also on average larger than those for other groups (Mallander 1999). People with mental disorders, on the other hand, often must resort to a room in a shared flat (see, e.g., Stockholm City 1997), which is presumably quite stressful when coresidents are psychotic or depressed. Substance abusers are often referred to category houses (mostly not included in the statistics of special housing) where they experience similar problems when they are sober, while their neighbors are drinking or taking drugs.

Many municipalities have come to regard group housing and category housing for drug abusers, alcoholics, and people with mental illnesses as permanent, and despite deficient tenure security and integrity, and sometimes substandard housing quality, their residents are not included as "homeless" in counts. The probable reason is that homeless people are counted—nationally and locally—not because of any pure interest of knowledge, nor in order to assess the need for improved planning or allocation of housing, but rather to get an idea of the number of people who are possible clients of the contemporary, social-work-based homelessness policy.

Hence, the social workers' three roles in relation to their homeless clients—social workers, landlords, and informants—might explain a great deal of their promotion of the current asocial lifestyle account of local homelessness problems, as well as its impact on the government discourse.

REPRODUCING HOMELESSNESS: THE ZERO-SUM GAME OF HOUSING CONTROL

Homelessness historically has been approached from two competing or sometimes complementary perspectives: one that focuses on the lack of suitable, affordable, and accessible housing, and another—following the vagrancy policy—that focuses on asocial lifestyles as the core and cause of the homelessness problem.[18] Each tradition brings out a consistent set of ideas regarding prevention and solution of homelessness and is claimed by different authorities. As with other social problems, it is the "owner" of homelessness that defines its roots as well as suitable measures to combat it (Sahlin 1992).

Beginning in the 1930s, a long tradition of controlling and punishing vagrants was replaced by the conception of homelessness as a housing problem to be combated with public control over housing production and allocation. Beginning in the mid-1980s, however, a new shift occurred, with the recent turn of social and housing policies. These changes include dismantling the housing policy, including public control over housing allocation and planning, on the one hand, and depreciating benefits and sharpening eligibility criteria within social security, on the other hand. In addition, the interpretation of the general right to social assistance has become more restrictive in the 1990s. Since 1994 disabled people—which in principle includes also people with severe social difficulties—have a right to housing with special services, if they need it. This does not, however, include a right to normal housing.

Gaps, mismatches, and contradictions in policies and rights produce unsafe spaces in which individuals may lose their homes or fail to access housing. These contradictions should not be regarded as policy mistakes. Rather, the political intention is that the individual should not be 100 percent safeguarded against poverty and homelessness. Landlords claim the right to evict in order to keep the discipline and rent-paying morale high among their tenants; social authorities want discretion and the right to refuse help in order to promote a change of lifestyle, which they consider more important for their clients' housing situation in the long run. Emile Durkheim (1893) pointed out that the function of punishment for rule breaking is to keep the norms alive, which in turn reinforces social bonds and a sense of community. What is significant in the current Swedish situation, however, is that the central and local state have withdrawn their influence from the housing market, and homelessness is no longer considered too harsh a punishment for the social authorities to execute. Surveillance of the homeless has substituted for control of the market.

Granted that the housing market excludes people, and social and housing policies allow homelessness occasionally to strike poor people, the role of contemporary homelessness policy in Sweden is ambiguous. Its core element is to provide training in independent living in subleased flats with reduced security. Although it is intended to reduce homelessness, it instead reproduces the problem through promoting the image that their tenants and those literally homeless are incapable of independent living. Furthermore, through this secondary housing market, the number of people who are homeless in the sense of lacking basic control over their living space increases. The growing number of homes in special housing are often substandard and reduce the residents' integrity. At the same time, public landlords are relieved of their social responsibility, while their power over tenants and housing applicants is reinforced.

These varieties of authority-managed housing with high rents, but impaired privacy and security of tenure, are justified through comparison with either literal homelessness or old-fashioned total institutions—and through the notion that their inhabitants are "incapable" of normal housing. However, this account is deceptive. The revival of night shelters in Sweden in the last decade is rather an unintended effect of the tendency among authorities to arrange their secondary housing market as a staircase of transition, which requires a lowest step to which evicted and rejected clients may be referred. And it was not the case a few decades ago that people with mental illnesses and substance abuse problems lived all their lives in hospitals or total institutions; most of them had regular homes to return to in periods when they did not need care.

In the secondary housing market, as well as in the neo-institutions called special housing, residents are deprived of tenants' rights to tenure security, integrity, privacy, and self-determination.[19] When housing is used as a means of control in order to alter people's lifestyles, it necessarily occurs at the cost of the clients' own control over their homes. In this way, control over a specific home is a zero-sum game. The social worker and the tenant cannot both ultimately decide, for instance, who should be let in or locked out and what rules should govern life inside its walls.

No doubt, this situation would gain attention as a public problem and as part of the homelessness issue, if the landlords were not authorities. However, these clients/tenants are typically not included in counts of homeless people, which today completely rely upon social workers as informants. The public image of homelessness, as an inevitable problem rooted in individual deficiencies such as substance abuse and mental illness, is founded and reproduced in national surveys. The choice of investigators, respondents, definitions, and questions all contribute to the reinforcement of an image of homeless people as problematic "others" who need control, support, and special housing, but not normal homes or normal conditions. The charity organizations' campaigns for alms to their shelters reinforce this message.

In summary, homelessness in Sweden is affected by two interrelated policy tendencies. First, the possibilities for homeless people to gain access to normal housing have been reduced. Estate owners have reinforced their "border control" through rejection of risky tenants and expulsion through eviction, while public control over housing allocation has diminished. Increased rents contribute to the exclusion, as does the growing share of the population with very low income. At the same time, evictions of tenants who are considered incapable of independent living have been facilitated.

The other tendency is for a growing number of people to live in insecure conditions as tenants of local social authorities, where the goal of (re-)inclusion in the housing market is either uncertain and facing many obstacles, or eventually abandoned by the authorities. These tenants suffer from deficient tenure security and lack of privacy.

The recent development of Swedish homelessness may be summarized in the following way: For the majority of people, the housing situation has improved regarding both the control and quality of dwellings. The minority of people who continuously sleep rough or in temporary shelters—the literally homeless—has probably increased somewhat but are still rather few. A much larger middle group has probably similar standards as in previous decades but considerably less control over their homes. The predominant part of this group stays temporarily with friends or relatives or with families they want to break away from because they cannot afford or are not trusted to rent vacant flats; only a few of these households are known to social authorities and reported in the surveys.

Another part resides in the local social authorities' special housing or secondary housing market and is not considered "capable" of anything better and hence not counted in among the homeless.

This regulated lack of housing control should by no means be regarded as a residual problem, but rather as the deliberate result of current homelessness policies. The winners of these games are the landlords, who have increased their discretionary power over housing applicants and tenants and reduced their responsibilities and economic risks. The fourth party, the central government, has withdrawn from the game in order to help out the market forces and the budget deficits.

A number of steps might counteract homelessness in Sweden. First, a right to (normal) housing should be introduced, handled, and secured by housing authorities, detached from social work. Second, the state should regain public control over housing allocation in order to facilitate mediation of vacant flats according to need and also to enable homeless people to obtain full tenancy rights and normal homes. Third, municipalities should use their housing companies as means for a fair and comprehensive housing supply, instead of as a source of profit. Fourth, people who are currently housed by the local social authorities should be acknowledged with full tenancy rights; these should be valid irrespective of the status of the landlord. Fifth, the already existing right to support in housing, for those who want it, should be respected regardless of tenure. Sixth, and finally, landlords' rights to evict need to be restricted and circumscribed.

With such a policy, homelessness could be avoidable in Sweden.

REFERENCES

Ågren, G., E. Berglund, E. Finne, and P. Franér. 1997. *Hemlösa i Stockholm 1996* (Homeless in Stockholm 1996). FoU-rapport 1997:9, Stockholm City: Research and Development Department, Social Services in Stockholm City.

Avramov, D. 1995. *Homelessness in the European Union: Social and Legal Context of Housing Exclusion in the 1990s.* Brussels: Feantsa.

Bengtsson, B., and E. Sandstedt, eds. 1999. *Systemskifte i bostadspolitiken?* (System shift in housing policy?). Boinstitutets Årsbok 1999. Stockholm: Boinstitutet.

Bergenstråhle, S. 1999. *Boende och välfärd 1986–97* (Housing and welfare 1986–97). Stockholm: Boinstitutet.

Boréus, K. 1994. *Högervåg: Nyliberalismen och kampen om språket i svensk offentlig debatt 1969–1989* (The shift to the right: Neo-liberalism and the struggle about the language in Swedish public discourse). Stockholm: Tiden.

Busch-Geertsema, V. 1998. *Rehousing Projects for Single Homeless Persons: Innovative Approaches in Germany.* National Report 1997 for the European Observatory on Homelessness. Brussels: Feantsa.

Christensen, A. 1994. *Hemrätt i hyreshuset* (Right to one's home in the rental house). Lund: Juristförlaget.

CSA (Centralförbundet för socialt arbete/Central Association for Social Work). 1907.

Reformlinjer för svensk fattigvårdslagstiftning (Principles of reform of Swedish legislation on poverty). Stockholm.

Durkheim, É. 1984 [1893]. *The Division of Labor in Society.* New York: Macmillan.

Finne, E. 1997. *Socialtjänstens kontakter med missbrukare, psykiskt störda och hemlösa 1996* (Local social authorities' contacts with substance abusers, mentally diseased, and homeless in 1996). FoU-rapport 1997:15. City of Stockholm.

Flyghed, J. 1995. "Vräkt till hemlöshet? Vräkningar i Sverige 1982–1994" (Evicted into homelessness? Evictions in Sweden 1982–1994). *Socialvetenskaplig Tidskrift* 2, no. 2:99–116.

Flyghed, J., and S. Stenberg. 1993. *Vräkt i laga ordning* (Legally evicted). Rapport 1993/94:1. Vällingby: Konsumentverket (National Consumer Authority).

Foucault, M. 1985 [1972]. *Madness and Civilization.* New York: Vintage Books.

Government Bill 1992/93:115. 1993. *Om ändringar i jordabalkens hyresregler* (On changes in the tenancy legislations).

Government Bill 1992/93:242. 1993. *Om minskad statlig reglering av kommunernas ansvar för boendefrågor* (On reduced governmental regulation of the municipalities' responsibility for housing issues).

Government Directives 1998:56. 1998. *En bostadssocial beredning* (A commission for housing social issues).

Government Directives 1998:108. 1998. *Nya former för stödåt hemlösa* (New forms of support for the homeless).

Hertting, N., E. Sandor, Jr., H. Szemzo, and I. Tosics. 1999. *Strategies to Combat Homelessness in Western and Eastern Europe: Trends and Traditions in Statistics and Public Policy.* Manuscript. United Nations.

———. 2000. *Homelessness in Western and Eastern Europe: Trends and Traditions in Statistics and Public Policy.* Working Paper no. 31. Govle: Institute for Housing and Urban Research.

Johansson, A. 1962. "Bostadspolitiken" (The housing policy). In *Hundraår under kommunalförfattningarna 1862–1962* (Hundred years with municipality statutes, 1862–1962), 509–96. Swedish Rural Municipality Association, Swedish County Association, and Swedish Town Association.

Juhila, K. 1992. "Bottom-of-the-Barrel Housing Markets: Discourse Analysis of the Practices of the Municipal Housing and Social Authorities." In *Hemlöshet i Norden* (Homelessness in northern countries), ed. M. Järvinen and C. Tigerstedt, 183–94. NAD-publication no. 22. Helsingfors: Nordiska Nämnden för Alkohol-och drogforskning.

Lext, G. 1968. *Mantalsskrivningen i Sverige före 1860* (Census registration in Sweden before 1860). Gothenburg: Department of Economic History.

Lind, H. 1999. "Bostadspolitikens förändringar: Pendelrörelse eller dialektisk process?" (Housing Policy Changes: Oscillation or a dialectical process?). In *Systemskifte i bostadspolitiken?*, ed. B. Bengtsson and E. Sandstedt, 38–53. Stockholm: Boinstitutet.

Main, T. J. 1996. "Analyzing Evidence for the Structural Theory of Homelessness." *Journal of Urban Affairs* 18, no. 4:449–58.

Mallander, O. 1999. *De hjälper oss tillrätta: Normaliseringsarbete, självbestämmande och människor med psykisk utvecklingsstörning* (They help us out—Normalization work, self-determination and people with learning disabilities). Lund: School of Social Work.

Sweden 59

Mossler, K., J. Torége, and A. Öström. 1999. "120 000 barn berörs av långvarigt socialbidrag" (120,000 children affected by durable welfare reception). *Välfärdsbulletinen* 2.

NBHBP (National Board of Housing, Building, and Planning [Boverket]). 1991. *Bostadsmarknadsläget 1991* (The situation on the housing market 1991). Boverket Media 1991:38. Karlskrona: NBHBP.

———. 1998. *Bostadsmarknadsläge och förväntat bostadsbyggande 1998–99. Kommunernas bedömning* (The housing market situation and expected housing building 1998–1999. The municipalities' estimates). NBHBP-Report 1998:1. Karlskrona.

———. 2000. *Bostadsmarknadsläge och förväntat bostadsbyggandeår 2000–2001* (The situation on the housing market and expected housing building 2000–2001). Karlskrona.

NBHW (National Board of Health and Welfare [Socialstyrelsen]). 1993. *Hemlösa i Sverige. En kartläggning* (The homeless in Sweden: A mapping). Socialstyrelsen följer upp och utvärderar 1993: 13. Stockholm.

———. 1998. *Reformens första tusen dagar. Årsrapport för psykiatreformen 1998* (The first thousand days of the reform: Annual report on the psychiatry reform). Stockholm.

———. 1999a. *Verksamheter inom vård och omsorg om äldre och funktionshindrade 1998* (Activities in community care services for the elderly and disabled persons 1998). Stockholm.

———. 1999b. *Kartläggning av hemlösa i Sverige* (Mapping of homeless people in Sweden). Questionnaire and letter to the respondents in the 1999 homelessness survey, Dnr 62–621/99.

———. 1999c. *Socialstyrelsen kartlägger antalet hemlösa: 1 200 är uteliggare eller bor på härbärge* (The NBHW maps the number of homeless: 1,200 sleep rough or stay in shelters). Press release no. 45, 30.8.1999.

———. 2000. Hemlösa i Svenge 1999. *Vilka är de och vilken hjälp får de?* (The homeless in Sweden 1999. Who are they and what help do they get?). Stockholm.

NBHW and NBHBP. 1994. *De bostadslösas situation i Sverige* (The situation of the homeless in Sweden). Socialstyrelsen följer upp och utvärderar 1994:15. Stockholm.

Palme, J. 1999. "Swedish Social Security in the 1990s—Dismantling the Welfare State?" Paper presented at the meeting of the Swedish Sociological Association, Stockholm, January 28–29, 1999.

Sahlin, I. 1992. *Begreppet "hemlös": En kritisk granskning av använda definitioner* (The concept of homeless: A critical review of used definitions). Karlskrona: NBHBP.

———. 1993. *Socialtjänsten och bostaden: Redovisning av en enkätundersökning om socialtjänstens metoder och resurser att lösa klienternas bostadsproblem* (Social authorities and housing: Report on a survey about the social authorities' methods and resources for solving their clients' housing problems). Research report. Lund: Department of Sociology.

———. 1996. *På gränsen till bostad: Avvisning, utvisning, specialkontrakt* (On the border of housing: Rejection, expulsion, and special contracts). Lund: Arkiv.

———. 1998a. *The Staircase of Transition.* Swedish report to European Observatory on Homelessness 1997. Brussels: Feantsa.

———. 1998b. "Klara eget boende" (Incapable of independent living). In *Vardagsbegrepp i socialt arbete* (Everyday concepts in social work), ed. V. Denvall and T. Jacobson, 207–22. Stockholm: Norstedts Juridik.

————. 1999. *Supported Accommodation*. National Report to the European Observatory on Homelessness 1998. Brussels: Feantsa.

Sahlin, I., and C. Thörn. 2000. *Women, Exclusion and Homelessness*. National Report from Sweden to the European Observatory on Homelessness 1999. Brussels: Feantsa.

SOSFS (NBHW's Collection of Statutes). 1998:11. *Socialstyrelsens allmänna råd om försörjningsstöd* (General advice from NBHW on support for subsistence), 11.

SOU (Statens offentliga utredningar, or Government's Official Investigations). 1962:22. *Samhällsfarlig asocialitet* (Asociality dangerous to the society). Stockholm.

SOU 1995:104. *Skattereformen 1990–1991. En utvärdering* (The tax reform 1990–1991. An Evaluation). Commission for Evaluation of the Tax Reform. Stockholm.

SOU 1996:156. *Bostadspolitik 2000—från produktions-till boendepolitik* (Housing policy 2000—From production policy to housing policy). In Slutbetänkande av bostadspolitiska utredningen (Final report from the Commission on Housing Policy). Stockholm.

SOU. 2000:3. *Välfärd vid vägskäl. Utvecklingen under 1990-talet*. (Welfare at the crossroads: The development in the 1990s). The Commission for Welfare Account. Stockholm.

Statistics Sweden. 1990. Tables. <http://www.SCB.se/befovalfard/befolkning/fob/fob-typl.asp>.

————. 1999a. *Inkomstspridningen ökar men en liten ljusning för ungdomar* (The income gap increases but a slight improvement for youth). Press release no. 1999: 101.

————. 1999b. *Färre tomma lägenheter* (Fewer vacant flats). Press release no. 1999: 126.

Stockholm City. 1997. *Program för beredande av bostäder och boendestöd till hemlösa* (Program for supplying of housing and support in housing for the homeless). Utlåtande 1997:145 RVI.

"Stora brister i kommunernas socialtjänst" (Great deficiencies in the municipalities' social services), *Sydsvenskan*, June 18, 1999.

Swärd, H. 1998. *Hemlöshet: Fattigdomsbevis eller välfärdsdilemma?* (Homelessness: Proof of poverty or a dilemma of welfare?). Lund: Studentlitteratur.

Turner, B. 1999. "Bostadspolitikens blinda fläckar—om de fördelningspolitiska verkningarna av den förda politiken." (The blind spots of housing policy—On the distribution policy effects of the policy that is carried on). In *Systemskifte i bostadspolitiken?*, ed. B. Bengtsson and E. Sandstedt, 140–62. Stockholm: Boinstitutet.

BIBLIOGRAPHIC ESSAY

In order to give a fresh overview of the current housing and homelessness policy in Sweden, I have made use of several official printings and even of not yet published manuscripts. However, many of these references are bound to be obsolete as soon as new data are processed and published, or the policy changes. Other references function as examples of the prevailing discourse on homelessness, which I criticize. However, some books and articles which have inspired me and my understanding of the Swedish homelessness problem will probably have a more lasting interest and provide information of relevance also for other countries.

In "Bottom-of-the-Barrel Housing Markets. Discourse Analysis of the Practices of the Municipal Housing and Social Authorities," Kirsi Juhila shows how social workers in Finland tend to talk about their homeless clients, whom they regard as "incapable of independent living," in two different but interrelated ways. In the "rehabilitation discourse" the homeless client is regarded as curable through social work, such as training and support. When clients "fail" to improve in the intended way, however, the same "incapability" is viewed as permanent and is therefore embedded in a "discourse of hopelessness." Those who are described in this way are offered only "bottom of the barrel housing," that is, shelters, temporary accommodation, hostels, and institutions. This analysis is very convincing and has inspired and confirmed my own research on this topic in Sweden.

Volker Busch-Geertsema provides, in *Rehousing Projects for Single Homeless Persons: Innovative Approaches in Germany*, an encouraging account of well-founded research on working solutions for the homeless. Like Sweden, Germany has a modern housing stock and a well-developed social policy but still a number of homeless people. In this report, Busch-Geertsema reviews two pilot schemes for the provision of permanent housing to single homeless men with severe social difficulties. The projects were very successful, despite the fact that many of the tenants had been homeless for more than ten years and many feared that they would not be "capable of independent living." Evaluations showed that when these people obtained normal tenancy rights and only voluntary support (without having to be tested in various preparative steps), most of them succeeded in keeping their homes and becoming integrated into the society. One of the interesting features of these projects was that they targeted the "worst" among the homeless, instead of those with the best prospects to succeed. Projects oriented to the more "promising" individuals never impress those who are convinced that a great share of the homeless is "hopeless."

Two references should be mentioned because they deal with the problematic relationship between data on homelessness and definitions, namely Dragana Avramov's *Homelessness in the European Union: Social and Legal Context of Housing Exclusion in the 1990s*, based on national reports from the European Union, and Nils Hertting et al., *Strategies to Combat Homelessness in Western and Eastern Europe*. Because of their comparative perspective, both of these books are indirectly helpful for an understanding of the complicated relationship between policy and exclusion, as well as among numbers, definitions, and the recognition of homelessness as a social problem.

The titles mentioned above are all in English, but, finally, I would like to mention one of the few books on the topic in Swedish, namely, Hans Swärd, *Hemlöshet, Fattigdomsbevis eller välfärdsdilemma?* Besides giving a summary of Swedish and American debates and research on homelessness and a longitudinal register study of night shelter guests in a Swedish town in the 1990s, Swärd presents his own qualitative research on individual paths to homelessness and how these interact with structural changes in Sweden.

NOTES

1. The Swedish homelessness rate has been estimated to be higher than the median level among EU member countries (Avramov 1995, 92; Hertting et al. 1999, 17).

2. Although the definitions and the surveyed institutions and organizations differed somewhat, NBHW concluded from a comparison of its national surveys in 1993 and 1999, respectively, that the number of homeless people in Sweden was rather similar in both of these years, as was the number of literally homeless individuals (NBHW 2000, 6, 8). However, the number of individuals on the secondary housing market who are not officially included among the homeless but nevertheless lack tenure security and ordinary tenants' rights has increased from 8.580 in 1990 (Sahlin 1996, 195) to 13.180 in 2000 (NBHBP 2000, 29).

3. Ironically, poor people who yet had a place to live had to surrender their homes to the local poverty board when they could not support themselves. Their cottages were subsequently used for housing other paupers, who were homeless (Sahlin 1996).

4. This system prevails. However, in many regions the tenants' associations have agreed that local rent deals should also reflect the market value of the site.

5. In 1998 a minimum sum was stipulated in law. Nevertheless, municipalities often pay less (*Sydsvenskan,* June 18, 1999). A heated debate has centered around the meaning of "cannot satisfy their needs in other ways" and on establishing reasonable conditions for assistance. It is currently common that welfare recipients are referred to unpaid "job practice" (e.g., picking up litter), or that they have to prove that they personally applied for a certain number of jobs during the week. Those who fail or refuse to live up to the stipulated demands are denied assistance.

6. Of all Swedish households in 1990, 41 percent lived in owner-occupied homes and 15 percent in housing associations (the right to dispose of such a flat is tied to a share of the association, and it is bought and sold on an unregulated market, but the owners pay monthly fees for running and capital costs for the estate). The remaining 40 percent lived in rental flats, about half of which were owned by municipality housing companies (Statistics Sweden 1990). No census has been taken in Sweden since 1990.

7. This law was almost never applied to a concrete case, but it is a general perception that the mutual knowledge of its existence gave municipalities a favorable power position in negotiations with local landlords, although it also had some unintended political consequences (see Sahlin 1996).

8. That this shift took place at the ideological level in the 1980s has been evidenced by, among others, Boréus (1994). Whether or not there has actually been a system shift or only gradual, quantitative changes in housing policy is debated, as is reflected in the title of a recent anthology (in translation) *System Shift in Housing Policy?* (Bengtsson and Sandstedt 1999).

9. The number of children in families dependent on social welfare for at least ten months of the year more than doubled between 1990 and 1996 (Mossler, Torége, and Öström 1999).

10. In March 1999, 4.4 percent of all rental flats were vacant and 3.7 percent were available for immediate rent. The latter share was somewhat higher in 1998 (4 percent) but less than 1 percent in the years between 1987 and 1991 (Statistics Sweden 1999, 126).

11. Another important factor is the current recovery of the labor market in big cities, which do in fact have a shortage of housing today, while the depression prevails in many other regions and towns. Thirty-seven percent of the municipalities considered demolishing vacant rental flats to reduce their costs for the buildings in 2000, and in 1998, 3,600 flats were destroyed (NBHBP 2000, 20). High local vacancy rates do not, however, reduce homelessness rates—it is rather the other way around (Sahlin 1993).

12. In *Hemrätt i hyreshuset* (1994), law professor Anna Christensen commented on the bill in the following way: "The examples given by the Chief of the Department on how the new system is supposed to be applied give . . . the impression that exactly those persons 'who are incapable of independent living' should be taken away from the ordinary rental buildings" (170). See also Sahlin 1998b.

13. The definition appended to the questionnaire in April 1999 was as follows:

Homeless in this investigation means that the individual has no owned or rented home and is not permanently lodged or subleasing a home, and is obliged to resort to temporary housing alternatives or to sleeping rough. An individual who is staying in a prison or in a social or health institution should be included if he/she is expected to leave the institution within three months but has no dwelling to move to. An individual who temporarily stays with acquaintances should also be included if he/she, because of homelessness, has been in touch with the respondent during the week. (NBHW 1999b, Letter to Respondents)

The definition is very similar to the one used in the 1993 investigation, despite the fact that respondents obviously interpreted the latter differently.

14. However, the analysis of responses to a survey of local social authorities in all 284 municipalities in 1990 revealed that frequent formal and informal cooperation between local social authorities and landlords was *positively* correlated with local rates of homelessness and rates of clients regarded "incapable of independent living." In addition, more of the "incapables" were literally homeless in towns with intense and frequent landlord-authority cooperation (Sahlin 1993).

15. The secondary housing market did not grow out of evaluated projects and has shown, in most municipalities, to be quite immune to the shortage of scientific backing and positive results. German research on alternative schemes would otherwise have given reason to doubt (Busch-Geertsema 1998). In the scheme for permanent housing provision for homeless people, homeless people were "provided with normal and cheap housing at normal building standards, with usual tenancy agreements, situated in non-stigmatized surroundings" (Busch-Geertsema 1998, 11).

16. Some of the projects within the German research scheme for permanent housing targeted single men with severe social difficulties who had been homeless for many years. One of the interesting evaluation results was that clients whom social workers thought would not succeed in living independently actually did fine in their new homes: "At the end of the evaluation period, residents who had been expected to have a considerable need of care and a rather high risk of problems proved to be quite stable and needed only little care, whereas for some other cases the opposite turned out to be true" (Busch-Geertsema 1998, 19).

17. Actually, 3.6 percent of these homes consist of shared bedrooms, which corresponds to at least 7 percent of the residents. Another 10.1 percent of the homes have no cooking or sanitary facilities (NBHW 1999a, Table 2), which is otherwise considered essential for a dwelling.

18. It is common to distinguish between "structural" and "individual" paradigms within homelessness research (e.g., Swärd 1998; Main 1996). However, my distinction refers not only to causal theories, but also to policies and solutions. Furthermore, both "housing-related" and "lifestyle-related" causes and solutions may be traced back to power relations and decisions that are structurally determined and at the same time realized and expressed in individual actions.

19. Although more humane and comfortable, there is a certain resemblance to the great incarceration of the poor and deviant in the beginning of the seventeenth century, so thoroughly analyzed by Foucault (1985 [1972]), which was repeated in the expanding number of poorhouses 300 years later.

3

Understanding Homelessness and Social Policy in Denmark

TOBIAS BØRNER STAX

In researching the field of homelessness in Denmark, two questions recur. The first expresses skepticism about the existence of the phenomenon of homelessness at all. The second relates to the quantitative dimensions of such a phenomenon. However, both questions have been asked with varied frequencies over the years. Several years ago, the first question was often posed, followed by explanations of why such a question was relevant: either no such phenomenon was observed that necessitated social political interventions, or it would be argued, if a few persons were without shelter or in need of support for housing, such support could and would be provided in accordance with current social legislation. However, this first question is being asked less and less frequently, which raises the question: Why is that?

The second question, regarding the number of homeless people, has been asked far more frequently in recent years. By reflecting upon this question—as well as the often overlooked question about whom we are categorizing as socially excluded in general, and homeless in particular—I shall try to provide an insight into the current understanding of homelessness and social exclusion[1] in Denmark and explore whether the decline in the frequency of questioning the social political relevance of the concept of homelessness is a consequence of a quantitative development among the socially excluded.

WHO ARE THE HOMELESS IN DENMARK?

Estimating the numbers within the field of social exclusion in general and homelessness in particular is an activity in which many participate. But it is also an activity wherein many participants have no explicit, nor clear, conceptualization of whom they are estimating. Furthermore, many, if not most, of the estimates are based on rather dubious methods and questionable assumptions so that the results are inaccurate. The estimates of various subgroups of homeless people are worth considering for two reasons: they take on political significance in the sense that they are used in political debates to formulate social policies, and they indicate a range of estimates that provide insight into some public understanding of the quantitative extent of homelessness. The common understandings of homelessness and social exclusion in Denmark can be defined by two general approaches, often used in combination, that are based on the following categorizations: homelessness as place and homelessness as types of people.

Homelessness as Place

There are understandings of homelessness that take as their point of departure the actual whereabouts of people. One might capture the Danish understanding by constructing a continuum ranging from life on the streets to life in a flat over which one has juridical secured rights. The continuum of today is shown in Figure 3.1.[2] This understanding of a continuum can be traced in the social policies concerning the socially excluded. The categories included in this continuum change over time as do the demarcations of which groups are considered socially excluded or homeless. For example, looking back about five or ten years, the category of homeless people living in supported shared dwellings did not exist. During the 1990s, shared dwellings became a popular measure to provide for the homeless. This arrangement was regarded as one that could provide its tenants with the capabilities necessary for moving into an independently owned dwelling. However, in the newly enacted social legislation, there is a change in regard to the use of shared dwellings: these are now understood as possible places for permanent residence, and the inhabitants of shared dwellings are thus not necessarily considered homeless any more.[3]

Using actual place as the basis for estimating the number of homeless people in Denmark is the approach that underlies most count estimates. In regard to the category of people sleeping at shelters or similar institutions, it is possible to find yearly recurring counts from *Statistics Denmark*. These figures are presented in Table 3.1

These figures provide the only regular attempt at counting. Three of the changes that can be found in the table are a significant increase in the number of day users, a significant increase in the number of institutions, and a significant increase in the number of employees at these institutions. First a word on the increase in day users. The institutions have, over the years, taken on the role of a place where former inhabitants come to work for a longer or shorter time during the day. It is a new group of users within the institutional system. Looking at the other changes one might—with the relatively steady number of 24-

Figure 3.1
Homelessness Understood According to Place of Residence

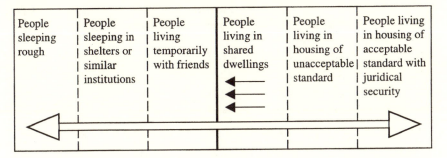

hour users and the increase in the number of institutions—think of a tendency toward establishing smaller institutions: the average number of beds per institution has dropped from 57 in 1977 to 28 in 1998. Along similar lines, an increase in staff size per 24-hour user can be calculated from 1982 to 1997: in 1982 there was 0.43 staff per user; in 1998, the equivalent number was 0.65. It has been pointed out, however, that identifiable changes are more the result of a changed inclusion under Section 105 in the social legislation[4] rather than a change among the existing institutions and groups of users.[5] The larger institutions for homeless people did not, until 1998, experience a development toward smaller units, nor did they experience an increase in staff size.[6] An alternative explanation could be that some small, more staff-intensive institutions have come into existence and that these have been administratively placed under Section 105 in the Social Assistance Act.[7] This does raise a significant concern regarding the usability of the numbers—at least the validity is questionable if one intends to use the figure as an illustration of a quantitative development. Furthermore, one of the seemingly interesting findings in these years' counts might be that the 24-hour users, from 1982 onward, continually take up about 90 to 100 percent of the beds, despite the fluctuation in the number of beds. It might be concluded that there are people enough to fill the beds available. This, again, questions the validity of using the figures as estimates of anything but the number of beds at institutions, established in accordance with the former Section 105 in the Social Assistance Act. Finally, attention should be drawn to the two types of institutions that are included under Section 105: institutions for the homeless and centers for battered women.[8] How many of which type of institutions existed in various years is not simple to figure out retrospectively. Only over the last several years has the distinction been included in the statistical information available. In 1998, 20 out of the 86 institutions were centers for battered women. These 20 centers had 334 beds, equivalent to 14 percent of all beds provided under Section 105.

Some estimates of the overall number of people using institutions for the

68   Europe

Table 3.1
Developments at Institutions for the Homeless (1977–1998)

Year	Institutions	Beds	24-Hour Users	Day Users	Total Users	Staff Size*
1977	40	2,288	1,975	n.a.**	n.a.	n.a.
1982	47	2,383	2,118	314	2,432	903
1987	65	2,577	2,510	367	2,877	1,219
1992	76	2,588	2,425	522	2,947	1,338
1993	74	2,549	2,503	489	2,992	1,415
1994	76	2,470	2,337	454	2,791	1,342
1995	78	2,435	2,218	552	2,770	1,321
1996	80	2,330	2,138	718	2,856	1,357
1997	83	2,323	2,332	952	3,284	1,417
1998	86	2,377	2,412	849	3,261	1,562

Notes: The numbers were gathered during one week in January for each year. It is thus a yearly
    estimate of the number of users during a seven-day period.
*The staff size is calculated in full-time positions.
**n.a. = not available.
Source: Järvinen 1993; *Statistics Denmark* 1982, 1988, 1993, 1995, 1996a, 1996b, 1996c, 1997a,
    1997b, 1998a, 1998b.

homeless during a year have been provided as well. In his 1992 work, T. Fridberg discusses various types of socially excluded people: "Nationally one can
estimate, with some uncertainty, that during one year between 12,000 and 13,000
persons have stayed at a §105 institution.[9] Half of these are probably in Copenhagen" (Fridberg 1992, 45, author's translation). This is an estimate based on
figures of users and repeat users during a year at some of the institutions included under Section 105. Again one should be very careful regarding the accuracy of the estimates: the calculation of repeated use of institutions includes
only users returning to the same institutions. Furthermore, in some institutions,
repetitive use is registered only if the person is recognized, not because of any
official registration (e.g., social security number). Finally, as Fridberg writes,
the estimated rate of repetitive use varies significantly between different institutions.

One further estimate, provided by the Ministry of Social Affairs, is included
as a source for quantitative information on the population in the ministerial
guidelines for implementing newly enacted social legislation.[10] In a memorandum from the ministry (1996), it is estimated that about 11,000 people use the
institutions established in accordance with the former Section 105. The ministry
then concludes that there is no increase in the number of users of the institu-

tions—on the contrary, they write (Ministry of Social Affairs 1996). The basis for this conclusion is the findings, four years earlier, by Fridberg. Not only can it be argued that this conclusion places too much certainty upon the numbers provided by Fridberg, it can be argued that the conclusion places entirely too much emphasis upon their own findings, which, based upon the methods described in the memorandum, are at least as uncertain as those provided by Fridberg. However, the conclusion does provide us with a tentative answer to the question of why, from these estimates of the number of people using institutions, we do not get the impression that the number of homeless people in Denmark has increased.

Other estimates of homeless people are categorized according to the actual places they inhabit; perhaps they will provide us with conclusions that might sustain an understanding of homelessness as a phenomenon on the rise in Denmark. One attempt to estimate the number of people in the other categories included in Figure 3.1 was carried out by P. Brandt[11] who, based on different methods and previous studies, approximated the number of homeless people in different places in the Copenhagen metropolitan area during an average day (Brandt 1994). According to Brandt, approximately 450 people are sleeping rough, about 1,000 are sleeping in institutions for the homeless, and around 2,000 are dwelling erratically (e.g., with friends or family) because they are not in possession of their own dwelling. From these approximations, he estimates the total homeless population in the Copenhagen metropolitan area to be around 3,600. Taking Brandt's estimations as valid, the rate of homelessness would be 2.12 per 1,000 people (Brandt 1994). These approximations, however, are also encumbered with a high degree of uncertainty, especially due to the methodology used in collecting the figures. For example, to estimate those sleeping rough Brandt contacted people living on the streets in 1991 and asked them how many they thought were in the same situation. The figures provided by the people asked differed between 300 and 600. Likewise the number of people sleeping erratically is a rough estimate based on Brandt's previous experiences with the homeless environment and his reflection on macro statistics for Copenhagen.

Recent estimates made in regard to the group of people sleeping rough in Copenhagen show no indications of an increase: in spring 1999, Brandt estimated the number of people to be around 500 (Brandt, in Christensen 1999).

Homelessness as Types of People

The second understanding in the Danish discourse on homelessness, an understanding which is often complementary to the first one described, is an approach to homelessness through a definition of the ideal typical characteristics of various subgroups of a group which is then constructed as the homeless population. It is possible to construct a typology of the different types that are included in these understandings. In an article by Koch-Nielsen and Stax five such types of homeless are identified[12]: bag ladies, traditional homeless, users of illegal substances, mental patients, and street children.

Bag Ladies

This group is the most conspicuous group in the cities. Despite being known as bag ladies they can also be men. They have severe mental problems and are almost impossible to contact. Because they stay in the same public place day after day, they are well known to the public. Brandt has estimated that there are about 50 people in this category (1994).

Traditional Homeless

These comparatively well-functioning, middle-aged men stay at reception centers for longer periods, but they could move out either to a private flat or probably to a sheltered flat connected to the center. These users are well acquainted with reception centers. Their actual reason for staying at the center might be the split up of a partnership, perhaps caused by violent behavior, alcohol abuse, or a combination of the two. Because of indebtedness and a consequent inability to borrow money for a requested down payment, some have no possibilities of finding another flat. During some periods, the heavy alcohol abuse may come under control, and for some a capacity to perform daily and regular activities might be restored during the stay at the institution.

Users of Illegal Substances

These are the most marginalized type, and the type most difficult to reach from the welfare system. In this category we find men as well as women mainly in the age group of 16 to 40 years. They might have a removed child with a present or former partner. Often they have no ties to a family of origin; such a connection in many cases was broken many years ago. Accordingly, their social network consists of other abusers. They will almost never have been in touch with the labor market, having lived on social assistance since they left school. Due to their use of various illegal drugs, they are regularly involved in criminal activities or prostitution. They might also suffer from a borderline psychosis or from a neurosis, perhaps caused by substance abuse. They live on the streets, with acquaintances, or sometimes in reception centers, where they are frequently ejected because of use of illegal drugs or frightening behavior.

Mental Patients

These people, with a chronic psychosis, have repeatedly been discharged from a psychiatric institution to either their parents' or their own flat. Either because of conflicts with the parents, or the housing association, or because they cannot cope with living alone, they will leave their place of residence and turn to a reception center, perhaps after living for a period on the street. Others dare not go out and will stay isolated for a long time in solitude in a flat until either neighbors or social workers manage to remove them. They have had almost no relations with the labor market, and they have often been granted an invalid (disability) pension. They will appear confused and, at times, also frightening and incomprehensible to others. Furthermore, a personal contact might be impossible to establish because of use of illegal substances.

Street Children

Finally, Koch-Nielsen and Stax mention the group of street children. These are youngsters under the age of 18 living away from their families without living with another family who has been given parental responsibility, or at an institution established as a place for permanent residence for youngsters. In the early 1990s street children were the focus of various political and scientific fields (Ertmann 1991; Juul and Ertmann 1991; Juul 1992; Nissen 1994, 1996a, 1996b; Plougmand 1990; Ploeg 1990). At that time it was estimated that between 300 and 350 youngsters were homeless in Copenhagen (Juul and Ertmann 1991). The interest in this group of people has almost disappeared since then, but there is no evidence that the problem no longer exists.[13]

Besides an estimate by Brandt (1994) that around 50 people fit the first category—the bag ladies—I am not aware of any attempts at estimating the population in these categories, but it seems to me that the Danish discourse on social exclusion might be grasped through an understanding of these ideal typical characteristics together, with an understanding of a continuum of actual whereabouts. I shall return to this correlation later in this chapter.

One group of people that neither Koch-Nielsen and Stax nor Brandt touch upon are battered women. There has been a tendency in Denmark to see homelessness as more than a housing issue. Homeless people have been understood as having more complex problems than the lack of an abode (e.g., the lack of an abode in combination with a mental disturbance or the use of illegal substances). It has been the understanding that people in need of a dwelling—should that be the only problem—to a large degree were provided with such. Having to leave a home as a result of violence was not taken as an impediment to the capability of living in a dwelling. With this understanding, the people using centers for battered women were placed somewhat marginally within the group of homeless people. They have not been considered as *real* homeless people, and their problems have often been seen as solvable through social legislation, which did include possibilities for providing dwellings. In general, the problems of violence in a household, or the problem of household breakdown has, to a larger degree, been part of studies on families rather than studies on social exclusion. This exclusion of battered women from the group of homeless could be taken as an illustration of a continuously discursive categorization that influences the formulation of social policy as well as the social research.

DANISH SOCIAL POLICY FOR HOMELESS PEOPLE

In 1998 Denmark experienced a seemingly radical change in its social legislation. The Social Assistance Act enacted in 1976 was replaced by four new bills that now constitute the central elements of social assistance in particular as well as the social policy in general.[14]

The period from the beginning of the 1970s to the mid-1970s might be described as the completion of the Social Democratic–inspired social policy.[15] This completion can be identified in the Social Assistance Act from 1976, the bill that was replaced in 1998. A central part of the Social Assistance Act was the provision of universal coverage and the abandonment of the strategy of withholding individuals' civil rights when receiving welfare benefits.

Around the beginning of the 1980s, a reconsideration of the welfare state and its social policy gained momentum. This reconsideration began with an understanding that the welfare state was experiencing a crisis in legitimacy and financing: The public sector was heavily criticized for being expensive, expansive, and creating dependence, and efforts to modernize it were introduced. However, in most cases, the argument that there was such a crisis was not followed by arguments for a so-called dismantling of the welfare state. Rather the argument was to reform the actual functioning of the welfare state, thus attempting to adapt the costs to an economy that was understood to be in significant difficulty, primarily because of public deficit and a large foreign debt. Furthermore, the argument went, the answer was to solve the legitimacy crisis through a change in the criteria for receiving public transfer income and through a change in the demands put upon recipients. The hope was to keep both expenditures and the number of recipients at bay. These arguments continued, with different nuances, into the 1990s, and one of the latest outcomes of this process has been the four new bills making up the new social policy.

Three features of the development are of special importance:

• From universalism toward targeting services
• From institutions toward supported housing arrangements for different disadvantaged groups
• From passive income support toward activation

Social Legislation Today

The social legislation that is of most relevance for social support and housing includes an attempt to assess levels of need and target interventions. The social support, or the various social services, are organized into three levels. §1. The aim of this legislation is

1. To offer counseling and support toward the prevention of social problems
2. To offer various common services that might have a preventive aim as well
3. To consider the demands which follow from reduced physical or mental function ability or from special social problems (Jurainformation 1998).

On the *first level*, or the level of least intervention, it is the intention to provide counseling and support to prevent social problems. At this level, specific supportive measures are not directed toward particular groups. Instead, there is a general right, carried by each and every one covered by the social legislation, to be informed about possibilities and to be counseled in regard to possible choices.

On the *second level*, the bill deals with measures that are general in character, available to all, independent of the existence of some kind of disability. Here we find nontargeted measures, or obligations, to be taken care of by the municipalities. For example, of special relevance for the homeless, is a general obligation by the municipality to provide shelter.

The *third level* of social support is the level of most direct relevance for homeless people. At this level we find targeted measures, or measures provided for people considered to have special needs.

In the first section of the law, there are initial hints of the aim of the social legislation as well as an idea of a placement of responsibilities. After presenting the three levels of support, the section continues:

Stk.2. The aim of support provided through this legislation is to advance each individual's possibilities for taking care of him/her self, or to ease the daily life, or to increase the quality of life.

Stk.3. The support in accordance with this legislation is based upon the individual's responsibility for her/him self and her/his family. The support is provided according to the individual needs and premises and in cooperation with the recipient. (Jurainformation 1998)

In these two subclauses, we can trace an understanding of support to influence a process toward normalization. Perhaps we can identify an acceptance of a degree of deviation as something that we shall recognize as a condition that requires social support to facilitate an individual's daily functioning. Furthermore, we can identify an understanding of an individual responsibility for one's own situation and for one's family, and we can find the currently politically correct version of how to formulate the decisions on supportive measures: the consideration of the individual's needs and the inclusion of the recipient in these considerations.

Shared Dwellings as a Possibility for the Socially Excluded

One measure provided through the social legislation regards the provision of dwellings of a more permanent character. Since 1995 the municipality has been legally obliged to provide shelter in an acute situation for both families and singles. Prior to 1995 the obligation did not cover single people. The shelter can be temporary, but in that case the municipality shall attempt to find alternative measures, and measures of a more permanent character if needed.

Whereas the providing of shelter under acute circumstances is not a targeted measure for housing those considered socially excluded, it does provide a generally formulated right that is applicable to the homeless as well as other citizens. Specific measures are, however, directed toward people categorized as socially excluded, or people with special social difficulties, as they are referred to in the legislation. One of these measures regards the provision of places where homeless people can stay.

Prior to 1995 the possibilities for providing shelter to people with social difficulties, or homeless people, was limited to the obligation of providing a room in a Section 105 institution. A few housing projects, financed by the public sector, were available, but they were experimental.

During the 1980s a development in the discourse on social housing took place: a general disbelief in the benefit of institutions evolved from the psychiatric sector. A process of deinstitutionalization was initiated with the closing of larger mental hospitals and the opening up of local psychiatric centers that were to take care of the mentally challenged during the daytime.[16] Some of the former patients were now provided with places in what came to be known as "shared dwelling."[17] Quoting the Ministry of Social Affairs: "A shared dwelling in its typical form is assumed to be a flat in a living quarter that is shared by 3 to 5 persons and with a weekly supervision/inspection with the possibility of summoning assistance."[18]

However, not until 1995 did the social legislation include these housing arrangements as measures for the socially excluded. With the legal change of 1995, the municipalities were enabled to establish shared dwellings for people otherwise sheltered in accordance with Section 105, and the law provided the municipalities with the possibility of connecting help (professional or voluntary) to these dwellings (Ministry of Social Affairs 1994a). In the same memorandum as quoted above, it was estimated that there was a need for approximately 800 places in shared dwellings (Ministry of Social Affairs 1994b). This type of housing became the politically correct approach to compensate for the housing, as well as the social, problems understood to be present among people living as socially excluded.

An idea of the aims of the support and housing provided can be obtained in some guidelines provided by the Ministry of Social Affairs from 1995:

The aim of the social support is to be part of the provided assistance that enables self-help, both in regard to practical matters and on a personal level, thereby enabling the inhabitants to take care of the largest number of tasks possible in a moderately protected environment.

Therefore the assistance should support, through counseling and guidance, ordinary daily functions like cleaning, personal hygiene, and economy. But it is also important to support participation in occupational and leisure activities. Furthermore, the support can concern the establishment of contact with the surroundings, friends and family ... or public and private measures, e.g., places for treatment of physical or mental disabilities or of substance abuse. (Ministry of Social Affairs 1995, author's translation)

During the debate on the bill, which added the section enabling the providing of shared dwellings, the Minister of Social Affairs stated, "The basic attitude in the present bill is that we shall provide these people with an offer, which is somewhere in-between an institution and taking care of one self in one's own home. . . . The whole idea is to build on some of the positive elements that are present in the §105 institutions" (*Folketingets forhandlinger* 1995, 2,449, author's translation).

Three basic expectations ground the popular belief in the shared dwelling:

- First, it is meant to enable the homeless to live in what feels like their own dwelling, with their own room, and access to a kitchen, a living room, and so on.
- Second, it is supposed to avoid (or minimize) the feeling of being isolated or fearful. The belief is that somebody else is around without intruding into one's private sphere.
- Finally, the shared dwelling, when needed, is intended to include a staff member who provides intensive support for the inhabitants.

With the most recent changes of the whole social legislation, a further step toward establishing shared dwellings as the ordinary measure for homeless people was taken: the term institution was abandoned in reference to measures aimed at adults: "The previously used concept of institutions in areas concerning adults is abolished thus making it possible for the municipalities and the regional counties to organize the provision of measures with respect to the individual, independent of the type of dwelling in which she or he is living" (Ministry of Social Affairs 1998, author's translation).

In reality, however, the institution as a praxis was not abandoned, and still has not been. The name might have been changed, but currently the buildings and the rooms used for sheltering are almost identical to the old-type institutions. Furthermore, to clarify how great the gap was between rhetoric and reality, it was stated, in the comments to the section in the legislation dealing with the provision of housing arrangements, that the measures provided in the future might be the same as those provided prior to the legislative change (Ministry of Social Affairs 1998).

One thing that has changed, however, is that various kinds of support and various types of housing have been separated. Previously, there was a connection between which measures were to be provided at which institutions. With the legal change of 1998, the two became separated, and different measures can be provided independently of housing arrangements—also in an independently owned dwelling, like a normal flat, if that is considered beneficial. The Ministry of Social Affairs argued that

the separation of the rules in accordance with section 73 and the regulations on the housing arrangements are to be seen as one step further in the direction of equaling the possibilities for, and treatment of, people with physical and mental disabilities or persons with special social problems independent of housing arrangements. (Jurainformation 1998, author's translation)

Thus no support shall be an integral part of one type of housing or sheltering and not available for people living at different types of arrangements. Instead, there shall be, according to the legislation, an individual evaluation of needs for support, and measures aimed at the needed support shall then be provided.

The Idea of Activation

A second central theme of relevance for most people in contact with social legislation is the idea of activation. The political catchphrase could be from *passive* to *active* support. Generally speaking, the understanding is that the system of welfare benefits previously did not lead to any development on behalf of the individual; quite the contrary, it had the effect of fostering passivity among recipients. Attempts have been made to change this through a coupling of benefits with activation.[19] The idea of activation can be thought of as the process of normalizing the excluded in relation to the labor market, just as the idea of shared dwellings can be understood as the process of normalizing them to the housing market. In the idea of activation, we can identify an understanding of connection to the labor market as something that can be gradually lost or gained, and an understanding that this loss or gain can be influenced by a mixture of pressure and assistance by the public.

But what does this tell us about the understanding of the people included in the population of this report? It indicates a current understanding of how the problem is conceptualized, how it should be solved, what is thought to be the cure, and who is expected to do what. It is clear from the social legislation that activation is thought to play a critical role in impacting homeless people. In the comments on the legislation, the municipality is directed to take into consideration the fact that some people may have social problems apart from their relationship to the labor market, and that this may influence the offer of activation as well as the sanctions in regard to an eventual nonfulfillment of such offers. It is, however, clear from the legislation that an understanding of part of the problem of social marginalization is considered connected to a loss of contact— or no contact at all—to the labor market. Hence the strategies used focus on pushing and pulling the socially excluded back into contact with the labor market.

PROBLEMS IN THE CURRENT SOCIAL POLICY AND IN THE UNDERSTANDINGS OF SOCIAL EXCLUSION

At first it may appear that the understanding of homelessness as a multifaceted problem has guided the formulation of the recently enacted legislation. There are arguments for the adaptation of the measures provided to the needs of the individual homeless. There are requirements that the municipalities become involved in the organization of social support, not in accordance with some a priori formulated principles, but in accordance with what is understood as the actual needs of the person facing the social worker. We can identify a change from an obligation to provide a bed at a large institution to an obligation to provide a place where the person might benefit from living and where supportive measures needed are provided—in many cases a shared dwelling—and, again, this must be conducted in accordance with an assessment of the needs of the individual person. One might be seduced into believing that the formulation of the new social legislation accepts that socially excluded people are a diverse group with a diverse spectrum of problems, and that the legislation provides the legal framework for becoming involved according to these accepted diversities. On the surface, all these ideas and all the arguments appear convincing.

But, there are blind spots in the understandings of the socially excluded and in the provision of measures, and alternative understandings are marginalized. While certain aspects of the social legislation make reference to some causes of exclusion, there is a closing down of alternative perspectives which takes a critical systemic view; in fact, the current understanding of homelessness and the development of a social policy can be seen as a discursive practice that fits the development of the legitimization of social support, in particular, and the welfare state, in general.

It is possible to see the categorization of homeless persons as correlated with a changing idea of what welfare should be provided and with changing the understandings of the causes for deviation. There is a useful fit between an understanding of social exclusion, as caused by a range of diverse factors, owing to individual deficiencies and pathologies, and the development of a view of change in the organization of the welfare state, from universal coverage to a specific coverage with predefined targeting of the various measures provided. With the construction of social exclusion as something that is not suitable for generally formulated measures, but instead reflects factors individual in character, a targeting of measures becomes the evident solution, and the obvious approach for the provision of services. According to M. Järvinen (1993), a tendency to focus upon factors ascribed to social-psychological conditions immanent to the individual, or ascribed to the early childhood experiences, has been present in recent Danish understandings of homelessness.[20] According to Järvinen, we are currently experiencing an increased attention along lines that she calls *homelessness through a perspective of marginalization* (Järvinen 1993). Marginalization means that social exclusion is caused by misfits between the demands of given sectors and the capabilities possessed by the excluded individuals. It is through the construction of an understanding of marginalization that it becomes possible to construct a continuum, both a continuum of understood types of dwellings and a continuum regarding relations of persons to the labor market. By using a psychological focus, it becomes possible to locate the misfit in causes within the individual, and not in the structure or the organization of the sector in relation to which the misfit occurs. Thus, on the one hand, there is a comparability between the understanding of homelessness through a typology that outlines the current state of the people, as well as through the construction of a continuum that organizes the provision of measures into a process of normalization or stabilization. On the other hand, the development from universal to residual and targeted measures can target the exact problems constructed through the typology and do so at the appropriate place understood through the continuum. Here the shared dwelling plays an interesting double role: it is a provided measure that serves as a position on the continuum capturing the actual place, but it has also become a construct of acceptability. It is thus not a social political problem to have people living in such housing arrangements. Rather it is the cure, or the best place, to compensate for the deviations that are immanent in those who are excluded.

The understandings identified in the Danish discourse on social exclusion are, however, not evident, and they are understandings that at other times and in other spatialities have been less prevalent.[21] Furthermore, this placing of the causes of homelessness upon factors inscribed in the individual's psychic character and in past experiences, rather than in the current relations between the socially excluded and those who are not considered excluded, or in discursive understandings of exclusion, leads to the provision of measures supposed to ease the living conditions of the homeless or to reintegrate them through providing them with capabilities to compensate for their deviance. But this understanding closes off a social political critique and other approaches which consider systemic causes of social exclusion. The social policy becomes more focused upon compensating for the missing capabilities than it focuses upon compensating, or even preventing, the causes of exclusion, not to mention that the understanding of homelessness closes off criticism that it is the organization of the policy itself that influences the exclusion process. This critique could be taken further by arguing that an understanding of social exclusion along the lines outlined in the beginning of this chapter makes sacred the organization of the different sectors of our society. When we place the causes of exclusion in early childhood or in abnormalities immanent in the excluded's social-psychological characteristics, we close off causes that can be ascribed to the structure of the housing market, or the structure of the labor market, or the organization of the social policy.[22] These sectors are, instead, understood primarily as being reintegrative. It could be argued that we hereby are closing off aspects of exclusion that might throw a different light upon social exclusion.

Finally, the understanding of social exclusion plays a political role. With the construction of the socially excluded as a diverse group of people with differentiated needs, a seemingly obvious approach for providing measures would be the provision of relatively wide ranges of possibilities, for example, abolishing the provision of certain types of institutions only, or avoiding connecting certain types of support to certain types of housing. However, this does leave the assessment of the needs of the socially excluded up to the last administrative level that deals with individual homeless people. This assessment could be part of a struggle over sparse resources, and people categorized as socially excluded in this struggle could have an unfavorable position from which to fight. If this is the case, then the move from certain defined measures, that the local government is obliged to provide, to a system based on assessing the specific needs of the individual homeless might in some localities place the socially excluded in an even worse position.

The construction of the group of people considered socially excluded cannot be understood without including the political context, and without reflecting on political development in general. It is necessary to understand how people living as homeless are living under certain conditions that we cannot accept in our welfare state anno 2000. They also comprise a category of people which functions as a political argument in the formulations of social, labor, and housing policies. It is important to recognize that the definition, at any given time and in any given space, is provided as part of a broader policy.

The current policy is unfortunately not discussed as policy. Rather it is presented as the provision of the necessary measures derived from characteristics inscribed in the socially constructed category of the socially excluded—but inscribed as given rather than as constructed. This has unfortunate implications for the discussion of the socially excluded in Denmark because it narrows and closes off political attention to, and critique of, both understanding and practice that do not fit into the current dominant discourse.

REFERENCES

Andersen, C., et al. 1997. *Vanskeligt stillede sindslidende*. Copenhagen: Socialt Udviklingscenter.

Avramov, D., ed. 1999. *Coping with Homelessness*. Aldershot, UK: Ashgate. An anthology with articles presented through the EUROHOME research network. Covers relations between poverty, social exclusion, and homelessness; existing research on homelessness; values and policies in relation to homelessness; and services for homeless people.

Børner, T. 1997a. *Om hjemløshed: Begreber, typer, tal og metoder*. Working paper (www.sfi.dk). Copenhagen: Danish National Institution of Social Research. A study of the different understandings of homelessness which have been present in Denmark with a representation of the various existing quantitative information that is flourishing in the public debate. The working paper includes reflections upon further possible research.

———. 1997b. *Youth Homelessness in Denmark*. Brussels, Feantsa (www.sfi.dk).

Børner, T., and I. Koch-Nielsen. 1996. *Homelessness in Denmark*. Brussels: Feantsa (www.sfi.dk).

Brandt, P. 1992. *Yngre hjemløse i København*. Copenhagen: FADL. A social-psychiatric study of the causes of homelessness based on a registration of all users between 18 and 35 years of age of shelters at Copenhagen during one year in the late 1980s. Collects quantitative data on age, sex, type of institution used, number of visits during a year, and so on. Combines the quantitative data with qualitative interviews focused around mental health and use of illegal substances.

———. 1994. Personal correspondence.

———. 1997. Personal correspondence.

Breakey, W. R., and P. J. Fischer. 1990. "Homelessness: The Extent of the Problem." *Journal of Social Issues* 46, no. 4:31–49.

Christensen, S. K. 1999. "Omstilling med problemer." *Danske Kommuner* 12:24–25.

Dørup, A. B., et al. 1996. *Lad målet styre midlerne.* Copenhagen: Munksgaard.

Ertmann, B. 1991. *Gadens Børn.* Copenhagen: Fremad.

Folketingets forhandlinger. 1995. *Folketingets Forhandlinger*, no. 13, Transcription of National Parliament. Copenhagen: Schultz Grafisk A/S.

Fridberg, T. 1992. *De socialt udstødte.* Copenhagen: Danish National Institution of Social Research, 92:12.

Hr. Berg. 1982. *På herberg i København.* Copenhagen: Socialpolitisk Forenings Små-skrifter, 57.

Järvinen, M. 1993. *De nye hjemløse.* Holte, Denmark: SOCPOL. A social constructivist analysis of the understandings of homelessness which have been present in Denmark over time with special attention to the recent understanding that a new kind of homelessness has appeared. In the second half, the focus is primarily on the situation of excluded women in Denmark today.

Jensen, M. K., et al. 1997. *Sociale boformer.* Hørsholm, Denmark: Statens Byggefor-skningsinstitut, 281.

Jurainformation. 1998. *Ny sociallovgivning 1. juli 1998.* Copenhagen: Jurainformation.

Juul, S. 1992. *Young: Street Children in Denmark.* Copenhagen: Danish National Institute of Social Research, f.u.5.

Juul, S., and B. Ertmann. 1991. *Gadebørn i Storkøbenhavn.* Copenhagen: Danish National Institute of Social Research, 91, no. 9.

Koch-Nielsen, I., and T. B. Stax. 1999. "The Heterogeneity of Homelessness and the Consequences for Service Provision. In *Coping with Homelessness*, ed. D. Avramov. Aldershot, UK: Ashgate.

Larsen, J. E., and I. H. Møller, eds. 1998. *Socialpolitik.* Copenhagen: Munksgaard.

Lauridsen, J. T. 1996. *Fra udstødte til anbragte 1500–1950.* Copenhagen: Royal Library.

Middelboe, T., and E. T. Jacobsen, eds. 1994. *Kommunerne og de sindslidende.* Copenhagen: Dansk Sygehus Institut, 94, no. 9.

Middelboe, T., and S. Juul. 1994. *Sindslidende i samfundet.* Copenhagen: Dansk Sygehus Institut, 94, no. 10.

Ministry of Social Affairs. 1994a. *Forslag til Lov om ændring af lov om social bistand m.v.* (bill no. L8). Copenhagen: Ministry of Social Affairs. Includes comments and enclosures.

———. 1994b. *Notat om økonomien i lovædring vedr. styrkelse af indsatsen for socialt udstødte m.v. (3. udgave).* Copenhagen: Ministry of Social Affairs, Økonomisk-statistsik kontor, J.nr: 5029–15 from 02.05.94.

———. 1995. *Vejledning om bestemmelser i bistandsloven om husvilde (§31) og for personer med særlige sociale vanskeligheder (§68b) om medhjælp i boligen og om væresteder o.lign. samt om udvidelse af forsøgsreglerne (§138e).* Copenhagen: Ministry of Social Affairs, from 31.03.95.

———. 1996. *Undersøgelse af indsatsen for hjemløse m.fl.* Copenhagen: Ministry of Social Affairs.

———. 1998. *Vejledning: Den sociale indsats for de mest udsatte voksne: Sindslidende, Stof-og alkoholmisbrugere, Hjemløse m.fl.* Copenhagen: Ministry of Social Affairs.

Munk-Jørgensen, P., et al. 1992. "Hjemløse psykisk syge, en registerundersøgelse af klienter på herberg og forsorgshjem." *Ugeskrift for Læger*, 154:1271–75.

Nissen, M. 1994. "Projekt Gadebørn-status pr. september 1994." Unpublished internal memorandum.

———. 1996a. *Midtvejsevaluering af Projekt Gadebørn*. Draft (forthcoming).

———. 1996b. "Hjælp og selvhjælp i behandling af udstødte unge. Om Projekt Gadebørn i København." *Nordisk Sosialt Arbeid*.

Nordentoft, M. 1990. "Afinstitutionalisering og hjemløshed blandt psykisk syge i historisk perspektiv." *Nordisk Psykiatrisk Tidsskrift* 44:435–41.

Ploeg, J. D. van der. 1990. "Hjemløse unge i Holland." In *"Udskudte" børn og unge*, ed. H. Bros. Copenhagen: Socialstyrelsens Informations—og konsulentvirksomhed.

Plougmand, O. 1990. "Enhver er sin egen lykkes smed?" In *"Udskudte" børn og unge*, ed. H. Bros. Copenhagen: Socialstyrelsens Informations—og konsulentvirksomhed.

Reintoft, H. 1998. *Træd varsomt: Dansk socialpolitik ved en skillevej*. Copenhagen: Hans Reitzels Forlag.

Sahlin, I. 1998. *The Staircase of Transition*. Brussels, Feantsa.

Shinn, M., and B. C. Weitzman. 1990. "Research on Homelessness: An Introduction." *Journal of Social Issues* 46:1–13.

Soulet, M. H. 1999. "Theoretical Uses and Misuses of the Notion of Social Exclusion." In *Coping with Homelessness*, ed. D. Avramov. Aldershot, UK: Ashgate.

Statistics Denmark. 1982. Sociale ressourcer. *Statistik for amtskommuner, 1982:2*. Copenhagen: Statistics Denmark.

———. 1988. Den sociale ressourceopgørelse 13.januar 1988, kommunefordelt opgørelse. *Socialstatistik 1988:10*. (Statistikservice). Copenhagen: Statistics Denmark.

———. 1993. Den sociale ressourceopgørelse 15.januar 1992 kommunefordelt opgørelse. *Socialstatistik 1993:1*. (Statistikservice). Copenhagen: Statistics Denmark.

———. 1995. Den sociale ressourceopgørelse 13.januar 1993 kommunefordelt opgørelse. *Socialstatistik 1995:4*. (Statistikservice). Copenhagen: Statistics Denmark.

———. 1996a. Den sociale ressourceopgørelse 19.januar 1994 kommunefordelt opgørelse for ældreområdet mv. *Socialstatistik 1996:5*. (Statistikservice). Copenhagen: Statistics Denmark.

———. 1996b. Den sociale ressourceopgørelse 18.januar 1995 kommunefordelt opgørelse for ældreområdet mv. *Socialstatistik 1996:10*. (Statistikservice). Copenhagen: Statistics Denmark.

———. 1996c. Den sociale ressourceopgørelse januar 1996, kommunefordelt opgørelser for ældreområdet mv. *Socialstatistik 1996:12*. (Statistikservice). Copenhagen: Statistics Denmark.

———. 1997a. Den sociale ressourceopgørelse januar 1997. Kommunefordelt opgørelser for ældreområdet mv. *Socialstatistik 1997:7*. (Statistikservice). Copenhagen: Statistics Denmark.

———. 1997b. Den sociale ressourceopgørelse januar 1997. Kommunefordelt opgørelser for dagpasningsområdet mv. *Socialstatistik 1997:10*. (Statistikservice). Copenhagen: Statistics Denmark.

———. 1998a. Den sociale ressourceopgørelse januar 1998. Kommunefordelt opgørelser for ældreområdet mv. *Socialstatistik 1998:7*. (Statistikservice). Copenhagen: Statistics Denmark.

———. 1998b. Den sociale ressourceopgørelse januar 1998. Kommunefordelt opgørelser for dagpasningsområdet mv. *Socialstatistik 1998:8*. (Statistikservice). Copenhagen: Statistics Denmark.

Stax, T. B. 1998a. "Youth Homelessness in Denmark?" In *Youth Homelessness in the European Union*, ed. D. Avramov. Brussels: Feantsa.

———. 1998b. *From Shelter to Dwelling: A Re-integrative Project at Mændenes Hjem*. Brussels: Feantsa (www.sfi.dk).

———. 1999a. "Homelessness in Denmark." In *Homelessness in United States, Europe, and Russia*, ed. C. O. Helvie and W. Kunstmann. Westport, Conn.: Bergin and Garvey.

———. 1999b. *Support and Housing: Two Complementary Aspects of a Social Policy*. Brussels: Feantsa (www.sfi.dk).

———. 2000. *Én gang socialt marginaliseret*. Copenhagen: Danish National Institute of Social Research, 99, no. 21. A study of the life-stories of people who used shelters in Copenhagen ten years ago. The study identifies pathways followed out of homelessness as well as institutional and organizational barriers that make the following of such pathways difficult. Through register-based research and qualitative interviews, the project uncovers contacts with various types of institutions (e.g., the law enforcement agencies and the welfare office), and the study excavates the housing situation since life at institutions as well as general socioeconomic characteristics are illustrated.

Uggerhøj, L. 1996. *Hjælp eller afhængighed*. Ålborg, Denmark: Ålborg Universitetsforlag.

Vranken, J. 1999. "Different Policy Approaches to Homelessness." In *Coping with Homelessness*, ed. D. Avramov. Aldershot, UK: Ashgate.

Zobbe, K., and T. J. Hegland. 1992. *Analyse af bofællesskaber o. lig. for voksne med handicap: Beretning-Bilag 3*, landsudvalget vedrørende den sociale opgavefordeling. Ålborg, Denmark: Ålborg Universitetscenter.

NOTES

1. As should become clear in the discussion that follows on the understandings of homelessness and the socially excluded, there are no clear distinctions between the two terms. A homeless person might be referred to as socially excluded and vice versa. The reason for this lack of clarity between the two terms is that the dwelling is taken to constitute only part of the problem among the people categorized as socially excluded or homeless. It can, for example, be seen in the legislation pertaining to the area. Here the term homeless has been abandoned and replaced with the term "people with special social problems."

2. The understanding of a continuum depending on the actual whereabouts can be found in Swedish literature as well. In one paper, I. Sahlin identifies the understanding among local administrators of the housing market as represented by the metaphor of a staircase (Sahlin 1998).

3. In Stax (1999a) and in Børner and Koch-Nielsen (1996) several actual dwellings

are described in English. For the reader with the capabilities for understanding Danish, an evaluation by Jensen et al. (1997) is recommended.

4. Section 105 is the section in the social legislation which, prior to the recent legislative change, included the obligation for providing institutions for people considered socially excluded or homeless. Since the recent legislative change, the equivalent paragraph would be Section 94 in the Legislation on Social Service.

5. For example, Järvinen (1993).

6. However, due to the new social legislation that took effect on July 1, 1998, the larger institutions for homeless people are currently experiencing change. Some are transforming parts of their space into more permanent types of dwellings, some are transforming some sections into shared dwellings, and some are being subdivided into smaller institutions. It is too early yet to pinpoint how these very recent changes will affect the provision of shelters, centers for battered women, half-way houses, and so on, in Denmark. But that the whole area is currently undergoing a transitional period seems evident.

7. For a discussion of the numbers, see Børner (1997b).

8. Distinguishing between the two types of institutions using the terms "centers for battered women" and "institutions for homeless" explicates a blurred distinction in the Danish political and scientific understanding of homelessness.

9. Institutions established in accordance with Section 105 in the Social Assistance Act. After the July 1998 legislative change, these institutions are referred to as section 94 institutions.

10. In a ministerial document on the administration of the new social legislation, there are references to and a presentation of some of the numbers pertaining to social exclusion (Ministry of Social Affairs 1998). Thus, by official decree, we now have a certain number of homeless people—an approach toward estimating the number of homeless which underscores the political and arbitrary character of the estimates.

11. Brandt is the former head social psychiatrist at the largest institution for the homeless in Denmark and the current leader of a project directed toward helping people who are living rough.

12. Koch-Nielsen and Stax (1999). Another typology on homelessness in Denmark is provided by Fridberg (1992). An example of an American approach along similar lines can be found in Breakey and Fischer (1990).

13. The most recent literature on the topic would be Børner (1997b) and Stax (1998a). This is not primary research, but it summarizes and discusses previous research in a Danish context in English.

14. In regard to the socially excluded, it shall be mentioned that quite a few of the measures aimed at these people were introduced through a legislative change in 1995 and were carried over into the new social legislation.

15. For further information about the recent history of Danish social policies, see Dørup et al. (1996); Larsen and Møller (1998); Reintoft (1998); Stax (1998b, 1999b); Uggerhøj (1996).

16. See, for example, Middelboe and Jacobsen (1994); Middelboe and Juul (1994).

17. See, for example, Andersen et al. (1997); Zobbe and Hegland (1992).

18. Ministry of Social Affairs (1994b, author's translation). See also Ministry of Social Affairs (1995).

19. Activation is understood, in the legislation, to be any activities that aim at raising the recipient's abilities to establish or reestablish a connection to the labor market (Jurainformation 1998).

20. See Brandt (1992); Munk-Jørgensen (1992); Nordentoft (1990).

21. See Järvinen (1993); Hr. Berg (1982); Lauridsen (1996) for discussions of the changing understandings of homelessness and social exclusion over time in Denmark. The discussion can be found in other settings as well: Shinn and Weitzman (1990); Soulet (1999); Vranken (1999).

22. For an analysis of the interaction between the socially excluded and public institutions as well as an analysis of the life stories of 1,000 people who, ten years ago, used the institutions for homeless, see Stax (2000).

4

Homelessness in Germany: Housing Poverty in a Wealthy Country

VOLKER BUSCH-GEERTSEMA

THE "SUCCESS STORY" OF HOUSING IN GERMANY

Germany is one of the wealthiest countries in the world. In 1996 Germany's gross national product was ranked sixth in the world (preceded by Luxembourg, Switzerland, Japan, Denmark, and Singapore, and followed by the United States of America) (Weidenfeld and Wessels 2000, 430). Among the members of the European Union, Germany, with a total area of about 137,700 square miles, is the fourth largest country and, with about 82 million inhabitants, has the highest population figure. About 15 million inhabitants live in the area of the former GDR (East Germany) which was united with West Germany (about 67 million inhabitants) in 1990. Since then Germany has consisted of 16 states (*Bundesländer*, 5 in the east and 11 in the west).

German housing politicians deplore the relatively small ratio of owner occupation in Germany. Only 38.9 percent of the overall 32.3 million dwellings in Germany were owner occupied in 1993, the remaining stock (61.1 percent) was rented (Schewe 1995, 361).[1] Germany has the lowest ratio of owner occupation in the European Union. In looking at the countries with the highest proportions of owner occupation (Ireland, Spain, and Greece), it becomes obvious that a high ratio of owner occupation is no indicator of great wealth (IFS 1998, 2). On the contrary, the only European country with an even lower ratio of owner occupation than Germany is Switzerland (not a member of the European Union), the second wealthiest nation per capita in the world (Stabu 2000, 351).

In particular, in West Germany, the average quality of housing has been

Table 4.1
Space per Person in West German Dwellings

Year	Housing space per Person in square feet
1950	161.5
1960	208.8
1966	240.0
1968	256.2
1972	284.2
1978	334.8
1980	350.9
1982	361.7
1985	380.0
1987	382.1
1993	406.9
1996	412.3

Source: Stabu 1996, 34; Stabu 1998a, 240; author's calculations.

steadily improving since World War II. During the war, almost a quarter of the housing stock was destroyed, and in the first ten years after the war about 12.5 million refugees required housing. Since then the number of dwellings has almost doubled in West Germany. In 1950 the average space per head in a dwelling was 161.5 square feet; in 1996, it was 412.3 square feet (see Table 4.1). In 1993, 98.3 percent of all dwellings in West Germany had a bathroom or a shower, and 98.7 percent had a toilet inside (Schewe 1995, 365).

Although the average housing space per head is definitely smaller in East Germany (it was 350.9 sq. ft. in 1996) and the dwellings have fewer amenities (89.1 percent had a bath or shower and 87.4 percent had a toilet inside the dwelling), housing provision in the east had improved immensely since the war. However, in the former GDR, the construction of new housing was strongly prioritized to the disadvantage of redeveloping and modernizing old housing, which resulted in high costs for the redevelopment of rotten, old buildings after the German unification.

All in all, one can say that the housing provision for the majority of the German population is very good. However, a large number of persons in Germany are homeless, which has created a recurring discourse on the housing shortage in Germany. At the beginning of the 1980s, the housing shortage was obvious, and the number of homeless persons was high (see DST 1980). After an easing of the situation of the housing market in the mid-1980s, homelessness figures again increased dramatically at the end of the 1980s. At the beginning of the 1990s, a new peak was reached, and the number of homeless persons was estimated at one million (see Berthold 1993). Although there has been another decrease in homelessness figures in West Germany since the middle of the 1990s, there is scant hope that this trend will persist. In East Germany homelessness increased significantly after the German unification, but it is still under the quantitative level of West German municipalities (see Busch-Geertsema and Ruhstrat 1997b).

THE DEFINITION OF HOMELESSNESS AND THE PROBLEM OF COUNTING HOMELESS PEOPLE

There is no legal definition of homelessness in Germany, but experts and policy makers generally agree that the definition of homelessness should not be reduced to people sleeping rough and that the problem goes beyond being without a dwelling. In 1987 the head association of German municipalities published a paper (DST 1987) including a definition of homelessness as being "people in urgent need of housing" (*Wohnungsnotfaelle*), which has been widely accepted and has served as a basis for a number of research projects and reports.

The population in urgent need of housing and of administrative support can be divided roughly into three groups:

- People who are homeless
- People who are threatened by homelessness
- People who live in unacceptable housing conditions.

Homeless people in Germany, the first group, includes all people who have no regular tenancy contract for a normal dwelling and, therefore, are provided with temporary accommodation by local authorities, or live in special institutions because they are homeless, or share housing temporarily with friends or relatives, or sleep rough. This definition includes immigrants as far as they have the right to take up residence in Germany (this excludes asylum seekers until legal proceedings have been completed, but includes repatriates of German nationality, called *Aussiedler*).

People threatened by homelessness, the second group, are mainly persons against whom legal action for eviction has been taken or who are threatened by immediate eviction.

People in unacceptable housing conditions, the third group, suffer from extreme overcrowding, very low housing standards (like missing sanitary equipment in the dwelling or housing conditions that are injurious to health), unbearable rent burdens, and tenancies with escalating social conflicts.

Official data on the extent of homelessness or on the number of people in urgent need of housing are not available in Germany. Some studies, based on the definition above, have tried to assess numbers of people in urgent need of housing in single German *Bundesländer* (Koch, Hard, and Tristram 1993; Busch-Geertsema and Ruhstrat 1994; Evers and Ruhstrat 1994; Schuler-Wallner et al. 1996; Busch-Geertsema and Ruhstrat 1997b).

For many years experts and politicians have been asking for national and annual statistics on people in urgent need of housing in order to provide data on a nationwide and continuous basis.[2] As a first step, the Federal Statistical Office published a feasibility study in 1998 (Koenig 1998), using the broad definition given above as a starting point. While it says, on one hand, that many of the above-mentioned subgroups cannot be assessed in official statistics, it admits, on the other hand, that it would be possible to make a statistical assessment of those homeless persons who are accommodated by municipalities and service providers in the voluntary sector, in temporary accommodation, or in special institutions. Households affected by legal action for eviction could also be continuously assessed.[3] It is still uncertain whether such statistics will actually be collected in Germany.

The only official statistics that register a subgroup of the homeless population on a fixed day each year (June 30) are taken in North Rhine-Westphalia, Germany's most densely populated *Bundesland*. These statistics (*Obdachlosenstatistik Nordrhein-Westfalen*), however, assess only those homeless persons who are accommodated by municipalities in municipal shelters and temporary accommodation according to police law (*Ordnungsbehördengesetz*). Homeless persons accommodated in institutions for the homeless in the voluntary sector are not assessed and neither are other subgroups of the homeless. Unfortunately, no other *Bundesland* has comparable statistics.

The total figure of homeless persons in Germany can be estimated only this far. The latest estimation for West Germany, based directly on a scientific questioning of municipalities (mainly in North Rhine-Westphalia), dates from 1992. The number of homeless persons in West Germany on a fixed date (June 30, 1992) was estimated at from 520,000 to 580,000 persons (including from 260,000 to 320,000 "repatriates" in temporary accommodation). Approximately 200,000 persons were affected by legal action for eviction in 1992 in West Germany (Busch-Geertsema and Ruhstrat 1994, 73).

As the first number only comprises persons known as homeless to municipalities on a fixed date, the National Coalition for the Homeless made its own estimations on the basis of these data, which included an assumed underestimation of homeless persons not known to municipalities, as well as the assumed number of homeless persons in East Germany, and then calculated the total number of all persons affected by homelessness within one year. For 1992 this number, estimated by the National Coalition, amounted to about 800,000 homeless persons in Germany (see Specht-Kittler 1994, tables 16, 17).

THE HISTORICAL BACKGROUND: THE PERCEPTION OF HOMELESS PEOPLE AND THE DEVELOPMENT OF SERVICES FOR THEM

In Germany the service system for the homeless is characterized by a separation of responsibilities and service types between municipalities, on the one hand, and service providers in the voluntary sector on the other. This separation, deeply rooted in history, is reflected in the German system of law.

Because rooflessness is traditionally regarded as a danger to public security and order, German municipalities are obliged by police law to avert this danger by providing roofless persons with temporary accommodation at minimal standards. Until the late 1960s, it was possible to force roofless people into such shelters, but then respective legal provisions were considered as infractions of the constitutional right to individual liberty and thus abolished. What remained was the unconditional obligation of municipalities to provide roofless persons who are not able to help themselves with temporary accommodation. Whereas homeless families once were accommodated in special estates built for the homeless (in suburbs, near railway tracks, or close to refuse dumps; congested dwellings with deliberately designed low standards, without inside bathrooms or toilets and without central heating), it has by now become more common to provide temporary accommodation (especially for families) in decentralized forms of housing rented or owned by municipalities. Hostels, hotel rooms, shacks, containers, military barracks, and so on are still used by municipalities to temporarily accommodate homeless people.

In the course of the last 20 years, many municipal estates for the homeless were demolished, redeveloped, or changed into normal, permanent, rented housing. However, as homelessness increased in Germany at the end of the 1980s, many new emergency shelters were erected. (For further details concerning temporary accommodation of homeless people see Busch-Geertsema 1999a.) Nevertheless, as early as the 1980s, the head association of German municipalities stated their intention to avoid temporary accommodation as far as possible by improving the prevention of homelessness and by arranging normal, permanent housing on the basis of tenancy agreements for homeless people (DST 1987).

In many towns, temporary accommodation by municipalities on the basis of police law concentrates on providing accommodation for evicted families and, sometimes, but not everywhere, for single persons evicted from their former dwellings. Persons who are homeless for other reasons, and in particular those who became homeless outside the border of the municipal district, are referred to institutions in the voluntary sector. The greatest part of these institutions belong to voluntary organizations of the two most important churches in Germany, the Protestant and Catholic churches. Their institutions for nonlocal, single, homeless persons have existed for more than a hundred years (see Scheffler 1987; John 1988; Treuberg 1989).

Institutions for the itinerant poor were set up everywhere in Germany by private welfare agencies in the second half of the nineteenth century, especially after 1880. There were many itinerant poor at that time, and Christian hostels and work places for itinerant people provided temporary accommodation as well as board, for which the poor had to work. Most of the rural labor colonies accommodated and boarded unemployed itinerant workers for a longer time to make them work hard and save them from demoralization and idleness. Labor colonies served as private unemployment relief and as Christian institutions of "moral improvement" at the same time. The first labor colony, Wilhelmsdorf, was founded by the most important German protagonist of vagrant welfare in the late nineteenth century, Protestant minister Friedrich von Bodelschwingh, in Bethel near Bielefeld. His main maxim was "work in place of alms." A network of institutions for itinerant persons, the enforced introduction of record books for each of them, as well as the punishment of "work-shy persons" by the state, were designed to ensure a regulated itinerancy, while jobs offered in labor colonies served as "work tests" to pick out "honest itinerant workers" from the mass of beggars and vagrants.

During the first decades of the twentieth century, the discourse shifted from the moral to the psychological, and mental deviations were perceived to be the cause of the "unsettled living" of many itinerant unemployed. Welfare institutions for vagrants aimed at permanent "custody" of these men, who were now declared pathological and impeded in their ability to work. In institutions for "persons without a settled way of living," in the voluntary sector, this approach survived in combination with the original aims of welfare for vagrants until the 1970s, in spite of the brutal practice during German fascism when thousands of homeless beggars were arrested and deported to concentration camps, where these "persons without a settled way of living" were sterilized and later exterminated as psychopaths (Ayass 1995). Most of these institutions, including labor colonies, continued to exist, as well as the national associations to which they belong. Supported by scientific research, they tried to "settle down deficient persons" (Busch-Geertsema 1997). This was to be achieved by interning the homeless in homes and institutions and by rewarding compulsory work with a small allowance. Only in the 1960s and 1970s were the most important legal provisions for compulsory action against "work-shy persons," "predelinquents," and vagrants abolished. The professionalization of social work led to a modernization of the concept of pedagogical and therapeutical rehabilitation of homeless people.

However, at the end of the 1970s, and in the course of the 1980s, a fundamental change of values took place within the voluntary sector. The idea of integration was taken seriously, and it was reflected by legislation. Article 72 of the Federal Welfare Act stipulates "assistance in overcoming extraordinary social difficulties" for persons who need such assistance. It mandates securing the economic situation of homeless people and providing them with normal housing. It was accepted that most persons without a settled way of living were not as mobile as implied by this term. Furthermore, the system of homeless institutions with limits of stay for "short-stay accommodation for people on the move," with social welfare allowances on a daily basis, and with benefits intending to drive the homeless out of municipalities (culminating in giving out tickets to the next town) were acknowledged as important causes of their mobility (Marciniak 1977). Homelessness was classified as a structural problem of poverty and lack of housing, and the phrase person without a settled way of living was replaced by the term "single homeless person." "Stationary" institutions were criticized as "total institutions" (Goffman 1973). They were supplemented more and more by "ambulant" advice centers which were to help the homeless realize their claims to legal minimum standards and to assist in integration. Their aim was to integrate them as soon as possible into normal, permanent housing. It was realized that overcoming homelessness and providing permanent housing are basic requirements for an integration of homeless people into society and for the success of further social and therapeutic action.

It is unfortunate that, at the same time that this idea was gaining ground, and when "ambulant" advice centers for single homeless persons were opened everywhere in Germany, the housing shortage was growing worse, and single homeless people had no chance of finding affordable dwellings within the stock of normal housing, even when they were supported by social workers. Some welfare organizations of the voluntary sector reacted by becoming increasingly involved in housing policy and appealed to the state to give priority to providing disadvantaged persons with normal housing. A small number of them started to provide permanent housing for the homeless on their own, either as "brokers" or even as builders or purchasers of housing which they then let to homeless persons. If necessary, the rehoused homeless were also offered further individual care. However, although the number of ambulant advice centers for homeless persons has increased greatly (there were about 310 such advice centers and independent day centers in Germany in 1997), the number of places in homeless institutions in the voluntary sector is still at about 15,700 (in 290 institutions) (BAG Wohnungslosenhilfe 1998a, 10). A considerable number of them belong to former labor colonies with their century-old tradition of surveillance and moral training.

After highlighting the deeply rooted separation of services and responsibilities, this argument now has to be qualified. In recent years, German jurisdiction has clearly pointed out that the municipal obligation of accommodating homeless persons on a temporary basis is also applicable to single homeless persons (not only to families). Meanwhile, many municipalities provide accommodation for single homeless persons. According to the Federal Welfare Act, agents of social welfare are obliged to finance accommodation and care for homeless persons (homeless persons who have their own incomes have to contribute to the costs). Nowadays institutions of the voluntary sector are financed mainly by the state. However, the implementation regulations of Article 72 of the Federal Welfare Act still distinguish between persons without a settled way of living, accommodated in institutions at the cost of financing agents at the level of the *Bundesländer*, and other homeless persons who fall under the financial responsibility of municipalities. Although the redefinition of persons without a settled way of living into single homeless persons has often confused responsibilities, it has also enlarged the number of persons for whom institutions in the voluntary sector feel responsible. Finally, the traditionally separated organization of support for single homeless persons, on the one hand, and homeless families, on the other, has been increasingly questioned (see Evers and Ruhstrat 1993; Specht-Kittler 1997).

In summary, it can be said that, since the 1970s, services for homeless people have been liberated at least in tendency from the outdated view of homelessness as a consequence of individual deficiencies, pathological disposition, or offenses against public security and order. Furthermore, the traditional division of support into municipal accommodation directed mainly to evicted families, and institutions in the voluntary sector directed especially at nonlocal single homeless people (persons without a settled way of living) has begun to crumble. Punitive and controlling approaches, combined with the pedagogical and therapeutic, served both to help and to marginalize homeless people. This practice has more frequently been criticized and replaced by efforts to enable homeless people to lead a life as normal as possible and to integrate them successfully into society. It has been acknowledged that providing homeless people with permanent housing is an essential requirement of any possible supportive service. An increased emphasis on the prevention of homelessness and providing people with normal housing have become the key goals of policy.

Although single women, with or without children, are a minority among the single homeless, their proportion has grown in recent years and is estimated to be at around 21 percent (BAG 1997).[4] Reasons given by feminist researchers include the discriminatory nature of the male-oriented service system for the single homeless and therefore a lack of advice centers, hostels, and support services for women only[5] and the tendency of women to hide their homelessness as long as possible and seek private solutions (for example, by accepting insecure and temporary accommodation with male acquaintances including the danger or experience of sexual exploitation or domestic violence) (see BMFSFJ 1999; Enders-Dragässer 1998).[6]

There are other reasons, too. One of them is the fact that refuges for women fleeing from domestic violence are not part of the service system for the homeless in Germany (and domestic violence is one of the main reasons for women to become homeless). According to an unpublished survey of the coordinator of these refuges, in 1998 there were about 390 women's refuges in Germany with about 9,200 places for women and children (the number of places in institutions of voluntary service providers for the single homeless was about 15,700). These institutions do not define their clients as homeless (although the women are actually without a secure dwelling and can therefore be included in the definition of homelessness as it is accepted in Germany) and are quite reluctant to cooperate with the sector of services for the homeless. The same holds true for institutions that care exclusively for young single mothers with children.

Another reason for a relatively low number of women among the single homeless is the fact that women, in case of divorce or family breakdown, often keep the children, and lone mothers have a certain priority in the allocation of social housing, although allocation procedures vary locally. On one hand, some single mothers, who are homeless, run the risk of having to leave their children in foster care or in youth welfare institutions, on the other hand, there is a positive discrimination of single mothers at least in the sector of social housing. Generally, the chances of single mothers getting a social dwelling are much greater than those of single men.[7]

The majority of homeless, single mothers with children—like other homeless families—will be found in municipal temporary accommodation, but the numbers of women in institutions of voluntary organizations are growing. Recent studies criticize the traditional stereotypes of single homeless women as "shopping bag ladies" or extremely marginalized and destitute persons living on the street by stating that these persons account for only a tiny minority among the different groups of homeless women of which the majority live in "concealed" homelessness.

SOCIOECONOMIC BACKGROUND

Unemployment and Poverty

The numbers of unemployed persons and of recipients of social assistance (*Sozialhilfe*) have increased enormously in recent years. The annual average number of persons officially registered as unemployed in Germany rose from 2.6 million in 1991 to 4.38 million in 1997. There was a slight decrease in 1998 with an annual average of 4.28 million persons registered as unemployed, or 11.1 percent of the population (without soldiers).[8]

At the end of 1997, 2.89 million people in Germany relied on social assistance payments, 3.5 percent of the total population. This proportion is nearly four times higher than in the 1960s when the system of social assistance was introduced and when less than 1 percent of the population received social assistance. The proportion of young people receiving social assistance has clearly risen; the rate of recipients of social assistance is definitely higher in children and young persons up to 18, where it amounts to 6.8 percent, than in the group of elderly persons (older than 70) where only 1.2 percent receive social assistance. More women (3.9 percent) than men (3.2 percent) claim social assistance. Above all, single parents often receive social assistance. Almost every third single mother (28.3 percent) received social assistance at the end of 1997. Among immigrants living in Germany, the poverty rate of 9 percent is clearly higher than among the German population with 3.0 percent (Seewald 1999, 96, 97).

Table 4.2
Population of Germany (in millions of inhabitants)

Year	East Germany	West Germany	East- and West Germany
1987	16.64	61.08	77.72
1988	16.67	61.45	78.12
1989	16.61	62.06	78.67
1990	16.11	63.25	79.36
1991	15.91	64.07	79.98
1992	15.73	64.87	80.60
1993	15.65	65.53	81.18
1994	15.56	65.86	81.42
1995	15.51	66.16	81.67
1996	15.45	66.44	81.89
1997	15.37	66.69	82.06
1987 – 1997	-1.27	+5.61	+4.34

Source: Stabu 1998a, 45.

Demographic Trends

The German population was fairly stable at about 78 million persons between the early 1970s and the late 1980s (about 17 million living in the east and about 61 million in West Germany), but there was a significant growth in population after the late 1980s (see Table 4.2). From 1987 (77.7 million inhabitants) until 1997 (82.1 million inhabitants), the German population increased by more than 4 million people. However, this increase in population only affected West Germany (where the population figure increased by more than 5 million); the population figure in East Germany dropped by about 1 million inhabitants. While the natural population change would have produced a decline of the German population in the 1990s (in West Germany, too), this trend was reversed by external migration. One of the main immigrant groups is German repatriates (*Aussiedler*), persons of German origin who had lived in different Eastern European countries after World War II and moved back to Germany in the past years. *Aussiedler* have a legal claim to German citizenship. Their immigration to Germany was approved for political reasons until the late 1980s and supported and promoted by numerous forms of state financial assistance. When their numbers increased significantly after the political changes in Eastern Europe and the

Figure 4.1
Migration to Germany[1]

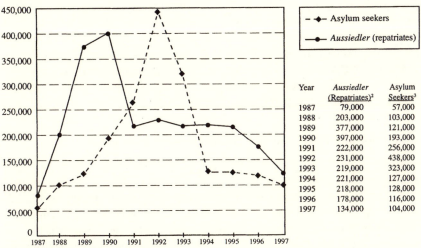

Year	Aussiedler (Repatriates)[2]	Asylum Seekers[3]
1987	79,000	57,000
1988	203,000	103,000
1989	377,000	121,000
1990	397,000	193,000
1991	222,000	256,000
1992	231,000	438,000
1993	219,000	323,000
1994	221,000	127,000
1995	218,000	128,000
1996	178,000	116,000
1997	134,000	104,000

[1]Until 1990 only for West Germany.
[2]*Source*: Stabu 1998a, 83.
[3]*Source*: Stabu 1998a, 67.

former Soviet Union, and reached a peak in 1990 at almost 400,000 *Aussiedler*
entering Germany, legal procedures were changed, and a maximum contingency
of around 220,000 repatriates were allowed to come to Germany every year.
From 1987 until 1997, about 2.5 million *Aussiedler* returned to Germany (see
Figure 4.1).[9]

Asylum seekers and other refugees are another important group of immigrants. Asylum seekers are allowed to stay in Germany only for the time of
their asylum procedures, and they have to leave Germany if their application
for asylum is rejected (which is the case in more than 90 percent of all decisions). After a large increase in asylum seekers (in 1992 their annual number
reached a peak with 438,000), legal conditions were changed radically, and the
number of asylum seekers coming to Germany has declined sharply.[10]

The increase in population seems to have stopped in 1998 when a first decline
of around 0.1 percent of the population was registered. In 1997, for the first
time since 1985, the number of foreign migrants leaving Germany was greater
than the number of newly immigrated foreigners (Sommer and Voit 1998, 975).

Even more important than the increases and decreases in the population figure
is the increase in the number of private households in Germany. While the
number of inhabitants in West Germany increased by around 10 percent between
1970 and 1997, the number of households increased by nearly 40 percent (from
22 million in 1970 to 30.6 million in 1997 in West Germany; there were alto-

gether 37.5 million private households in Germany in 1997 (see Stabu 1998a, 65). The average household size in West Germany decreased from 2.74 persons per household in 1970 to 2.18 in 1997. The percentage of small households has increased steadily. In 1997 more than 68 percent of all private households in Germany were one- and two-person households. Several factors have contributed to the trend of smaller households: the growing number of childless adults, a declining birthrate, a declining number of marriages, an increasing number of divorces, and the growing percentage of elderly couples living together without children, a result of increased life expectancy.

The Housing Market, Rent Rises, and Problems of Access

A decrease in housing construction, especially in West Germany, in the 1980s, against the background of the above-mentioned demographical trends, contributed to the housing shortage which became obvious at the end of the 1980s.[11] There was an estimated shortage of 2 million. An all-time low of housing construction in West Germany was reached in 1988 when just over 200,000 new dwellings were constructed. Afterward, the construction of new housing increased again (in 1996 a new peak, since the year 1974, was reached with more than 600,000 newly constructed dwellings). Between 1988 and 1996, the total housing stock in Germany grew by 3 million dwellings (from 33.4 to 36.5 million) (Manzel 1995, 351; Stabu 1998a, 234, 240). Construction of new housing, a decrease in immigration, and a subdued demand for more housing space caused by the continuous economic recession have considerably eased the situation of the housing market since the middle of the 1990s. However, this trend is much more descriptive of dwellings with high rents than in the sector of cheap dwellings where local shortages still occur.

As a consequence of the housing shortage of the late 1980s, rents rose significantly in Germany. This increase of rents has reduced since 1994, but the increase of rents is still definitely greater than the increase of other costs of living and of wages. For many households, the rent burden has actually been growing (BMBAU 1997, 21, 41). Rent allowances made by the state, however, were not increased between 1990 and 1999. As the number of homeless people peaked at the beginning of the 1990s and declined considerably in the second half of the 1990s, the number of households affected by rent arrears and threatened by home loss increased.

The benefits to the homeless resulting from the easing of the housing market are limited. First of all, the segment of the housing market available to people with low incomes or no incomes at all is small. Social welfare offices accept an assumption of rent cost only up to a fixed *appropriate* limit, and housing allowances are only paid up to fixed amounts. Besides these financial barriers, many homeless persons confront social barriers, such as landlords, who doubt their contractual fidelity (punctual and continuous rent payments, careful use of the dwelling) and fear conflicts with neighbors. In particular, those homeless persons who have already been evicted once have poor chances of finding a dwelling in the housing market. Finally, there still is a strong disproportion of supply to demand of dwellings for single households—housing policy and social housing construction clearly favor families.[12]

Eventually, it is questionable whether the easing of the housing market will last: the future development of important factors affecting the demand of housing is uncertain. It is difficult to make any prognosis about future trends of immigration to Germany. The number of households is still increasing. Any improvement of the economic situation might easily cause a larger demand for more housing space by the more affluent part of the population, as it has been the case several times since World War II (Ulbrich 1991). As to the supply of housing, building activities have been clearly decreasing since 1996. In particular, in the sector of social housing construction, the number of subsidized, newly constructed dwellings has been far smaller than in previous years. At the same time, allocation rights and rent restrictions of social housing (which are limited in time in Germany because public subsidies are paid only for a limited period, and social obligations cease to be in force when the period is over or cheap credits are paid back) are currently running out on a large scale, with the result that the total stock of social housing has been rapidly diminishing.[13] While there were about 4 million social dwellings in West Germany in 1980, in 1998 it was assumed that their number was going to be halved to about 2 million by the year 2000. Another division in half to only one million of social dwellings is expected by the year 2005 (see GDW 1998, 23). Most parts of the remaining housing stock are concentrated in large housing estates in the suburbs. Also, many municipalities sold their shares in housing enterprises in past years after serious financial difficulties and therefore lost influence in the allocation of dwellings. As allocation rights have to be concentrated on a still diminishing stock of social housing, the debate on emerging "ghettos" or "overstrained neighborhoods" (title of a current study on behalf of the Association of Building Societies, GDW 1998) is becoming more vehement, and "problematic" tenants are increasingly excluded even from those housing stocks for which municipalities still possess allocation rights.

THE LEGAL FRAMEWORK

There is no legal right to permanent housing in Germany; however, municipalities have the unconditional obligation to provide roofless persons, who are not able to help themselves, with temporary accommodation. A modern version of the principle of averting a danger to public security and order points out that the dangers connected with rooflessness mainly affect individual rights of the roofless (human dignity and protection of health and life) (Luebbe 1993). Standards required of temporary accommodation are very low (van Aken and Derleder 1994), although there are great differences in the practice of providing accommodation. Homeless people who are provided with temporary accommodation are still treated as homeless persons. Even if they are accommodated in normal housing, they have no legal rights as tenants. They can be transferred to other shelters at any time, and they remain obliged to look for permanent housing.

While police laws force municipalities to provide temporary accommodation, there is no obligation for municipalities to refer to police laws when accommodating homeless people. Instead, municipalities are entitled and advised to give priority to arrangements of temporary accommodation in dwellings rented and sublet to homeless people by municipalities, according to the Federal Welfare Act (see Luebbe 1993).[14] Agents of social welfare are obliged, by the Federal Welfare Act, to pay the costs of accommodation and care as well as minimum allowances to homeless persons with no incomes. This affects accommodation in municipal shelters as well as accommodation in institutions of the voluntary sector. Furthermore, agents of social welfare are obliged, by the Federal Welfare Act, to grant support and assistance "in overcoming extraordinary social difficulties" to all homeless persons with such difficulties (Article 72, Federal Welfare Act). This assistance means material support as well as personal support (advice, care). Types of assistance that are explicitly mentioned by this article are support of job training, assistance in gaining access to jobs and keeping them, and support in acquiring and maintaining dwellings.

While municipalities are not obliged to provide permanent housing, they are obliged to take over the full amount of housing costs for tenants who are recipients of social assistance (*Sozialhilfe*) "as far as they (the costs) are appropriate" (Article 3, implementing order to Article 22, Federal Welfare Act). However, neither the Federal Welfare Act nor the corresponding implementing order define the meaning of "appropriate," so municipalities have a rather free hand in fixing the upper limits of housing costs. In practice, there are considerable local differences. Besides the costs of accommodation, social assistance covers the current costs of living up to a level acknowledged to be the minimum standard of living. Social assistance is strictly considered subsidiary to other types of income and claims to alimony against relatives.

If unemployed persons were employed for at least 12 months within the past three years and paid into the social insurance, they can claim unemployment benefits (insurance payment amounting to 67 percent of their former net incomes if they have children, 60 percent if they have no children). Usually unemployment benefits are granted for 12 months (and longer in cases of elderly unemployed persons). One condition for the payment of unemployment benefits is the readiness of the unemployed to accept reasonable job offers. After these 12 months, unemployed persons may have a claim to unemployment assistance that is means tested and financed by taxes. For unemployed persons with children, it amounts to 57 percent of their last net income; for unemployed persons without children, it amounts to 53 percent.

Another source of income is housing allowance (*Wohngeld*), which is financed 50 percent by the central government and 50 percent by the *Länder* (regional states). This assistance supports households in paying rent costs, if their incomes are below a fixed ceiling. The amount of housing allowance depends on the number of family members belonging to the household, on the total sum of family income, and on the amount of officially accepted housing costs. As a matter of principle, the housing allowance may only be a contribution to the rent and may never cover its full amount. Owner occupiers may also receive a housing allowance as a contribution to the financial burden caused by capital and managing costs. However, according to the latest statistics on housing allowances, this affects fewer than 5 percent of all recipients. This illustrates the fact that housing property is of little importance to people with low incomes.

Although there is a legal claim to a housing allowance, it is granted only on the application of the entitled person. Many people entitled to a housing allowance do not pursue their legal claims; similarly, many people do not apply for social assistance although they are entitled to it. The proportion of all persons entitled to a housing allowance is estimated by experts to be between 40 percent and 50 percent (Ulbrich 1992; Hauser and Huebinger 1993, 151). Furthermore, housing allowances are updated only at long intervals, so rent increases during these intervals enlarge the financial burden of the recipients. For example, ceilings for officially accepted rents and rates of state contribution were not changed between 1990 and 1999, despite sharp rent increases.

German tenancy law (as part of the civil code) allows a rather good protection against notice to quit to tenants. Only under special conditions, which are laid down by law, is a landlord legally entitled to give notice to quit (for example, if landlords want to use the dwellings for themselves or for relatives, or if tenants offend against contractual rules). Usually certain periods of notice have to be observed. This is not the case, however, if rent arrears amount to more than one monthly payment. There are strong legal restrictions for tenancy contracts limited in time. If no explicit reason for a limitation in time is given (like an intended renovation or demolition of the dwelling), tenancy contracts limited in time have to be continued on tenants' demands.

A legal regulation central to the prevention of home loss is laid down in Article 15a of the Federal Welfare Act (BSHG/Bundessozialhilfegesetz). It says that it is possible to grant social assistance in order to "secure an accommodation." Therefore rent arrears can be assumed by social assistance offices in cases of threatened home loss. This regulation of the Federal Welfare Act is the complementary counterpart of Article 554 of the civil code which allows a "cure" (*Heilungsmöglichkeit*) in cases of notice to quit on the ground of rent arrears. If the landlord is promised an assumption of rent arrears by institutions of social assistance, a notice to quit can be declared void. The respective landlord has to receive this announcement by the institution of social assistance within one month after taking legal action against his tenant, and tenants may use this right only once within two years. Social assistance offices may either pay rent arrears from their own funds or assume them by granting a loan to the tenant, who

Table 4.3
Causes of Actions for Eviction in the First Months of 1993 (35 selected lower district courts in North Rhine-Westphalia)

cause of action	number of actions for eviction	
	absolute	%
default of payment	1,506	67.9
notice to quit on the ground of tenants' behavior	179	8.1
use of flat contrary to tenancy agreement	107	4.8
notice to quit on the ground of landlord's personal interest in the flat	212	9.6
other causes	214	9.6
total	2,218	100.0

Source: Busch-Geertsema and Ruhstrat 1994, 87.

may be obliged to pay it back, possibly in installments (for further details see Busch-Geertsema 1996).

WHY DO PEOPLE BECOME HOMELESS AND WHERE DO THEY WANT TO LIVE?

One of the main causes of home loss in Germany is eviction. Surveys have shown that the main reason for evictions is rent arrears: there is a detailed study of reasons for legal actions for eviction during the first half of 1993 based on cases of lower district courts (*Amtsgerichte* with jurisdiction over minor civil and criminal cases) in North Rhine-Westphalia. From a total number of 2,218 legal actions for eviction, 67.9 percent resulted from default of payment, 9.6 percent were based on a personal interest of the owner in the flat, 8.1 percent were due to intolerable demeanor of tenants, and 4.8 percent resulted from use of the flat contrary to tenancy agreement (Busch-Geertsema and Ruhstrat 1994, 86–89). The results of this analysis are similar to the results of surveys conducted in the 1980s (Koch 1984, 38). Obviously, in more than two-thirds of all cases of evictions, arrears of rent are the cause of eviction (see Table 4.3).

Apart from cases of home loss where landlords applied for actions of eviction, there are many other routes to homelessness which are not known to the courts. They become apparent from interviews with homeless persons who were asked to state the reasons for their first experience of homelessness. Unfortunately, there are no recent results concerning homeless households as a whole. For homeless families and single persons accommodated in municipal institutions of temporary accommodation according to police law, a comparatively high rate of homelessness as a result of eviction and enforced eviction can be expected, because local authorities accommodate mainly evicted households into temporary accommodation. The following results are based on interviews with single homeless persons who do not belong to this group, but were counseled and accommodated by institutions and advice centers of nongovernmental welfare organizations.

Interviews with homeless persons from all parts of Schleswig-Holstein have shown that just under 29 percent of 254 interviewed persons became homeless as a consequence of notice to quit by landlords. More than 40 percent became homeless for the first time without any notice to quit or notice to leave, but following separation from (marital or quasi-marital) partners (23.6 percent), or death of a relative (2 percent), or because they had left their parents' homes (14.6 percent). Finally, 9.4 percent became homeless after they had left an institution (e.g., prison and hospital), and 6.7 percent after the loss of accommodation which is tied to employment (Evers and Ruhstrat 1994, 223–28).

The majority of homeless persons interviewed in this survey had occupied a flat of their own for some time, but many of them did not become homeless in the usual way (notice to quit, action for eviction, enforced eviction), but as a consequence of changes and conflicts in family, marital, or quasi-marital relationships (see Table 4.4).

Among the interviewed homeless women, almost 59 percent of first home losses were caused by divorce or separation from a marital or quasi-marital partner (33 percent) or by leaving their parents' homes (25.9 percent). In the questionnaire, there was no question concerning domestic violence, but there is ample evidence that a high proportion of women's homelessness is caused by domestic violence. In an evaluation of model support schemes designed exclusively for homeless women, users of these schemes between October 1995 and September 1997 were asked about experiences of violence. Ninety-two percent of 240 women who answered this question affirmed that they had such experiences (BMFSFJ 1999, 156).

Several surveys investigating the wishes and needs of homeless persons show that the majority of homeless persons want to live in self-contained dwellings. In interviews with single homeless persons in Lower Saxony in 1989, more than two-thirds of 726 interviewed persons stated that they wanted to live in small, self-contained dwellings, and 19.3 percent wanted to live in furnished rooms (see Ruhstrat et al. 1991, 89). Of 258 single homeless persons who were questioned in Schleswig-Holstein, in 1992, on their housing requests, 73.3 percent declared that they wanted to live in small, self-contained dwellings, and 17 percent wanted to live in furnished rooms. Only 5.4 percent wanted to continue their present way of living or did not want to live in a dwelling. Another important result of these interviews was the fact that only 1.6 percent of all questioned persons wanted to live in shared dwellings, and less than 1 percent wanted to live in stationary institutions (providing beds for temporary stays with no rent

Table 4.4
Reason for First-Time Homelessness of Single People (Schleswig-Holstein)

Reason/occasion	number	% (n = 254)
leaving without notice to leave / notice to quit	**116**	**45.7**
- separation of partnership	60	23.6
- leaving of parental home	37	14.6
- death of relative	5	2.0
- problems in paying the rent	4	1.6
- intolerable housing conditions	4	1.6
- other reasons	6	2.4
notice to quit by landlord	**73**	**28.7**
- arrears of rent	37	14.6
- landlord's personal interest in the flat	16	6.3
- tenants' behavior	13	5.1
- other reasons	7	2.8
notice to leave by tenant	**21**	**8.3**
- financial problems	6	2.4
- conflicts with landlord	4	1.6
- intended change of residence or flat	4	1.6
- other reasons	7	2.7
after stay in institutions	**24**	**9.4**
- imprisonment	12	4.7
- psychiatric clinic	2	0.8
- home	3	1.2
- hospital	4	1.6
- other institutions	3	1.2
after tied accommodation (in company flat, etc.)	**17**	**6.7**
other occasions/reasons	**3**	**1.2**
total	**254**	**100.0**

Source: Evers and Ruhstrat 1994, 224.

contract and therapeutic or rehabilitative aims) (Evers and Ruhstrat 1994, 241) (see Table 4.5).

Data from the electronic data system of the National Coalition of Services for the Homeless confirm a clear preference for standard housing by homeless persons. According to the latest published analysis, 72.9 percent of more than

Table 4.5
Requests Concerning Future Housing of Homeless Persons in Schleswig-Holstein According to a Survey of 1992

Requested housing	number	%
(small) self-contained dwelling	189	73.3
furnished room	44	17.0
shared housing/residents groups	4	1.6
stationary institution for the homeless	2	0.8
caravan/house-boat	2	0.8
others	1	0.4
dwelling not requested/continuation of present way of living	14	5.4
no answer	2	0.8
total	258	100*

*Deviation from 100 percent as a result of rounding off.
Source: Evers and Ruhstrat 1994, 241.

16,000 registered homeless persons stated, in 1996, that they wanted a dwelling of their own, and 8.9 percent wanted a furnished room (BAG Wohnungslosen-hilfe 1998b, 37; author's calculations).[15] In total, more than 80 percent of all homeless persons wanted a normalization of their housing situation. These data soundly disprove the frequently held assumption that a large proportion of the homeless population made deliberate decisions for life without a dwelling or refused reintegration into normal housing.

RECENT TRENDS IN HOMELESSNESS AND POLICIES

The Quantitative Development of Homelessness

As it has already been mentioned, there is only scarce data on the quantitative development of homelessness figures in Germany. Among the sources for these figures are statistics from North Rhine-Westphalia, which show a dramatic rise and then a clear reduction in the figure of a subgroup of homeless persons in the 1980s and 1990s. According to these statistics, the number of persons provided with temporary accommodation by measures of public order laws rose by almost 65 percent between 1988 and 1994, reached its peak on the statistical fixed day (June 30) in 1994 with 62,400, and has been declining since then. On June 30, 1999, the figure (29,700) was at a historical low (LDS NRW, various years) (see Figure 4.2).[16]

Developments were similar for the mainly single, homeless persons in institutions of welfare organizations in the voluntary sector, who are not included

Figure 4.2
Homeless Persons Temporarily Accommodated under Police Law
(*Ordnungsbehördengesetz*) in North Rhine-Westphalia (June 30 each year)

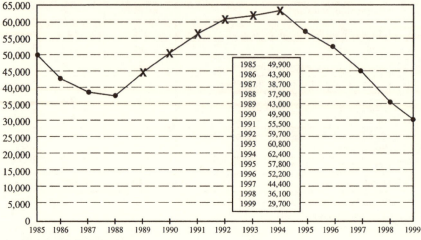

1985	49,900
1986	43,900
1987	38,700
1988	37,900
1989	43,000
1990	49,900
1991	55,500
1992	59,700
1993	60,800
1994	62,400
1995	57,800
1996	52,200
1997	44,400
1998	36,100
1999	29,700

Source: LDS NRW 1996–2000.

in the North Rhine-Westphalia statistics. At the end of the 1980s, residential institutions were occupied beyond their capacities, and new places had to be established. Since the mid 1990s, complaints have become frequent that residential institutions are not used to capacity and have vacant places.

In contrast to the development of homelessness figures in West Germany, first studies on quantity and development of homelessness in East Germany have shown a strong increase compared with low homelessness figures in the first years after the German unification. Numbers are still below the level of East German cities but are obviously approximating the quantity of homelessness in West Germany, particularly in larger East German cities (Busch-Geertsema and Ruhstrat 1997b).[17]

While the situation on the housing market has relaxed on the whole, other trends increase the risk of homelessness. Among them are the constantly high level of unemployment in Germany, the obvious increase of poverty, and the growing rent burden for many households. Other risk factors are over-indebtedness, high rates of divorce (and of domestic violence), sinking safety of social networks, cuts in state welfare benefits, and a tightening of requirements for claims to such benefits. However, the quantitative developments of recent decades in West Germany show that poverty and unemployment—which are definitely related to homelessness—do not necessarily have the same trend as homelessness: homelessness can be reduced in spite of growing risks like poverty and unemployment.

The reduction of homelessness is not only a consequence of a general easing of the situation of the housing market but demands special measures to prevent and remove homelessness and resolve the problem of access barriers to standard housing.

Innovation in Policies on Different Levels

In Germany at the present time, there is a mandate to provide homeless persons with standard housing, which has been broadly established in the sector of services for the homeless, at least in public statements, trendsetting declarations, and recommendations. Demands that government create a housing policy that accepts more responsibility for groups particularly disadvantaged in the housing market instead of leaving responsibility for them to social policy have had some effect.[18]

The Federal Ministry of Housing has participated in several research schemes; for example, on the incidence of homelessness and the prevention of homelessness in practice; on temporary accommodation and reintegration of homeless persons into normal housing (Busch-Geertsema and Ruhstrat 1994); on the feasibility of statistics on homelessness (Koenig 1998); and on housing acquisition by cooperation of housing enterprises, municipalities, and voluntary welfare organizations (BBR 2000). One research scheme, permanent housing provision for homeless people, part of the major scheme "Experiments in Urban Development" (*Experimenteller Wohnungs—und Städtebau*, or EXWOST) is especially important in this respect. It evaluates projects providing homeless people with normal and permanent housing at reasonable rents and normal building standards, with usual tenancy agreements, situated in nonstigmatized surroundings. In addition, the projects are of manageable size and combine housing provision with further assistance in social integration. Findings of several years' evaluation showed that even long-term homeless persons with considerable health-related and social problems could maintain their dwellings and clearly improve their situation under such conditions with adequate social support (see BBR 1998 for findings of the total research scheme; information on certain projects is given in Busch-Geertsema and Ruhstrat 1997a and in Busch-Geertsema 1998). In 1995 the Federal Ministry of Housing introduced a regulation providing that an annual sum of 50 million DM from the budget of federal subsidies to social housing should be invested into housing provisions for homeless people.

Plans for a reform of the Federal Housing Construction Act have been directed to include homeless persons as a special group in need of housing into the Act, and to concentrate on housing construction and allocation rights for particularly disadvantaged persons in need of housing.

Parliamentary reports on action against homelessness charging responsibility to the Federal Ministry of Housing have been introduced. The second report of the federal government published in 1998 takes up a clear position in respect to the aims of services for the homeless. On the one hand, it underlines the fact that providing and maintaining dwellings is often not sufficient in itself.

Although homelessness does not generally go along with further social difficulties and need of personal support, strategies for a permanent solution of the problem may not be restricted to housing provision, but their conception has to include services in support of housing from the start: aids and support to secure the standard of living, to organize everyday life, to restore and maintain health and to establish social contacts.

In the following, however, the report also highlights the relevance of normal housing for a further integration of homeless persons:

In principle, a provision with "normal housing" has to be the aim, meaning housing with usual standards in intact neighborhoods. Spatial and social exclusion do not serve integration but make effective support more difficult. Accommodation in shelters and other special forms of housing or a concentration of disadvantaged households in poor housing areas may rather increase social problems than solve them. Moreover, such forms of housing are in most cases especially expensive. (Deutscher Bundestag 1998, 2)

Social legislation also gave some positive directions, in spite of many changes for the worse.[19] For example, Article 15a of the Federal Welfare Act for the prevention of homelessness was reformed and now contains a stronger obligation for municipalities to intervene actively.

On the level of the *Länder*, special measures were taken, too. Several *Bundesländer* started schemes to promote housing projects for homeless persons. North Rhine-Westphalia is a model in this respect as it set up several innovative schemes. For example, between 1994 and 1997, it promoted projects that created new housing (by new construction or redevelopment of existing housing) in combination with employment schemes (see Busch-Geertsema and Ruhstrat 1999). By 1999 more than 30 of these projects have been carried out in North Rhine-Westphalia alone. Often homeless persons were able to benefit from these projects (as participants of employment schemes or residents, or both). Since 1997 the North Rhine-Westphalian model scheme Preventing Homelessness— Securing Permanent Housing has supported a multitude of other innovative activities by municipalities and voluntary organizations aiming at a more efficient prevention of homelessness, the development of new housing for homeless persons, and appropriate social and medical care (see Thabe 1999). The establishment of central agencies (*Zentrale Fachstellen*) at municipal administrations, which was recommended by the head association of German municipalities in 1987 (DST 1987), is crucial to both model schemes. The main idea of these central agencies for the prevention and eradication of homelessness is to focus competencies and resources related to ending homelessness. Responsibilities used to be spread among different offices: social welfare and youth welfare offices were responsible for the prevention of home loss, public affairs offices

for the accommodation of homeless persons, and housing offices for the reintegration of the homeless into permanent housing. A central agency, in contrast
to that, is responsible for all these problems and can cope with them faster, more
efficiently, and at lower cost, while giving priority to preventing and removing
homelessness (MASSKS 1999).

To reduce homelessness, increased efforts of municipalities to prevent cases
of home loss and to improve opportunities for the homeless persons to be provided with social dwellings are especially important. A growing number of municipalities have set up central agencies and make intensive efforts to reduce the
number of places in emergency shelters. Several surveys have proved that it is
cheaper to prevent homelessness than it is to accommodate homeless persons
(DST 1987), and providing homeless persons with standard housing and appropriate social care may also save costs to municipalities (Busch-Geertsema
1997a). Social support in normal housing is growing in importance for voluntary
organizations of social work (see Busch-Geertsema 1999b).

New Forms of Exclusion and New Target Groups of Homeless People

The high level of poverty and long-term unemployment and a change of
discourse about public order and security have also brought about new forms
of exclusion. American debates on "zero-tolerance strategies" have given rise to
German demands to use private security forces or the police to prevent begging
and public drinking as well as the loitering of socially unwanted persons (drug
addicts, vagrants, punks, and so on) in public areas, pedestrian zones, stations,
and so on. Since the legality of many of these demanded prohibitions is questionable (the prohibition of begging and vagrancy in penal legislation was explicitly abolished in 1974), public areas are being changed into private property
to allow the proprietor to make use of his domiciliary right (Behrendes 1998;
Ronneberger 1998; Wolf 1998).

New services for those who are excluded have been emerging (or sometimes
revived) in Germany as a reaction to the erosion of social rights, the insufficient
realization of legal claims, and the debate on the deconstruction (or reconstruction) of the welfare state. A rapidly growing number of new charitable action
groups have come into being in recent years. Relying on voluntary work, they
try to provide poor and homeless people with food, clothes, sleeping bags, and
so on. Some newly founded organizations, called "tables" (*Tafeln*), distribute
donated food to people in need, man soup kitchens for the poor, and set up
"furniture stocks" in many places. Donators' parliaments give permanent donators the right to decide together on the use of donations. It is a characteristic
of these charitable action groups that they keep their distance from the traditional
agents of social policy, state, and established voluntary organizations (even
though both try to influence the new pressure groups). These groups are evi-
dently influenced by communitarian ideas, which have been discussed and im-

plemented in Germany for some time. The tradition of Christian charity services for the poor and homeless in Germany is quite obvious. Because these efforts are a reaction to the erosion of social rights and the state's withdrawal from its social responsibility, there is a danger that they might add to this development by defining the needs of the poor and homeless at a very low level, by providing substitutes for legal benefits and thus enforcing dependence on voluntary donations instead of claiming legal rights, and by reviving a separation of people in need into the deserving and undeserving poor.

It is a rather new trend in Germany to set up special medical services for the homeless. Although homeless persons have a claim to medical care like other citizens, which is financed either by health insurance or the Federal Welfare Act, it is obvious that the state of health, in particular of those (single) homeless persons who are temporarily accommodated in shelters or who live in the streets, is often extremely bad and that many homeless persons do not receive or use appropriate medical care in spite of their serious health problems (see Locher 1990; Trabert 1995, 1999; Kunstmann 1999). In response to that initiative, groups have been founded in many places in Germany to set up medical care for homeless persons. They work in very different ways. Some of them call on homeless persons in the streets, and others offer consulting hours in shelters or have offices near stations. Sometimes these schemes are initiated by voluntary organizations, but in some places by doctors and health offices. It is the common aim of these services to offer homeless persons better access to medical care without barriers. The risk of these projects is that they might contribute to an exclusion of homeless persons from the general health system if they are referred to the new emergency services (see Kunstmann, Gerling, and Becker 1996).

A growing number of surveys have recently dealt with the high incidence of psychiatric diseases among the homeless (IFKP 1996; Greifenhagen and Fichter 1998; Quadflieg 1998). The samples of these surveys, which demonstrate an extraordinarily high prevalence of psychiatric diseases, are often reduced to single homeless persons living in the streets or in emergency shelters. Apart from methodological drawbacks of many psychiatric surveys in this sector (see Kunstmann and Becker 1998; Salize 1998), it is obvious that mental diseases and a lower self-help capacity, as a result of these diseases, poses a special risk to the homeless.[20] Another obvious point is that a reduction of the total number of homeless persons increases the proportion of those who suffer from special social and health-induced problems and are therefore particularly disadvantaged. It is not sufficient if they are provided only with housing. Additional social and medical support is necessary, and adequate measures must be developed.

The number of homeless women has clearly gained in significance. BAG (1999a) estimates their percentage among the homeless population without repatriates at about 30 percent. Recent studies point at the particular relevance of "hidden" homelessness for women (who may be put up by friends or live without tenancy contracts in insecure tenancies) and stress the importance of domestic violence, personal conflicts, and structural discrimination against women (high incidence of poverty, discrimination in the employment and income system, insecure housing situations) as causes for female homelessness (BMFSFJ 1999; Enders-Dragässer 1994, 1998; Rosenke 1996; Beinling et al. 1994).

Among the new target groups of the homeless is a rising number of persons of foreign nationality who make use of services for the homeless.

In recent years, much public concern has been focused on homeless children, young people, and young adults who stay at public places, have broken off relations with parents, school, and services of state youth welfare agencies, and have become delinquent. Several research and action schemes are dealing with the phenomenon of street children. This term, however, is rejected by most of them because it suggests misleading associations to conditions in poor countries (see Permien and Zink 1998; Hansbauer 1998). These young people, whose center of life is the street, are a special challenge to German youth welfare. Their number is estimated at between 5,000 and 7,000. The number of those children and young people who are accommodated with their parents in shelters and other forms of temporary accommodation for the homeless is much higher (see Busch-Geertsema 1997b; for housing problems of young people, see also Bendit, Gaiser, and Marbach 1999).

CONCLUSION

Despite great wealth and overall good housing provision for the majority of the population, there are many homeless persons in Germany. Experiences of recent decades have shown that their number depends on the development of supply and demand and on the effectiveness of access barriers in the housing market. It is certain that unemployment and poverty are important risk factors for the constitution of homelessness. The German example also shows that, even when poverty and unemployment rise, a significant reduction of homelessness is possible if the situation in the housing market relaxes and special measures are taken to prevent and eradicate homelessness. To further reduce, and permanently reduce, homelessness figures, preventive action must be made more effective, services of social care and support for those persons who need them must be strengthened and differentiated, and access to standard housing must be secured for socially disadvantaged persons permanently and at a sufficient rate. The decrease of housing with social obligations and thus of public influence on the allocation of dwellings, as well as financial cuts in the social sector, give little reason for optimism in this respect.

Ultimately, a further integration of socially excluded groups also depends on a successful struggle against poverty, unemployment, indebtedness, and social marginalization. If the state retreats from these urgent social responsibilities, further social exclusion and homelessness will be the inevitable result.

REFERENCES

van Aken, J. C., and P. Derleder. 1994. "Rechtliche Aspekte und Rahmenbedingungen im Zusammenhang mit der Wohnungsnotfallproblematik." In *Wohnungsnotfälle. Sicherung der Wohnungsversorgung für wirtschaftlich oder sozial benachteiligte Haushalte*, V. Busch-Geertsema E. U. Ruhstrat. Bonn: Bundesministerium für Raumordnung, Bauwesen und Staedtebau, and Bundesministerium Für Familie und Senioren.

Ayass, W. 1995. *"Asoziale" im Nationalsozialismus*. Stuttgart: Klett Cotta.

BAG Wohnungslosenhilfe, Bundesarbeitsgemeinschaft Wohnungslosenhilfe. 1997. *BAG Informationen: Weibliche Wohnungsnot*. Bielefeld, Germany.

———. 1998. *Jahres bericht der Geschäftsstelle 1997*. Bielefeld, Germany.

———. 1999. "Pressemiteilung der BAG Wohnungslsönhilfe: BAG Schätzung 1998 zur Zahl der Wohnungslosen." *Wohnungslos* 1: 44–45.

Bundesamt für Bauwesen und Raumordnung, ed. 1998. *Dauerhafte Wohnungsversorgung von Obdachlosen* (Authors: G. Schuler-Wallner, I. Mühlich-Klinger, and R. Greiff), Werkstatt: Praxis, Nr. 3. Bonn. Final report on the results of a three-year evaluation of seven pilot schemes at various places in Germany aimed at permanent rehousing of homeless people. One hundred and nine dwellings (in 13 buildings) were constructed especially for this project, and the report describes the different concepts, target groups, management, and financing, as well as different forms of organizing the rehousing process (regarding allocation, social support, and so on) and the results. Evaluation findings show that even those homeless persons who need personal care and are considered "risky tenants" can be provided with normal housing, and they are able to maintain tenancies if efforts are made to meet their need of support and to cover possible risks of tenancies. The whole evaluation scheme was financed by the Federal Ministry of Housing.

———. 2000. *Wohnraumbeschaffung durch Kooperation* (Authors: U. Behrendt, V. Eichener, and R. Höbel), Forschungen, Heft 96. Bonn.

Behrendes, U. 1998. "Kooperation zwischen Polizei und Sozialarbeit in Sicherheits-und Ordnungspartnerschaften?" *Wohnungslos* 2:41–48.

Beinling, M., A. Birk, G. Broszat, et al., ed. 1994. *Frauen und Kinder zuletzt?! Frauen in Wohnungsnot*. Bielefeld, Germany: Verlag Soziale Hilfe.

Bendit, R., W. Gaiser, and J. H. Marbach, eds. 1999. *Youth and Housing in Germany and the European Union. Data and Trends on Housing: Biographical, Social and Political Aspects*. Opladen: Leske & Budrich.

Berthold, M. 1993. "Winter 92/93: Mindestens 29 wohnungslose Männer und Frauen erfroren. Pressemitteilung der BAG Wohnungslosenhilfe e.V. vom 1.3. 1993." *Gefährdetenhilfe* 1: 39.

BMBAU, Bundesministerium für Bauwesen, Raumordnung und Städtebau. 1997. *Wohngeld und Mietenbericht 1997*. Bonn.

Busch-Geertsema, V. 1987. "Wohnungslosigkeit als 'Charakterschwäche'. Zur wissenschaftlichen Verarbeitung eines sozialen Problems." In *Wie Armut entsteht und Armutsverhalten hergestellt wird. Denkschrift und Materialien zum UNO-Jahr für Menschen in Wohnungsnot*. ed Autorengruppe. Bremen: Universität Bremen Selbstverlag.

———. 1996. *Insecurity of Tenure and Prevention of Homelessness in Germany. National Report 1995 for the European Observatory on Homelessness*. Brussels: Feantsa.

————. 1997a. *Normal Wohnen ist nicht nur besser, es ist auch billiger. Vergleich der Unterbringungskosten von Wohnungslosen in Einrichtungen und Sonderwohnformen mit den Kosten ihrer Versorgung in normalem Wohnraum.* Bremen: Gesellschaft für Innovative Sozialforschung und Sozialplanung.

————. 1997b. *Youth Homelessness in Germany. National Report 1996 for the European Observatory on Homelessness.* Brussels: Feantsa.

————. 1998. *Rehousing Projects for Single Homeless Persons. Innovative Approaches in Germany. National Report 1997 for the European Observatory on Homelessness.* Brussels: Feantsa.

————. 1999a. "Temporary Accommodation for Homeless People in Germany with Special Focus on the Provision for Immigrants and Asylum Seekers." In *Coping with Homelessness: Issues to Be Tackled and Best Practices in Europe,* ed. D. Avramov. Aldershot, England: Ashgate.

————. 1999b. *Homelessness and Support in Housing in Germany. Solution or Part of the Problem? National Report 1998 for the European Observatory on Homelessness.* Brussels: Feantsa.

Busch-Géertsema, V., and Ruhstrat, E. U. 1994. *Wohnungsnotfälle. Sicherung der Wohnungsversorgung für wirtschaftlich oder sozial benachteiligte Haushalte,* ed. Bundesministerium für Raumordnung, Bauwesen und Städtebau and Bundesministerium für Familie und Senioren. Bonn: Selbstverlag. This is the first study on behalf of the federal government (jointly commissioned by the Departments of Housing and of Social Assistance) that developed an integrated perspective on all homeless people (single homeless as well as homeless families). This is the only recent survey which has tried to provide a scientific and nationwide assessment of the number of homeless people in Germany based on empirical evidence. It gives an overview of the legal provision concerning homelessness, temporary accommodation, and the possible prevention of homelessness; discusses municipal efforts to prevent homelessness and rehouse homeless people; and includes a number of recommendations for improving policies at all different levels.

————. 1997a. *Wohnungsbau für Wohnungslose.* Bielefeld, Germany: Verlag Soziale Hilfe.

————. 1997b. *Wohnungslosigkeit in Sachsen-Anhalt. Umfang und Struktur von Wohnungslosigkeit in einem ostdeutschen Bundesland und Strategien zu ihrer Vermeidung und Behebung.* Bielefeld, Germany: Verlag Soziale Hilfe.

————. 1999. *Landesmodellprogramm Arbeiten und Wohnen. Beschäftigungsföderung und Wohnungsbau für Benachteiligte am Wohnungs-und Arbeitsmarkt,* ed. Ministerium für Arbeit, Soziales und Stadtentwicklung, Kultur und Sport des Landes Nordrhein-Westfalen. Düsseldorf.

Deutscher Bundestag. 1998. *Bericht der Bundesregierung über Maßnahmen zur Bekämpfung der OBDACHLOSIGKEIT.* Bundestagsdrucksache 13/10141.

DST, Deutscher Städtetag. 1987. *Sicherung der Wohnungsversorgung in Wohnungsnotfällen und Verbesserung der Lebensbedingungen in sozialen Brennpunkten— Empfehlungen und Hinweise.* Köln: DST-Selbstverlag.

DST, Deutscher Städtetag, ed. 1980. *Neue Wohnungsnot in unseren Städten.* Stuttgart.

Enders-Dragässer, U. 1994. *Frauen in Wohnungsnot. Endbericht der Studie 'Zur Situation alleinstehender wohnungsloser Frauen in Rheinland-Pfalz'.* Mainz: Ministerium für die Gleichstellung von Frau und Mann.

————. 1998. *Wohnungsnot und Wohnungslosigkeit von Frauen in der Wohnungslosenhilfe in Hessen, im Auftrag des Hessischen Ministeriums für Frauen, Arbeit und*

Sozialordnung. Frankfurt: Gesellschaft für Sozialwissenschaftliche Frauenforschung e.V.

Enders-Dragässer, U., B. Sellach, A. Feig, M.-L. Jung, S. Roscher, and Band 186 der Schriftenreihe des BMFSFJ 1999. *Frauen ohne Wohnung. Handbuch für die ambulante Wohnungslosenhilfe für Frauen,* ed. BMFSFJ, Bundesministerium für Familie, Senioren, Frauen und Jugend. Stuttgart: Kohlhammer. This recently published evaluation, financed by the Federal Ministry for Women, covers new support schemes (counseling, day shelters, hostels, support in housing) exclusively for homeless women and their needs, which are staffed by female social workers, in four German cities. It records a wide range of data of more than 450 users of these institutions. Some chapters focus and give advice on specific topics, such as health problems of homeless women, integration of homeless women into employment, public relations work of institutions working with homeless women, and quality management and quality assurance of such institutions. A list of addresses of 95 institutions for homeless women in Germany is included.

Evers, J., and E. U. Ruhstrat. 1993. "Abschied von der Eigenständigkeit der Hilfe für alleinstehende Wohnungslose." *Gefährdetenhilfe* 1: 1–13.

———. 1994. *Wohnungsnotfälle in Schleswig-Holstein. Im Spannungsfeld zwischen Sozial-, Ordnungs- und Wohnungspolitik.* Kiel, Germany: Ministerium für Arbeit, Soziales, Jugend und Gesundheit des Landes Schleswig-Holstein und Diakonisches Werk Schleswig-Holstein.

Fitzpatrick, S. 1998. "Homelessness in the European Union." In *European Integration and Housing Policy,* ed. M. Kleinman, W. Matznetter, and M. Stephens. London: Routledge.

GDW, Bundesverband deutscher Wohnungsunternehmen, ed. 1998. *Uberforderte Nachbarschaften. Zwei sozialwissenschaftliche Studien über Wohnquartiere in den alten und den neuen Bundeslaendern im Auftrag des GDW.* Köln: GDW.

Goffman, E. 1973. *Asyle. Über die soziale Situation psychiatrischer Patienten und anderer Insassen.* Frankfurt: Suhrkamp.

Greifenhagen, A., and M. Fichter. 1998. "Ver-rückt und obdachlos—psychische Erkrankungen bei wohnungslosen Frauen." *Wohnungslos* 3:89–98.

Hansbauer, P., ed. 1998. *Kinder und Jugendliche auf der Strasse, Analysen, Strategien und Lösungsansätze.* Münster, Germany: Votum.

Hauser, R., and W. Hübinger. 1993. *Arme unter uns, Teil 1: Ergebnisse und Konsequenzen der Caritas-Armutsuntersuchung,* ed. Deutscher Caritasverband. Freiburg i. B.: Lambertus.

IFKP, Institut für Kommunale Psychiatrie, ed. 1996. *"Auf die Strasse entlassen," obdachlos und psychisch krank.* Bonn: Psychiatrie-Verlag.

IFS, Institut für Städtebau, Wohnungswirtschaft und Bausparwesen. 1998. *Wohneigentumsquote leicht angestiegen—Ostdeutschland überholt die Schweiz, Pressemitteilung* vom 17.4.1998. Bonn (see also Sozialpolitische Umschau, Nr. 219, 18.5.1998).

John, W. 1988. *Ohne festen Wohnsitz—Ursachen und Geschichte der Nichtsesshaftigkeit und die Möglichkeiten der Hilfe.* Bielefeld, Germany: Verlag Soziale Hilfe.

Kärkkäinen, S. L. 1999. "Annual Survey on Homelessness in Finland: Definitions and Methodological Aspects." In *Coping with Homelessness: Issues to Be Tackled and Best Practices in Europe,* ed. D. Avramov. Aldershot, England: Ashgate.

Kleinman, M. 1996. *Housing, Welfare and the State in Europe. A Comparative Analysis of Britain, France and Germany.* Cheltenham, England: Edward Elgar.

Koch, F. 1984. *Ursachen von Obdachlosigkeit. Bericht über das Forschungsprojekt der Arbeitsgemeinschaft der Spitzenverbände der Freien Wohlfahrtspflege der Freien Wohlfahrtspflege des Landes Nordrhein-Westfalen.* Düsseldorf: Ministerium für Arbeit, Gesundheit und Soziales NRW.

Koch, F., G.: Hard, and P. Tristram. 1993. *Wohnungsnot und Obdachlosigkeit. Soziale Folgeprobleme und Entwicklungstendenzen.* Düsseldorf: Ministerium für Arbeit, Gesundheit und Soziales des Landes Nordrhein-Westfalen (Landessozialbericht, Band 2).

König, C. 1998. *Machbarkeitsstudie zur statistischen Erfassung von Wohnungslosigkeit.* Wiesbaden, Germany: Statistisches Bundesamt.

Kunstmann, W. 1999. "Germany." In *Homelessness in the United States, Europe and Russia: A Comparative Perspective,* ed. C. O. Helvie and W. Kunstmann. Westport, Conn.: Bergin & Garvey.

Kunstmann, W., and H. Becker. 1998. "Methodische Probleme der Erhebung psychiatrischer Krankheitsprävalenzen unter Wohnungslosen. Eine kritische Analyse am Beispiel der Münchner und der Dortmunder Studie." *Wohnungslos* 3: 106–13.

Kunstmann, W., S. Gerling, and H. Becker. 1996. "Medizinische Versorgungsprojekte für Wohnungslose. Ursachen und Konzepte." *Wohnungslos* 3: 103–12.

LDS NRW, Landesamt für Datenverarbeitung und Statistik Nordrhein-Westfalen. Different years. *Statistische Berichte. Die Obdachlosigkeit in Nordrhein-Westfalen am 30. Juni 19 . . .* Düsseldorf.

Locher, G. 1990. *Gesundheits-/Krankheitsstatus und arbeitsbedingte Erkrankungen von alleinstehenden Wohnungslosen.* Bielefeld, Germany: Verlag Soziale Hilfe.

Lübbe, A. 1993. *Wohnraumbeschaffung durch Zwangsmaßnahmen. Möglichkeiten und Grenzen kommunaler Wohnraumzwangsbewirtschaftung im Interesse der Unterbringung von Obadachlosen, Aussiedlern und Asylbewerbern.* Baden-Baden, Germany: Nomos.

MASSKS, Ministerium für Arbeit, Soziales und Stadtentwicklung, Kultur und Sport des Landes Nordrhein-Westfalen/KGSt, Kommunale Gemeinschaftsstelle für Verwaltungsvereinfachung/LAG Ö/F, Landesarbeitsgemeinschaft der Öffentlichen und Freien Wohlfahrtsflege in Nordrhein-Westfalen, ed. 1999. *Zentrale Fachstellen zur Hilfe in Wohnungsnotfällen. Ein Handbuch zur Umsetzung in den Kommunen.* Düsseldorf.

Manzel, K. 1995. Zur Entwicklung des Wohnungsbaus in Deutschland in der ersten Hälfte der neunziger Jahre." *Wirtschaft und Statistik* 5: 350–60. This handbook for municipalities recommends the reorganization of services for the homeless in an integrated and effective way. The handbook presents very detailed models of good practice in preventing homelessness and reintegrating homeless people into normal housing.

Marciniak, K. 1977. "Die ambulante Nichtsesshaftenhilfe." In *Phänomen Nichtsesshaftigkeit und die Anforderung an die Hilfe.* Bielefeld, Germany: Bundesarbeitsgemeinschaft für Nichtsesshaftenhilfe.

Permien, H., and G. Zink. 1998. *Endstation Strasse? Strassenkarrieren aus der Sicht von Jugendlichen.* Munich: Deutsches Jugendinstitut.

Quadflieg, N. 1998. "Psychische Störungen bei wohnungslosen Männern." *Wohnungslos* 3: 98–102.

Ronneberger, K. 1998. "Die Unwirtlichkeit der Städte." *Wohnungslos* 2: 48–51.

Rosenke, W. 1996. "Weibliche Wohnungsnot. Ausmaß—Ursachen—Hilfeangebote." *wohnungslos* 3: 77–81.

———. 1999. "Erhebung über den Bestand und den Standard kommunaler Übernachtungsmöglichkeiten für wohnungslose Frauen." *Wohnungslos* 3: 124–29.

Ruhstrat, E. U. et al. 1991. *"Ohne Arbeit keine Wohnung, ohne Wohnung keine Arbeit!" Entstehung und Verlauf von Wohnungslosigkeit,* ed. Evangelischer Fachverband Wohnung und Existenzsicherung. Bielefeld: Verlag Soziale Hilfe. This pioneer study on single homelessness in Lower Saxony analyzes the structural effects that cause homelessness and the negative results of a poorly designed support system. The core of the study consists of 17 in-depth interviews with single homeless persons about their life histories and their experiences with institutions. The study also provides quantitative data on the social structure (age, sex, education, income, employment, and so on) of several hundred single homeless persons, the reasons for their first experience of homelessness, their life situations, and their wishes for the future.

Salize, H. J. 1998. "Psychiatrische Wohnungslosenforschung in Deutschland—marginalisiert wie ihre Klientel?" *Wohnungslos* 3: 103–5.

Scheffler, J., ed. 1987. *Bürger & Bettler. Materialien zur Geschichte der Nichtsesshaftenhilfe in der Diakonie, Bd. 1, 1854 bis 1954, vom Herbergswesen für wandernde Handwerksgesellen zur Nichtsesshaftenhilfe.* Bielefeld, Germany: Verlag Soziale Hilfe.

Schewe, P. 1995. "Wohnungen und ihre Ausstattung. Ergebnis der 1%-Gebäude-und Wohnungsstichprobe am 30. September 1993." *Wirtschaft und Statistik* 5: 361–65.

Schuler-Wallner, G., I. Mühlich-Klinger, and R. Greiff. 1998. *Dauerhafte Wohnungsversorgung von Obdachlosen,* ed. BBR, Bundesamt für Bauwesen und Raumordnung. Werkstatt: Praxis, Nr. 3. Bonn.

Schuler-Wallner, G., R. Ulbrich, V., Ölbermann, R., Dilcher, and H. Schäfer. 1996. *Wohnungsnotfälle in Hessen. Problemumfang und Erfahrungen mit Konzepten zur dauerhaften Wohnungsversorgung. Untersuchung im Auftrag des Hessischen Ministeriums für Landesentwicklung, Wohnen, Landwirtschaft, Forsten und Naturschutz.* Darmstadt, Germany: Institut Wohnen und Umwelt.

Seewald, H. 1999. "Ergebnisse der Sozialhilfe-und Asylbewerberleistungsstatistik 1997." *Wirtschaft und Statistik* 2: 96–110.

Sommer, B., and H. Voit. 1998. "Bevölkerungsentwicklung 1997." *Wirtschaft und Statistik* 12: 971–77.

Specht-Kittler, T. 1994. *Housing Poverty in a Rich Society: Houselessness and Unacceptable Housing Conditions in Germany. A New Perspective on "Homelessness." National Report 1994 for the European Observatory on Homelessness.* Brussels: Feantsa.

———. 1997. "Wohnungslosenhilfe in der Krise. Neue Herausforderungen und die Suche nach Antworten auf dem Weg ins 21. Jahrhundert." *Wohnungslos* 4.

———. 1998. *Statistikbericht 1996,* ed. BAG Wohnungslosenhilfe, Bundesarbeitsgemeinschaft-Wohnungslosenhilfe. Bielefeld, Germany.

Stabu, Statistisches Bundesamt. 1996. *Fachserie 5, Bautätigkeit und Wohnungen. 1%-Gebäude-und Wohnungsstichprobe 1993, Heft 3, Haushalte—Wohnsituation, Mieten und Mietbelastung-.* Wiesbaden, Germany.

————. 1998a. *Statistisches Jahrbuch 1998 für die Bundesrepublik Deutschland*. Wiesbaden, Germany.

————. 1998b. *Bevölkerung und Erwerbstätigkeit. Fachserie 1, Reihe 3, Haushalte und Familien 1997 (Ergebnisse des Mikrozensus)*. Wiesbaden, Germany.

————. 2000. *Statistisches Jahrbuch 2000 für das Ausland*. Wiesbaden, Germany.

Steffen, J. 2000. *Die wesentlichen Änderungen in den Bereichen Arbeitslosenversicherung, Rentenversicherung, Krankenversicherung, Pflegeversicherung und Sozialhilfe (HLU) in den vergangenen Jahren*. Bremen: Arbeiterkammer und Angestelltenkammer.

Thabe, S. 1999. "Erste Erfahrungen aus dem Landesmodellprogramm in NRW." In *Der Ausgrenzung entgegenwirken—Überwindung sozialer Schwierigkeiten im brüchigen Netz sozialer Hilfen. Dokumentation der Bundestagung 1998 des Fachverbandes Evangelische Obdachlosenhilfe e.V.* Evangelische Obdachlosenhilfe e.V. Bielefeld: Verlag Soziale Hilfe.

Trabert, G. 1995. *Gesundheitssituation (Gesundheitszustand) und Gesundheitsverhalten von alleinstehenden, wohnungslsön Menschen im sozialen Kontext ihrer Lebenssituation*. Bielefeld, Germany: Verlag Soziale Hilfe.

————. 1999. "Soziale Dimension von Krankheit vernachlässigt." *Deutsches Ärzteblatt* 96, Heft 12: 756–60.

Treuberg, E. V. 1989. *Mythos Nichtsesshaftigkeit. Zur Geschichte des wissenschaftlichen, staatlichen und privatwohltätigen Umgangs mit einem diskriminierten Phänomen*. Bielefeld, Germany: Verlag Soziale Hilfe. This book presents an historical account of the "myth" of "persons with an unsettled way of life" and the ways in which homeless single men have been seen and handled as a group in the past.

Ulbrich, R. 1991. "Wohnungsmarktsituation in den westlichen Bundesländern." *Wohnungswirtschaft und Mietrecht*, Heft 5: 234–47.

————. 1992. "Verteilungswirkungen wohnungspolitischer Instrumente." In *Wohnungspolitik in sozialpolitischer Perspektive*, ed. F. Koch and C. Reis. Frankfurt am Main: Eigenverlag des Deutschen Vereins für öffentliche und private Fürsorge.

Weidenfeld, W., and W. Wessels, ed. 2000. *Europa von A bis Z. Taschenbuch zur europäischen Integration. Bundeszentrale für politische Bildung*. Bonn: Europa Union Verlag.

Wolf, J. 1998. *Das Recht des Lebens auf der Strasse: Ein Rechtsgutachten zur Privatisierung öffentlicher Flächen und zum Grundrechtsschutz wohnungsloser Menschen*. Dortmund, Germany: Institut für Landes und Stadtentwicklungsforschung des Landes Nordrhein-Westfalen.

NOTES

1. The latest statistical data available for the German housing stock are from 1993 and are based on a 1 percent random housing sample in all Germany by the federal statistical office. The ratio of owner occupation in West Germany is slightly higher (41.9 percent), but significantly lower in East Germany (26.1 percent). See Schewe 1995, 362.

2. A good example for the feasibility and the value of a national annual survey on homelessness is provided in Finland (see Kärkkäinen 1999).

3. The federal statistical office recommended not including persons in unacceptable

housing conditions in official statistics because there are no detailed and widely accepted criteria for defining unacceptable physical standard, overcrowding, rent burden, and so on.

4. This percentage relates to single homelessness. The German Coalition for the Homeless (Bundesarbeitsgemeinschaft Wohnungslosenhilfe) also provides an assessment of percentages of children (under 18) and male and female adults among all homeless people (except immigrants and *Aussiedler*). According to the latest assessment, 30 percent of the homeless are women, 39 percent are men, and 31 percent are children and young people under 18 (BAG 1999). There are some indicators that the percentage of single men is underestimated and that of children is overestimated by the coalition.

5. A recent survey shows that in about half of all municipal night shelters there are no separate bathrooms and showers for women, and separate shelters for homeless women are a rare exception (see Rosenke 1999). In 1997 only 15 advice centers for the homeless in Germany were focused on women.

6. There is ample evidence of a great number of women in situations of "hidden" homelessness. An objection of Fitzpatrick against the assumption that more women than men live in such situations (by temporary sharing with friends and relatives, etc.) also holds true for Germany: "I know of no research which compares hidden homelessness amongst men and women and therefore could substantiate the claim that men are *less* likely than women to seek a 'private' solution to their homelessness" (Fitzpatrick 1998, 208–9).

7. The shrinking of the social rented sector in Germany may have serious consequences for the risk of single mothers (and other homeless families) to become and stay homeless.

8. Percentages used for international comparisons are slightly lower because of differences in definition. The annual average quota of unemployment in Germany for 1997 was at 10.0 percent according to EUROSTAT.

9. It can also be seen as part of the German success story of housing that most of these repatriates have been integrated into permanent housing rather quickly. Nevertheless, about half or even more of all homeless persons in Germany in 1992 were repatriates in temporary accommodation.

10. For further details concerning migration and temporary accommodation for migrants in Germany, see Busch-Geertsema 1999a.

11. For an analysis of German housing policy in comparative perspective see Kleinman 1996.

12. Social housing in this respect has special importance for households with children. Some towns have managed to reduce family homelessness considerably by making contracts with providers of social housing.

13. As Kleinman rightly explains,

Social housing takes a very specific form in Germany. The term "social housing" therefore describes a method of *financing* housing together with a set of *regulations* and *responsibilities* about allocation of tenancies, rent levels and standards, rather than referring to a physically identifiable stock of dwellings. Flats which were at one time let as social housing can, once the subsidized loans with which they were built have been paid off, be let as non-social private rented housing. (Kleinman 1996, 91, emphasis in the original)

It has to be added that at this stage formerly rented social dwellings may also be converted into owner-occupied flats and sold.

14. However, temporary accommodation according to police laws is still predominant, as shown by the latest research findings from East Germany. In East Germany, this legal instrument was introduced at the time of German unification in 1990 (see Busch-Geertsema and Ruhstrat 1997b).

15. It is striking that the fraction of homeless persons who request furnished rooms is lower in more recent surveys than in previous ones. Although a direct comparison of findings is not possible because findings are related to different regions, it can be assumed that furnished rooms are less preferred because they have become a less frequent type of standard housing for the rest of the population as well. Shared dwellings, which are probably the most frequent type of supported housing for homeless persons, do not meet the housing requests of the majority of homeless persons either. In general, housing requests of homeless persons reveal a strong orientation toward social standards of normality.

16. However, families benefited much more from this trend than single homeless persons, so the ratio of single homeless persons to the total of homeless households increased from 44.4 percent on June 30, 1994, to 51.7 percent on June 30, 1998.

17. The National Coalition has continued its estimations from 1992 but assumed a further increase of homelessness in all Germany until 1996 (which might mean an overestimation of the total number) and acknowledged a slow decrease only for the time after 1996. For 1998, the National Coalition estimated a number of 690,000 homeless persons in all Germany (among them 150,000 repatriates). This is not a number estimated for a fixed date, but the total number of all persons affected by homelessness within one year (BAG 1999).

18. However, there is a frequent argument about the relevance of housing provision for the necessary support of homeless persons, and consequently on the responsibility of housing policy, municipal housing offices, and housing market for the problem of homelessness. By mentioning the fact that homeless persons are also afflicted by personal, social, and health problems—which is often true—it is attempted to narrow the range of responsibility for homeless persons to the sole responsibility of social policy and administration. A frequent argument is that these problems have priority and have to be coped with before a provision with standard housing will be possible, or that social policy is responsible to accommodate persons *unable to live in dwellings* outside the stock of standard housing at lower standards. The fact that social integration of one part of the homeless requires *more than just a dwelling*, however, does not diminish the importance of a normal, separate dwelling as a precondition for further integration. Despite continuous debates, this conclusion has been broadly acknowledged in recent years in Germany, although there are considerable deficits in its practical realization, which would mean direct promotion of provision of the homeless with standard housing, or provision of social support in dwellings.

19. A number of changes in the 1990s caused reduction of unemployment payments, restriction of increases in social assistance payments, the enforcement of social assistance recipients to work (and an automatic reduction of payments in case of refusal of job or training offers was introduced), and so on. For details see Steffen 2000.

20. Psychiatric diseases, on the other hand, may be exacerbated by a consequence of homelessness.

5

Homelessness in a Mediterranean Country: The Case of Greece

ARISTIDES SAPOUNAKIS

HOMELESSNESS IN THE GREEK CONTEXT

Homelessness in Greece has only recently been recognized as a social problem. The phenomenon of homeless people wandering around or sleeping in the streets in big cities is indeed fairly new. Until the beginning of the 1990s, the general public tended to believe that homelessness did not exist in Greece or at least that it was not a social problem with significant dimensions. Similar attitudes were even expressed by government officials responsible for social welfare. It is only very recently that homelessness has escalated as a result of, to a great extent, the influx of large numbers of immigrants mainly from Albania, the countries of Southeastern Europe, and the Middle East. The problem has, therefore, only recently been acknowledged and attracted attention and publicity; any attempts to address its present form and extent through service provision remain, as yet, insufficient and fragmentary.

Despite the lack of proper firsthand research on the issue, it must be acknowledged that evidence indicates that the homeless population in Greece is roughly 15,000 people. This figure does not include people with ownership problems in regard to their dwelling, those staying with another person or family while being capable of having a home of their own, Gypsies living in tents, and people in substandard housing conditions. The above figure also ignores the homeless economic refugees, who are estimated to be around 100,000 people, with similar housing conditions who are not officially considered as homeless. The number of the homeless population in Greece, as indeed in most European countries, varies and is very difficult to specify.

Despite this recent interest in the issue, no institute, nongovernmental organization, or public authority in Greece deals with homeless people as a special group. Although the Greek constitution states that the provision of accommodation to people who are homeless or housed in unsuitable conditions constitutes a special task for the state,[1] and a legal framework for the provision of social housing to people of low income exists, there is no statutory obligation of the local authorities or the central government to provide accommodation and support to any individuals or social groups defined as "vulnerable."

Greece has generally followed the pattern of other Southern European countries in that social welfare—housing being an important aspect of it—has tended to be primarily a responsibility of the family rather than the state. In other words, family solidarity has filled the gaps left by insufficient welfare provisions. It is therefore a widespread and acceptable feature of Greek society that accommodation problems are solved within families, and reliance on services is usually a last resort for those who lack family support.

As poverty and unemployment figures have risen, the housing conditions of sizable portions of the population have deteriorated. As far as rental accommodation is concerned, increased unemployment and a rise in rent prices make it increasingly difficult for many tenants to keep their homes or even find suitable, cheaper accommodation. The threat—or reality—of homelessness and substandard housing is becoming increasingly urgent.

Despite evidence of these trends in recent years, very little systematic research has taken place, and these changes are thus difficult to quantify. Collection of data by various services used by homeless people is fragmentary, and the data available do not lead to any conclusions regarding the extent and nature of the problem.

As noted above, the incidence of homelessness has tended to be attributed to illegal immigrants, the majority of whom live in substandard, overcrowded conditions. The dimensions of the illegal labor force in Greece, as well as its impact on Greek society, have not yet been properly addressed.[2] Still, Albanian and other economic refugees are not regarded as homeless, insofar as they have "put themselves into this situation" by leaving their own homes in order to seek better economic gains elsewhere. Moreover, foreign laborers are not generally economically excluded from the housing and rental market, but rather they themselves are often reluctant to spend the money they earn on rent so that at the end of the day they can save it and export it to their homeland—a custom that has often been implied in interviews. Nevertheless, their case needs to be mentioned as, in recent years, they have had a strong impact on the housing market, especially where low-cost rental accommodation is concerned, and because they tend to share the housing problems of the rest of the homeless population in Greece.

A last introductory note is due in relation to the recent history of access to housing for the poor in Greece in view of the country's rapid urbanization process during the second half of the twentieth century. In the absence of housing policies, this change has been indirectly supported by measures and policies aimed at the encouragement of private building activity by keeping construction costs low, inflating plot ratios in the cities, and allowing urban sprawl to expand (Economou 1987).

The housing needs of the labor force that converged on big urban centers during the 1950s and 1960s exerted heavy pressure on cheap suburban land. Agricultural estates on the periphery of Athens were cut into parcels and sold to newcomers who then constructed dwellings, often by using their own hands. The outdated legal framework of the early 1920s and state tolerance allowed landowners to achieve maximum exploitation by producing as many building plots as possible at the expense of open spaces, public amenities, and so on.

On the other hand, newcomers were never actually discouraged from building illegally since the houses they constructed not only escaped demolition but were readily connected to urban utility networks. The changing role of the state was put into effect during the late 1970s through laws 947/79, 1337/83, and recently 2508/97, which aim to organize urbanization and to ensure the quality of development. Although surely beneficial to urban development, these legal instruments have not as yet enabled the state to regulate the pressure on land, particularly as far as vacation housing is concerned. On the other hand, the main instrument to achieve housing access for the poor in the postwar period (i.e., through self-housing) has now become too difficult to practice.

THE ROLE OF THE FAMILY

In Greece, as indeed in the majority of Mediterranean countries, the role of the family in filling the gap of a poorly developed welfare state is crucial. With regard to housing, a stable system of family solidarity has developed over time, which aids family members in need. The recipients of such help—often available to extended as well as immediate family—are, naturally, the ones in greatest need: newly wedded couples and elderly, lonely, or disabled relatives. Phenomena that are related to the malfunctioning of the family—for example, domestic violence and out-of-wedlock births—have only very recently become apparent or at least reported; normally such behavior would be kept within the family.

The most common form of housing provision is the "dowry," that is, the allowance granted to nearly every married couple by the bride's family, which often amounts to the provision of a house or flat. Even though the dowry was abolished in the legal sense during the early 1980s, it remains a strong element of the Greek tradition, and most Greek families provide a house or flat to a newly married couple whenever financially possible.

Cohabitation of parents and adult children, as well as among other family members, is also very common in Greek families. It is partly directed by financial necessity as few young people are able to afford independent housing. To some extent, however, it is also due to the fact that the extended, and not the nuclear, family is still the most dominant form of family organization in Greek society. In most Greek families, adult children would not be expected to leave the family home before marriage, and elderly relatives would normally come to live with the younger generation, especially after the death of one spouse.

Close family bonds are also manifest in the support available to family members facing insecurity of tenure. Support often takes the form of help with rental payments for young couples seeking housing—usually offered by the bride's family in cases when provision of a flat or house is not possible—or assistance to other members of the extended family. In recent years, as houses are becoming smaller in size and family bonds are gradually slackening, cohabitation is often being replaced by financial assistance to those family members in need.

On the whole, family solidarity has always played a crucial role in the prevention of homelessness within Greek society, especially for young people. As statutory supportive mechanisms for housing access remain poorly developed, there is evidence that family contributions to housing costs for young adults exceeds, by far, any action by the state (Maloutas 1990).

HOUSING POLICY AND HOMELESSNESS IN GREECE

The Right to Proper Housing

The Greek constitution allows for social housing, yet this remains theoretical as it does not correspond to concrete policies relating to housing, especially for the poor. The right to social housing falls into the broad category of non-directly enforceable social rights which were introduced into the Greek legal order through the constitution of 1975. Similar provisions are found in the constitutions of other Mediterranean countries as, for example, in Portugal.

A combined interpretation of two specific provisions in the Greek constitution (paragraphs 3 and 4 in article 21) leads to the conclusion that the protection of low-income groups forms a main objective of public action regarding housing. According to paragraphs 3 and 4, "The State will care for the health of citizens and will adopt special measures for the protection of young people, elderly, handicapped as well as for the relief of the needy"; and "For those without any or with insufficient accommodation, housing is subject to specific statutory measures." These provisions correspond to the primary legal basis for public housing policies in Greece, but their vague nature has yet to be further specified through programs and measures (Amitsis 1994).

Social Housing Provision in Greece

Despite the existence of a fairly well-established legal framework, the actual provision of social housing by the state in Greece has remained modest. The most active body in this field is the Workers' Housing Association (OEK). The responsibility of the OEK is to provide owner-occupied permanent accommodation to its beneficiaries, that is workers and other employees with a more or less consistent working record. Its construction programs of ready-made dwellings are distributed via a lottery system. OEK beneficiaries may enjoy the privilege either of acquiring a house through this system or of being offered a subsidized housing loan in order to buy, refurbish, or construct the house they wish, provided they are first-time buyers. A recently introduced rent subsidy scheme constitutes an important measure against insecurity of tenure for nearly a tenth of OEK beneficiaries (20,000 out of 200,000) who are eligible for it. Despite its limitations, the OEK offers an important service to its beneficiaries, who are usually low-income employees with a more or less consistent working record. It is not, however, in any way connected to services for homeless people and is not, in effect, concerned with the poorest section of the population. It is also important to note that there is no rental sector of public housing in Greece.

The second body responsible for the provision of social housing in Greece is the Welfare Section of the Ministry of Health and Welfare. Like the issue of housing itself, the ministry's contribution is multifaceted. The first two categories of housing provision address, on the one hand, the needs of refugees from Asia Minor during the early 1920s through the 1930s and, on the other hand, housing assistance to Greece's disaster-stricken populations who have lost their homes as a result of droughts, earthquakes, fires, or other disasters, the incidence of which has taken alarming dimensions in the recent past. The third and most important activity of the Ministry of Health and Welfare concerns housing provision for the poor. This is based on law 775/64, which addresses the housing needs of low-income classes through a housing policy called Popular Housing. The ministry's housing policy concerns the housing needs of the homeless population as well as of people living in inadequate conditions because of economic reasons.

Households who qualify for support are those who are homeless or who live below the threshold of poverty, and are permanent Greek citizens, who reside in the regional department in which new dwellings are going to be constructed. Ready-made apartments are given, actually sold, to tenants at cost prices; repayment is due in 40 biannual payments. The beneficiaries of these programs are selected on the basis of social and economic criteria such as the household's low income, its housing condition, the amount of people it comprises, and so on. If the number of beneficiaries exceeds the amount of new houses, a lottery system similar to the one followed by the OEK is organized, the difference being that the procedure is repeated for three-member households (aiming at two-roomed flats), four-member households (aiming at three-roomed flats), and so on.

Policies include the provision of ready-made dwellings, via modest, small-scale programs for urban areas as well as the provision of sites for new settlements in rural areas. Until 1986 the ministry offered subsidized loans for the construction of houses. Funds to support housing programs come almost exclusively from the state, and, for this reason, after a long period of inactivity between 1985 and 1993, construction of new dwellings has only recently resumed.

On the whole, it must be noted that social housing provision in Greece, although important for many people in need, is not in any way linked to emergency or transitory housing services for homeless people. Clearly, the criteria for eligibility for social housing have not been updated to take into account more recent features of homelessness such as its link with unemployment. As a result, social housing provision in Greece excludes young people who are particularly affected by unemployment as well as other groups of homeless people who may be in desperate need but do not meet the criteria for becoming beneficiaries of welfare organizations. One may note, however, the recent rise of public awareness of specific target groups like street children. The impact on government policy of this particular concern led to the establishment of a hostel for street children in the capital.

Housing Loans

Although the construction industry has been beneficial to the country's economy, the housing loan system in Greece has always tended to remain underdeveloped as a result of the banks' credit policies; access to housing has been primarily achieved through people's own savings. Thus credit institutions have not generally affected the manner in which the broader public has satisfied its housing needs; only a small percentage of people have used their services to obtain a house. On the other hand, another rather small percentage of beneficiaries enjoyed the privileges of subsidized loans either through the OEK, or through the housing programs of the Ministry of Health and Welfare. Yet, both bodies were indeed at first more interested in providing ready-made dwellings rather than lending money to their beneficiaries.

Housing loans in Greece may be separated into four categories according to the manner in which the loan is concluded and the degree of insecurity of tenure involved. The first category of housing loans relates to unsubsidized loans granted by banks of the public or private sector in the open loan market. Although unfavorable in terms of interest, these loans are usually repaid without problems as the banks always check the beneficiaries' repaying capacity beforehand through their IRS declaration. The second category of housing loans concerns the uncommon yet favorable loans granted by banks to their employees or to civil servants. Repayments are usually subtracted from the beneficiaries' monthly salaries thus protecting against repayment default unless the recipients suffer job loss.

The third category of housing loans, the majority of which are granted by the National Bank of Greece (which has in 1998 become a conglomerate with the National Mortgage Bank and the National Housing Bank, two public institutions specializing in housing loans), constitutes those in which the beneficiaries are selected according to their household condition and income.

The main difference between these loans and those of the first category is that they are characterized by a socially minded approach which is rather atypical of private credit institutions. This important divergence in tendency is reflected both in the selection of beneficiaries and the way in which creditors pursue repayment of defaulted loans.

The fourth category of housing loans relates directly to the social housing programs of the two main housing institutions: the OEK and the Popular Housing program of the Ministry of Health and Welfare. Such loans are only technically implemented by the National Mortgage Bank of Greece, now the National Bank of Greece, which does not interfere with their repayment.

It is remarkable to note that OEK beneficiaries do not generally pay back the loans they receive, even though these loans are the most favorable in the subsidized market. A similar practice is observed when beneficiaries are asked to contribute the small share demanded from them by the OEK when they receive a ready-made dwelling after a lottery procedure. Apparently, these loans do not generally lead to repossession or auction, although this is a practice that is under serious consideration by the OEK.

To sum up, although not very extensive, the existing system of housing loans includes specific instruments that aim at promoting access to housing for the poor. These loans are directly or indirectly linked to social housing policies, insofar as they aim to address the housing needs primarily of working people with low income. Housing loans, however, are not directed toward people who do not have a regular job and income, and who are not, therefore, capable of repaying them. In this sense, it may be argued that their contribution to the prevention of homelessness tends to remain minimal.

The Rental Market

In order to attain an accurate picture of the pattern of owner-occupied housing in Greece, one should note the fragmentation in land ownership, a pattern that exists both in rural and urban property. Although many people do make money exclusively from renting their property,[3] the market is characterized by an abundance of middle- and often low-income owners who rent their apartments. This explains the rate of house ownership in Greece, which is among the highest in the European Union. Eighty percent of Greek families own at least one dwelling, and 70 percent stay in their own house. Economic insecurity has inclined Greeks to invest their capital in housing rather than in the stock market or other forms of industry.

With reference to evictions, 13 percent of all households surveyed were asked to vacate their lodgings. In analyzing this indicator, one notices that the threat of eviction has been exerted on 21.7 percent of the unskilled workers, 17.91 percent of the unemployed, and 15.66 percent of the pensioners of lower categories—all of these groups showed percentages slightly higher than the average. Discrepancies are more evident in Athens where 15 percent of all households faced the threat of eviction, but only 9.59 percent of self-employed professionals, compared to 17 percent of pensioners and 19 percent of the unemployed, faced such threats. It should again be noted that families with many members are more prone to eviction; 19 percent of couples with more than three children were asked to leave their houses (DEPOS 1990). In the absence of relevant statutory supportive mechanisms, evicted families will normally seek refuge within the extended family or through various forms of transitional or marginal accommodation.

Rents in Greece are quite expensive; the average amount paid is as high as 12 percent of the total average household expenditure. As shown by recent data on household expenditure in Greece, provided by the National Statistical Service (ESYE 1991), the average amount of money spent on housing rose from 10.21 percent of the average total household expenditure in 1987–1988 to 11.86 percent in 1993–1994. Comparing the two budgets and the differential distribution of costs, it is interesting to note that household expenses like housing, transportation, and education rose at the same time as expenditures for consumer goods like clothing and household appliances fell (Department of Housing and Public Works 1996).

Emergency Accommodation Services

Five statutory hostels provide emergency accommodation in Greece, all of them in Athens, with a total capacity of 360 beds. Three of them are organized by the Ministry of Health and Welfare and two by the Municipality of Athens. Apart from these, two small hostels (capacity of 15) provide for the urgent accommodation needs of battered women and HIV patients (Sapounakis 1998). Earlier this year, a new hostel provided shelter and care for street children in need.

The target group for statutory hostel beds is single homeless people from the streets, as well as people facing a range of personal and social problems that result in temporary or long-term homelessness, for example, young people (over 18) leaving care institutions, ex-prisoners, people who became homeless through a family crisis or breakup, and elderly people with no family support who need a place to stay until they can make a longer term arrangement. Shelter referrals are made by various welfare institutions, the church, children's homes, community organizations, and hospitals. They also accept self-referrals by homeless people. With regard to the criteria for admission, prospective residents have to be Greek nationals and must not suffer from any infectious disease or have any psychiatric problems or problems related to alcoholism or drug addiction. In the absence of a well-developed voluntary sector, excluded groups, such as illegal immigrants and substance abusers, are thus forced to make the best of the private rental housing market.

Inasmuch as services for specific target groups are concerned, there are many guest houses all over the country which provide shelter for elderly people in need. Some of these shelters are organized by the Greek Orthodox Church as well as the Roman Catholic Caritas. Other service providers belong entirely to the voluntary sector and rely on their own funding sources. Such institutions are either based on the origin of the users or are organized by public-minded people.

Housing Provision for Specific Target Groups

The most important housing provision policy relates to the accommodation of repatriates from Pontos,[4] whose number has escalated to over 100,000 during the last few decades, following the collapse of the socialist regime in the former Soviet Union. In 1990 a special body called EIYAAPOE was set up by the Ministry of the Exterior to support their integration into Greek society. In particular, EIYAAPOE provides emergency assistance to the repatriates upon their arrival to secure housing in the future and to promote their social integration, particularly their integration into the labor market, through the provision of training or retraining, education, and Greek-language lessons.

The three-phase program of EIYAAPOE includes the provision of accommodation as well as other forms of support (practical assistance, psychological support, training, and so on). In the first phase, repatriates are offered accommodation in specially designated shelters for up to a month, upon arrival, as well as specialized advice and support in relation to issues of immediate concern. At the end of this period, the repatriates are moved to specially organized "admission camps." These camps provide a number of services aimed at preparing repatriates for living in Greece and achieving social integration, and they may accommodate up to 1,000 people for a period of up to 6 months.

The final phase of the EIYAAPOE program concerns the housing resettlement of the repatriate population. Two types of housing support are offered to that effect: the first is a rent subsidy scheme. The percentage of the rent paid by EYIAAPOE decreases gradually until the family can manage to meet the costs of living independently. The second form of housing support concerns the construction of dwellings, by EYIAAPOE in cooperation with special construction companies, which are offered to repatriate families on very favorable terms. In addition to the above, a number of benefits have been introduced by various government departments to address the urgent financial needs of the repatriate population.

Apart from the accommodation of repatriates, the central government has been seriously involved in promoting the social integration of the Romani population in Greece.[5] Gypsies already enjoy full citizenship rights although it may be argued that, on many occasions, racism and prejudice against them may lead to their exclusion from the labor or the housing market.

The need to ameliorate their living conditions and the pressure they exerted on central and local authorities have led to the establishment of the Framework of Policy for the Social Integration of the Gypsies for the time period 1996–1999. The Greek government has already started to implement some measures toward improving the living conditions of the Romani population in Greece.

These measures include the establishment of temporary accommodation areas in regions considered to be "passages," which will include such amenities as a water supply, a sewage system, cooking utilities, electricity, and a system of refuse collection; the promotion of improvement works along with welfare works of Gypsy encampments; the establishment of organized Gypsy accommodation areas in Attica, around Athens; and the preparation of a National Master Plan that will deal with the issue of housing for this particular target group.

Other homelessness prevention policies will target people who are in the process of leaving institutions like mental hospitals and other kinds of asylums, including prisons. Evidence indicates that these policies are very important because they address target groups that are particularly vulnerable in terms of their ability to achieve access to proper housing and resettlement. Since the mid-1980s, a number of rehabilitation and community mental health services have been established. The programs generally combine housing rehabilitation with certain forms of vocational training. The housing provided is either in short-stay guest houses or in long-stay residential care hostels, with a longer term view of moving patients on to private rented, supported flats. Long-term housing resettlement, at least in theory, amounts to the former patient being able to live—either alone or with others—in private rented accommodation. It is important to note that the projects are currently at risk because European Union funding ran out in 1999, and no official commitment has been made by the Ministry of Health and Welfare concerning their future. In view of this, ex-patients may face the possibility of being forced to return to an asylum.

Deinstitutionalization difficulties are also faced by young people leaving care homes, ex-offenders coming out of prison, and people completing programs in drug rehabilitation centers. Evidence shows that for such people homelessness is often an unsurpassable obstacle toward social integration (Madianos 1994). Many of them lack family support and have particular difficulties in getting work which would allow them to pay for rented accommodation. Some people may find temporary accommodation in emergency shelters, yet there exists very little provision of long-term housing. The only service providers currently addressing this target group, especially young ex-offenders, are Arsis (Neon Hora 1996) and, to an extent, Onissimos. Lack of funding, however, an issue pertinent to nongovernmental organizations of the voluntary sector, has kept the output of these bodies minimal despite rising needs.

The last policy concerning supported accommodation relates to the settlement of the nearly 8,000 officially recognized refugees in Greece, who have come mainly from Turkey and the Near East. The policy is addressed to only a small portion of the illegal immigrants who have applied and are finally granted asylum. Indeed, asylum is granted only to people who qualify under article 14 of the Universal Treaty of Human Rights of 1948. The Greek government provides transitory accommodation as well as education and health care to up to 350 refugees in a specially designated refugee camp in Lavrion. The length of their stay varies, and it is estimated that approximately 75 percent of the refugees stay in Greece after leaving the camp. They are normally expected to get a job and move into rented accommodation, as there is no longer-term housing provision for them after they leave the camp.

Finally, there is no provision for the accommodation needs of illegal immigrants in Greece, that is for those who do not qualify as political refugees. Indeed, the phenomenon of the massive inflow of immigrants seeking employment has not generally triggered a response from the Greek government, apart from the continual deportation of economic refugees back to Albania since 1994 and the recent implementation of the green card system. Still, housing provision is definitely excluded from the government's policies.

EVALUATION OF POLICIES AND SERVICES

The measures and policies adopted by central and local government to enable access to housing for the poor vary greatly depending on the body responsible and the target group they address. Inasmuch as the housing program of the Workers' Housing Organization (OEK) is concerned, the delivery of ready-made apartments to its beneficiaries is far from satisfactory, as the construction program is too slow to cover the housing needs of all beneficiaries. Long waiting lists make this quite apparent. Budgetary restrictions obviously play a significant role in this situation. It has been reported that all available funds for this year have been consumed. On the other hand, there is a considerable delay from the Ministry of Finance, the central government institution responsible for supporting OEK's housing policies, in repaying the money spent by the collaborating National Mortgage Bank for housing loans organized by the OEK. In September 1998, the funds due for repayment were almost 10 billion drachmas and had been delayed for several months.

On the other hand, the housing program of the Ministry of Health and Welfare for people at risk of homelessness combines all the drawbacks of the OEK's programs, the most significant one being its modest output, which has confined its application to a fraction of the households in need. Indeed, this program is supposed to have a much wider appeal to the public than OEK's contribution, since it is meant to provide for the housing needs of all households in difficulty rather than just those with a consistent working record. A sound survey of poverty and housing needs in Greece would indicate the national dimensions of the problem and would specify the priorities required.

At the same time, the program of EIYAAPOE, which addresses the social integration of repatriates from Pontos, has had a very modest output; only one-tenth of the target group has finally benefited from it. Thus the vast majority of potential users has not managed to benefit from EIYAAPOE's integration program. Several times repatriates from Pontos have marched to the Ministry of the Exterior, the body responsible for EIYAAPOE, and demanded their rights to housing, education, employment, and social integration. Thus, even the one-tenth of the target group who do take part in the program are often disenchanted because of the delay involved in its implementation and the low-standard housing conditions in the intermediate stages. Additional dissatisfaction arises from the incapacity of the program's organizers to provide suitable employment for its users, as in many cases their training and employment have been in fields that may not easily be found in their new place of residence.

The repatriate community's disenchantment with Greek programs purporting to foster their integration into Greek society is also manifested in cases where the government has taken measures against those who do not participate in EIYAAPOE's program, who are trying hard, instead, to achieve access to housing by their own means. Since EIYAAPOE's programs, although quite ambitious, have only been able to cover the housing needs of a small percentage of the repatriate population, the majority are forced to seek assistance from friends and relatives or to cope on their own. Thus, apart from approximately 15,000 people who have participated in the housing program, as many as 20,000 Greek repatriates live with friends and relatives in the greater Athens area, about 10,000 live in caravans in deprived areas in the periphery of Athens, and, finally, another 20,000 to 30,000 are scattered all over the country, some of them having managed to find proper accommodation while others are still living in substandard conditions.

Deinstitutionalization programs, on the other hand, are too new to allow specific conclusions about the users' point of view. As far as reintegration after leaving a prison is concerned, the only service providers found in the country belong entirely to the voluntary sector; their contributions are basically funded by donations.

On the other hand, there has been an increased activity concerning the opening of mental institutions by placing the emphasis on resettlement policies. Since the early 1990s, the Ministry of Health has started to build up mechanisms to allow patients of the Leros Mental Hospital to become reintegrated in society by providing the means for independent living and a smooth insertion to the labor market. After the success of what is called "the Leros experiment," similar policies were adopted by other mental institutions in Greece as, for example, the hospitals in Chania, Crete, and Dafni near Athens.

The overall impression is that users are quite satisfied with the novel approach to reintegration they offer and are quite keen to take part in vocational training programs and the variety of available activities. The most important issue, which requires immediate attention on behalf of the Ministry of Health and Welfare, relates to funding difficulties faced by these programs, as most initially relied on European Union funding. In many cases, psychiatrists and other professionals were unpaid for several months and eventually left the deinstitutionalization programs.

Different attitudes are held by the country's Romani population, who are used to dwelling in substandard conditions and who do not expect much from the state. The integration program for Gypsies has only very recently been put into effect, and people are quite apprehensive about it as they feel that it may again consist of measures promised, but not implemented, for purely political reasons.

Incidents have already occurred which illustrate that the Greek society is not particularly prepared to accept the new approach toward the improvement of the Romani population in the country. Even though there is evidence to suggest that a significant percentage of the Romani population is prepared to undergo changes in customs and behavior in order to become socially integrated (Sapounakis 1993), it appears that discrimination against Gypsies in Greece is latent or sometimes overtly expressed, on both local and political levels.

In relation to emergency accommodation, statutory shelters for the provision of urgent accommodation and other services to homeless people in general are welcomed by people in need. Services for the elderly and services for other homeless people are considered adequate in quality but not in quantity. For this reason, the Ministry of Health and Welfare is planning to extend its program of provision of emergency accommodation through the establishment of additional shelters which will provide for the diversified needs of the homeless population. Since the overview of existing services has shown that there is a need for emergency services for specific groups of people, the program includes shelters for women, either experiencing domestic violence or with dependant members; shelters for the young, especially for those who are between 16 and 18 years old; and shelters in Thessaloniki, a city that appears to have as many as a hundred rough sleepers.

Guest houses for the elderly may have good to average living standards, but they are surely insufficient to meet the rising demands. It is estimated that private and public shelters and clinics for the elderly in Greece represent 0.8 percent of the population as compared to from 8 to 11 percent in Western Europe. This divergence has traditionally been an outcome of the role of the extended family in Greece. According to an EOP (Ethnikos Organismos Pronias) survey, 93.4 percent of the younger generation still feel obliged to keep the older members of the family in their own homes, but their limited income does not often allow them to do so (EOP 1992). Thus the need for additional shelters for the elderly is gradually becoming more pressing.

Finally, a new encampment is planned for political refugees because the existing one in Lavrion is inadequate to meet the temporary accommodation needs of people qualifying for asylum in Greece. In addition to this, new measures are about to be taken concerning the integration of people who choose to stay and work in Greece. These measures, currently aimed at providing full rights of medical care, should be extended to cover all aspects of integration.

RECOMMENDATIONS

Inasmuch as support for housing and the provision of social housing in general is concerned, state intervention has tended to remain too modest compared to the level of need. Housing loans on favorable terms and various welfare benefits are available only to social groups that meet specific criteria relating to status and employment record and who are not necessarily the most needy.

As housing integration is an important component if not a prerequisite for wider social integration, a growing portion of the population tends to become socially excluded. In most cases, homelessness is paired with an inability to work as a result of individual circumstances or high unemployment affecting certain groups, for example, young people, single mothers with dependent members, people aged 55 to 65, those suffering from chronic diseases, and people who have just come out of an institution such as a prison, reform school, or mental hospital. Such vulnerable social groups find it particularly difficult to cross the bridge toward integration and are forced into poverty and social exclusion as a result.

It has become apparent that the number of people facing housing problems is growing. Indeed the situation appears more serious than ever as more and more population groups find it difficult to attain proper housing and may be considered vulnerable. In view of this, a number of measures and policies need to be taken at both central and local government levels.

There is no state, nongovernmental organization, or any other body that deals with the homeless as such. This absence is evident both at the level of survey and analysis of the issue and at the level of policy making. Homelessness in Greece has already increased sufficiently to convince governmental officials to develop more positive measures to cope with it. The establishment of an organization, which may not necessarily belong to the public sector but must surely have the state's broader support, appears to be absolutely essential toward this end.

The emerging trend of the weakening of extended family bonds, which has become apparent in the country, and the need for the development of welfare state mechanisms must clearly be taken into consideration by statutory officials. A number of policies aimed at preventing homelessness must then be prepared and implemented. The contribution of research on the issue is clearly significant to this end.

Furthermore, the experience of social shelters shows that there is a gap between urgent accommodation and proper housing. People turn to social shelters for a short period of time, usually in the middle of a personal crisis. Housing programs usually aim at those with a more or less consistent working record, and banks would lend no money unless ensured they will get it back. There appears a need for the provision of permanent accommodation with minimum costs, which will be used by people with little money to spend and by those not always ready to cooperate. The development of mechanisms of supported accommodation in Greece that will act as a stepping stone between emergency and proper accommodation will definitely contribute to this direction. The organizational problems involved need an altogether different approach from central and local government in order to be dealt with effectively. This approach must rest on the understanding of the role that nongovernmental organizations in Greece may play and their potential in contributing to the implementation of both action and prevention policies.

REFERENCES

Amitsis, G. 1994. "Minimum Income Policy and Housing Law." Unpublished paper for the European Observatory on Minimum Income Policy, Athens, 1994.

Department of Housing and Public Works. 1996. *National Report for Greece*. Document prepared for the Habitat II Conference in Istanbul, June 1996.

DEPOS. 1990. *Condition and Trends in the Housing Market in Large Urban Areas in Greece*, vol. 2; *Discrepancies According to Social Categories and Groups of Households*. Athens: Public Corporation for Housing and Urban Development (DEPOS). In Greek.

Economou, D. 1987. "Housing Policy During the Post-war Period in Greece." *Social Research Review* 64. National Centre of Social Research (EKKE), Athens. In Greek.

EOP. 1992. Unpublished extracts of the survey on social and economic parameters conducted in 1991 in Greece by the National Technical University of Athens (EMP) for the National Organisation of Welfare (EOP). Athens: EOP.

ESYE, National Statistical Agency. 1991. Unpublished results of the 1991 population and housing survey, Athens. In Greek.

Madianos, M. 1994. *Psycho-social Rehabilitation—From the Asylum to the Community*. Athens: Greek Letters. In Greek.

Maloutas, T. 1990. *Athens, Housing, Family: Analysis of the Post-war Housing Practice*. Athens: Exantas. In Greek.

Ministry of Housing, Environment and Public Works. 1995. *National Report for Greece*. Document prepared by DEPOS in view of the Habitat II Conference held in Istanbul in June 1996.

"Neon Hora"—Annual Report 1995. 1996. Athens: Arsis. In Greek.

Sapounakis, A. 1993. "Housing Condition of New Settlers: The Case of the Gypsy Settlement of Aliveri in Volos, Greece." Paper presented at the conference organized by the Poverty 3 Programme in Perama. Athens, April. In Greek.

———. 1998. "National Report on Homelessness in Greece." Report prepared for the European Observatory on Homelessness, organized for the European Commission DGV by Feantsa, Athens.

NOTES

1. Greek Constitution 1975, article 21.

2. It is estimated that nearly 800,000 economic refugees are currently in Greece and only half of them have applied and received the "green card" that grants them legal status inasmuch as employment in Greece is concerned.

3. This generally applies to people who received ready-made apartments after having their plot developed by usually small-scale developers, a widely followed practice during and after the 1960s–1970s private housing boom.

4. Pontos is a vaguely defined region that covers the area surrounding the northeastern coast of the Black Sea. It is now part of the Republics of Georgia, Ukraine, and Armenia.

5. A significant portion of the nearly 350,000 members of the Romani population (Gypsies) of Greece are expected to be willing to become socially integrated.

6

Housing and Homelessness in England

KATHERINE DUFFY

INTRODUCTION

In earlier years, homelessness was thought to be a question largely of housing shortage; however, recently there has been a trend toward the view that homelessness is not a housing problem, and that the personal characteristics of the homeless are key to understanding homelessness (Randall and Brown 1999, 4). Using the concept of the three dimensions of the "welfare triangle"—state, market, and civil society (Duffy 1998b)—this chapter suggests that the housing environment has become more risky for vulnerable people and households. Pressures on family and personal networks, increased income inequality, reductions in the supply of social housing and tightened eligibility criteria for entry to it have all increased the risks of housing exclusion. Decentralization of some housing policy implementation to local communities may increase the difficulties experienced by the most vulnerable in securing permanent housing. Without a significant change in government economic and welfare policies, vulnerability and housing insecurity are likely to be increasingly evident in England.

A THEORY OF SOCIAL EXCLUSION APPLIED TO HOUSING

To understand homelessness, one must address the causes and triggers of homelessness, for both the insecurely housed and the street homeless. Using the concept of social exclusion is a fruitful way to analyze the relationship between housing and homelessness. The model of a "welfare triangle" (Duffy 1998b) illustrates how individuals experience social integration and exclusion. Social exclusion is not a condition, but a dynamic process; it is exclusion from a place where you stood before (Xiberras 1993). It is a consequence of the interactions between changes in the three dimensions of the welfare triangle: civil society (families and personal networks), the state (governments), and the capitalist markets (including the labor and housing markets). Social exclusion is about risk and the increases in exposure to social risk that are occurring in many societies which have embraced a more neoliberal model of social organization. There is a risk of social exclusion for those who have weak links to one of these dimensions of welfare. People at risk include those with weak attachment to the labor market (for example, the unemployed and the low skilled), or those stigmatized or excluded from state social protection (for example, asylum seekers). However, as for poverty, one can distinguish relative from absolute exclusion. Most people are not permanently poor (Spicker 1998, 14–15); neither are they likely to be permanently excluded. The risks of entry to and exit from some situations, for example teen unemployment, may be quite high. Those with weak links to all three elements of the welfare triangle are likely to be at serious risk of long-term social exclusion; their social disqualification (Paugam 1993) ossifies into a new excluded place, and there is no route back (Pieretti 1994). Applied to housing, those with weak relationships to one dimension may be vulnerable on the housing market, but street homelessness is likely to arise from weak relationships in all three dimensions. For the street homeless, both entry and exit risks to their situation may be low. Low exit opportunities imply that preventative policies are most effective in combating street homelessness.

There is considerable dispute about the causes of homelessness, and about which factors are contingent and which are underlying causes. By using evidence from six cities in four Northern European countries during the 1970s to the 1990s, B. O'Flaherty has argued that increasing homelessness is due to changes in the housing market linked to increasing income inequality. He rejected a number of factors commonly put forward as causes of homelessness, including the decline in public house building because it is not targeted at the poorest, and changes in income maintenance programs, because of U.S. evidence that there are very different rates of homelessness in different states.[1] He also rejects deinstitutionalization because it occurred before homelessness rose significantly (O'Flaherty 1996, cites in Carter 1998, 276).

Although the importance of income inequality in exacerbating the conditions that result in homelessness cannot be ignored, it is important to look beyond the economic factors for a full understanding of the causes of increasing homelessness.

First, the decline in public house building has had the effect of further "balkanizing" the housing market, and supply shortages have led to tighter eligibility criteria which have contributed in two dimensions to increasing the risks of homelessness. Government recognition that communities have become "unbalanced" has led them to an increased focus on area-based policies. In devolving some powers to communities and providing social landlords with new powers to manage their housing stock for its asset value, they have increased the risks of exclusion from permanent housing for some categories of the insecurely housed and homeless.

Second, broad measures of changes in income maintenance may not be effective tools in understanding changes in homelessness; it may be necessary to examine a variety of specific welfare policy changes. In addition, the reliability of the homelessness statistics and the variation in other factors may disguise the impact of welfare policy. Certainly, for England,

researchers generally agree that a number of changes in social security policy (e.g. the abolition of grants for rent deposits and furniture, and of board and lodging payments) in the late 1980s were closely associated with a squeeze on the ability of single people on low incomes to gain access to suitable housing. . . . [While] one of the common aims of these policies has been to discourage young people from leaving home to set up on their own . . . these changes and the single room rent restrictions are widely thought to have increased the number of rough sleepers. (Social Exclusion Unit 1998a, 6)

Furthermore, while O'Flaherty considers and rejects deinstitutionalization as a source of homelessness, he does not consider the potential impact for the mentally ill and newly vulnerable, of their failure to access the sanctuary of institutions. This may exacerbate their illness and increase the risk of homelessness for those without community support.

Third, it's important to consider the personal characteristics of the insecurely housed and the street homeless. Those living in insecure housing, especially the street homeless, suffer from social isolation and weak family and personal networks. A. Marsh and D. Mullins have drawn attention to the risks of social exclusion inherent in the breakup of nets of social relations (1998, 752). P. Somerville has argued that an "improved understanding of the dynamics of the domestic economy is essential for explaining key housing processes such as leaving home, becoming homeless and returning home" (Somerville 1998, 778). Furthermore, "social exclusion in a housing context is likely to arise where . . . the system of domestic exploitation has broken down" (1998, 776).

Homelessness is triggered by the breakdown of habitual sources of domestic care, such as parenting and other family relationships. Somerville's discussion of domestic life is couched in terms of the labor process (1998, 71). Though it is beyond the scope of this chapter to discuss the nature of patriarchal relations, the evidence of this chapter suggests that it would be fruitful for other authors to analyze the shift in social housing policy to the concept of "priority need" within this framework. The policy both excludes from access to social housing those outside patriarchal notions of dependency, and inhibits the reconstitution of nuclear families from "split" elements.

ADEQUACY AND AFFORDABILITY: HOUSING PROVISION AND HOUSING NEED

The adequacy, affordability, and accessibility of social provision (the "Triple A" model in Duffy 1998b, 139–42) are the three criteria that can be used to assess the relationship between housing and homelessness. Changes in adequacy and affordability have increased housing insecurity for some groups vulnerable on the housing market. These include increasing income inequality arising from the markets, and government policies that have changed the responsibilities owed by the state to various groups vulnerable on the housing market.

Market Housing and Housing Need

In Shelter's *National Enquiry into Housing Need* (1998a), market housing is defined as all forms of housing available on the private market for rent or purchase. Affordable housing is socially rented housing provided by local authorities (municipalities), housing associations (not-for-profit housing providers), and subsidized home-ownership initiatives. It has been argued that social housing is "decommodified" housing and so is potentially less exclusionary on income grounds; access is on the basis of need (Somerville 1998, 772–73). The Shelter enquiry defines need in terms of those people who cannot access the market. In a society in which, increasingly, "pound notes are votes," exclusion from the market may result in citizen exclusion.

The Decline in the Supply of Social Housing

During the first two terms of the Thatcher government, 1 million council properties (i.e., social housing) were sold. Dwelling completion fell from 85,049 in 1979 to 528 in 1994 (Robinson 1998, 25). There were large changes in tenure during the 1980s, with little further change in the 1990s (Department of the Environment 1996d). In 1979, 32 percent (6.7 million) of all dwellings in Britain were local authority tenancies. By 1988, this had dropped to 23 percent (5.4 million) (Robinson 1998, 25). Between 1981 and 1994, the numbers of owner-occupiers increased from 9.1 million to 13.4 million (68 percent of all households). The number of council tenants fell from 5.1 million to 3.7 million, and private renters fell from 1.9 million to 1.6 million in 1989, before rising to 1.9 million (Department of the Environment 1996d, 1).

Research for the Department of the Environment, Transport and the Regions (DETR)[2] concluded that the most important determinants of regional house prices are income, interest rates, size of the housing stock, and demographic change (DETR 1998d). During the 1980s, Britain became wealthier, but income inequality rose and became one of the highest in any developed industrial country (Hills 1998). Increasing income inequality has created greater problems of access to market housing for low-paid, insecure workers and the unemployed.

A strategy of widening share ownership through encouragement to buy shares in privatized utilities became the basis of the "property-owning democracy." As incomes rose, housing became ever more an asset as well as a home. Those who could do so bought into a rising housing market in which inflation eroded the value of their debt. More households had the possibilities of acquiring a wealth stake in society, and wealth ownership was further distributed down the income scales through the Conservative government's "right to buy" policy (the right of tenants to buy their local authority-rented homes at very significant discounts). However, the policy reduced the stock of local authority housing (Shelter 1998a, para. 17). For example, the borough of Cheltenham in southern England lost 35 percent of its stock (Shelter 1998b, 14). For fifteen years, little social housing was built (Shelter 1998b, 9). Financial restrictions have meant that local authorities may take years to piece together bits of funding and small parcels of land or to extract some social housing units as "planning gain" from private developers, but only as one of a number of options from a limited pot (Shelter 1998b, 25, 27).

Markets respond to wants rather than needs. Planning requirements are formulated in terms of land, and there is no estimate of the distinction between numbers of households "in need" and those people whose requirements may be met through the market. For example, Hertfordshire overshot its house-building target by 33 percent and used up its available land on private housing development, but it still has not met the local need (Shelter 1998a, para. 14). Local authorities' stock transfers to other registered social landlords (RSLs), such as Housing Associations, has made it more difficult to assess housing need (Baker 1997,11; Butler 1998, 4). Yet the housing market is not efficient even at meeting wants. The private sector concentration on estates of high-density "starter homes" has produced high stock turnover and little commitment to local communities. The Shelter enquiry concluded that current planning and housing policies fail to ensure provision of sufficient affordable housing, that the key issue is finance, and that the prime responsibility rests with the government (Shelter 1998a, introduction).

However, meeting the gap between the demand and supply of affordable housing will not of itself meet housing "need." A shortage of affordable housing is not the only dimension of housing need. The supply of affordable housing was less than the demand in four of the five areas investigated by the Shelter[3] inquiry; the exception was Newcastle, in the northeast of England, which has experienced population decline. The "abandonment" of property and tenancies has been receiving increasing policy attention by the Joseph Rowntree Foundation.[4]

Demographic and social change have added to the impact of housing tenure segregation. In its evidence to the Shelter enquiry, Crisis (a voluntary organization for the single homeless) referred to the government's prediction of a requirement for 4.4 million new homes, 3 million for single persons, as a need not well addressed by the housing market (Shelter 1998b, 8). The same is true for the social-rented sector. In addition to a shortage of accommodation for single persons, there are not enough affordable large homes and ground floor accommodations. New stock is limited by spending rules and a desire to keep to a minimum, on any site, the amount of supported or special-needs housing (Baker 1997, 40–41).

The Changing Characteristics of Mortgagers and Renters

The greater impermanence of households has exacerbated the problems for the economically weaker households (and, of course, the two may be interdependent) in accessing market housing. The proportion of mortgagers living alone doubled from 0.6 million to 1.2 million between 1984 and 1995, but in 1995, 78 percent of mortgagers were still cohabitees or married couples. On the other hand, private renters in furnished accommodation were increasingly young, male, and single (and, by 1995, 28 percent were students). There was also a significant rise in adult children continuing to live at home (Department of Environment 1996d, 4). Those in unfurnished accommodations were mainly couples and one-person households (Department of the Environment 1996d, 1). However, a review of the accelerated evictions procedures[5] for assured short-hold tenancies shows the vulnerability of families inhabiting the private rented sector. Despite the low proportion of families in private-rented accommodation, the DETR found that two-thirds of those they interviewed concerning evictions were families with children, two-thirds were not working, and half had lived in the property for more than two years. Adding further to family distress, in order to avoid the charge of having made themselves intentionally homeless, and to be able to qualify for rehousing under homelessness legislation, some families had to stay in the property until court orders for repossession were granted (DETR 1998e, 1–3).

Over the same period (1984–1995), the characteristics of social renters greatly changed. The proportion of couples fell from 50 percent to 40 percent, and the proportion of single-parent households with dependent children rose from 9 percent to 14 percent. In 1995, 41 percent of social rented sector tenants were widowed, divorced, or separated people. Single parents and those living in "deprived" areas were the most dissatisfied with their area. Few social sector tenants (23 percent) expected to be able to buy a house, three-fifths for financial reasons. The lowest income group of mortgagers (under £200 per week[6]) spent 40 percent of gross income on their mortgage, and the highest (over £500 per week) spent 10 percent (Department of Environment 1996d, 2). Social rented sector tenants were twice as likely as private renters to be in receipt of Housing Benefit (subsidized rent).

The Balkanization of Housing and Households: The Impact of Housing Policy on Social Integration

The impact of economic changes originating in the markets and social changes in civil society have been exacerbated in the housing field by the role of government. Policies have had the net effect of spatially and socially entrenching the separation of single people from families, and men from women, as well as separating those working from those reliant on welfare benefits, and those better off from those who are poor. Evidence from London boroughs and from the northern city of Newcastle suggests that economically active people are moving out of social housing areas because of the limited variety of tenure types and the housing quality in their localities (Shelter 1998b, 10–11, 33).

Demographic and spatial concentration of those households not able to access even discounted-price homes has been a common feature of "marketization" of housing in Central and Eastern Europe (Duffy 1998b, ch. 6). The boundaries between those with an asset and those with merely a right to occupy accommodation have become more visible; for example, some new English housing developments have physically separated social and private market housing by roads or fences (Shelter 1998a, para. 18). Evidence submitted to Shelter's Enquiry into Housing Need suggested that funding constraints have forced local authorities to build social housing at high density, reduce living space, and limit forward building of infrastructure to support new housing areas. Even without the impact of job losses and withdrawal of private capital (banks, shops) from social housing areas, they were increasingly "desertified" spaces.

ACCESSIBILITY: "SUSTAINABLE" COMMUNITIES AND THE RISKS OF EXCLUSION FOR VULNERABLE INDIVIDUALS AND HOUSEHOLDS

Impoverished Communities

The overall outcome of the interaction of market, civil society, and state activity has been a "skew away from balanced communities in the last thirty years" (Shelter 1998a, para. 22). One example is the demographic composition of residents of Housing Association properties. Approximately 2,200 Housing Associations manage 900,000 homes for 1.5 million people, 20 percent of all social rented housing. They mainly provide homes for the homeless, elderly, disabled, young, single, low-income, and minority ethnic communities (Evans 1998, 713–14). Housing Associations, some of whom must accept 100 percent tenant referral rates from local authorities, have had little control over the residents of their housing stock, many of whom are those to whom the local authority owes a housing duty because they are defined as being in priority need. Cuts in public subsidy and rising rents have meant Housing Association properties are occupied mainly by Housing Benefit claimants stuck in the poverty trap. Most would need very large increases in gross income to be equally well off when responsible for paying their own rent. M. Blanc (1998) suggests that there is evidence of increasing pauperization of those in rent-supported (HLM) housing in France, and this has driven HLM landlords to undertake job creation and other housing "support" measures. Similarly, for a mixture of reasons—social purpose, protection of assets, and source of additional funding from the

Housing Corporation—some Housing Associations have taken up the initiative known as "Housing Plus," which involves social as well as housing management. However, various authors have suggested that Housing Plus is underresourced and relies heavily on economic regeneration organization for real resources. Projects are very often small scale, piecemeal, and opportunistic (Evans 1998, 6–23; Smith and Paterson 1999).

Sustainable communities matter in meeting housing needs. Blanc has suggested that social housing arose as a transactional output combining improved living conditions with no wage increase (1998). It was intended for the low-paid, stable worker and not for the very poor. Somerville argues that the notion of "trapped tenants" is a "myth" (Somerville 1998, 776), but as Spicker (1998) points out, it is the less poor, the less disadvantaged, who occupy the same areas as the very poor and disadvantaged, who are most likely to be long-term residents of an area. They are in large measure the "local community" which occupies the social space between the workplace and home. They are subject to the stresses of poverty and the risks of street and house crime in poor areas (Spicker 1998, 18). Along with unemployment, the institutionalized residential instability around them, which is a consequence of the system of social housing allocation and support, is part of the story of the loss of a sense of community.

Rebuilding Communities: A Risk of Exclusion for Stigmatized Groups

The DETR, which is the government department with primary responsibility for housing (and homelessness), has recognized the problems of areas with a relatively high proportion of poor and disadvantaged residents. Community involvement has been accorded with delivering more effective services. An evaluation of tenant-led Housing Management Organizations (HMOs) concluded that most tenant-managed organizations outperformed their local authority and Housing Association counterparts, and the most effective tenant-managed organizations were those where tenants had the most control (Department of the Environment 1995a). Thus the DETR's practitioners' guidance for those involved in urban regeneration now insists on community involvement as a means to enhance the effectiveness of its program delivery, achieved by collective community "ownership" of the process (but not the assets) (Department of the Environment 1995c; DETR 1997b; DETR 1998a).

Given the evidence on community effectiveness in program delivery, there has been an increasing government emphasis on targeted initiatives and community involvement. For example, there is a greater emphasis on community involvement in the fifth round of the Single Regeneration (DETR 1998a, paras. 3–4). The government has introduced a separate, more finely targeted initiative for the poorest and most disadvantaged areas based on the rankings in its Index of Local Deprivation (DETR 1998b). The New Deal for Communities (NDC) is a new fund worth £800 million over three years to "help turn around the poorest neighbourhoods" over a ten-year period (DETR 1998c, summary). It supports plans that bring together local people, community and voluntary organizations, public agencies, local authorities and businesses to tackle the problems of poor neighborhoods (DETR 1998c, 17). Its targets will be job prospects, investments in buildings and people, and neighborhood management and service delivery. The bid must show how local residents will be involved, and it is anticipated that at least half of bidding partnerships who succeed in getting funding will be led by bodies other than the local authority or the local Training and Enterprise Council (DETR 1998c, 15).

In the context of urban policy, K. Duffy and J. Hutchinson (1997) have discussed the conceptual problems with the British government's "turn to community." As a means of managing aspects of social housing and the social environment, this turn to community has two dimensions of interest to this chapter. The first is that communities are, by definition, exclusionary; it is not possible to conceive of a community that is not bounded, whether this is based on geography or some nonmaterial characteristic. P. Healey has argued the "need to understand social exclusion and cohesion as group-building and mobilising processes, which generate boundary making and breaking and create labels of 'we,' 'you' and 'they' " (quoted in Blanc 1998, 784). For example, B. Murtagh has written of Northern Ireland's enclave communities as a security choice by hostile communities, a voluntary segregation and exclusion, despite the Northern Ireland Housing Executive's attempt at "color-blind" housing policy (1998, 834–35). Neighborhood residents who have little choice of neighborhood, and consequently who their neighbors are, will find it difficult to build a common bond in geographic communities. If social exclusion is socially constructed (Somerville 1998, 762), then governments and communities create and re-create social exclusion, and new DETR programs enlarge the powers of the community to demand and enforce exclusion.

M. Blanc (1998) has drawn on G. Simmel's analysis (1964) of the dynamic tensions in social transactions to discuss the difficulties in social housing. One might suggest that, by following the increasing income inequality arising in the primary market, government reaction to the housing difficulties of the low-paid has destroyed the earlier social transaction involved in the offer of social housing to the working poor. They have made social housing a tenancy of last resort, and into this housing are decanted those people whose circumstances mean that the state owes them a duty of care. However, the increased powers over housing matters for community leaders and other partners in area-based regeneration policies (Duffy and Hutchinson 1997, 353–54) may increase the risks of exclusion for certain individuals and groups. It may be the outcome of a new "transaction" between some parts of communities and their landlords, as the price of new resources for these communities.

Maximizing Rents and the Risk of Exclusion

The second problem of the turn to community flows from this difficulty of establishing a common bond. Tight financial regimes and "skewed" and stressed "communities" mean that landlords confront difficulties in retaining the asset value of their stock and increasing the flow of rents. The government's Code of Guidance on Parts VI and VII of the Housing Act of 1996 indicates the balance of government priorities. It states that the social landlords' aim is "maximising rental income, and where possible, creating balanced communities" (Department of the Environment/Department of Health 1996, 5.1). Thus, social housing landlords are increasingly involved in controlling access to their stock and the social control of those living in it.

The Housing Corporation's 1997 Performance Standards state that "reasonable preference should be given to those in greatest need except where this would lead to unsustainable tenancies or unstable communities" (Baker 1997, 25). But, as one local authority in the east of England noted, "By definition those most often excluded are those least able to gain access to other tenures" (Baker 1997, 24). Recently, government has given higher priority to combating antisocial behavior. Part V of the Housing Act of 1996 gives local authorities more power in this field (Butler 1998, 9). Poor people are more likely to be victims of crime and nuisance (Home Office 1998). The government's Crime and Disorder Act of 1998 has provided new powers, civil orders (ASBOs), through which police and local authorities can apply to the courts for orders intended to prevent alarm, distress, or harassment by any resident. Breach of the orders' prohibitions is a criminal offense that can result in up to five years of imprisonment. Civil liberties groups are concerned about the broad and generalized scope of the orders, the lack of legal safeguards, and the lack of requirement for criminal law standards of evidence, despite the criminal law penalties. The first published recipients of the orders are a single mother and two juveniles. Therefore added to the risks of exclusion inherent in the community management of estates, there is a further risk arising from the pressure on social landlords to maximize rental income combined with their new powers to exclude.

In summary, there have been cuts in the adequacy of the supply of social housing, and government policies have exacerbated trends arising in markets and civil society. The need for affordable social housing has risen during a period in which the supply has been reduced. The results are twofold: first, there is a lengthening queue for social housing which is addressed by very restricted access criteria. The criteria have further weakened the scope for sustainable communities, yet have not succeeded in addressing housing insecurity and homelessness. Second, the tighter access criteria, primarily a shift from "need" to "priority need," are entrenching the dualisms and fragmentation arising in the other parts of the welfare triangle. The next section describes the characteristics of the homeless: those who are successful applicants to the social housing queue, those who fail to make it into the queue, and those most in "need"—long-term street homeless who are excluded from permanent homes.

ACCESSIBILITY: HOMELESSNESS AND THE ROUTES TO SOCIAL HOUSING

Homelessness

The government defines a person as homeless if they have no right to occupy a property, as owner or tenant. Those in temporary accommodation are, therefore, technically homeless (Social Exclusion Unit 1998a, 3).

Characteristics of Applicants for Housing under the Homelessness Legislation

In the last decade, 4.3 percent of heads of household in England experienced homelessness, but only 2.5 percent were accepted as such by local authorities (Birrell 1998, 855). There are a number of groups with priority, but homeless people are the only group with a statutory right to housing. The local authority has a statutory obligation to provide permanent housing if the applicant is homeless, in priority need, and not intentionally homeless (Robinson 1998, 26). In addition, the local authority can impose discretionary criteria, such as whether the applicant has a local connection. "Priority need" includes families with dependent children, pregnant women, the vulnerable old, the mentally ill, and those with learning difficulties, physical disabilities, and people in certain "emergency" situations.

Between 1992 and 1994, the Department of the Environment tracked 2,474 applicants under the homelessness legislation who were resident in nine local authorities. They were most commonly living in someone else's house (51 percent), and 46 percent were childless, three-quarters were less than 35 years old, and only 2 percent were over 65. Only 29 percent of applicant households had someone in employment. Of those who applied, 48 percent were accepted as eligible, 36 percent got an offer of housing, and 31 percent were permanently rehoused by the end of the survey. For 54 percent, the reason for rejection was that they were not in priority need; 34 percent were not deemed to be homeless; and 3 percent were deemed to be intentionally homeless.

The personal characteristics of those accepted as homeless demonstrate the impact of the priority needs criteria. Those accepted (and those who withdrew) were twice as likely to be households with children or pregnant women and were half as likely to be single and childless. Those accepted were least likely to be households with someone in employment, had lower incomes, and were most likely to be in receipt of income support and Housing Benefit (Department of the Environment 1996b, 1–3). Clearly, homelessness acceptance policy has a profound impact on who gains access to the remaining stock of social housing and therefore contributes to "the skew away from balanced communities" both demographic and economic.

Access to Social Housing for Split Households

Four percent of all homeless applicants to local authorities are recorded as "split households," however this is likely to be a considerable underestimate; need is often "hidden." There seems to be an important difference between the presenting problem that is recorded and the underlying issue. For example, in a three-month period in 1995, only one in six split households visiting Shelter Housing Aid Centres were recorded as such, since it was infrequently given as the main or secondary "housing" problem. The usual main problem recorded was "homeless"; the secondary problem was often given as finances or problems at home (Baker 1997, 14).

Split households are of three kinds: families where a child or parent is absent, married and unmarried couples who wish to live together, and people who wish to live with a caregiver. A survey of local authorities found that 74 percent of split households are families with children, and they have very low incomes: three-quarters depend on welfare benefits for their income (Baker 1997, 15). There are questions about the right to human dignity arising from their insecure housing situation (living with parents, living with friends, living apart from partners and caregivers). Baker's interviews illustrate their feelings of hopelessness and their difficulties in maintaining relationships, protecting children, and achieving privacy and security (Baker 1997, 25–26).

According to Part III of the Housing Act of 1985, which deals with homelessness, families should not have to separate solely because they do not have a home. However, two-thirds of split households who make a homeless application are not accepted for rehousing by local authorities, despite the fact that half are living in temporary or insecure accommodation (Baker 1997, 1–3). A key barrier to fulfilling homelessness requirements is that split families cannot show that they "normally" live together if they have never shared a home. Reforming couples and "step" families will find this hurdle difficult to overcome (Baker 1997, 6–8).[7]

The problems faced by split households in accessing social housing reinforce the unbalanced demographic structure of social housing communities. The difficulty faced by split families in reconstituting nuclear households from "split" elements also shows the contradictory nature of government policy. While attempting to rebuild communities, government policies inhibit the rebuilding of family and personal networks that help to integrate people and buffer them from life "shocks." The bitterness of exclusion may undermine other attempts at social integration: as one interviewee said, "I'm now telling my children that they owe this country absolutely nothing" (Baker 1997, 23).[8]

Poor Health and Access to Housing through the "Vulnerability" Route to Priority Need

Homeless people have worse health and poorer access to health services. Mortality rates for homeless people aged 45–64 are 25 times those of the general population. However, a 1995 survey indicated that only one-quarter of general practitioner doctors (GPs) (and 4 percent of fund-holding GP practices) would fully register a homeless person seeking treatment. In some parts of London, the wait for drug rehabilitation is four months, but maximum hostel occupancy before moving on is three months. There is a strong financial disincentive for GPs to register the homeless,[9] and people are likely to use "crisis" health services, occupying hospital beds because they are homeless (Social Exclusion Unit 1998a, 11–12; Randall 1998, 25). However, many psychiatric wards are discriminatory in their treatment of the homeless (Randall 1998, 23–24).

As "vulnerable" people, no sick people should be among the long-term homeless as they are in priority need. However, in interviews with 40 single homeless people in Edinburgh, D. Robinson found that the incorporation of medical priority into social housing is falling short (Robinson 1998, 30). Demand for access to social housing on medical priority grounds is high and rising. Housing managers rely on the advice of medical practitioners who do not work according to formal guidelines concerning housing-related problems, and housing officials are not trained to assess medical information. Homeless people themselves lack awareness of the relevant procedures, or they are not registered with a medical practitioner and consequently have no proof of their condition. Others have little expectation that their ill health would be considered sufficient grounds for medical priority, and so do not apply on those grounds (Robinson 1998, 30). Although the government is changing the procedures, in the queue for social housing, it is not possible for applicants to join more than one category of queue. Case officers doubtful of a successful outcome may not advise the homeless of the opportunity to apply under medical priority, since homeless applicants are frequently put in a separate, shorter queue through which local authorities fulfill their obligations under the legislation relating to the statutorily homeless. However, such housing is frequently hard to let, or poor quality and in unsuitable locations. Many of those in Robinson's study who had been offered a tenancy (and 84 percent of local authorities operate a one-offer policy) had refused it (Robinson 1998, 30). As one interviewee put it, "I just want something nice that I can move into and call a home" (Robinson 1998, 37).

Restrictions on Access to Social Housing Through the Housing Register

There are routes to housing other than application as homeless in the special "homeless" queue, including applying to get on the housing register (the main queue) and assessment panels. Just 5 percent of local authorities have assessment panels that can make judgments of individual need, which the household must demonstrate. This process has the advantage of flexibility in decision making on individual cases, but it is a process in which households have few rights (Baker 1997, 34).

Split families, frequently turned down for social housing through the homelessness route, also face problems in eligibility to get on the housing register, which is the main queuing route to social housing. It is difficult to get "living apart" recognized as itself a housing problem (Baker 1997, 33), and two-thirds of split households coming to Shelter were not on a waiting list (Baker 1997, 38).

Denial of access to the housing register seems to be emerging as a major problem. In 1998 Shelter's 45 Housing Aid Centers reported increasing numbers of people in housing need denied access to local authority housing registers. People are excluded by being refused access to, or by being removed from, the register; allowed on, but then suspended or deferred; or, finally, given low or no priority, so that in effect they will never receive an offer of housing (Butler 1998, 6). According to a local authority in the northeast, "The exclusion policy sends a much clearer message . . . that 'problem' tenants will not be tolerated and given access to the housing register" (Butler 1998, 13).

However, the "problem tenants" are not disruptive tenants. In practice, the biggest single cause of exclusion from the register is a result of social housing landlords' primary duty to maximize rental income. Butler has demonstrated that the vast majority of households are excluded for financial reasons (1998, 14, Table 3); in other words, they are debtors. A northeast local authority, in one of the poorest regions of England, excludes those "reasonably likely to persistently fail to pay rent"; another authority, in the southeast, said, "We have an anti-poverty strategy, so we would not exclude for arrears" (Butler 1998, 18). One local authority excluded for historic arrears to any landlord; 22 excluded for nonhousing debt, for example, consumer debt (Butler 1998, 19). In a questionnaire survey of all housing directors in England, Butler found that 44 of the 134 responding authorities had made most of the 32,971 recorded exclusions, 36 percent for rent arrears.

However, homeless households are denied access to the register as a result of subjective judgments or unproven allegations about behavior or likely behavior in a tenancy, including behavior of other household members and former partners. There appears to have been some impact from the 1996 Housing Act which increased local authority discretion and decreased stress on housing needs, instead emphasizing tenant responsibilities and exclusion for antisocial behavior (Butler 1998, 8). Twenty-four local authorities had excluded people for *believed*, as opposed to *proven*, antisocial behavior (Butler 1998, 19). There are no records of what subsequently happens to those excluded from the register (1998, 4–5).

After debt, age restrictions are the second most common reason for excluding people from the register (66 local authorities) (1998, 20). This can affect young people owed a duty of accommodation by Social Services or through referral arrangements. It is particularly damaging for young people leaving social care and conflicts with the government's integration aims through the New Deal for the Young Employed. However recent government announcements suggest that all 16- and 17-year-old care leavers with no support will be deemed "vulnerable" and therefore eligible for rehousing.

ACCESS TO HOUSING FOR ROUGH SLEEPERS

"Rough sleepers are a potent symbol of social exclusion."
                                           Social Exclusion Unit (1998a, 1)

The DETR defines street homelessness as "people sleeping or bedded down in the open air (such as on the streets, or in doorways, parks or bus shelters); and people in buildings or other places not designed for habitation (such as barns, sheds, car parks, cars, derelict boats, stations of 'bashes' [makeshift sleeping shelters of cardboard or other available materials])" (Ruggieri 1998, 4).

The Characteristics of Rough Sleepers

There was a rapid rise in rough sleeping in the early 1990s, and there is a continuing problem of rough sleeping in some large British cities. It is estimated that between 2,000 and 3,000 may sleep rough on any night. In a London survey, the majority were male (83 percent) and white (90 percent). One-quarter were less than 25 years old, and 85 percent had experienced more than one episode of sleeping rough (Randall and Brown 1999, 5). Half of rough sleepers had been in prison or on remand, one-quarter had been in the armed forces, and 28 percent had been excluded from school. Ninety percent were unemployed, and only 38 percent had any school qualifications, compared to 66 percent of the general population (1999, 14–15). The percentage of rough sleepers who are of black or minority ethnic origin is consistent with their population share. However, their small absolute numbers may mean that their needs are neglected. There is so far little written on homeless black and ethnic minority people, but there is research ongoing under the "Words from the Street" initiative (see Ruggieri 1998).

Although studies made of rough sleepers usually find that they are mostly male and mostly white, female rough sleepers are often hidden from view. Most counts take place in day centers, hostels, and winter shelters, or in visible places. Women rough sleepers, who often have a history of disruption in their early family lives, leave home at an early age, often at 14 or 15, to live with friends or boyfriends, and "this appeared to be accepted by parents, especially if relationships at home were strained" (Jones 1999a, 19). Some women are reluctant to seek help; for example, young women who are afraid of being sent back to the parental home, and women with their lives "in a mess" who said they did not care (Jones 1999a, 20–36). A few women find sleeping rough liberating after enduring abusive relationships or care homes. Some, usually young women, find positive friendships on the streets (Jones 1999a, 48).

Older people do not make much use of services such as day centers and hostels, partly from a fear of intimidation by younger residents, and partly because of the severity of their own mental illness. Two-thirds of those M. Crane met had reported or observed mental health problems, mostly unreported and untreated (Crane 1997, 28). Many older homeless had lived on the streets for years, or in hostels, and had never been resettled. Half of those who were re-settled became homeless again because they could not cope, and two-thirds experienced difficulties coping following resettlement. Crane found no specific policies and few services for older people (1997, 6).

Vulnerability to Street Homelessness: The Impact of Weak Family and Social Networks

S. Ruggieri's interviews indicate that young people with family problems who become homeless might move in with a girlfriend or boyfriend, but if this ar-rangement broke down, they would not have a family support network to help them. Furthermore, sleeping on friends' floors is a strategy only for those new to sleeping rough or who have a support network (Ruggieri 1998, 27, 36). A. Jones reported that those who stayed for a time with friends or someone in their family suffered from feeling that they were imposing upon them and left after a few weeks (Jones 1999a, 48). One-quarter to one-third of young homeless are care leavers, and up to 50 percent of care leavers lose their tenancies. Parents of young homeless are more likely to have mental health problems or to be substance abusers (Randall and Brown 1999, 10–11), and therefore their children may have less reliable sources of support.

In the United States, studies suggest that homeless women typically experience residential instability rather than constant homelessness over long periods: "You get used to leaving things behind" (Jones 1999a, 68). Jones's schema for 77 women interviewed indicated that the reasons for the current or the most recent episode of homelessness were usually related to family breakdown and absence of social networks (1999a, 21, fig. 2.1). Although, for women as a whole, the third most common reason for homelessness was eviction, it was not uncommon to say that this was caused by their partner's or ex-partner's behavior. For young women, most commonly cited reasons were "kicked out" or left due to rela-tionship breakdown. Mothers are relatively protected from rough sleeping by priority-needs access to social housing, although the government is currently considering limiting housing access for teen mothers to hostel accommodation. However, women without children are excluded from the priority-need category for access to social housing. Twenty of the 77 women interviewed by Jones said they had children who usually had been placed in care or left with relatives. When women become categorized as single homeless, because they have no statutory right to rehousing, it is difficult to get their children back (1999a, 23).

Crane's study of older homeless people (defined as people aged over 55), a convenience sample in four cities, led her to typify them as of three kinds, each with their own "triggers," or contingent causes, of homelessness. For the *lifetime homeless*, triggers included disturbed family homes and discharge from orphan-ages and from the armed services. For the *midlife homeless*, the main triggers were found to be death of a parent, marital breakdown, a drift to transience, and less secure work and housing. For the *late-life homeless*, widowhood, marital breakdown, retirement, loss of tied accommodation, and increasing severity of mental illness were the triggers (Crane 1997, 5). In 1991, 10 percent of those over 55 in England and Wales were single, and 5 percent were divorced. This is compared to 60 percent of homeless men and 40 percent of homeless women who were single, and 30 percent of homeless men and 50 percent of homeless women who were divorced or separated.

The majority of older homeless people met by Crane were men; two-thirds were single, and most others were separated or divorced. For older homeless people, transience is a minority characteristic: 75 percent of women and 50 percent of men had remained in one town since becoming homeless. Mental illness was common, especially among women and those sleeping rough (Crane 1997, 28). They were usually unemployed or working in unskilled jobs. The majority had no living relatives or were estranged. Of the few women who had children, fewer brought them up to the age of 16 (Crane 1997, 24, 26). Many older people had no contact with their families or with services for the homeless. Crane refers to disaffiliation and the shredding of the web of human relationships. Older homeless people are closer to G. Pierreti's absolutely excluded for whom "there is no route back" (1994), rather than the marginal lifestyle which is more typical of certain young homeless.

Crane argues that whereas family breakdown is frequently the trigger, mental illness is the underlying cause of homelessness for many older people. Nevertheless, she states that "a person may have a mental illness, not be able to manage independently, and receive support from a parent or spouse. While the support is maintained, the person is unlikely to become homeless" (Crane 1997, 36). Furthermore, she notes that neither mental illness nor discharge from a psychiatric hospital is itself the cause of homelessness, but it is a cause of complicating stressful events. "One notes again that homelessness occurs when habitual support breaks down" (1997, 39).

The cause of homelessness does not appear to be vulnerability per se, whether in relation to the markets or personal health, but a lack of support and protection from its likely effects. The weakness of family and personal networks is most evident among the street homeless. Without sustained alternatives to these sources of support for some, and help in rebuilding these sources of support for others, street homeless people are unlikely to be able to get off and stay off the streets. As one person living on the street said, "If you are on your own you've got no chance really, no chance at all" (Ruggieri 1998, foreword).

The Link between Appropriate Social Services Support and Sustainable Housing Occupation

Reasons given for rough sleeping include the freedom to drink and take drugs and to avoid rent, bills, and hassles; "It's OK when you know how to do it" commented one respondent (Randall and Brown 1999, 7). Self-exclusion from conventional social networks may be the response of some people to their experience of oppression in personal relationships or their inability to cope with social life. Some, particularly older rough sleepers, both male and female, hide themselves from public view. However, according to the Social Exclusion Unit, surveys show that only 5 percent of rough sleepers do so by choice (1998a, 9). Standard psychiatric tests indicate that 60 percent of rough sleepers may have mental health and substance-abuse problems, but only a fraction of these had ever received help. Agencies consider some conditions untreatable, and therefore there are no support services. Others with multiple needs fall between services (Randall and Brown 1999, 11–12, 14). According to the Social Exclusion Unit, 88 percent of the homeless mentally ill were mentally ill before becoming homeless (1998a, 5). Mental illness can lead to isolation, and the government has allocated £6 million over three years for the Homeless Mentally Ill Initiative (HMII), which provides intensive support and is carried out in partnership with voluntary organizations. Three-quarters of interventions with HMII clients failed if only accommodation or mental health issues was tackled; if both were tackled, only 10 percent failed (Randall 1998, 25).

The government aims to cut rough sleeping by two-thirds within three years. It is clear from the description above that, because of their ill health and chaotic lives, many rough sleepers have weak relations with the formal labor market and therefore limited legal sources of income. They have weak family and personal networks, and therefore they are also without emotional "buffers" against life shocks. As mainly single adults, many rough sleepers have been a low priority for reintegration assistance through permanent housing. Despite the evidence of multiple problems and the reasons given above for choosing to become or remain rough sleepers, the government has suggested that the New Deal for the Unemployed initiative will provide an "opportunity to break the no job-no home cycle" though it is likely to be concentrated on those who are under 25 (who were a significant cause of the rise in rough sleeping in the early 1990s) (Social Exclusion Unit 1998a, 2).

Homeless people need homes, not only accommodation. Most evidence suggests that intensive one-to-one long-term support is essential to successful integration of longer-term homeless people in stable homes (Crisis 1998). However, in interviews with problem drinkers and housing management staff, Shelter found that isolation from support networks was likely to induce depression and relapse. Problem drinkers found difficulty coping but did not get continuing support after moving into a tenancy. Some had not been assessed under the Community Care legislation, and therefore were not receiving a care package, and some had been put in general needs accommodation despite special care needs, resulting in a greater risk of tenancy breakdown. The homeless mentally ill are not included as such in strategic plans or commissioning processes for social services (Randall 1998, 31). A Shelter study found that housing officers had not received appropriate training, were not aware of local services, were not able to access social work support for problem tenants, and that a small number of problem drinkers on their "patch" took up a lot of time (Shelter 1996, 4–5).

Clearly, those rough sleepers rehoused on priority-needs grounds because they are vulnerable are at serious risk of the tenancy breaking down. Up to half of tenancies of rough sleepers are abandoned within a year, according to a survey quoted by the Social Exclusion Unit (1998a, 11). Some rehoused former rough sleepers continue to spend a lot of time on the streets where they have their only network of social relationships. Furthermore, the new ASBOs increase the risk that vulnerable people will be excluded from housing. Alcohol misuse is already estimated to contribute to one-sixth of all evictions and 10 percent of all tenancies that are abandoned (Shelter 1996, 27). Simmel's notion of competing legitimacies, discussed earlier in this chapter, is very evident in the way in which landlords, and ultimately government, deal with rough sleepers. The government's concern about the perceived "moral hazard" of assistance to the homeless may undermine initiatives to support their integration into permanent housing. Thus,

it is essential that contractors have incentives to pitch their services at the right level; not so skimpy that they are ineffective, but not so attractive that they draw in more clients for whom London becomes a more appealing destination. . . . Make the New Deal for under 25s or the new over 25s program a condition of the hostel place. (Social Exclusion Unit 1998a, 24)

This concern with moral hazard is evident in the Code of Guidance on Parts VI and VII of the Housing Act, especially those sections concerning social fund loans (rather than rent guarantees) and intentional homelessness (Department of the Environment/Department of Health 1996). "Warehousing" of those who have become street homeless, particularly the older homeless, in hostel accommodation, often for years, will probably continue. This situation itself creates perverse incentives. The operation of the social housing sector blocks the route out of temporary accommodation for many homeless people. Hostel rents are high, Housing Benefit regimes and hostel life inhibit work incentives, and the wait for housing is long for single hostel dwellers. There has been a weakening of the local authority duty to provide permanent housing, and there is no access to permanent social housing for single people outside of the London Rough Sleepers Initiative (the year 2000 extended in whole or in part to some other cities).

Hostel residents are stuck in the poverty trap, unable to access market housing and unable to access permanent social housing. However, those most in need, with multiple problems, have difficulty in accessing hostels on any particular night because of the slower turnover in better quality, smaller hostels and the refusal of admission to those who lack identity papers and established benefit claims. There are only a few "wet" hostels (in which people can drink alcohol) and a gap in provision for those with multiple problems (Randall 1998, 28). "There needs to be a specific route into permanent housing for rough sleepers; general access through homelessness allocations, or even quotas for single homeless, will not ensure they gain access" (1998, 30).

CONCLUSION

Social exclusion provides a fruitful framework for the analysis of housing marginalization and homelessness. Individuals and households may have weak links to the three dimensions of the welfare triangle: state, markets, and civil society. The process is dynamic, and "social disqualification" may be the result of multiple risk in all three dimensions. At the extreme, there may be no route back, no place in social life. The risks of housing marginalization and exclusion are greater because of the developments, which themselves may be interrelated, in all three dimensions of the welfare triangle. The effects of increasing income inequality on the affordability of market housing, the effects of policy changes and resource restrictions on the adequacy and accessibility of social housing, and demographic and social change have resulted in a "skew away from balanced communities." Some perverse effects for social housing accessibility have arisen from the government's reaction to this situation. The department of government responsible for housing and area regeneration has taken a rather communitarian approach to community sustainability (in so doing it has given community representatives more power to exclude certain people from access to housing). Government has also increased landlords' social control over tenants through stronger legal powers to remove people from housing. However, at other levels of policy making, government has differing and conflicting approaches that impact housing and homelessness.

For example, former governments have encouraged a market-driven approach to the finance, supply, and affordability of housing, and the present Labor government has made little change to this approach. On the other hand, although the UK has no constitution requiring them, UK governments have had a social democratic welfarist responsibility for ensuring access to a suite of social rights, including a right to housing. The consequence has been long queues for access to the housing, especially social housing. Within the framework of monetarist government budget orthodoxy, the government has addressed the housing need by redefining its welfare responsibility from "need" to "priority need." The underlying principle concerns the state of housing, vulnerability. When considering the main housing register route to social housing, vulnerability is largely attributed to women with children. This perhaps reflects a patriarchal version of state responsibilities, though it has been beyond the scope of this chapter to develop this theme. Perversely, despite general expressed government concern with the family as a basic unit of community and social stability, the government's redefined welfare responsibilities have increased the residential segregation of poor men and children. This is reinforcing the "skew away from balanced communities" which has emerged from the labor market (impact of unemployment and low pay) and changes in civil society (increases in divorce and never-married motherhood).

For those already economically or physically vulnerable, or with little right to state support, evidence suggests that strong links to the structures of civil society, particularly family, protect against homelessness and assist in providing a route back to a home for those who have lost accommodation. Without family and community ties, or other intensive long-term social support, housing marginalization is likely to result in long-term homelessness. Single adult, especially male, access to social housing often requires evidence of multiple risks to mental and physical health, and often involves a segregated "homeless" route to social housing. These tenancies are likely to break down and are, in the future, more likely to end in eviction. The most disadvantaged are likely to end up as long-term hostel users and as street people with no route to permanent housing.

There is almost an inverse relationship between the extent of social exclusion, and in particular housing exclusion, and the likelihood of accessing secure accommodation in which people can be supported to live at home. Weak relationships to all three dimensions of the welfare triangle ossify people's place on the margins of society, or outside of all society in the case of the isolated, hidden homeless with mental health problems. In these circumstances, only the government can take the initiative to provide a legal, institutional, and resource environment within which individuals can help themselves and agencies can support people in permanent homes. However, this environment is unlikely to emerge for as long as welfare policy is strongly influenced by a neoliberal approach to the responsibilities of actors, including the government, business, civil society, and the housing disadvantaged themselves. The situation is further confounded by the conflicting principles of legitimacy raised by neoliberal, patriarchal, and communitarian approaches to housing policy and housing entitlements.

REFERENCES

Andrusz, G. 1998. Book Reviews: D. Clapham, J. Hegedus, K. Kintrea, I. Tosics, and H. Kay, 1996, *Housing Privatisation in Eastern Europe*; and D. Douglas, 1997, "A Change of System: Housing System Transformation and Neighbourhood Change in Budapest," *Housing Studies* 13, no. 6: 849–52.

Baker, L. 1997. *"Divided Lives": Split Households and Homelessness Policy and Practice.* London: Shelter.

Birrell, W. D. 1998. Book Review: R. Burrows, N. Pleace, and D. Quilgars, eds., 1997, *Homelessness and Social Policy*, Routledge: London. *Housing Studies* 13, no. 6: 854–57.

Blanc, M. 1998. "Social Integration and Exclusion in France: Some Introductory Remarks from a Social Transaction Perspective." *Housing Studies* 13, no. 6: 781–92.

Butler, S. 1998. " 'Access Denied': The Exclusion of People in Need from Social Housing." London: Shelter, June.

Carter, T. 1998. "Review Essay: Perspectives on Homelessness—Characteristics, Causes, Solutions." *Housing Studies* 13, no. 2: 275–81.

Crane, M. 1997. *Homeless Truths: Challenging the Myths About Older Homeless People*. London: Crisis/Help the Aged.

Crisis. 1998. *Now is the Time to End Street Homelessness* (Annual Review 1998). London: Crisis.

Crisis/Shelter. 1998. *Street Homelessness Outside London: English Local Authority Responses*. London: Crisis/Shelter.

Department of the Environment. 1994. *Private Renting for Single Homeless People: An Evaluation of a Pilot Rent Deposit Fund*. Housing Research Summary no. 25. London: HMSO.

———. 1995a. *Tenants in Control: An Evaluation of Tenant-Led Housing Management Organisations*. Housing Research Summary no. 40. London: HMSO.

———. 1995b. *Outreach and Resettlement Work with People Sleeping Rough*. Housing Research Summary no. 42. London: HMSO.

———. 1995c. *Involving Communities in Urban and Rural Regeneration: A Guide for Practitioners*. Housing Research Summary no. 46. London: HMSO.

———. 1996a. *Evaluation of the 1991 Homelessness Code of Guidance*. Housing Research Summary no. 43. London: HMSO.

———. 1996b. *Study of Homeless Applicants*. Housing Research Summary no. 49. London: HMSO.

———. 1996c. *The Provision and Use of Hostels by Local Authority Housing Departments*. Housing Research Summary no. 50. London: HMSO.

———. 1996d. *Housing in England 1994/5*. Housing Research Summary no. 55. London: HMSO.

———. 1996e. *Models of Practice in Housing Advice Services*. Housing Research Summary no. 61. London: HMSO.

———. 1997a. *Local House Condition Surveys*. Housing Research Summary no. 64. London: HMSO.

———. 1997b. *Evaluation of the National Homelessness Advice Service*. Housing Research Summary no. 68. London: HMSO.

Department of the Environment/Department of Health. 1996. *Code of Guidance on Parts VI and VII of the Housing Act 1996: Allocation of Housing Accommodation: Homelessness*. Revised 20 December 1996. London: Department of the Environment.

DETR. 1997a. *Involving Communities in Urban and Rural Regeneration: A Guide for Practitioners*, 2d ed. Rotherham, England: DETR, September.

———. 1997b. *Summary: Involving Communities in Urban and Rural Regeneration*. London: DETR, November.

———. 1998a. *Single Regeneration Budget Bidding Guidance: A Guide for Partnerships*. <http: //www.regeneration.detr.gov.uk/srb5/2.htm>.

———. 1998b. *1998 Index of Local Deprivation: A Summary of Results*. Summary no. 15. London: Stationery Office.

———. 1998c. *New Deal for Communities: Phase 1 Proposals: Guidance for Pathfinder Applicants*. London: DETR, September.

———. 1998d. *Modelling Regional House Prices: A Review of the Literature*. Housing Research Summary no. 84. Reading: DETR.

———. 1998e. *The Accelerated Possession Procedure: the Experience of Landlords and Tenants*. Housing Research Summary no. 89. London: DETR.

————. 1998f. *Local Authority Powers for Managing Unauthorised Camping*. Housing Research Summary no. 90. London: DETR.

Duffy, K. 1995. "Social Exclusion and Human Dignity: Background Report for the Proposed Initiative by the Council of Europe," CDPS (95) 1 Rev., Steering Committee on Social Policy (CDPS) Activity II 1b on Human Dignity and Social Exclusion. Strasbourg: Council of Europe.

Duffy, K. 1998a. "The Concept of Social Exclusion." In *Coping with Homelessness: Problems to be Tackled and Best Practice*, ed. D. Avramov. London: Ashgate.

————. 1998b. *Opportunity and Risk: Trends of Social Exclusion in Europe*. Strasbourg: Council of Europe, HDSE (98): 1.

Duffy, K., and J. Hutchinson. 1997. "Urban Policy and the Turn to Community." *Town Planning Review* 68, no. 3: 347–62.

Evans, R. 1998. "Tackling Deprivation in Social Housing Estates." *Housing Studies* 13, no. 5: 713–26.

Harrison, M. 1998. "Theorising Exclusion and Difference: Specificity, Structure and Minority Ethnic Housing Issues." *Housing Studies* 13, no. 6: 793–806.

Hills, J. 1998. *Income and Wealth; the Latest Evidence*. York: Joseph Rowntree Foundation.

Home Office. 1998. *The Crime and Disorder Act*. London: Home Office Communications Directorate, July.

Jones, A. 1999a. *Out of Sight, Out of Mind? The Experiences of Homeless Women*. London: Crisis.

————. 1999b. *Out of Sight, Out of Mind? Homeless Women Speak Out*. London: Crisis.

Marsh, A., and D. Mullins. 1998. "The Social Exclusion Perspective and Housing Studies: Origins, Applications and Limitations." *Housing Studies* 13, no. 6: 749–59.

Morrish, P. 1996. *Preventing Homelessness*. London: Shelter.

Murtagh, B. 1998. "Planning for Anywhere: Housing Policy in Northern Ireland." *Housing Studies* 13, no. 6: 833–39.

O'Flaherty, B. 1996. *Making Rooms: The Economics of Homelessness*. Cambridge, Mass.: Harvard University Press.

Paugam, S. 1993. "La Dynamique de la disqualification social." *Science Humaines* (Paris): May.

Pieretti, G. 1994. "Extreme Urban Poverty as a Salient Phenomenon." In *Understanding Social Exclusion in Europe*, a conference supported by the Commission of the European Communities. Organized by PSI, London, 24–26 November.

Randall, G. 1998. *Rough Sleeping: A Review of the Research*. London: DETR.

Randall, G., and S. Brown. 1999. *Prevention Is Better Than Cure*. London: Crisis.

Ratcliffe, P. 1998. "Race, Housing and Social Exclusion." *Housing Studies* 13, no. 6: 807–18.

Robinson, D. 1998. "Health Selection in the Housing System: Access to Council Housing for Homeless People with Health Problems." *Housing Studies* 13, no. 1: 23–41.

Ruggieri, S. 1998. *Words from the Street: The Views of Homeless People Today*. London: Crisis.

Shelter. 1996. *Preventing Homelessness: Supporting Tenants with Alcohol Problems*. London: Shelter.

————. 1998a. *An Urban and Rural Renaissance: Planning for the Communities of the Future: The Conclusions of Shelter's National Enquiry into Housing Need in Urban and Rural Areas*. Vol. 1. London: Shelter.

————. 1998b. *An Urban and Rural Renaissance: Planning for the Communities of the Future: Evidence Submitted to Shelter's National Enquiry into Housing Need in Urban and Rural Areas*. Vol. 2. London: Shelter.

Simmel, G. 1964. *The Sociology of Georg Simmel*, ed. K. Wolff. New York: Free Press.

Smith, P., and B. Paterson. 1999. *Making It All Add Up: Housing Associations and Community Investment*. York, England: Joseph Rowntree Foundation.

Social Exclusion Unit. 1998a. *Rough Sleeping: Report by the Social Exclusion Unit*. London: Stationary Office, Cm 4008, July.

————. 1998b. *Bringing Britain Together: A National Strategy for Neighbourhood Renewal*. London: Stationery Office, Cm 4045, September.

————. 1999. *What's the Unit for?* <http://www.cabinet.gov.uk/seu/index/more.html>.

————. 1998c. *Truancy and School Exclusion*. London: Stationary Office, May.

Somerville, P. 1998. "Explanations of Social Exclusion: Where Does Housing Fit In?" *Housing Studies* 13, no. 6: 761–80.

Spicker, P. 1998. *Housing and Social Exclusion: A Discussion Paper*. Edinburgh: Shelter Scotland, December.

Xiberras, M. 1993. *Theories de l'exclusion sociale*. Paris: Meridiens Klincksieck.

NOTES

1. In the United States, housing cuts (80 percent) during the Reagan years accounted for widespread homelessness and deinstitutionalization in the 1990s.

2. The DETR was formerly the Department of Environment before the creation of the new superministry by the current Labor government.

3. Shelter is a large, voluntary organization in Britain concerned with housing and homelessness.

4. The Joseph Rowntree Foundation has interests as a housing association, as a foundation committed to combating the causes of poverty, and as a large funder of social policy research.

5. The accelerated evictions procedure was introduced to make it easier for private landlords to reclaim their property (but not rent due, for which separate court proceedings are required).

6. At current exchange rates, £1 equals $1.64.

7. Section 22 of the Housing Act offers some assistance to large families living in overcrowded or unsanitary conditions under the "reasonable preference" rules.

8. Two other pieces of legislation, the Children Act 1989 and the NHS and Community Care Act 1990, should assist in securing accommodation for certain vulnerable groups. The former establishes a duty to children with no accommodation; however, Social Services do not provide housing and cannot assist whole families. The latter is relevant to those who require care at home, but according to Baker it has not worked in harmony with the homelessness legislation (Baker 1997: 9).

9. GPs are not paid for a patient unless the patient remains on their register for three months or more.

AUSTRALIA

7

"Share the Spirit": Homelessness in Australia

ANNA RUBBO

> Recent resolutions of the United Nations Economic and Social Council reaffirmed the right of every man, woman and child to a safe and secure place to live in peace and dignity. This should set the framework for the way we approach housing issues and in particular homelessness in this country.
> —Chris Sidoti, Australian Human Rights Commissioner (1996, 3)

> When (Australian) governments say they cannot afford it, that is a lie. . . . I am working in fifty countries at the moment, mainly in Africa, Asia. Former constituent elements of the Soviet Union in Central and Eastern Europe and there is not a country that comes within a bull's roar of being as fortunate or having anything like the resources we have in this country. . . . Are our priorities with our homeless people, with our indigenous people, with our young people with disabilities, with our people in pain because they suffer from mental illness, who self medicate with drugs and alcohol and sometimes an unholy combination of those in order to cope with the pain.
> —Brian Burdekin, special adviser to the UN Commissioner for Human Rights (James et al. 1999, 1)

INTRODUCTION

Recent figures estimate the number of homeless people in Australia to be 103,304, around 0.5 percent of the nation's population. On census night 1996 there were 73,000 households in the homeless population. Families accounted for 10 percent of homeless households, couples 14 percent, and single persons 76 percent (Chamberlain 1999, 7).[1]

In preparation for the Sydney 2000 Olympics, the plight of the homeless—

in Sydney at least—was thrown into sharp relief as the city made its final preparations for this hallmark event. Hallmark events often invite rather drastic planning measures, as was evidenced by the removal of Atlanta's homeless during the 1996 Olympic games (Beaty 1999, 46). Sydney also planned to accommodate its homeless well away from their homes in the CBD (central business district) as described in an article in the *Sydney Morning Herald*, "They're All Going on a Summer Holiday."[2]

In New York or London in the 1980s the exponential growth in street dwellers was shocking; today there are enough people sleeping rough and panhandling on Australian streets for all—not just the community, religious, and government organizations involved—to be aware that the problem has well and truly arrived in Australia. Homelessness has arrived amidst great affluence, at a time when the distribution of income has never been so unequal (Barrett et al. 1999; Whiteford 1998). Homelessness has come of age at a time when the question of reconciliation with Australia's first inhabitants, the Aboriginals, is very much on the political agenda.[3] It has also arrived at a time when a new homeless population is emerging in Australia. They are the thousands of illegal immigrants, mainly from Asia, who have arrived by small boats and are now detained in remote, rural enclaves. Like many Western countries, prison populations are also growing, and they also experience a form of debilitating metaphorical homelessness which often transfers into real homelessness when they reenter society (Carnaby 1998). Homelessness in any of these forms poses difficult moral, ethical, and political questions, as they must also be considered in terms of human rights and social justice.

In 1993 Australia, along with every other country in the world, agreed that "economic, social and cultural rights, the right to food, the right to shelter, the right to housing, and the right to education, were just as important, indeed, were integrally linked, and indivisible from civil and political rights" (Burdekin 1999, 1). Brian Burdekin, formerly the Human Rights and Equal Opportunities Commissioner responsible for the groundbreaking 1989 national inquiry *Our Homeless Children* and now special adviser to the UN Commissioner for Human Rights, believes it is simply a question of priorities. During a speech given at the 1998 "Homelessness: The Unfinished Agenda" conference, Burdekin stated, "When [Australian] governments say they cannot afford it, that is a lie" (Burdekin 1999, 1).

This chapter seeks to provide an overview of homelessness in Australia and how it is defined and measured, and to highlight its history and character, locating the phenomenon within debates about housing, poverty and citizen rights. It will outline government support that is available principally through the Supported Accommodation Assistance Program (SAAP) and focus to some degree on Australia's premier city, Sydney, where gentrification, tourism and the 2000 Olympics have impacted significantly on the availability of housing for low-income people.

In looking at homelessness today, the prevalence of mental illness and substance dependence is also a factor in understanding the cause of homelessness and in determining the appropriate responses. In this regard, and in relation to family breakdown as well as a lack of education and employment opportunities, homelessness in Australia today bears some similarities to homelessness in other advanced capitalist countries, especially the United States.

Structural problems associated with the labor and housing market (and income support for those not in the labor market) always underpin homelessness, regardless of the country in which it occurs. Unless these problems can be resolved, homelessness will remain as a major social issue in any society. However, the provision of not-for-profit accommodation and whole-of-life type assistance are also necessary for some people, if they are not to slip into chronic or episodic homelessness. (Neil 1999, 17)

The concluding sections of this chapter will summarize the recent thinking of the major political parties and offer reflections about some design strategies that may be helpful. The Australian literature on homelessness is largely "placeless." It is not about making places or harnessing the skills of a wider community, including design professionals, who might assist in the making of livable places, drawing perhaps on some societal practical idealism. Debates operate largely within the arena of policy making and planning, yet one can't help thinking that if there were more commitment to empowering the homeless in physical home building, there could be positive results. Just as so many of the poor in the Third World build for themselves effectively, it is reasonable to expect that with adequate resources the poor in the so-called developed world could do the same. However, just as the conservative aspects of self help have been critiqued in developing countries, so is there a necessity for caution in the so-called developed world.[4]

The issue of homelessness in Australia is complex and ideological. Any solution to homelessness needs a holistic and whole government approach. It requires public support and genuine empowerment of the homeless to engage in home building—home building not just in the sense of physical space, but the building blocks required to construct an effective life.[5] Homelessness is often tied to poverty, but it is also connected to lack of opportunity, destructive and nonsustainable relationships, poor health, and, quite often, plain bad luck. In today's volatile employment (and all too often downsizing) market and lifestyles often sustained by credit, more people realize they might also be vulnerable to homelessness. The argument here is not that people are responsible for their homelessness, or that they should be charged with resolving it. As will become clear, there are different types of homelessness in Australia, and different types of responses are required.

A CONTEXT FOR HOMELESSNESS

Australia has experienced only a relatively brief period of European settlement. Settled first by convicts and later free settlers from the United Kingdom, followed by post-World War II immigrants from Europe, and recently by people from Asia and the Pacific islands, Australia is a remarkably stable and by and large successful example of twenty-first century multiculturalism. One might say contemporary Australia has been a successful home-building experiment as many diverse people have created productive lives under a national identity umbrella which embraces such concepts as a "fair go" (a fair and reasonable course of action; the expectation that a person will receive reasonable treatment), and a tolerant "she'll be right mate" attitude (an expression of confidence to a friend that everything will go well) (*Macquarie Dictionary* 1990). This is, of course, a somewhat outmoded caricature, and European settlement was predicated on the notion of *terra nullius* (literally, empty land) in regard to the indigenous population.

The Aboriginal view is that modern Australia was built on a foundation of injustice and dispossession. Some, but by no means all, of the European population accept this view. As Aboriginal elder Lowitja O'Donoghue wrote, "From an indigenous point of view white settlement of Australia was a home invasion. . . . From our perspective our entire people were made homeless 200 years ago. For us, homelessness is not just about shelter—about bricks and mortar and galvo. It is about dispossession, alienation and trauma" (O'Donoghue 1998, 7,8). This dispossession has been compounded by policies that removed between one in three and one in ten indigenous children from their families and communities from 1910 until 1970 (HEROC 1997, 37).[6] In considering the history of homelessness in Australia, the Aboriginal definition must be taken into account as well as the experience of Aboriginals in their journey to contemporary homelessness. Continuous dispossession, Third World standards of living with regard to poverty levels, health, and well being, and employment have compounded this experience. This contested, colonized landscape, and quite different views of the meaning of the place, are explored by a number of authors, for example David Tacey (1995), Bruce Chatwin (1987), Henry Reynolds (1998, 1981), and Tim Flannery (1994).

For some people homelessness may be a choice. Not long ago in the Sydney suburb of Newtown, a woman approached a disheveled homeless man. She was distressed to see him living on the street, and she told him she would like to help him if he wanted to find housing. He replied, "I don't want any help. I choose to live like this. Bugger off." Another noted Sydney homeless "identity" was the "Umbrella Man" who lived in the city's Botanical Gardens. Apparently a former gallery director with family difficulties, who preferred isolation, he took to the parks and sheltered under his umbrella. His story became known after he was murdered—at "home."

All societies have rebels and eccentrics, as well as people who seek alternative ways of living. Some, such as Sydney's Arthur Stace and Bee Miles, contribute to creating urban myths through their living in urban public space. The eccentric Bee Miles frequented the streets and pubs and joined Sydney's libertarians in their critique of society from the 1950s (Coombs 1996). Stace was not homeless, but he made the city his home by inscribing the word "eternity" on footpaths and walls throughout the city. The word eternity figured highly on the Sydney Harbour Bridge for the 2000 New Year's Eve fireworks display. Mythical rural characters include bushranger Ned Kelly, who has been immortalized in Australian cultural history through literature but also in the paintings of Sidney Nolan.[7] Another mythic character is the swagman in the popular song "Waltzing Matilda," who jealously guarded his (homeless) independence and camped under the stars by the side of a billabong. When accused of stealing sheep by a policeman, he jumps into the billabong and drowns. The song is about being free and slightly outside the law. Today he might be called a homeless person; through the song he became something of a national hero, a person in the billabong who was independent, unencumbered, not bound by convention, and rebellious. Such was his powerful presence in the landscape that the song finishes with his ghost repeating he'll never be caught alive.

Kelly, the swagman, Bee Miles, Arthur Stace, and the Umbrella Man symbolize aspects of a perhaps now fading Australian archetypal ideal—a sense of independence from the state, society, and convention laced or combined with antiauthoritarian attitudes. In their lack of attachment to property in a country where people are preoccupied with it, they have something in common with indigenous Australians. Aboriginals, however, have powerful attachments to the land and their own people, a fact that was recognized by white Australia in 1992. The High Court of Australia's decision in favor of Aboriginal Eddie Mabo's land claims led to recognition of the previous ownership of Australia by indigenous people. Aboriginal culture is also in transition, a theme that is explored in some detail by David Tacey (1995, 138–47). Some of that transition is expressed by Aboriginal poet Oodgeroo of the tribe Noonuccal, formerly Kath Walker, "We are nature and the past, all the old ways. Gone now and Scattered" (Tacey 1995, 138).

In varying forms, homelessness has been a feature of Australia since settlement. There have always been "winos" and the "swaggies": the archetypal single, and often older, homeless men. There were the dispossessed in the 1930s depression. It was not until the 1970s, however, that the new forms of homelessness began to emerge. Youth and women escaping domestic violence were new faces among the homeless. As a result of poverty or misfortune, families swelled the numbers. Later, and in part as a result of deinstitutionalization, people with mental disorders became a significant sector of the homeless. Aboriginals are present in all these diverse groups.

Homelessness in Australia has never been easily or adequately resolved. In 1991, for example, Bettina Cass observed, "23,000 families were turned away from NSW Women's Refuges in 1987–88" (Cass 1991, 59). A four-week study conducted in inner Melbourne in 1999 revealed that two-thirds of people seeking emergency accommodation were being turned away. "Homeless swamp centers" announced the *Age* newspaper article. "1617 households—comprising 800 adults and 400 children—had applied for accommodation at least once. Disturbingly, 1374 of these households had nowhere to stay for that particular night. But despite their pleas for accommodation, the six inner city crisis centers that took part in the survey could meet the needs of only 373 households" (Farouque 1999, 9).

Melbourne exhibits a pattern common throughout major Australian cities where the gentrification of the inner suburbs pushes the poor to the fringes. Some of this housing turns into higher income rental property. Over the past ten years, Melbourne's private rental stock has increased by 22 percent but this has been accompanied by a 22 percent decline in cheap private rentals. As in all cities, people on lower incomes compete for a smaller proportion of the rental stock, often paying between 45 and 55 percent (and sometimes more) of their low income. According to the survey, the vast majority of the homeless come from the suburbs. Having failed to keep up in the private rental market in the outer suburbs and in some cases ex-urban metropolitan areas (such as the Central Coast in New South Wales), they gravitate to the inner urban area crisis centers. This begins the downward drift, or spiral, into painful and often debilitating crises. It is a process which affects single people, families, and couples. For some, it is transient or cyclical; for others, it is a one-way journey into an underclass and social exclusion (Mingione 1996, 3–41).[8] Further study would be required to illuminate the difference between people facing marginal affordability challenges and people living on the street.

A major issue in the homelessness debate in Australia is the availability of "exit point" housing, that is, affordable and secure housing for low-income people, or people who have experienced a housing crisis—in a shelter, refuge, or on the streets. There is far too little available stock and little incentive to the private sector to provide it. There is insufficient public housing and too little affordable private rental accommodation. Inner-city boarding houses, for example, once provided housing for low-income people. These houses have been disappearing, having been converted to apartments, single private residences, and tourist accommodations (Cox 1999, 69).[9] It is this lack of suitable, affordable accommodation that contributes to the 23,000 families mentioned being turned away from refuges. There simply are not enough places for them to go after the end of short stays in refuges and emergency accommodations.

DEFINING AND MEASURING HOMELESSNESS

In Australia a range of definitions for homelessness has been used. Cecily Neil and Rodney Fopp, in their 1992 book *Homelessness in Australia: Causes and Consequences*, consider homelessness a lot more than "houselessness." In coming to a definition of homelessness, they consider two issues: the notion of home and whether objective or subjective criteria provide a more appropriate definition. Drawing on the work of Sophie Watson, they conclude that the concept of home "incorporates a range of different attributes. Gender, cultural background and age also, they argue, crosscut it, with different attributes emphasized by different groups and household members. What is a home for one individual may not be a home for another, even within the same household. It is, therefore very difficult to define what is a home and what is not" (Neil and Fopp 1992, 6). Just as "home" is difficult to define, so too is "homelessness." Sleeping rough is the traditional description, yet much broader definitions can also apply. For example, is the person who sleeps on a friend's sofa homeless, or the person who pays most of his or her income in rent?

Historically the concept has tended to be used in a narrow sense, favoring those with children over those without, and men over women. . . . In choosing a definition, it is useful to think in terms of a continuum of housing. At one end is the accommodation which meets all the criteria of a home and, at the other, there is sleeping rough. In between there are all sorts of forms of housing and experiences of housing, which may or may not be defined as homelessness. The point along the continuum at which people are defined as homeless will depend on the individual concerned, on gender and cultural background, on the historical period and the policy issues in question. (Neil and Fopp 1992, 6)

In the 1999 publication *Counting the Homeless: Implications for Policy Development*, author Chris Chamberlain asserts that "there can be no meaningful public debate about the best policy to assist homeless people, unless there is reliable information on the number of homeless people in the community" (Chamberlain 1999, 1). Chamberlain and MacKenzies' (1992) work has been very important in this area, and their 1992 definition of homelessness was adopted in the 1996 census. This was the first time such a measure was used. Their definition of homelessness identifies three segments in the homeless population: primary, secondary, and tertiary homelessness. According to Chamberlain, there is an emerging consensus on these definitions, including definitions for youth homelessness. The 1995 Report of Youth Homelessness, for example, used similar categories to frame its policy recommendations (Chamberlain 1999, 13). Chamberlain and MacKenzie's categories are as follows:

Primary homelessness
People without conventional accommodation, such as people living on the streets, sleeping in parks, squatting in derelict buildings, or using cars or railway carriages for temporary shelter.

Secondary homelessness
People who move frequently from one form of temporary shelter to another. It covers: people using emergency accommodation (such as hostels for the homeless or night shelters); teenagers staying in youth refuges; women and children escaping domestic violence (staying in women's refuges); people residing temporarily with other families (because they have no accommodation of their own); and those using boarding houses on an occasional or intermittent basis.

Tertiary homelessness
People who live in boarding houses on a medium to long-term basis; residents of private

boarding houses do not have a separate bedroom and living room; they do not have kitchen and bathroom facilities of their own; their accommodation is not self-contained; and they do not have security of tenure provided by a lease. (Chamberlain 1999, 1)[10]

Accordingly, on census night 1996, there were 111,300 homeless people in Australia: almost half (48,500 people) were staying with other households; one-fifth (26,600 individuals) were staying in improvised dwellings, tents, or sleeping out, 22 percent (23,300) were staying in boarding houses, and 12 percent (12,900 people) were in refuges, hostels, shelters, and other types of emergency accommodation funded by the Supported Accommodation Assistance Program (SAAP) (Chamberlain 1999, 26).

Seventy percent of homeless people had not had secure accommodation for six months or more. There were 73,000 homeless households on census night. Seventy-six percent were single person households (55,000 people); 14 percent were couples, and 10 percent were families. The 7,200 families included 10,752 parents and 16,928 children (Chamberlain 1999, 29). The estimates of young people aged 19 to 24 and 12 to 18 are 15,700 and 21,000, respectively. School students account for around 36 percent of the homeless population aged 12 to 18 (Chamberlain 1999, 26, 27).[11]

The homeless population is spread unevenly around the country. In the southern states (Victoria, Tasmania, and South Australia) and the Australian Capital Territory, there were between 40 and 50 homeless per 10,000 of population. In Western Australia and Queensland, there were between 70 and 80 homeless people per 10,000 of population. The highest rate is in the Northern Territory (523 per 10,000 or 9,900 people). This was due to the large number of Aboriginal people living in improvised dwellings. The lowest rate was in the Australian Capital Territory (40.3 per 10,000 population).

SYDNEY AND THE HOMELESS

Sydney is Australia's largest and most international city, but it is also the city with by far the highest housing prices and rents in Australia. The phone records of people calling the Homeless Persons Information Center (HPIC) in Sydney reveal more detail about people in crisis, and the growing numbers of people in trouble. Based on incoming calls for assistance by homeless people, the HPIC recorded an increase of 23.7 percent across the Sydney metropolitan area in 1998. Their records also show, from 1996 to 1998, for people calling from the City of Sydney Local Government Area (LGA):

• A 91 percent increase in homeless people, from 917 to 1,755 people.

• A tripling of the number of homeless people on disability support pension, from 100 to 304.

• A 416 percent increase in the number of people with a psychiatric disability, from 36 to 185.

• A 400 percent increase in the number of people with a current drug or alcohol problem, from 33 to 183.

- A 104 percent increase of homeless people who had come from country NSW or interstate, from 217 to 443.
- A 146 percent increase in the number of people who had slept on the street the night before, from 217 to 534.
- A tripling in the number of homeless who slept in a crisis refuge the night before, from 60 to 198.
- A 250 percent increase in the number of single homeless men, from 193 to 675.
- A 137 percent increase in Aboriginal homeless, from 53 to 126.

During 1998 there were 18,703 calls on behalf of 26,106 people. Looking more closely at the individuals involved, 12.8 percent were aged 31 to 50, and 18.3 percent were 18 to 30. Children aged 0 to 2 years formed the next highest percent (5.3 percent). In terms of household types, the major groups were adult women with children (35 percent), adult men (24.9 percent), adult women (14.4 percent), and adult men and women with children (12.8 percent). Predominantly, people had initiated the calls themselves (64 percent) with referrals being provided for a minority from the Department of Housing (5.9 percent), the government employment agency Centrelink (5.3 percent), other SAAP services (4.3 percent), and nongovernmental organizations (NGOs) (4.8 percent).

Nearly ten percent of callers (9.7 percent) were from 89 diverse ethnic backgrounds. Most highly represented were New Zealanders (291), Vietnamese (108), Lebanese (106), Samoans (80), Fijians (52), Chinese (49), and British (49).

According to HPIC's records, the contributing reasons for homelessness were financial difficulty (37.6 percent), family breakdown (6.8 percent), interpersonal conflict (6.7 percent), overcrowding (5 percent), psychiatric illness (4.7 percent), long-term homeless (4.7 percent), and substance abuse (3.9 percent). Crisis evictions accounted for 1.4 percent and affected 3,269 people.

Further detail on Sydney's homeless people is provided by the 1998 report, *Down and Out in Sydney: Prevalence of Mental Disorders, Disability and Health Service Use among Homeless People in Inner Sydney* (Hodder et al. 1998).[12] The findings are sobering and alarming. Many homeless people have a mental disorder, and the rate of mental disorder among the homeless is substantially higher than for the general community. Many have chronic illnesses, and on most measures of morbidity the young are at least as impaired as the older population. The ages of people interviewed ranged from 18 to 37 years. Of those sampled, one in ten people preferred to speak a language other than English, and one in twenty were Aboriginal or Torres Straits Islanders. According to the study,

- Seventy-five percent of people have at least one mental disorder. The expected prevalence rate of at least one mental disorder in the Australian general population is 18 percent.
- Twenty-three percent of men and 46 percent of women have schizophrenia. The expected prevalence rate for the Australian general population is from 0.5 to 1 percent.

- Forty-nine percent of men and 15 percent of women have an alcohol use disorder. The expected prevalence rates in the Australian general population are 9 percent and 4 percent, respectively.
- Thirty-six percent of people have a drug use disorder. The expected prevalence rate in the Australian general population is 2 percent.
- Thirty-three percent of people have a mood disorder. The expected prevalence rate in the Australian general population is 6 percent.
- Twenty-six percent of people have an anxiety disorder. The expected prevalence rate in the Australian general population is 10 percent.
- Ten percent of people have a cognitive impairment. The expected prevalence rate in the Australian general population is one percent (Hodder et al. 1998, 9).

The researchers also found that

- Ninety-three percent of people reported at least one experience of extreme trauma in their lives.
- One in two women and one in ten men reported they had been raped.
- One in two people have at least one chronic illness.
- Nine percent of people reported they are seropositive for Hepatitis B or C. The prevalence rate in the Australian general community is approximately one percent (Hodder et al. 1998, 18).

In summary, the homeless in New South Wales is a growing population with a much higher than average prevalence of mental disorder. Young people under 24 account for nearly 20 percent of the homeless population.

YOUTH

Youth deserve special comment. The 1989 national inquiry *Our Homeless Children* (known also as the Burdekin report) brought the plight of homeless youth to the public, just as the *Bringing Them Home* inquiry (HEROC 1997) into the stolen generations of Aboriginal children did a decade later. Both inquiries have had profound impacts on Australians in general. The first promoted a number of measures to deal with homelessness; the second has stimulated a process of reconciliation and the desire and opportunity for many Australians to apologize.[13]

The Burdekin report (1989) unveiled a sad story about the experiences and life chances of many homeless children. Young people's pathway to homelessness often stems from an abusive family, to state care, and then to further abuse on the streets. The report paid special attention to the situations of Aboriginal children and young refugees and focused on children not living in family situations. Many young people leave damaging families and, as one homeless young woman from an immigrant family said, "My dad bashes my two brothers and me. Last time I had two black eyes and bruises. My dad's really strict. Really violent. He's still living in the 1940s in Cyprus." Another young woman explained why she and others left home: "Just to get away from the hassles at home. Most of it starts at home. Parents fight between each other. That all gets taken out on us. I think the main problem is alcohol. Father comes home and has a disagreement and belts into you. The only choice you've got is to leave home or keep getting bashed" (Burdekin Report 1989, 88).

While all young homeless people have housing difficulties, it appears that racism, ignorance, and discrimination are some of the biggest factors affecting refugees and other NESB (non–English speaking background) young people's access to housing. Refugee children seem to have suffered particularly, especially those who were sent from Vietnam. At the time it was common for children to be sent with relatives or friends or whoever would take them—just to get the children out of the country. Children under these circumstances often suffered the anxiety of an uncertain future and the stress of learning a strange language, the difficulty of understanding a new culture, the loss of their parents, and the memory of a traumatic homeland.

As the Burdekin report showed, Aboriginal children often had special difficulties. A significant number of street kids have been fostered or adopted into non-Aboriginal families who, when they become teenagers, question their identity, often with disastrous results leading to the breakdown of that placement. These young children do not have any links with their family or communities, nor do they have an extended family to fall back on (Burdekin Report 1989, 13). The totally disproportionate number of Aboriginal deaths in custody, often young men, support O'Donoghue's views about an eternal and deep-seated homelessness. The suicide of a 15-year-old Aboriginal boy in prison for a minor offense in March 2000 has occasioned the inquiry of the United Nations in mandatory sentencing laws.

Life on the streets and homelessness often lead to prostitution, drug dealing, and other criminal activities. David Goldie's 1989 film *Nobody's Children* and its sequel *Somebody Now: Nobody's Children Seven Years On* (1996) followed the lives of children living on Sydney's streets (*On Call Directory* 1998, 171).[14] More recently studies have revealed children's involvement in crime and the extent to which they are both the victims and perpetrators of violence (National Crime Prevention 1995, 5).

Frankly I do believe we are now at a crisis point in our community, certainly from the point of view of our young people, many of whom have lost faith in our system. . . . At least that is the perception of many thousands of our young people, that we have become a society driven by economics, not a society driven by compassion and a balanced soil agenda. The reason many of our young people are disillusioned or extremely cynical is their belief that our system has lost its capacity to deliver equity and justice. That, I suggest to you is a very dangerous position for any democracy. The vast majority of our young people care. (Burdekin 1999, 11)

FAMILIES

Some special issues pertain to families and their ability to house themselves. A 1992 study of 33 homeless Melbourne families indicated how diverse are the pathways to homelessness (McCaughey 1992). The causes are complex, often linked, deep seated, and difficult to resolve. Like so much of the literature, the study shows that homelessness often has its roots in family hardship that began in childhood, and then was repeated in adulthood. The causes were poverty, violent and often drunken fathers, sexual abuse, the difficulty of single mothers, the loss of a parent, parents separating and repartnering, relationship conflicts, and the trauma of children being made wards of the state or being put into foster care. These stories give some insight into the cause of homelessness, and the experience of it.

I was in a home until I was eight, then my mum took me back, but my stepfather hated and resented me. He used to belt me up all the time and sexually abused me. At 13 I climbed out of the window, joined a lot of other kids and never went back.

A family with two children living on an invalid pension reported:

We lived in a one-room flat for a couple of years. For about the first year and a half it was $90 a week then all of a sudden it's gone bang, and he upped it to $148. Well we sort of really couldn't afford it, but we couldn't afford to move either. We couldn't find the $1600 for the bond and four weeks rent it would have cost us. We were in a hopeless situation. (McCaughey 1992, 20)

WOMEN

Women escaping violence have become another group of people in need. It was only in the 1970s that leaving a bad marriage became a realistic option for many women when the sole parent's pension gave women some financial security if they chose to leave. Anne Summers, one of the founders of Sydney's first women's refuge, Elsie, recounts the story and importance of these safe places. Up until this time domestic violence took place mostly behind closed doors. Early one morning in March 1974, a group of women assembled in a park in the inner city neighborhood of Glebe in Sydney in preparation for taking over an empty house owned by the Church of England. Taking over the building was relatively easy but without funds or expertise the refuge itself was soon in crisis: "It was overflowing with women and kids." She continues:

Over endless cigarettes and milky tea at a kitchen table where the veneer was peeling and there was nothing so nice as a tablecloth, they (the women) started to tell one another stories. Dorrie, for instance, was shocked to learn other women had endured even worse beatings than hers. "They'd been unconscious for days in hospital," she said. "They'd be black and blue all over." Bobbie, another of Elsie's early residents, told of her incredulity at discovering that all the other women had been through "the violence and abuse and emotional controlling" that she had experienced. That was when they realized, there can't be something wrong with all of us. And once that started to happen, the story of Elsie moved inexorably beyond the women who maintained the roster and answered the phones and kept the place going, and became the story of the women who sought refuge there and who together learned the strength to move on to new lives of independence and dignity. (Summers 1999, 329)[15]

Thus, the context of homelessness is a varied one. From the 1970s, when women and youth were groups with great need, there have been other groups as well: refugees, intact families, and now a growing number of people with mental disorders. These changes can be traced back to the politics of war (e.g., Vietnam refugees), to policies of deinstitutionalization (people with psychological disabilities), and more recently to ever-increasing family breakdown, poverty, and despondency among younger people. Older single men, some of whom eked out marginal existences between the street and often run-down boardinghouses, have been declining. They are being replaced by younger people for whom boardinghouses are less of an option and who often will not accept the rules and regulations of shelters and other forms of emergency accommodation.

HOUSING, POVERTY, AND CITIZEN RIGHTS

This section provides an overview of housing, its provision and the policies affecting it. In 1993 Chris Paris, author of *Housing Australia*, wrote, "Australians enjoy one of the highest standards of housing in the modern world and so, in general it is difficult to approach the study of Australian housing fired up by a strong sense of injustice." He notes, however, "that many inequities remain within Australian housing, some of which are heightened if not wholly caused by public policy. Within an overall analysis we need to examine the extent and nature of such inequalities and to explore ways in which an affluent society might ensure that all its citizens could be adequately housed" (Paris 1993, ix, x).

From its early beginnings, Australia was a very urbanized nation with its population concentrated first in the major port cities of Sydney and Melbourne in the nineteenth centuries, and later with expansion to Perth, Adelaide, and Brisbane in the early twentieth century. Inner-city worker housing was built at high densities, while the middle classes spread out to the suburbs. The majority of Australians live in suburbs. K. Gibson and S. Watson (1994), in a collection of essays, *Metropolis Now: Planning and the Urban in Contemporary Australia*, reexamine the suburb as a postmodern phenomenon and the meaning of urban life.

The major growth in housing took place after World War II when a great deal of building activity took place in the 1950s and 1960s, and there was a steady increase in home ownership from 1945 until the mid-1960s. A safety net for the poor in the form of public rental housing was developed. With heightened investment in the mid-1960s, a substantial private rental sector developed. Most people aspired to the Australian dream of home ownership, and about 75 percent of the population achieve this. Paris (1993, 9) has coined the expression "housing career ladder": people move along a path or ladder from living with parents to private rental to first-time buyer, then second-time buyer, and then outright owner. Such a path depends on steady and rising incomes and, increasingly, on two household incomes. For those who do not follow this ladder, the path would be from living with parents to private tenant to public tenant. Divorce, unemployment, or personal problems might lead some back down the ladder. Home ownership and subsequent intergenerational transfers of wealth have been very important features of social differentiation (Paris 1993, 51, 52). Although this has tended to favor middle and upper income groups, it may provide mobility for working people. Children of older working people may also benefit.

Frank, a long-term working class resident of the now gentrified inner city foreshore suburb of Balmain in NSW, died in late 1999. Frank, a tradesman and once member of the Communist party, had worked on the wharves and on nearby Cockatoo Island since returning from WWII. He bought the house 25 years ago for $14,000. Recently the termite-ridden house sold for $620,000, and it will be demolished. His three adult children, themselves working class, have come into a quite generous "superannuation" package. (Paris 1993)

By the end of the 1970s the public share of housing varied from nearly 20 percent in the Northern territory, through 13 percent in the Australian Capital Territory, 10 percent in South Australia, 5–6 percent in West Australia and New South Wales, and 2–3 percent in Victoria and Queensland (Paris 1993, 197). Public housing remains at around 5–6 percent of the total Australian housing stock. For many years this housing provided affordable housing at less than market rents. By the late 1970s there was sufficient opposition to public housing that the 1978 Commonwealth State Housing Agreement (CSHA) introduced the concept of market rents. No subsidies accompanied these rises, and market rents were used to force out the wealthy tenants, ensuring that only the very poor would seek public housing. Thus, what had been a form of collective home ownership became welfare housing. Today public housing tenants are primarily the unemployed, single parents, and other pensioners. In New South Wales, beginning in April 2000, new tenants will pay 25 percent of their income for public housing, and existing tenants' rents will increase by 1 percent a year until they become 25 percent of income in 2004.

Throughout Australia, public housing waiting lists continue to grow. These figures covering the past 18 years illustrate this vividly. From 1982 to 1992, the number of applicants added to waiting lists in a year rose by 36 %, from 86,000 to 117,000 (Foard et al. 1994, 7). In 1991–1992 across Australia there were 216,339 applicants on the waiting list; and 117,000 were added to the list;

49,347 households were accommodated. In New South Wales, the country's most populous state, there were 71,458 applicants on the list in 1991–1992, and 3,000 were added to the list. Some 30,000 were accommodated that year (Foard et al. 1994, 131). By 1999 these lists had grown even longer. There are 96,000 households on the New South Wales Department of Housing waiting lists. About 2,000 households were approved for priority housing in the past year. Many, however, are not so fortunate as to find long-term housing, and in 1995 4,500 people were assisted with temporary accommodation under the rent assistance scheme (Westacott 1999, 32).

Due to the lack of affordable housing, there is a high incidence of housing stress. This happens as more people house themselves in an overheated rental market with few controls, and statutory regulations and practices that favor land-lords over tenants. Housing stress is defined as an income unit in the lowest 40 percent of the income distribution, which spends 25 percent or more of its income on housing. In 1990–91, 34 percent of all income units in New South Wales experienced financial housing stress, followed by Victoria (35 percent), Queensland (20 percent), Western Australia (9 percent), South Australia (8 per-cent) and Tasmania (3 percent) (Foard et al. 1994, 35). According to Housing Industry Association (HIA) figures for 1998, about 47,000 single-parent families were paying more than 35 percent of their weekly income in rent; nearly one-quarter were expending in excess of 50 percent of their income in rent (Paris 1993, 232). Rent assistance can provide relief, but even so significant numbers of households still pay over 30 percent of their income in rent. In Sydney around 50 percent of rent assistance recipients pay over 30 percent of their income in rent; in the Australian Capital Territory around 45 percent, Brisbane 38 percent. The problem is least severe in South Australia, where around 28 percent pay more than 30 percent of their income in rent, after rent assistance (Raper 1999, 5). A critique of the rent assistance program is that the levels of assistance are too low, especially in Sydney, and that taxpayer money is lining the pockets of private sector landlords in an inflated rental market.

Speaking at a conference in 1999, Michael Raper, president of the Australian Council of Social Services stated,

Cuts to unemployment payments for young people through Youth Allowance, the im-position of longer waiting periods and penalty periods for the unemployed, and restric-tions on social security payments for newly arrived migrants, will exacerbate the already great difficulties that people on low incomes have in accessing secure and affordable housing. . . . Tax reform is a critical factor in housing policy—not simply the taxation arrangements for investment in residential property, but the importance of a secure and reliable revenue source for the provision of housing assistance. Our public revenue base has shrunk by at least $10 billion per annum since the mid 1980s and will continue to decline without thoroughgoing tax reform.

Without a secure revenue base, the squeeze of funding for programs to prevent and address homelessness—including SAAP, CAP, CSHA funding of public and community housing and Rent Assistance—will become more and more serious. Housing is already an extremely vulnerable area, one that the (Liberal) federal Government has indicated willingness to cut (Raper 1999, 6,7).[16]

Despite such protestations, there has been little commitment to providing more public housing or significantly more affordable housing. As policies have changed, there have been innovative approaches, such as spot purchase programs in an attempt to get away from the image of the large public housing project. There has been some commitment to cooperative housing through the Local Government and Community Housing Program. An example of a capacity to provide affordable housing in Sydney has been demonstrated by the nongovernmental organization ARCH (Association to Resource Cooperative Housing). ARCH has successfully facilitated a number of co-ops, including those for people with specific needs. The involvement, for example, of members of an elderly Vietnamese community in the process resulted in high levels of satisfaction and culturally responsive housing.

The National Housing Strategy

A major initiative in assessing housing inequalities as well as the changing priorities in housing was undertaken by the Keating Labor government in the early 1990s. The National Housing Strategy was carried out by the Commonwealth Department of Health Housing and Community Services. This in-depth study—the first undertaken since 1945—was initiated by Minister Brian Howe and directed by Meredith Edwards. It opened up avenues for a major reconsideration of housing policy, and it presented a vision of housing and urban reform to take Australia into the twenty-first century. Its overall objective was to propose policies to ensure that all Australians have better access to more affordable and appropriate housing throughout their lifetime, and it was closely linked to four national imperatives for change: demographic, social justice, economic, and environmental.[17] The strategy has been informally referred to as the national women's housing strategy because women, and women with children, have accounted for some of the most disadvantaged groups in Australian society.

Among those who have theorized housing in relation to women, Sophie Watson (1988, 21) developed a feminist analysis of Australian housing. She has argued the necessity of analyzing "the processes within a housing system, be it local, regional, state or national, which served to produce and reproduce patriarchal relations to the detriment of women." With high divorce rates, women, especially older women, often experience the "downward drift" that may end up in homelessness. Single-parent families are frequently at risk. In general, the financial status of women is lower, hence their capacity to ride out marital breakdowns or simply the vicissitudes of old age (often without the benefit of superannuation) rendering women in a difficult position (Watson 1988, 21).[18]

Three strategic objectives have emerged from the National Housing Strategy's review processes and consultations:

- Expand the range and supply of secure, affordable, and appropriate housing choice accessible to all Australians, particularly those on lower incomes.
- Develop more efficient and more effective housing provision and land development.
- Achieve urban forms and structures that support broader national goals and create safe, quality, and sustainable environments in which people can live (Edwards 1992, x).

Of special relevance to the discussion of homelessness is the first objective but implementing it is easier said than done. With respect to the rental market, tax breaks which accrue through negative gearing overly favor investors, while doing little to increase the supply of affordable housing. In terms of citizens' rights, renters need greater protections against summary evictions, rent increases, and discrimination.

Assisting the Homeless

SAAP is Australia's flagship program to assist homeless people. It began in 1985 when the diverse range of programs for people who were homeless or experiencing domestic violence was brought under one umbrella. The commonwealth, state, and territory governments fund the program, with recurrent funds of $220 million in the 1996–1997 financial year distributed to 1,200 SAAP agencies nationally. On census night 1996, SAAP accommodated 40 percent of homeless people in Canberra, 20 percent in Victoria, Tasmania, and South Australia, 10 percent in Queensland, Western Australia, and New South Wales; and 2 percent in the Northern Territory (Chamberlain 1999, 5).

There has been a debate whether SAAP can achieve its goal of housing the homeless. The 1999 National Evaluation of SAAP reported that independent living is difficult for many SAAP clients as most were unemployed or not in the labor force when they left SAAP. Major concerns were also expressed about the adequacy of exit points and affordable and secure housing. In 1996–1997, 40 percent of SAAP clients moved to independent living (26 percent into private rental accommodation, 11 percent into public housing, and 3 percent to owner-occupied homes) (Chamberlain 1999, 5).[19]

For over a decade SAAP service providers have reported an increasing incidence of clients in "high need" in addition to their lack of accommodation. These high needs are often one or more of the following difficulties: mental illness, substance disorder, alcohol disorders, behavior disorder and intellectual disability, sexual abuse, and chronic health problems. The program has progressively sought to focus on the needs of individual clients and has developed a national case management strategy in order to secure appropriate outcomes for individuals. Successful case management depends on good linkages between SAAP and other relevant services such as mental health and drug and alcohol services. A recent report written for the Department of Family and Community Services by Bisset, Campbell, and Goodall (1999) discusses appropriate responses for homeless people requiring a high level of service provision.

A number of organizations in Australia assist people in crisis, according to the Australian Council for Social Services, or ACOSS (1998). Major church and charitable organizations include the nondenominational Christian Sydney City Mission, which is part of Mission Australia (1995); the Salvation Army; Bernard's; the Society of St. Vincent de Paul; the Anglican and Uniting churches; and the Smith Family, the Haymarket Foundation, women's refuges, and the Youth Accommodation Association. Hanover Welfare services is a peak body in Victoria and may provide leadership and direction to others. Shelter is a national organization with more than 20 years of experience in Australia. Shelter NSW is a community-based, peak housing organization that is working toward a fairer, more just housing system (Roden 1997, 3).[20] The National Youth Coalition for Housing (NYCH) is an Australia-wide peak body, which brings together state and territory youth accommodation coalitions. NYCH works on issues relating to young people, and it is active in youth affairs and housing policy areas (Shelter NSW 1999, 16).

The Council for Homeless Persons Australia is the national peak body. Recently, and in light of the report *Counting the Homeless*, the council has called "for a major expansion for federal Government programs to support the homeless, saying the ABS [Australian Bureau of Statistics] findings demonstrate current policies are based on inadequate information on the size of the homeless problem" (Shelter NSW 1999, 16). In 1999 a peak body addressing issues affecting homeless people was formed, which brought together the Council for Homeless Persons, the Women's Emergency Services Network, and the National Youth Coalition for Housing, with the aim of enabling key stakeholders to contribute to the development of policy and strategies to eliminate homelessness (Smith 1999, 74).

Poverty in Australia

Poverty is a major contributing factor to homelessness in Australia. The most common indicator of poverty is income. Poverty has been, and continues to be, extensively studied in Australia. Essays in the recently published *Poverty in Australia: Then and Now* (Fincher and Nieuwenhuysen 1998) look at trends over time. Comparisons are made between the results of the Ronald Henderson Commissions of Inquiry into Poverty 1975 and the 1996 STINMOD study.

On the centrally important income measure, Henderson found 12.5% of income units to be very poor (with incomes below the poverty line) and a further 8.1% to be rather poor (with incomes up to 20% above the poverty line). The corresponding estimates in 1996 showed that the proportion of income units in poverty had increased by about one-third (16.7% below the poverty line and a further 13.7% classified as rather poor) to a total of 30.4% in 1996 compared with 20.6% in 1973. (Fincher and Nieuwenhuysen 1998, 5)[21]

It is true that redistributive programs have helped limit the rise of poverty, but recent reductions in these programs, such as restrictions on the youth allowance or waiting periods for immigrants, do not bode well for the poor. Unemployment has been a major contributing factor to this rise, and while unemployment levels are currently falling, there is a shortage of employment for those affected by poverty. The skewed distribution of available jobs in an increasingly global economy may do little to ease the joblessness in key groups: youth and single-parent families, for instance.

Single-parent poverty has already been alluded to. Sheila Shaver in an excellent paper, "Sole Parent Poverty: How Does Australia Compare?" claims that poverty among Australian sole parents is high by comparison with similar countries in Europe and North America (Shaver 1997, 66–82, footnote).[22] According to one mode of measurement, the incidence of single-parent poverty among unemployed women is 71.7 percent in Australia, 12.5 percent in the Netherlands, 24 percent in Sweden, and 73.6 percent in the United States. Where women are employed, the incidence of poverty is still significant in Australia, and even more so in the United States: the incidence of single-parent poverty among employed women is 25.9 percent in Australia, 7.6 percent in the Netherlands, 3.5 percent in Sweden, and 31.8 percent in the United States (Shaver 1997, 78). Relating these figures to policies, Shaver argues that the key pointers to effective social policy are "a secure platform of universal support for children, policy arrangements ensuring the maintenance of support from non-custodial parents, and support enabling sole parents to participate in paid employment" (80). Another pointer must be the availability of suitable and appropriate work, a factor of equal importance to males and females in increasingly service- and technology-oriented economies. It is disingenuous to blame the victim as is often the case when there are powerful structural reasons emanating from the changing labor market that inhibit a dignified form of citizenship, and governments which are reluctant to take sufficient responsibility for those in need—often not of their own making.

Australia can take little pride indeed in these international comparisons. . . . In Australia the greatest prospects for improving the circumstances of sole parents lie in increasing their income from paid work . . . The framework of the sole parent pension gives real scope for part-time employment, underpinned by the security of income support. Viewed in their best light, these developments represent a move towards a policy framework to support combining social policy support with income from employment. (Shaver 1997, 80)

The numbers of homeless women, and women seeking emergency services, outlined below, paint a slightly less sanguine picture. Poverty can also be looked at from the point of view of housing affordability. The findings of the National Housing Strategy are salutary. Among low-income home purchasers, single parents spent around 40 percent of their income on housing. Rent payments for low-income renters exceeded 40 percent of income for nearly all age and income type units. By comparison, all Australian income units spent on the average 12.6

percent of their income on housing. In 1988, 53 percent of single-person income units were experiencing housing stress followed by couples with dependents (18.1 percent) and single parents (16.9 percent). In terms of age, the proportion of income units in greatest housing stress were aged 15–24 (21 percent), 25–34 (26.4 percent), and 35–44 (17 percent) (Edwards 1991, xi, x, 30).[23]

Contrasted against the rising poverty levels is the growing polarity between rich and poor. Severance packages for chief executive officers, or CEOs, which may leave workers high and dry and without their superannuation entitlements, are all too common. The Australian Bureau of Statistics figures show clearly that there is a growing inequality (Barrett et al. 1999). In Australia the myths surrounding the concept of "fair go" and a classless society are severely challenged in the current climate.

Citizen Rights

Homeless children and indigenous people experience considerable disadvantage in relation to housing rights and other human rights, and as has been noted already with regard to indigenous Australians, homelessness is linked to relocation and dispossession. The mentally ill, inasmuch as many are regarded as unemployable and isolated from the rest of the community, constitute another special constituency for whom housing should be a right and not a privilege. Whether or not housing was a right or a privilege was a major issue before and during the 1996 world conference on housing, Habitat II.

A few countries led by the United States wanted to use the Habitat II Conference to renege on the right to housing, and much of the conference became absorbed in that discussion and interpretations of the right to housing. The final declaration came out with something weaker than the UN statement. Commenting on the outcome the Australian Human Rights Commissioner, Chris Sidoti said he thought it

affirmed the "full and progressive realization of the right to housing." This seems to have satisfied both sides of the debate. Importantly the declaration affirmed governments' obligations to facilitate housing and referred to what specific policies and actions are required. . . . The Australian Government statement itself did not include any of the 50 proposed commitments developed through the Australian NGO forums or the Habitat II national consultative committee. (Sidoti 1996, 6)

During the lead-up to Habitat II, Sidoti addressed the 1996 National Conference on Homelessness. There he re-asserted a tenet of the 1948 United Nations Universal Declaration of Human Rights when he said, "Everyone has the right to a standard of living adequate for the health and well-being of himself and his family . . . including housing" (Sidoti 1996, 2).

In the aftermath, of Habitat II, Sidoti urged a return to the rights-based approach in dealing with housing provision in Australia: "Recent resolutions of the United Nations Economic and Social Council reaffirmed the right of every man, woman and child to a safe and secure place to live in peace and dignity. This should set the framework for the way we approach housing issues and in particular homelessness in this country" (Sidoti 1996, 3).

Today the number keeps rising. The governing Liberal/National conservative coalition party, and society at large, does not seem to have the will to take adequate action. The declaration of the Rights of the Child was agreed by unanimous vote of the General Assembly of the United Nations on November 20, 1959. It was the principles established in the declaration that the Burdekin Report (1989) examined in relation to children in Australia. The commission took as its brief that children have the right to "grow up in the care and responsibility of their parents wherever possible; adequate housing; enjoy the benefits of social security; protection from all forms of neglect, cruelty and exploitation; and special protection" (Burdekin Report 1989, 33).

While one would be wary in predicting that a Labor government today would do much better, social justice in relation to housing was on the agenda of previous governments. In 1975 the Labor government introduced the first-of-its-kind Homeless Persons Assistance Scheme, and in 1985 it brought in the SAAP. In 1983 the Labor government introduced a Social Justice Strategy (SJS) with the aim of developing a fairer, more prosperous, and just society. Social justice was one of the imperatives of the innovative 1992 National Housing Strategy. Director Meredith Edwards wrote, "Social justice is about quality of life; it is about choices and opportunities for people at different times in their lives; and it is about ensuring people can participate fully in economic, social and political life" (Edwards 1992, 10). The National Housing Agenda proposed that sustainable social justice outcomes could be fostered through a number of mechanisms (Edwards 1992, 11). Further, the strategy's objectives saw it as important in the interests of social justice that "those people who are not in home ownership enjoy some of its benefits, particularly security of tenure." The strategy proposed that the supply of social housing available for rent at the lower cost end of the market be expanded, and public housing authorities and community housing organizations provide this. Of special importance to the homeless was "better targeted housing assistance, together with increased levels of assistance to alleviate financial housing stress."

POLITICAL PARTIES

On the subject of homelessness, there seems to be some congruence between two of the major parties, the Democrats and the Labor party, but neither of them are in power. The leader of the Australian Democrats, Meg Lees, appears to agree with the Burdekin view on homelessness.

We are massively rich in resources on whatever scale or however you want to measure it. . . . So we can not make excuses. There are no excuses. Despite what the Coalition

(John Howard's liberal government) tells us, we do not have a debt problem. . . . We need specific planning, we need money, and we need commitment. It is a realistic dream. We must never give up dreaming it. The Democrats are committed to keeping it on the national agenda even if at the moment it is not the flavor of the month. (Lees 1999, 86)

Referring to the ruling Liberal party, she said, "In the past year we have heard a great deal from government about the need to reform the tax system, about how we have to reduce debt. But as we move towards the next century, we hear very little about how to reduce inequality. . . . In pursuit of these fundamentals the Howard Government has cut about seven billion dollars from Government programs over the last couple of years" (Lees 1999, 86).

The Labor party has a history of introducing liberal and social justice initiatives, principally seen in the Homeless Persons Scheme (1975) and SAAP (1985). To a great extent, the 1945 Commonwealth State Housing Agreement (CSHA) provided a platform for the development of visionary plans for public housing in Australia. The 1991 National Housing Strategy was a major initiative in housing policy and reshaping directions. According to the Shadow Minister for Housing, Belinda Neal, the elimination of housing stress is firmly on their future agenda (Neal 1999, 76–81).

While to date the record of the Liberal party and Prime Minister John Howard is not good on social policy—witness the slash/burn/privatize approach to public universities—it behooves us to look at what they might do in the future. Now in their second term and very confident, the Howard government believes it has fixed the economy and will now shift toward social policy and the "decent society."

I have always believed that a strong economy will provide greater opportunities for all Australians, but clearly not everyone is sharing equally in the benefits flowing from our current economic strength.

At the same time I have remained true to a modern conservative approach to social policy that supports bedrock social institutions such as the family and promotes enduring values such as personal responsibility, a fair go and the promotion of individual potential. Australians are decent and fair-minded. Decent communities find within themselves to mutually support each element of their societies. . . . Most of all the social coalition is firmly rooted in notions of mutual obligation—that those who have done well have an obligation to those who are less fortunate, and those that are supported by the community should give something in return. (Howard 2000, 11)

It will be worth waiting to see what this means. Will Howard's "decent" community want to deal with homelessness? What mutual obligations might he have in mind for homeless people? While most people are more aware of homelessness today and regularly encounter panhandlers in the streets, it is less likely that they have any real idea about who are the homeless, as people, or that the homeless might often be quite like themselves. A community that understands might be more willing to act. Creating more awareness and encouraging active responsibility may be the only way to ensure action on this growing problem. As has already been stated, eliminating homelessness requires political will. But it is the people through their elected representatives who must steer the political agenda.

PROPOSED SOLUTIONS

An example of building awareness occurred through a student architectural project in 1999 when a national design ideas competition was held for architecture, art, and design students to address the issue of homelessness through design (UNSW 1999).[24] The competition attracted some 200 entries from around the country. Most of the entrants had had nothing to do with homelessness previously, and they were distressed when they started to find out about it. Architecture students on this competition visited refuges and church organizations, and they worked in soup kitchens. For their projects the students wanted to do two things: to make the general public aware of what they now knew and to make a difference through design.

The results were interesting, and some of them were achievable. In making people aware, a series of ideas were put forward. One was an electronic board located at bus stops where information could be readily gained about the homeless, and where a person might find out how to become a volunteer. Drawing on ideas from the New York Homeless Projection project (Deutsche 1996, 45), another proposed to place holographs of the homeless in key sites around the city, a play on the attitudes that would prefer to have the homeless out of sight and out of mind. A third student designed stone pillows to be placed around the city, as a reminder that what is private for most people—sleeping—is public for others. In various ways, they contested the exclusion of homeless people from the public social space.

The making a difference project also drew out some interesting ideas. One student designed a fold-up bed for use in shelters. The bed folded into a vertical box on castors, so that people could leave their belongings locked up during the day. At night they could move the units into position and create rooms, or groups of friends. This was a simple and economic improvement on a bare floor and a cupboard which the church allowed people to use for their daytime storage. This may not seem a major contribution to the question of homelessness at first glance, but it did address significant issues of belonging and personal space that are so absent in shelters.

Another idea was to take over the roof space of city buildings, by attaching new lift cores on the external face of office towers. Showers, cafes, and gardens could be installed on unused rooftops. Yet another idea was to turn over the Olympic Village after the 2000 Games to people in housing need. Another proposed well-designed shower cum laundromat blocks in public parks. Why, students asked, should it be so hard for the homeless to have access to such basic necessities as a shower or a place to wash clothes? Another proposed

Internet cafes, suggesting that some of the more isolated and withdrawn people might find a virtual community sustaining. There are already plenty of homeless websites. Yet another suggestion was electronic directories for use by the homeless, to save them from having to walk unnecessarily. It is probably not a well-known fact that the homeless people—at least in Australia—often have problems with their feet because of all the walking they do to find food and shelter. Well-placed electronic directories could help them know what was available and where.

None of these ideas address the structural causes of homelessness that Cecily Neil speaks of, nor would they help provide the medium and long-term affordable housing that is so badly needed. It might, however, be just as interesting to challenge other sectors of the community to do something that would make a difference. There are many committed people working to alleviate homelessness in Australia in government and nongovernmental organizations. The work done by charitable organizations, compassionate individuals, and the churches is crucial. Drawing other people into a circle of action and understanding, such as happened with the design students, may well be effective in reestablishing the Australian ethic of a fair go.

Australian playwright David Williamson, for long a commentator on Australian life, might disagree. His most recent play, *The Great Man*, depicts the abandonment of traditional Labor party values where community and mateship predominated in favor of a self interested approach guided by the expediencies determined by global markets. Globalization is a permutation of the modernity that has characterized the twentieth century. The modernity so eloquently described by Marshall Berman helps us understand the marginal position of the homeless person in relation to modernity, and now globalization.

To be modern is to find ourselves in an environment that promises us adventure, power, joy, growth, transformation of ourselves and our world—and at the same time, that threatens to destroy everything we have, everything we know, everything we are. Modern environments and experiences cut across all boundaries of geography and ethnicity, of class and nationality, of religions and ideology: in this sense, modernity can be said to unite all mankind. But it is a paradoxical unity, a unity of disunity: it pours us all into a maelstrom of perpetual disintegration and renewal, of struggle and contradiction, of ambiguity and anguish. To be modern is to be part of a universe in which, as Marx said, "all that is solid melts into air." (Berman 1983, 15)

CONCLUSIONS

Homelessness in Australia is a growing social, economic, and human rights problem. Homelessness is much more than shelter, and its successful resolution is very much a question of political and community will. As previously mentioned, it would be useful to empower homeless people in the activity of home building in more tangible and independent ways than appear to be possible at the moment. In no way, however, should this suggestion be seen to obviate the need for effective policy, or to relieve federal, state, or local government of its responsibility to the homeless.

Of the estimated 103,304 homeless people on census night 1996 many, it would seem, would be more than capable of taking charge of their lives. The definitions of homelessness provided by Chamberlain and MacKenzie make that clear. The findings in *Down and Out in Sydney* make it equally clear that there are people who need substantial and ongoing assistance. This should be a right, not a privilege.

I have endeavored to provide a context for understanding more about homelessness in Australia, by briefly reviewing its recent growth, the way it is defined, who are the homeless and how homelessness is counted, and the ways in which government as well as nongovernmental organizations have sought to intervene. I have described the housing market, which simply does not provide enough affordable housing. With only 6 percent of housing in the public sector, and an inflationary housing market, low-income people are locked out of home ownership and affordable, secure accommodation in the private market. There is an urgent need for rent reform to protect low-income tenants. Rent assistance is often inadequate, and the more politically difficult measures, such as increased public housing or taxation measures that would address housing procurement, do not appear to have either political or general public support.

The complexity of the problem is evident nowhere more so than in the profiles presented of the homeless: the young, the physically disabled, the struggling families, and the people with psychological disabilities. Amongst all groups are people with "high needs." As Jean McCaughey says with regard to families, "The pathways to homelessness are easy to identify, but the forces which carry families along the downward spiral are hard to change or resist" (McCaughey 1992, 68). The same is true for individuals. With the young some of the issues raised over a decade ago in the Burdekin Report (1989) have yet to be seriously addressed, for example, youth access to state housing and adequate income support for young people who are forced to live independently.

In summing up the 1998 conference "Homelessness: The Unfinished Agenda," executive director of the National Community Housing Forum Adam Farrar recommended a number of key action items:

- Ensure that resources fully match needs.
- Coordinate all aspects of policy, program, and service delivery.
- Ensure that appropriate services are available.
- Improve awareness and understanding of homelessness.
- Ensure the human rights of homeless people.
- Enact legislation to reduce the incidence of homelessness.

On receipt of the watershed 1989 Burdekin Report, *Our Homeless Children*, then Labor Prime Minister Bob Hawke said that no Australian child would be living in poverty after 1990. Many still do. On the advent of the 1989 stolen generations report *Bringing them Home*, many Australians genuinely expressed their regret. It would be heartening if the Australian community could really "share the spirit" and bring as much energy, enthusiasm, and hard work as has gone into the Sydney Olympics, to support social justice and equality for society's most disadvantaged members: the homeless. It would be heartening if the maelstrom that modernity has brought for disadvantaged people, and that globalization now threatens to bring, could be mediated by traditional Australian values of equality and a fair go.

POSTSCRIPT

Since writing, the Sydney 2000 Olympic Games and Paralympics have come and gone. Some of the pessimism expressed at the beginning of this chapter did not eventuate. The organization Shelter NSW reported on radio that many of the homeless participated in the city-wide enthusiasm for the games. Balmy weather and a festive atmosphere created in part by the numerous live television sites around the city helped. While a full report has yet to be published, an interim report (Vinson 2000) details a varied picture. Of the 189 men interviewed, 42 percent said that they had noticed changes in the ways the authorities had been treating people, especially those in the under-40 age group. A teenager remarked, "I've had four checks today in the street," while a man in his thirties commented, "If anything they've been more friendly." Overall, it would seem that relative to the experience of the homeless in other Olympic cities, Sydney's homeless experienced a relatively fair go.

REFERENCES

Ackland, R. 2000. "They're All Going on a Summer Holiday." *Sydney Morning Herald*, January 14.

Australian Council of Social Service (ACOSS). 1998. *Crisis Services in Australia: A Scoping Study*, Working paper no. 19.

Barrett, G., T. Crossley, and C. Worswick, 1999. "Consumption and Income Inequality in Australia," presented to the 1999 Symposium of the Academy of the Social Sciences in Australia, *Facts and Fancies of Human Development*, November 8.

Beaty, A. 1999. "The Homeless Olympics." In *Homelessness: The Unfinished Agenda, Proceedings of the Conference, August 3–4, 1998*, eds. C. James et al., pp. 46–52. Ian Buchan Fell Housing Research Centre, University of Sydney.

Berman, M. 1983. *All That Is Solid Melts into Air: The Experience of Modernity*. London: Verso.

Bisset, H., S. Campbell, and J. Goodall. 1999. *Appropriate Responses for Homeless People Whose Needs Require a High Level and Complexity of Service Provision*, Ecumenical Housing Inc., prepared for the Department of Family and Community Services, Canberrra.

Burdekin, B. 1989. *Our Homeless Children: Report of the National Inquiry into Homeless Children*. Canberra: Human Rights and Equal Opportunity Commission.

————. 1999. Keynote Address in *Homelessness: The Unfinished Agenda, Proceedings of the Conference, August 3–4, 1998.* eds. C. James et al., pp. 9–17. Ian Buchan Fell Housing Research Centre, University of Sydney.

Burgess, R., M. Carmona, and T. Kolstee. 1997. *The Challenge of Sustainable Cities: Neoliberalism and Urban Strategies in Developing Countries.* London: Atlantic Highlands, N.J. Zed Books.

Carnaby, H. 1998. *Road to Nowhere: A Report on the Housing and Support Needs of Women Leaving Prison in Victoria.* Melbourne; Flat Out Inc.

Cass, B. 1991. "The Housing Needs of Women and Children." Discussion paper, National Housing Strategy, Commonwealth of Australia.

Chamberlain, C. 1999. *Counting the Homeless: Implications for Policy Development.* Occasional Paper, Australian Bureau of Statistics, Commonwealth of Australia.

Chamberlain, C., and D. MacKenzie. 1992. "Understanding Contemporary Homelessness: Issues and of Definition and Meaning." *Australian Journal of Social Issues* 27(4): 274–97.

Chatwin, B. 1987. *The Songlines.* London: Picador.

Chesterman, C. 1988. "Homes Away from Home: Final Report of the National Review of the Supported Accommodation Assistance Program." Canberra: AGPS.

Coombs, A. 1996. *Sex and Anarchy: The Life and Death of the Sydney Push.* Ringwood Victoria: Viking.

Cox, G. 1999. *Ready! Set! Go!: One Year to Go. It's Time for Action on Housing and Homelessness for the 2000 Olympics.* A report to the New South Wales State Government, Shelter NSW.

Crawford, M. 1991. "Can Architects Be Socially Responsible?" In *Out of Site: A Social Criticism of Architecture*, ed. D. Ghirardo. Seattle: Bay Press.

Deutsche, R. 1996. *Evictions: Art and Spatial Politics.* Cambridge Mass.: MIT Press.

Edwards, M. 1991. *National Housing Strategy: The Affordability of Australian Housing.* Commonwealth of Australia.

————. 1992. *National Housing Strategy: Agenda for Action.* Commonwealth of Australia.

Farouque, F. 1999 "Homeless Swamp Centres." *The Age*, November 9, p. 9.

Fincher, R., and J. Nieuwenhuysen, eds. 1998. *Australian Poverty: Then and Now.* Victoria: Melbourne University Press.

Flannery, T. 1994. *The Future Eaters.* Chatswood, New South Wales: Reed Books.

Foard, G., R. Karmel, S. Collett, E. Bosworth, and D. Hulmes. 1994. *Public Housing in Australia.* Canberra: Australian Institute of Health and Welfare.

Fopp, R. 1996. "No Where to Go: An Analysis of the Supported Accommodation Assistance Program." *Australian Journal of Social Issues* 31(2).

Gibson, K., and S. Watson, eds. 1994. *Metropolis Now: Planning and the Urban in Contemporary Australia.* Sydney: Pluto Press.

Hage, G. 1997. "At Home in the Entrails of the West: Multiculturalism, 'Ethnic Food' and Migrant Home-building." In *Home/World: Space, Communality and Marginality in Sydney's West*, eds. H. Grace, G. Hage, L. Johnson, J. Longsworth, and M. Symonds. Sydney: Pluto Press.

————. 1998. *White Nation: Fantasies of White Supremacy in a Multicultural Society.* Sydney: Pluto Press.

HEROC (Human Rights and Equal Opportunity Commission). 1997. *Bringing Them*

Home. Report of the National Inquiry into the Separation of Aboriginal and Torres Straits Islander Children and Their Families. Commonwealth of Australia.

Hodder, T., M. Teesson, and N. Buhrich. 1998. *Down and Out in Sydney: Prevalence of Mental Disorders, Disability and Health Service Use among Homeless People in Inner Sydney.* New South Wales: Sydney City Mission.

House of Representatives. 1995. *A Report on Aspects of Youth Homelessness.* Canberra, AGPS (The Morris Report).

Howard, J. 2000. "Quest for a Decent Society." *The Australian* <www.news.com.au>, Jan. 18, p. 11.

Inglis, K. 1999. *Observing Australia 1959 to 1999.* Victoria: Melbourne University Press.

James, C., et al. 1999. *Homelessness: The Unfinished Agenda, Proceedings of the Conference, August 3–4, 1998.* Ian Buchan Fell Housing Research Centre, University of Sydney.

Lees, M. 1999. "Response to Proposition: 'That Australia Lacks the Political Will to Eliminate Homelessness,' " In *Homelessness: The Unfinished Agenda, Proceedings of the Conference, August 3–4, 1998,* eds. C. James et al., pp. 82–86. Ian Buchan Fell Housing Research Centre, University of Sydney.

McCaughey, J. 1992. *Where Now? Homeless Families in the 1990s.* Australian Institute of Family Studies, Policy Background paper no. 8.

The Macquarie Dictionary. 1990. New South Wales: Macquarie University.

Mingione, E., ed. 1996. *Urban Poverty and the Underclass: A Reader.* Oxford; Cambridge, Mass.: Blackwell, especially Chapter 1, "Urban Poverty in the Advanced Industrial World: Concepts, Analysis and Debates," pp. 3–41.

National Crime Prevention. 1995. *Living Rough: Preventing Crime and Victimization among Homeless Young People.* Commonwealth of Australia.

National Housing Strategy. 1993. Canberra: Australian Government Publication.

Neal, B. 1999. "Response to Proposition: 'That Australia Lacks the Political Will to Eliminate Homelessness.' " In *Homelessness: The Unfinished Agenda, Proceedings of the Conference, August 3–4, 1998,* eds. C. James et al., pp. 76–81. Ian Buchan Fell Housing Research Centre, University of Sydney.

Neil, C. 1999. "The Unfinished Agenda: Reconciling Agendas, and Intended and Untended Outcomes." In *Homelessness: The Unfinished Agenda, Proceedings of the Conference, August 3–4, 1998,* eds. C. James et al., pp. 17–26. Ian Buchan Fell Housing Research Centre, University of Sydney.

Neil, C., R. Fopp, with C. McNamara and M. Pelling. 1992. *Homelessness in Australia: Causes and Consequences.* Victoria; CSIRO.

Nolan, S., and R. Melville. 1964. *Ned Kelly: 27 Paintings by Sidney Nolan,* London: Thames and Hudson.

O'Donoghue, L. 1998. *Can We Call Australia Home?* Fifth F. Oswald Barnett Oration, November 5. Ecumenical Housing Inc. and Copelen Child and Family Services, Victoria.

Paris, C. 1993. *Housing Australia.* South Melbourne: Macmillan Education Australia.

Raper, M., 1999. Opening Address. In *Homelessness: The Unfinished Agenda, Proceedings of the Conference, August 3–4, 1998,* eds. C. James et al., pp. 4–7. Ian Buchan Fell Housing Research Centre, University of Sydney.

Read, P. 1996. *Returning to Nothing: The Meaning of Lost Places.* Melbourne, Australia: University of Cambridge Press.

Reynolds, H. 1981. *The Other Side of the Frontier.* Queensland: James Cook University.

————. 1998. *The Whispering in Our Hearts*. Victoria: Allen and Unwin.

Rickard, J. 1999. *Australia: The Present and the Past*. London and New York: Longman.

Roden, W. 1997. *Building a Fairer Housing System: Shelter NSW Submission to the Senate Inquiry into Housing Assistance*. Sydney: Shelter NSW Co-op Ltd.

Serageldin, I. ed. 1997. *The Architecture of Empowerment: People, Shelter and Livable Cities*. London: UK: Academy Editions.

Shaver, S. 1997. "Sole Parent Poverty: How Does Australia Compare?" In *Poverty in Australia: Dimensions and Policies*, ed. Michael Bittman, pp. 66–82. Social Policy Research Centre Reports and Proceedings no. 135.

Shelter NSW. 1999. "Stop Press: New Homeless Report." In *Around the House, The Newsletter of Shelter NSW, Inc.* 37 (September–December): 16. Sydney: Shelter NSW Co-op Ltd.

Sidoti, C. 1996. *Housing as a Human Right*. Sydney; Human Rights and Equal Opportunity Commission.

Smith, W. 1999. "Response to the Proposition: 'Australia Lacks the Political Will to Eliminate Homelessness.' " In *Homelessness: The Unfinished Agenda, Proceedings of the Conference, August 3–4, 1998*, eds. C. James et al., pp. 70–75. Ian Buchan Fell Housing Research Centre, University of Sydney.

Social and Economic Research Centre (SERC) and Australian Housing and Research Institute (AHURI). 1999. *National Evaluation of the Supported Accommodation Assistance Program (SAAP)*. Canberra: Department of Family and Community Services.

Stewart, D. 1985. *Ned Kelly* (1943). In *Three Australian Plays*, ed. A. Sykes. Melbourne: Penguin.

Summers, A. 1999. *Ducks on the Pond: An Autobiography 1945–1976*. Ringwood, Victoria: Viking.

Sydney City Mission. 1995. *Shadow People: The Reality of Homelessness in the 90's*.

Tacey, D. 1995. *Edge of the Sacred: Transformation in Australia*. North Blackburn, Victoria: Harper Collins.

Turner, J. 1976. *Housing by People: Towards Autonomy in Building Environments*. New York: Pantheon Books.

Vinson, T. 2000. "Counting the Street Homeless: Interim Report—Covering Weeks 1 and 2. Survey of Sydney's Homeless during the Olympics." September unpublished.

Watson, S. 1988. *Accommodating Inequality: Gender and Housing*. Victoria: Allen and Unwin.

Westacott, J. 1999. "The Unfinished Agenda: Reconciling Agendas, and Intended and Unintended Outcomes." In *Homelessness: The Unfinished Agenda, Proceedings of the Conference, August 3–4, 1998*, eds. C. James et al., pp. 32–38. Ian Buchan Fell Housing Research Centre, University of Sydney.

Whiteford, R. 1998. "Is Australia Particularly Unequal? Traditional and New Views." In *Contesting the Australian Way: States, Markets and Civil Society*, P. Smyth and B. Cass. Cambridge, Melbourne: UK: Cambridge University Press.

Williamson, D. 2000. *The Great Man*, unpublished.

NOTES

The author wishes to thank Harvey Volke and Adam Farrar for comments on a previous version of this paper.

1. C. Chamberlain, in *Counting the Homeless: Implications for Policy Development* provides a thorough analysis of the number of homeless in Australia. The 1996 Census targeted the homeless population by employing a special enumeration strategy which used a cultural definition of homelessness proposed by Chamberlain and MacKenzie in 1992.

2. For a very thorough analysis of the Sydney housing market and the social impact of the Olympic Games, see Gary Cox, *Ready! Set! Go!: One Year to Go. It's Time for Action on Housing and Homelessness for the 2000 Olympics*. See also C. James et al., *Homelessness: The Unfinished Agenda* and media reports: *Sydney Morning Herald* <www.smh.com.au> "Home Rents Soar near Olympic Sites, Jan. 7, 2000; 'They're All Going on Summer Holiday,' " Jan. 14, 2000; "Boarders Left Homeless in Olympic Rush," Jan. 19, 2000.

3. For example, this year the Council for Aboriginal Reconciliation will host Corroboree 2000 (May 28) with a People's Walk for Reconciliation across the Sydney Harbour Bridge. See www.austlii.edu.au/car/ for strategies to advance reconciliation.

4. For discussions about the poor building for themselves, see, for example, Turner (1976) and Seragelin (1997). Rod Burgess, a critic of Turner, has argued that Turner's position too easily allows governments to renege on their responsibilities.

5. Anthropologist Ghassan Hage has developed interesting ideas in relation to psychological and physical homebuilding among migrant communities in Australia. See Hage (1997, 1998).

6. The preface of the 689-page report *Bringing Them Home. Report of the National Inquiry into the Separation of Aboriginal and Torres Straits Islander Children and Their Families*, states, "This report is a tribute to the strength and struggles of many thousands of Aboriginal and Torres Straits Islander people affected by forcible removal. We acknowledge the hardships they endured and the sacrifices they made. We remember and lament all the children who will never come home."

7. See, for example, Douglas Stewart's play *Ned Kelly* (1943) and the Nolan paintings in Nolan and Melville, *Ned Kelly: 27 Paintings by Sidney Nolan* (1964).

8. See Mingione (1996), especially Chapter 1, "Urban Poverty in the Advanced Industrial World: Concepts, Analysis and Debates," pp. 3–41. Of particular interest are the issues he raises in regard to poverty and citizenship, and the chains of events that activate "malign circuits." New forms of poverty exclude a growing number of individuals from full citizenship. Mingione writes,

The problem is not the revolt of the poor, who are such also because they have no voice or political representation, but rather a weakening of the social bond as a whole in a situation where solidarity and certainties are fading away even for those who are not poor. The aim . . . is to discuss the impact of the phenomenon as a critical factor with regard to social cohesion in the process of transformation that is affecting citizenship systems of the advanced industrial world. . . . Both employment and the family are becoming less stable and thus more problematic and selective in protecting individuals from falling into malign circuits of impoverishment. These transformations create new tensions on, the welfare intervention front, which is already troubled by fiscal and financial difficulties. (1996, 12, 13)

9. See Cox (1999, 69). The Department of Urban Affairs and Planning commissioned a study into inner Sydney boardinghouses in 1997. Out of 785 properties investigated, only 255 remained as boardinghouses. New uses were apartments (51 percent), single private residences (23 percent), and tourism (10 percent).

10. These definitions were developed by Chamberlain and MacKenzie in 1992.

11. Chamberlain (1999) points out the difficulty in accurately counting homeless young people who are more likely to sleep rough, and hence more likely to avoid being counted, go to squats, or stay with other families because they have left or have been thrown out of home.

12. The Research Group in Mental Health and Homelessness carried out this study, in 1997. It was funded and supported by the Sydney City Mission, Society of St. Vincent de Paul, Salvation Army, Wesley Mission and the Haymarket Foundation; Center for Mental Health, New South Wales Department of Health; and St. Vincent's Hospital, Sydney. 210 homeless people, aged 17–87 were interviewed. Interviews were conducted in any of the eight major hostels providing emergency accommodation in inner Sydney. These included Campbell House, Edward Eager Lodge, Foster House, Matthew Talbot Hostel, Samaritan House, Venetian Village and The Women's Place. The sample included people sheltered in the hostels, people seeking food, clothing and support while living on the street, or in cheap accommodation.

13. Sorry books were made up around the country and were signed by thousands of people. Notably Prime Minister John Howard refuses to say "sorry" on behalf of the nation, to the detriment of the reconciliation process.

14. David Goldie directed, wrote, and produced two ABC (Australian Broadcasting Commission) films on homeless children.

15. Anne Summers was a founding member of the Women's Liberation Movement in Australia. Her autobiography provides interesting insights into the period in which homelessness has been a feature of the Australian political and social landscape. Coombs (1996), Rickard (1999), and Inglis (1999) also provide insights into a traditional, and changing, Australia which help establish a context for contemporary homelessness.

16. CAP is the Crisis Accommodation Program, and CSHA is the Commonwealth State Housing Agreement, the mechanism by which the states and federal government negotiate their commitment to housing procurement and provision.

17. The National Housing Strategy was the most comprehensive review of Australian housing since 1945. As such they are an important source of data pertaining to housing and housing policy for low-income people.

18. These issues are taken up in Watson (1988). Her focus is not homelessness, but the book provides an excellent comparative analysis of women in England and Australia, raising the criticality of questions about gender and housing in relation to divorce, income status, and old age.

19. SAAP's capacity to achieve its goals is discussed in Chesterman (1988), Fopp (1996), and more recently (1999) by the Social and Economic Research Center (SERC) and the Australian Housing and Research Institute (AHURI).

20. Shelter NSW promotes the exchange of ideas between organizations through forums and seminars, promotes and lobbies for development of government housing policy with effective involvement of the NGOs, prepares reports and newsletters, and conducts research in helping to develop NGO housing services networks. Shelter NSW has a membership of over 120 individuals and organizations, including tenants advice services and community housing organizations.

21. *Australian Poverty: Then and Now* (1998) is a comprehensive collection of essays on all aspects of poverty in Australia with special tribute to the work of Ronald Henderson, known for his development of the Poverty Line and his commitment to challenging the "lack of caring in Australian society." He wrote in McCaughey et al. (1977),

quoted in Fincher, "Welfare policy is conceived not simply as a matter of institutions and serves for the poor and vulnerable, important though these are. It is to be seen above all as strengthening the social fabric in which we all live." Henderson was director of the Institute of Applied Economic and Social Research at the University of Melbourne from 1962–1979. He chaired the 1972 Commonwealth Commission of Inquiry into Poverty. He also established the quarterly *Australian Economic Review*, through which he and colleagues were influential in economic policy debate, especially on the labor market, efficiency and productivity, and the ideal of equitable income distribution.

22. Shaver (1997) discusses the difficulties of measuring poverty, some of the shortcomings of the Henderson model (HPL) and the LIS, and new models for assessing poverty.

23. Housing stress is assumed to exist if an income unit pays more than 30 percent of its income on housing and is in the lowest 40 percent of the income distribution range.

24. The competition, "In the Shadow of Neon Light: Homelessness and the City," was part of the National Students' Conference, Flashpoint 99, University of New South Wales, July 1999. There is considerable literature on social responsibility in relation to homelessness and the potential for design professionals and artists to act in a socially responsible manner. See, for example, Crawford (1991). Deutsche (1996) documents a major project in New York, The Homeless Projection, which she interprets as a symbolic declaration of new rights for the homeless people who have been effectively excluded from urban social space.

THE AMERICAS

8

Poverty Amidst Plenty: Homelessness in the United States

BARBARA DUFFIELD

You think you know what homeless mean but you don't know nothin' 'bout homeless. You think homeless mean you ain't got no apartment, you ain't got no bed for yourself, ain't got no place to wash off when you soil or you be sweaty. Well, bein' homeless mean more than all that.

It mean you don't got no next-door neighbor, no best friend no more. You don't got no favorite place to play or hide your candy money. You don't even got your own seat in your own classroom, you be movin' so many time. Don't know the teacher name. So who care? She don't know your name either.

You ain't got no good memories of holidays or the movies or even rides.

You ain't even got yourself bad memories. You know why? You bet you don't! 'Cause one shelter look like the next, and soon you can't remember how long you been in this one or that one. Anyway, it don't make no difference. Not after a whiles it don't. You know why? 'Cause you be doublin' up so many nights in the same bed covers, sharin' the same potty so many nights, that one mornin' you wake up and you ain't sure who you is anymore. Maybe you still you, maybe you turn into the other person.

So don't tell me you knows 'bout homeless kids. And don't ask me if I understand what happenin' to my family bein' we got no home. They invisible and so is me. I not here anymore. I died three year ago. Hey, you wastin' your time talkin' to a dead person.

—Tape-recorded statement of an eleven-year-old girl as she was approached
by a social worker at an emergency shelter, Seattle, WA (Quint 1994)

At the turn of the century and the dawn of the new millennium, there is perhaps no greater irony than the growing number of men, women, and children suffering the most abject form of poverty—homelessness—in the wealthiest, most powerful country in the world. This chapter will explore the rise of homelessness in the United States; its impact on various populations; policy and programmatic responses to homelessness; and recommendations for eliminating homelessness.

THE RISE OF HOMELESSNESS IN THE UNITED STATES

The word "homeless" did not gain popular currency in the United States until the 1980s, when large numbers of men, women, and children became visible either on city streets or seeking emergency shelter. Indeed many communities doubled or tripled their shelter capacity in the 1980s and early 1990s in order to respond to increasing homelessness: in Boston, shelter capacity increased by 246 percent between 1983 and 1995, increasing from 972 to 3,362 beds; in Los Angeles, shelter capacity more than tripled between 1986 and 1996, increasing from 3,495 to 10,800 beds; and in the state of Minnesota, the number of persons in homeless shelters on one night more than quadrupled between 1985 and 1997 (National Coalition for the Homeless 1997).

Prior to the 1980s, homelessness was confined primarily to the skid row areas of major cities: sections of town containing cheap hotels, lodging houses, pawnshops, and other businesses. In the latter part of the nineteenth century, skid row was inhabited by low-skilled workers for industries with highly seasonal demand, such as large-scale agriculture, lumbering, and railroad and highway construction (Rossi 1989). Skid rows were located near railroad freight assembly yards, warehouses, and trucking terminals that employed many residents. Because of the physical nature of this work, the laborers were almost exclusively men.

The Great Depression of the 1930s caused a surge in homelessness, mainly young men traveling from place to place in search of employment. Families, too, experienced homelessness, such as those memorialized in John Steinbeck's *The Grapes of Wrath*. These families left the central dust bowl states to look for work in the West. World War II and the booming postwar economy alleviated homelessness for the vast majority, leaving the skid rows of American cities to harbor the remaining homeless people. Thus, the skid rows in the 1950s and 1960s were inhabited primarily by older white men who had never been married, were extremely poor, suffered disabilities through age, alcoholism, or illness, and lived in cubicle rooms in "flophouse" hotels or in cheap single-room occupancy (SRO) hotels.

The word "homeless" in reference to the residents of skid row was used by researchers at the time to refer to the fact that these men lived outside of the family unit, not to their lack of shelter (Rossi 1989). Indeed, very few of the homeless men in skid row of the nineteenth or early twentieth century were without any shelter; the vast majority lived in inexpensive—and inadequate— hotels. Similarly, the men and families displaced in the Great Depression were known as "transients" and typically sought shelter at "transient camps" provided by federal relief agencies, or with relatives or friends.

It was not until the late 1970s and early 1980s that homelessness came to describe a widespread and growing phenomenon: people who literally had nowhere to sleep, no shelter of any kind—no home. Unlike the homeless people of previous decades, the new homeless population was younger and contained disproportionate numbers of minorities as well as many women and children. No longer concentrated in skid row, homeless people appeared throughout downtown areas, in suburbs, and in rural areas. Thus, contemporary homelessness was born. In the following decades, it grew unabated, and today, in many communities, it persists at record levels.

THE CAUSES OF HOMELESSNESS IN THE UNITED STATES

Two trends are largely responsible for the rise in homelessness in the United States: a growing shortage of affordable rental housing and a simultaneous increase in poverty. Federal policy choices and economic transformation underlie both trends.

Of particular significance was the ascendance of conservative Republicans to power in 1980, led by President Ronald Reagan. From tax policy to social deregulation to the assault on organized labor, the Reagan administration sought to spur economic recovery by enacting policies that benefited U.S. businesses and the wealthy at the expense of the poorest Americans. These policies created the preconditions for many poor people to experience homelessness. In addition, some Reagan-era policies had a more direct role in causing homelessness, particularly the massive cutbacks in almost every social program. The cumulative impact of these policies is staggering: during the Reagan years, cash aid to poor families (the Aid to Families with Dependent Children, or AFDC, program) was slashed, and eligibility tightened, three times, resulting in the elimination of 442,000 people (approximately two-thirds of whom were children) from the national caseload; 491,000 disabled people receiving Supplemental Security Income and Social Security Disability Insurance were removed from the rolls; and 1 million people lost food assistance (food stamps), while the remaining 20 million had their food stamp benefits reduced (Blau 1992). Housing programs received some of the largest cuts during the Reagan years: indeed, of all domestic cutbacks in the administration's first two years, 50 percent came from subsidized housing programs. The number of households receiving housing assistance dropped by nearly three-quarters under the Reagan administration, and production of new housing units plummeted (Blau, 1992).

Thus, Reagan-era polices played a critical role in the mushrooming homeless population of the 1980s. Moreover, economic transformation (increasing global competition and the shift to a service-based economy) and the continuation of federal policies benefiting business interests and scaling back social programming by subsequent administrations helped to fuel the growth of homelessness in the decade that followed.

The Declining Supply of Affordable Housing

The declining supply of affordable housing, and the limited scale of housing assistance programs, are the two most significant underlying causes of homelessness in the United States.

Between 1973 and 1993, 2.2 million low-rent housing units disappeared from the market. These units were abandoned, converted into condominiums or expensive apartments, or became unaffordable because of cost increases. Loss of affordable housing continued into the 1990s. Despite a rapidly growing economy, the affordable housing gap grew by 1 million between 1991 and 1995 (Daskal 1998). By 1995 the number of low-income renters in America outstripped the number of low-cost rental units by 4.4 million rental units—the largest shortfall on record. In 1997, for every 100 households at or below 30 percent of median income, only 36 units were both affordable and available for rent (U.S. Department of Housing and Urban Development 1999b).

The current paradox of economic growth and a worsening housing crisis can be explained by the fact that the strong U.S. economy has caused rents to soar, putting housing out of reach for the poorest Americans. Thus, at the current turn of the century, rents are rising at twice the rate of general inflation; they are also rising faster than income for the American households with the lowest incomes (U.S. Department of Housing and Urban Development 1999b). This has resulted in a significant loss of housing: between 1991 and 1997, 372,000 rental units affordable to very-low-income families were lost, a reduction of 5 percent. The loss of affordable housing for the poorest households puts increasing numbers of people at risk of homelessness.

Lack of affordable housing also has led to high rent burdens (rents which absorb a high proportion of income), overcrowding, and substandard housing. These phenomena, in turn, have not only forced many people to become homeless; they have put a large and growing number of people on the brink of homelessness: 5.3 million unassisted, very-low-income households had "worst-case needs" for housing assistance in 1995 (U.S. Department of Housing and Urban Development 1998).[1] This figure is an all-time high.

Government housing assistance programs can make the difference among stable housing, precarious housing, or no housing at all. However, the demand for assisted housing far exceeds the supply: only about one-third of poor renter households receive a housing subsidy from federal, state, or local governments (Daskal 1998). The limited level of housing assistance means that most poor families and individuals seeking housing assistance are placed on long waiting lists. In the late 1990s, the time households spent on waiting lists for federal housing assistance grew dramatically (U.S. Department of Housing and Urban Development 1999a). Lengthy waiting lists for public housing mean that people must remain in shelters or inadequate housing arrangements longer. Consequently, there is less shelter space available for other homeless people, who must find shelter elsewhere or live on the streets.

A housing trend with a particularly severe impact on homelessness is the loss of SRO housing. In the past, SRO housing housed many poor individuals, including poor persons suffering from mental illness or substance abuse. From 1970 to the mid-1980s, an estimated 1 million SRO units were demolished (Dolbeare 1996). The demolition of SRO housing was most notable in large cities: between 1970 and 1982, New York City lost 87 percent of its $200 per month or less SRO stock; Chicago experienced the total elimination of cubicle hotels; and by 1985, Los Angeles had lost more than half of its downtown SRO housing (Koegel et al. 1996). From 1975 to 1988, San Francisco lost 43 percent of its stock of low-cost residential hotels; from 1970 to 1986, Portland, Oregon, lost 59 percent of its residential hotels; and from 1971 to 1981, Denver lost 64 percent of its SRO hotels (Wright and Rubin 1997). Thus the destruction of SRO housing is a major factor in the growth of homelessness in many cities.

The loss of affordable housing in the United States, and the subsequent rise in homelessness, is directly linked to the decline in federal support for low-income housing. Budget authority for federal low-income housing programs peaked in 1978, at $66.6 billion in inflation-adjusted dollars, or 6.4 percent of all federal budget authority (Dolbeare 1999). Approximately 80 percent of this amount was spent on the provision of additional subsidized units or households. In the same year, outlays for low-income housing assistance cost $7.8 billion. Housing-related tax expenditures, primarily home-owner deductions, cost $33.4 billion. Between 1980 and 1988, however, the federal budget authority for low-income housing was cut by over 50 percent, from $64.9 billion to $31.6 million. The FY2000 budget calls for only $20.7 billion in low-income housing budget authority, or 1.4 percent of total budget authority. In contrast, housing-related tax expenditures, primarily home-owner deductions, 75 percent of which benefit households in the top fifth of income distribution, cost $105.8 billion.

The entitlement to deduct mortgage interest from income for tax purposes is, in fact, the largest federal housing program. This accounts for the fact that, in 1994, the top fifth of households received 61 percent of all federal housing benefits (tax and direct), while the bottom fifth received only 18 percent. In short, while federal policy makers have failed to respond to the needs of low-income households, they have enacted policies that disproportionately benefit the wealthiest Americans.

Persistent Poverty

Poverty in the United States is more prevalent in the late 1990s than it was during the 1970s, despite significant economic growth. Even more significant for discussions of homelessness is the proportion of poor people living in *extreme* poverty: in 1998, 13.9 million people—40 percent of all poor persons—

had incomes of less than half the poverty level (U.S. Bureau of the Census 1999a).

Two factors help account for increasing poverty: eroding employment opportunities for large segments of the workforce, and the declining value and availability of public assistance.

Work and Homelessness

Record economic growth and low unemployment rates mask a number of important factors that explain why homelessness has persisted or worsened in the United States. These factors include stagnant or falling incomes and less secure jobs that offer fewer benefits.

While there has been growth in real wages at all levels in the late 1990s, these increases have not been enough to make up for a long pattern of stagnant and declining wages in the 1980s and much of the 1990s. Low-wage workers have been particularly hard hit by these long-term wage trends. Despite recent increases in the minimum wage, the real value (that is, the inflation-adjusted value) of the minimum wage in 1997 was 18.1 percent less than in 1979 (Mishel, Bernstein, and Schmitt 1999). Factors contributing to wage declines include a steep drop in the number and bargaining power of unionized workers; the failure of the federal government to raise the minimum wage to keep up with inflation; a decline in manufacturing jobs and the corresponding expansion of lower-paying service-sector employment; globalization; and increased nonstandard work, such as temporary and part-time employment.

Declining wages, in turn, have put housing out of reach for many workers: in every state, metropolitan area, county, and town, more than the minimum wage is required to afford a one- or two-bedroom apartment at fair market rent (FMR)[2] (National Low Income Housing Coalition 1999). In fact, the median wage needed to afford a two-bedroom apartment is more than twice the minimum wage. Thus, 40 percent of households with worst-case housing needs—households paying over half their incomes for rent, living in severely substandard housing, or both—have at least one working person. This represents a 32 percent increase in working households with worst-case housing needs from 1993 to 1995 (U.S. Department of Housing and Urban Development 1998).

The connection between impoverished workers and homelessness can be seen in homeless shelters, many of which house significant numbers of full-time wage earners. A survey of 30 U.S. cities found that more than one in five homeless persons is employed (U.S. Conference of Mayors 1999). In a number of cities not surveyed by the U.S. Conference of Mayors, as well as in many states, the percentage is even higher (National Coalition for the Homeless 1997).

Moreover, the future of job growth does not appear promising for many workers: a 1998 study estimated that 46 percent of the jobs with the most projected growth between 1994 and 2005 pay less than $16,000 a year; these jobs will not lift families out of poverty (National Priorities Project and Jobs with Justice

1998).[3] Moreover, 74 percent of these jobs pay below a livable wage ($32,185 for a family of four).

Public Assistance and Homelessness

The declining value and availability of public assistance is another source of increasing poverty and homelessness. Until its repeal in August 1996, the largest cash assistance program for poor families with children was the Aid to Families with Dependent Children (AFDC) program. Between 1970 and 1994, the typical state's AFDC benefits for a family of three fell 47 percent, after adjusting for inflation (Greenberg and Baumohl 1996). The Personal Responsibility and Work Opportunity Reconciliation Act of 1996 (the federal welfare reform law) repealed the AFDC program and, with it, poor families' entitlement to cash assistance. The AFDC program was replaced by a block grant program called Temporary Assistance to Needy Families (TANF). TANF benefits and food stamps combined are below the poverty level in every state; in fact, the median TANF benefit for a family of three is approximately one-third of the poverty level. Thus, public assistance in the United States does not provide relief from poverty. Nor does it protect families from homelessness: a survey of homeless families in 22 U.S. communities found that 57 percent were receiving welfare (Homes for the Homeless 1999).

Welfare caseloads have dropped sharply since the passage and implementation of welfare reform legislation. However, declining welfare rolls simply mean that fewer people are receiving benefits—not that they are employed or doing better financially. Early findings suggest that although more families are moving from welfare to work, many of them are faring poorly due to low wages and inadequate work supports. Only a small fraction of welfare recipients' new jobs pay above-poverty wages; most of the new jobs pay far below the poverty line (Children's Defense Fund and the National Coalition for the Homeless 1998).

As a result of loss of benefits, low wages, and unstable employment, many families leaving welfare struggle to get medical care, food, and housing. Many lose health insurance, despite continued Medicaid eligibility: a recent study found that 675,000 people lost their health insurance in 1997 as a result of the federal welfare reform legislation, including 400,000 children (Families USA 1999). Housing is rarely affordable for families leaving welfare for low wages, yet subsidized housing is so limited that fewer than one in four TANF families nationwide lives in public housing or receives a housing voucher to help them rent a private unit. Thus, for most families leaving the rolls, housing subsidies are not an option. As a result, former welfare families experience increased housing instability: a seven-site survey of former and current welfare recipients seeking human services found that former recipients were more likely than current recipients to have doubled-up living arrangements to save money (25 percent compared to 15 percent), more than twice as likely to have moved because they could not pay the rent, and nearly twice as likely to report that a child had to change schools because of a family move (Children's Defense Fund and the

National Coalition for the Homeless 1998). In some communities, former welfare families appear to be experiencing homelessness in increasing numbers. A survey of homeless families in 22 cities found that 37 percent had their welfare benefits cut or reduced in the last year; among families who had their benefits cut or reduced, 20 percent said they became homeless as a result (Homes for the Homeless 1999).

A sizable portion of the welfare population experience domestic violence at any given time: estimates of the percentage of women recipients who experience abuse range from 20 to 80 percent (Institute for Women's Policy Research 1997). In the absence of cash assistance, and without affordable housing, women who experience domestic violence may be at increased risk of homelessness or compelled to live with a former or current abuser in order to prevent homelessness.

While research on the impact of welfare reform is still in its infancy, census data indicate one clear outcome: an increase in extreme child poverty. In 1996 family income from cash assistance and food stamps kept more than 3.6 million children above half of the poverty line. By 1997, however, these two programs kept fewer than 3 million children from extreme poverty—652,000 fewer children than the year before. Had cash assistance and food stamp income remained constant, the number of extremely poor children would have shrunk by 226,000 in 1997, owing to rising employment and growth in non-welfare income among the poorest families (Children's Defense Fund 1999). Instead, the weakening of assistance allowed 426,000 more children to fall into extreme poverty. Together, food stamps and cash assistance programs for low-income families reduced the child poverty gap (the total amount by which the incomes of all children who are poor fall below the poverty line) by 37 percent in 1995, but only by 27 percent in 1998. Consequently, the average amount by which poor children fall below the poverty line increased between 1995 and 1998, reaching the highest level recorded since data on this issue first were collected in 1979 (Porter and Primus 1999).

In addition to the reduction in the value and availability of welfare benefits for families, recent policy changes have reduced or eliminated public assistance for poor single individuals. Several states have cut or eliminated cash assistance for single impoverished people, despite evidence that its availability reduces the prevalence of homelessness (Greenberg and Baumohl 1996).

Disabled people, too, must struggle to obtain and maintain stable housing. In 1998, on a national average, a person receiving Supplemental Security Income (SSI) benefits had to spend 69 percent of his or her SSI monthly income to rent a one-bedroom apartment at fair market rent; in more than 125 housing market areas, the cost of a one-bedroom apartment at fair market rent was more than a person's total monthly SSI income (Technical Assistance Collaborative and the Consortium for Citizens with Disabilities Housing Task Force 1999).

As with housing, the paradox of economic growth and persistent poverty becomes obvious. The benefits of economic growth have not been equally distributed; instead, they have been concentrated at the top of the income and wealth distributions. Income inequality remains at its highest level since the U.S. Census began tracking the data in 1947. With the economy performing very well by most indicators, this suggests that inequality is highly intractable, and that more will have to be done on a policy level to address it.

Thus, in summary, a rising tide does not lift all boats, and in the United States today, many boats are struggling to stay afloat.

Other Factors Contributing to Homelessness in the United States

Particularly in circumstances marked by poverty and lack of affordable housing, certain additional factors enhance the chances of becoming homeless. These include lack of affordable health care, domestic violence, mental illness, and addiction disorders.

Lack of Affordable Health Care

For families and individuals struggling to pay the rent, a serious illness or disability can start a downward spiral into homelessness, beginning with a lost job, depletion of savings to pay for care, and eventual eviction. In 1998 approximately 44.3 million Americans had no health care insurance (U.S. Bureau of the Census 1999b). More than a third of persons living in poverty had no health insurance of any kind. The coverage held by many others would not carry them through a catastrophic illness.

Domestic Violence

Battered women who live in poverty are often forced to choose between abusive relationships and homelessness. Lack of affordable housing and long waiting lists for assisted housing mean that many women and their children are forced to choose between abuse at home and the streets. Nationally, an estimated 18 percent of homeless parents who had previously lived in their own apartments reported that they left their residences because of domestic violence (Homes for the Homeless 1999). In addition, 58 percent of cities surveyed by the U.S. Conference of Mayors identified domestic violence as a primary cause of homelessness (U.S. Conference of Mayors 1999).

Mental Illness

Approximately 20 to 25 percent of the single adult homeless population suffers from some form of severe and persistent mental illness (Koegel et al. 1996). Despite the disproportionate number of severely mentally ill people among the homeless population, increases in homelessness are not attributable to the release of severely mentally ill people from institutions. Most patients were released from mental hospitals in the 1950s and 1960s, yet vast increases in homelessness did not occur until the 1980s, when incomes and housing options for those living on the margins began to diminish rapidly. According to the Federal Task Force on Homelessness and Severe Mental Illness, only 5 to 7 percent of homeless persons with mental illness need to be institutionalized; most can live in the community with the appropriate supportive housing options (Federal Task Force on Homelessness and Severe Mental Illness 1992). However, many mentally ill, homeless people are unable to obtain access to supportive housing and other treatment services. The mental health support services most needed include case management, housing, and treatment.

Addiction Disorders

The relationship between addiction and homelessness is complex and controversial. While rates of alcohol and drug abuse are disproportionately high among the homeless population, the increase in homelessness over the past two decades cannot be explained by addiction alone. Many people who are addicted to alcohol and drugs never become homeless, but people who are poor and addicted are clearly at increased risk of homelessness. During the 1980s, competition for increasingly scarce low-income housing grew so intense that those with disabilities, such as addiction and mental illness, were more likely to lose out and find themselves on the streets. The loss of SRO housing, a source of stability for many poor people suffering from addiction and mental illness, was a major factor in increased homelessness in many communities.

Addiction does increase the risk of displacement for the precariously housed; in the absence of appropriate treatment, it may doom one's chances of getting housing once on the streets. Homeless people often face insurmountable barriers to obtaining health care, including addictive disorder treatment services and recovery supports. The following are among the obstacles to treatment for homeless persons: lack of health insurance, lack of documentation, waiting lists, scheduling difficulties, daily contact requirements, lack of transportation, ineffective treatment methods, lack of supportive services, and cultural insensitivity. An in-depth study of 13 communities across the nation revealed service gaps in every community in at least one stage of the treatment and recovery continuum for homeless people (National Coalition for the Homeless 1998).

Even when disabling conditions such as addiction or mental illness are treated, homeless addicts and mentally ill people must compete with all other poor people for a dwindling supply of low-income housing. Homelessness can thus be seen as a perverse game of musical chairs, in which the loss of "chairs" (low-cost housing) forces some people to be left standing (homeless). Those who are least able to secure a chair—the most disabled and therefore the most vulnerable—are the most likely to be left without a place to sit.

WHO BECOMES HOMELESS? THE DEMOGRAPHICS OF AMERICAN HOMELESSNESS

The population of people who experience homelessness in the United States is diverse; it encompasses all age and ethnic groups. However, persons living in poverty are most at risk of becoming homeless; demographic groups that are more likely to experience poverty are also more likely to experience homelessness. The homeless population in the United States is therefore disproportionately young, nonwhite, and disabled.

According to the U.S. Conference of Mayors 1999 study of homelessness in 26 American cities, the urban homeless population is composed of single men (43 percent); single women (13 percent); families with children (37 percent); and unaccompanied youth (7 percent). It is also 50 percent African American, 31 percent Caucasian, 13 percent Hispanic, 4 percent Native American, and 2 percent Asian.

Research indicates that 33 percent of homeless men have served in the armed forces, as compared to 31 percent of the general adult male population (Burt et al. 1999). The majority of these men (78 percent) served before or after the Vietnam era.

Homelessness in the United States is often assumed to be an exclusively urban phenomenon, because homeless people are more numerous, geographically concentrated, and visible in urban areas. However, many people experience homelessness and housing distress in America's small towns and rural areas. Understanding rural homelessness requires a more flexible definition of homelessness, given the few shelters in rural areas. People experiencing homelessness in rural areas are less likely to live on the street or in a shelter, and more likely to live in a car or camper, or with relatives in overcrowded or substandard housing. Studies comparing urban and rural homeless populations have shown that homeless people in rural areas are more likely to be white, female, married, currently working, homeless for the first time, and homeless for a shorter period of time (U.S. Department of Agriculture 1996). Other research indicates that families, single mothers, and children make up the largest group of people who are homeless in rural areas (Vissing 1996). Homelessness among Native Americans and migrant workers is also largely a rural phenomenon. Studies also reveal higher rates of domestic violence and lower rates of alcohol and substance abuse among the rural homeless population (U.S. Department of Agriculture 1996).

Homeless Families with Children

Perhaps the most shocking trend in American homelessness is the growing number of homeless families with children. The number of poor people increased 41 percent between 1979 and 1990; families and children under 18 accounted for more than half of that increase (U.S. House of Representatives 1992). Today, families with children constitute approximately 40 percent of people who become homeless (Shinn and Weitzman 1996).

Single mothers head approximately 85 percent of homeless families; the average homeless family comprises a young woman with two young children (Better Homes Fund 1999). Like homeless individuals, homeless families are extremely poor; the estimated average income of homeless families is less than half the federal poverty level (Burt et al. 1999). Unsurprisingly, homeless mothers suffer from higher rates of depressive disorders and other illnesses such as asthma, anemia, and ulcers, than other women. An estimated 39 percent have been hospitalized for medical treatment (Better Homes Fund 1999).

Homelessness breaks up families. Families may be separated as a result of shelter policies that deny access to older boys or fathers. Separations may also be caused by placement of children into foster care when their parents become homeless. In addition, parents may leave their children with relatives and friends in order to save them from the ordeal of homelessness or to permit them to continue attending their regular school. Nationally, 60 percent of homeless women are parents of minor children, but only 39 percent live with at least one of them; 41 percent of homeless men are parents of minor children, but only 7 percent live with one or more of their children (Burt et al. 1999). One-fifth of homeless children are estimated to be separated from their parents (Better Homes Fund 1999).

Children are more vulnerable to deep poverty and homelessness than any other population in the United States. In New York City and Philadelphia, for example, children are more likely to experience homelessness than the general population: nearly 8 percent of the cities' African American children used the public shelter system over a three-year period in Philadelphia and a five-year period in New York City. Nationally, children make up 39 percent of people living in poverty, but only 26 percent of the total population (U.S. Bureau of the Census 1999a). In fact, the poverty rate for children is almost twice as high as the poverty rate for any other age group.

It is not surprising, therefore, that a growing number of children are without homes. In some states, children under the age of 18 represent the majority of persons who are homeless; for example, 50 percent of all sheltered homeless persons in Minnesota, 64 percent of those seeking shelter in Oregon, and 55 percent of homeless people in Iowa (Duffield 2000). In 1997 states reported 625,330 *school-age* homeless children (U.S. Department of Education 1999). Alarmingly, it is estimated that over 40 percent of children in shelters are under the age of five (Homes for the Homeless 1999). Based on these numbers, the National Coalition for the Homeless estimates that over 1 million children in the United States experience homelessness over the course of a year.

Homelessness wounds children. Homeless children are in fair or poor health twice as often as other children; they suffer three times as many stomach problems, five times as many diarrheal infections, fifty percent more ear infections, and twice as many hospitalizations (Homes for the Homeless 1999). Homeless children are four times more likely to be asthmatic (the number one cause of school absences); twice as likely to experience hunger; and four times more likely to have delayed development (Better Homes Fund 1999). More than one-fifth of homeless children between three and six years of age have emotional problems that are serious enough to require professional care. School-age homeless children struggle with serious mental health problems: nearly one-third have a major mental disorder that interferes with daily activities, compared to 19 percent of other children. Despite these higher rates of mental health problems, less than a third of homeless children who might benefit from treatment actually receive it (Better Homes Fund 1999).

Homeless children also face numerous barriers to educational success. Deep poverty, high mobility, and school requirements often make attending and succeeding in school a challenge for homeless students. Residency requirements, guardianship requirements, delays in transfer of school records, lack of transportation, and lack of immunization records often prevent homeless children from enrolling in school. Moreover, homeless children and youth who are able to enroll in school face barriers to regular attendance: the FY1997 U.S. Department of Education Report to Congress reported that 45 percent of homeless children and youth were not attending school on a regular basis during their homelessness (U.S. Department of Education 1999).

In addition to enrollment problems, the high mobility associated with homelessness has severe educational consequences. Homeless families move frequently owing to limits on the length of shelter stays, or in search of safe and affordable housing or employment, or to escape abusive partners. All too often, homeless children have to change schools because shelters or other temporary accommodations are not located in their school district. An estimated 40 percent of homeless children attend two different schools, while 28 percent attend three or more different schools (Better Homes Fund 1999).

Every time a child has to change schools, his or her education is disrupted. According to some estimates, 4 to 6 months of education are lost with every move (Homes for the Homeless 1999). It is estimated that 14 percent of homeless children repeat a grade because they have moved to a new school, compared with 5 percent of other children (Better Homes Fund 1999). Homeless children are thus at high risk of falling behind in school as a result of their mobility. Overall, homeless children are twice as likely as other children to repeat a grade, and often perform below grade level because of frequent moves and school absences.

In response to these barriers, the U.S. Congress passed the Stewart B. McKinney Homeless Assistance Act in 1987. Title VIB of the McKinney Act entitles homeless children and youth to a free, appropriate education, and it also provides funding for states and school districts to help homeless children and youth enroll, attend, and succeed in school. According to the most recent U.S. Department of Education Report to Congress, 88 percent of homeless children and youth are enrolled in school, a significant increase in school access.

Despite these federal protections, many barriers to homeless children's enrollment and success in school remain. Continuing barriers to enrollment in school include guardianship and immunization requirements, transportation problems, and school fees (Anderson et al. 1995). Barriers to success in school include family mobility, poor health, and lack of food, clothing, and school supplies. These barriers remain, in large part, owing to the pitiful amount of funding allocated to the McKinney Act's education program: only 4 percent of all school districts in the country receive McKinney Act funding to help homeless children and youth enroll, attend, and succeed in school (National Association for the Education of Homeless Children and Youth and National Coalition for the Homeless 1999). As a result, states were able to provide direct services only to 37 percent of their estimated populations of homeless children in the 1997–1998 school year.

As the data above powerfully illustrate, homeless children's lives are marked by trauma—trauma that can damage their opportunities for healthy, stable lives as adults. It should come as no surprise that experiencing homelessness as a child significantly increases one's chances of being homeless as an adult: in a recent national study, 21 percent of homeless adults reported childhood experiences of homelessness; 27 percent lived in foster care; and 22 percent were forced to leave home (Burt et al. 1999).

POLICY AND PROGRAMMATIC RESPONSES TO HOMELESSNESS

In the early 1980s, the initial responses to widespread and increasing homelessness were primarily local. Homelessness was viewed by the Reagan administration as a problem that did not require federal intervention. In 1983, the first federal task force on homelessness was created to provide information to localities on how to obtain surplus federal property for homelessness assistance; this task force did not address homelessness through programmatic or policy actions.

In the years that followed, advocates around the country demanded that the federal government acknowledge homelessness as a national problem requiring a national response. With this goal in mind, the Homeless Persons' Survival Act was introduced in both houses of Congress in 1986. This act contained emergency relief measures, preventive measures, and long-term solutions to homelessness. Only small pieces of this proposal, however, were enacted into law. The first, the Homeless Eligibility Clarification Act of 1986, removed permanent address requirements and other barriers to existing programs. Also in 1986, the Homeless Housing Act was adopted. This legislation created the Emergency Shelter Grant program and a transitional housing demonstration program; the Department of Housing and Urban Development (HUD) administered both programs.

In late 1986, legislation containing Title I of the Homeless Persons' Survival Act—emergency relief provisions for shelter, food, mobile health care, and transitional housing—was introduced as the Urgent Relief for the Homeless Act. After an intensive advocacy campaign, the legislation was passed by large bipartisan majorities in both houses of Congress in 1987. After the death of its chief Republican sponsor, Representative Stewart B. McKinney of Connecticut, the act was renamed the Stewart B. McKinney Homeless Assistance Act. It was signed into law by a reluctant President Ronald Reagan on July 22, 1987.

Today, the McKinney Act remains the only major federal legislative response to homelessness. It authorizes programs that provide emergency shelter, food assistance, transitional housing, primary and mental health care, and education, as well as job training for veterans. These programs have saved lives and helped hundreds of thousands of Americans to regain stability.

While inadequate funding clearly impedes the effectiveness of the McKinney Act programs, the McKinney Act's greatest weakness is its focus on emergency measures—it responds to the symptoms of homelessness, not its causes. In the absence of legislation addressing the lack of affordable housing and livable incomes, homelessness in the United States has increased rather than abated.

The inadequacy of measures to address homelessness has led, in turn, to a new and increasingly common response to homelessness: criminalization. A survey of the 50 largest U.S. cities found that 86 percent have enacted anti-panhandling laws, and 73 percent have established anti-sleeping (on the street) laws (National Law Center on Homelessness & Poverty 1999). Some cities have even gone so far as to outlaw sitting in certain public areas. Over half of the cities surveyed responded to the problem of increased homelessness by conducting "police sweeps" to remove people who are homeless from the public eye. Homeless persons are either jailed or transported to suburban or rural areas where scarce resources and services for people who are homeless are even more difficult, if not impossible, to find. Even church activists and social service providers have come under attack for providing services to people who are poor, hungry, and homeless.

Anti-homeless activities are widespread in cities with admitted shortages of emergency shelter, affordable housing, and jobs that pay a living wage. Despite the tremendous expansion of the shelter system, demand for emergency shelter far exceeds supply throughout the country. Many homeless people have no choice but to live on the streets or other public places. The move toward the criminalization of homelessness by many American cities is a tragic statement—indeed a concession—of the nation's lack of progress toward addressing one of its most visible and persistent social ills.

RECOMMENDATIONS FOR ENDING HOMELESSNESS

Over the past twenty years, homeless advocates have developed recommendations for ending homelessness that, given its causes, appear obvious: affordable housing, livable income jobs, education and training for those jobs, adequate incomes for those who cannot work, accessible and affordable health care, and civil rights protections. These recommendations have been echoed in countless campaigns, policy proposals, programs, and legislation. While progress has been made in some areas, there has been no sustained effort to end homelessness in the United States.

This lack of success is attributable to numerous complex social, economic, and historical factors that transcend homelessness itself. Distrust of government and, particularly, of redistributionist policies; urban gentrification; ideologies of individualism, "self-help," and "personal responsibility"; and racism, sexism, and classism have all played their part in the debate on homelessness and the larger debate on poverty of which it is a part. Together, they have made achieving a political consensus on the measures for ending homelessness difficult, if not impossible. *In short, the problem has never been a lack of good ideas or well-crafted policy proposals to end homelessness; rather, it has been the complete lack of public and political will to implement them.*

Among the greatest barriers to effective action to end homelessness are lack of understanding and support from the American public. Americans know little about the causes and realities of homelessness. Media and politicians propagate stereotypes of homeless people as single adults disabled by addiction or mental illness who are to blame for their conditions and who choose homelessness as a lifestyle. Thus, the many faces of homelessness in the United States go unrecognized, as does the fact that in the United States, homelessness is a *poverty* problem. Its principal solutions involve measures to alleviate poverty, and, most important, that which defines homelessness—the lack of housing. Yet without a public will to end homelessness, there is no political will. As long as the American public is ignorant about the realities of homelessness and the devastation it brings, it will remain silent at the polls, or worse, continue to elect policy makers who demonize poor people and enact measures that deepen their suffering.

Some homeless advocates have embarked upon creative efforts to increase public understanding and support through media campaigns, street newspapers, the Internet, "awareness" weeks, and speakers' bureaus. While these activities have resulted in isolated victories, their long-term impact is difficult to gauge. Moreover, the scope of current public awareness efforts pales in comparison to what is needed to change the dialogue on poverty and homelessness in the United States. National, state, and local advocates must give priority to efforts to engage their communities in discussions of the realities of homelessness. They must work to create a dialogue between housed and homeless Americans—a dialogue that will bridge the ever-widening gulf between those who can afford housing and those who cannot. Only then will solutions to homelessness garner the public support, and thereby create the political will, to end homelessness in the United States.

There is another critical—indeed, essential—element missing from current efforts to end homelessness: the participation and leadership of poor and homeless people themselves. Homelessness in the United States is political; it has resulted from the choices of policy makers who have acted to protect the interests of their wealthy constituencies at the expense of the poorest citizens. Homelessness is thus a form of economic oppression and injustice. With similar forms of oppression in American history—those experienced by workers, African Americans, and women—change has occurred only as the result of protest movements led by those who are directly affected. Whites did not lead the civil rights movement; men did not lead women's struggle for equality.

Yet, with very few exceptions, current efforts to alleviate poverty and its extreme form—homelessness—are led by people who have never experienced poverty or homelessness. Homeless and formerly homeless people are involved in some advocacy organizations, from local coalitions to board membership on the National Coalition for the Homeless. However, in all but a handful of cases, they are not in leadership positions. The lack of widespread participation and leadership by poor and homeless people in efforts to end poverty and homelessness has led to a troubling phenomenon: the invisibility of poor and homeless people, and the absence of their voices from public debate on the subject. Rarely is a group of people so often *talked about*, rather than *talked to* as active participants in the dialogue about them. This in turn has led to the objectification and dehumanization of individuals who experience homelessness as "the homeless," a monolithic and static group that is easily stereotyped and patronized, even by those who are advocating on their behalf.

Service providers, advocates, and others must support poor and homeless people's active involvement as *decision makers* in efforts to alleviate poverty and end homelessness. This approach calls into question the role of professionals as "experts"; it also questions the operation of industries, such as homelessness research, service provision, and advocacy, which are dependent upon homelessness for their continued existence. Such industries may create conflicting interests and ultimately weaken advocacy efforts. Poor and homeless people have the best insights into their needs and interests; they therefore should be in the forefront of efforts to end the conditions from which they suffer.

A generation of Americans has grown up with widespread homelessness. No longer a "new" phenomenon demanding action, homelessness *appears* to be an intractable problem, an immutable aspect of the urban landscape. Without protracted efforts to push the issue of homelessness to the center of the American public's attention, and without poor and homeless people leading these efforts, the United States will continue to relegate increasing numbers of its most vulnerable citizens to the despair and misery of Third World conditions, making a mockery of its pretensions to be a land of justice, equal opportunity, and prosperity.

REFERENCES

Anderson, L. M., M. I. Janger, and K. L. M. Panton. 1995. *An Evaluation of State Local Efforts to Serve the Educational Needs of Homeless Children and Youth*. Washington, D.C.: Policy Study Associates.

Baumohl, J., ed. 1996. *Homelessness in America*. Phoenix, Ariz.: Oryx Press. This book is one of the most comprehensive and authoritative publications available on the broad social issue of American homelessness. It features 20 essays on key policy-related issues by 37 leading researchers, advocates, and other specialists.

Better Homes Fund. 1999. *America's New Outcasts: Homeless Children*. Newton: Better
    Homes Fund. This powerful report illustrates the devastation homelessness brings
    to young lives in statistical and human terms.

Blau, Joel. 1992. *The Visible Poor: Homelessness in the United States*. New York: Ox-
    ford University Press.

Burt, M., L. Aron, T. Douglas, J. Valente, E. Lee, and B. Iwen. 1999. *The Forgotten
    Americans—Homelessness: Programs and the People They Serve*. Washington,
    D.C.: Interagency Council on the Homeless.

Children's Defense Fund. 1999. *Extreme Child Poverty Rises by More Than 400,000 in
    One Year*. Washington, D.C.: Children's Defense Fund.

Children's Defense Fund and National Coalition for the Homeless. 1998. *Welfare to
    What: Early Findings on Family Hardship and Well-being*. Washington, D.C.:
    Children's Defense Fund and National Coalition for the Homeless.

Daskal, Jennifer. 1998. *In Search of Shelter: The Growing Shortage of Affordable Rental
    Housing*. Washington, D.C.: Center on Budget and Policy Priorities.

Dolbeare, Cushing. 1996. "Housing Policy: A General Consideration." In *Homelessness
    in America*, ed. Jim Baumohl. Phoenix, Ariz.: Oryx Press.

———. 1999. *Proposed Federal Housing Trust Fund*. Washington, D.C.: National Low
    Income Housing Coalition.

Duffield, Barbara. 2000. "Advocating for Homeless Students." In *Promising Practices
    for Educating Homeless Students*, ed. James Stronge. Larchmont, N.Y.: Eye on
    Education.

Families USA. 1999. *Losing Health Insurance: The Unintended Consequences of Welfare
    Reform*. Washington, D.C.: Families USA.

Federal Task Force on Homelessness and Severe Mental Illness. 1992. *Outcasts on Main
    Street: A Report of the Federal Task Force on Homelessness and Severe Mental
    Illness*. Delmar, N.Y.: National Resource Center on Homelessness and Mental
    Illness.

Greenberg, Mark, and Jim Baumohl. 1996. "Income Maintenance: Little Help Now, Less
    on the Way." In *Homelessness in America*, ed. Jim Baumohl. Phoenix, Ariz.:
    Oryx Press.

Hamberg, Jill, and Kim Hopper. 1984. *The Making of America's Homeless: From Skid
    Row to New Poor 1945–1984*. New York: Community Service Society. This
    classic work offers the definitive historical perspective on homelessness in the
    United States.

Homes for the Homeless. 1999. *Homeless in America: A Children's Story. Part One*.
    New York: Homes for the Homeless and the Institute for Children and Poverty.

Institute for Women's Policy Research. 1997. "Domestic Violence and Welfare Receipt."
    IWPR Welfare Reform Network News 4:1.

Koegel, P., M. A. Burnam, and J. Baumohl. 1996. "The Causes of Homelessness." In
    Homelessness in America, ed. Jim Baumohl. Phoenix, Ariz.: Oryx Press.

Kozol, Jonathon. 1988. *Rachel and Her Children: Homeless Families in America*. West-
    minster, Md.: Random House. Kozol's landmark book examines family home-
    lessness in America through narratives of individual homeless women and
    children.

Mishel, L., J. Bernstein, and J. Schmitt. 1999. *The State of Working America: 1998–99*.
    Washington, D.C.: Economic Policy Institute.

National Association for the Education of Homeless Children and Youth and National

Coalition for the Homeless. 1999. *Making the Grade: Successes and Challenges in Providing Educational Opportunities for Homeless Children and Youth.* Washington, D.C.: National Coalition for the Homeless.

National Coalition for the Homeless. 1997. *Homeless in America: Unabated and Increasing.* Washington, D.C.: National Coalition for the Homeless. Written on the occasion of the tenth anniversary of the McKinney Act, this report provides 10-year historical profiles of homelessness in 11 urban, rural, and suburban communities and four states. Every community profile includes an interview with a person who has worked in the community on homelessness issues for 10 years or longer. Community and national advocates discuss the past, present, and future, and provide insights into solutions to homelessness.

————. 1998. *No Open Door: Breaking the Lock on Addiction Recovery for Homeless People.* Washington, D.C.: National Coalition for the Homeless.

National Law Center on Homelessness & Poverty. 1999. *Out of Sight—Out of Mind?* Washington, D.C.: National Law Center on Homelessness & Poverty.

National Low Income Housing Coalition. 1999. *Out of Reach: The Gap between Housing Costs and Income of Poor People in the United States.* Washington, D.C.: National Low Income Housing Coalition.

National Priorities Project and Jobs with Justice. 1998. *Working Hard, Earning Less: The Future of Job Growth in America.* Northampton, Mass.: National Priorities Project and Jobs with Justice.

Porter, Kathryn, and Wendell Primus. 1999. *Recent Changes in the Impact of the Safety Net on Child Poverty.* Washington, D.C.: Center on Budget and Policy Priorities.

Quint, Sharon. 1994. *Schooling Homeless Children: A Working Model for America's Public Schools.* New York: Teachers College Press.

Rossi, Peter. 1989. *Down and Out in America: The Origins of Homelessness.* Chicago: University of Chicago Press.

Shinn, Mary Beth, and Beth Weitzman. 1996. "Homeless Families Are Different." In *Homelessness in America*, ed. Jim Baumohl. Phoenix, Ariz.: Oryx Press.

Street Sheet: A Publication of the Coalition on Homelessness, San Francisco. San Francisco: Coalition on Homelessness. *Street Sheet* is a monthly newspaper written by poor and homeless people in San Francisco, California. This unique publication offers news analysis, policy proposals, and personal commentary from the perspective of homeless individuals and families. It is sold on the streets of San Francisco by homeless vendors, who keep 100 percent of the money earned through their sales. Smart, engaging, and powerful testimony is provided in each and every issue.

Technical Assistance Collaborative, Inc., and the Consortium for Citizens with Disabilities Housing Task Force. 1999. *Priced Out in 1998: The Housing Crisis for People with Disabilities.* Boston, Mass.: Technical Assistance Collaborative.

U.S. Bureau of the Census. 1999a. *Poverty in the United States: 1998. Current Population Reports, Series P60–207.* Washington, D.C.: U.S. Bureau of the Census.

————. 1999b. *Health Insurance Coverage: 1998. Current Population Reports, Series P60–208.* Washington, D.C.: U.S. Bureau of the Census.

U.S. Conference of Mayors. 1999. *A Status Report on Hunger and Homelessness in America's Cities: 1999.* Washington, D.C.: U.S. Conference of Mayors.

U.S. Department of Agriculture. 1996. *Rural Homelessness: Focusing on the Needs of the Rural Homeless.* Washington, D.C.: U.S. Department of Agriculture.

U.S. Department of Education. 1999. *FY 1997 Report to Congress on the Education of Homeless Children and Youth.* Washington, D.C.: U.S. Department of Education.

U.S. Department of Housing and Urban Development. 1998. *Rental Housing Assistance—The Crisis Continues: 1997 Report to Congress on Worst Case Housing Needs.* Washington, D.C.: U.S. Department of Housing and Urban Development.

———. 1999a. *Waiting in Vain: An Update on America's Housing Crisis.* Washington, D.C.: U.S. Department of Housing and Urban Development.

———. 1999b. *The Widening Gap: New Findings on Housing Affordability in America.* Washington, D.C.: U.S. Department of Housing and Urban Development.

U.S. House of Representatives. Committee on Ways and Means. 1992. *Overview of Entitlement Programs: 1992 Green Book.* Washington, D.C.: U.S. Government Printing Office.

Vissing, Yvonne. 1996. *Out of Sight, Out of Mind: Homeless Children and Families in Small-Town America.* Lexington; University Press of Kentucky.

Wright, James, and Beth Rubin. 1997. "Is Homelessness a Housing Problem?" In *Understanding Homelessness: New Policy and Research Perspectives.* Washington, D.C.: Fannie Mae Foundation.

NOTES

1. Worst-case needs refers to those renters with incomes below 50 percent of the area median income who are involuntarily displaced, or pay more than half of their income for rent and live in substandard housing.

2. FMRs are the monthly amounts "needed to rent privately owned, decent, safe, and sanitary rental housing of a modest (nonluxury) nature with suitable amenities." 62 *Federal Register* 50724 (September 26, 1997). HUD determines FMRs for localities in all 50 states.

3. The poverty line for a family of three is $12,750; for a family of four, $16,813.

9

Bringing It All Back Home: Homelessness and Alternative Housing Policies among Urban Squatters in Buenos Aires, Argentina

VALERIA PROCUPEZ AND MARIA CARLA RODRIGUEZ

> Profound errors must predominate in the legislation of Latin American countries, when almost all the actions performed daily by millions of people in order to survive are considered illegal.
>
> —Jorge Enrique Hardoy

INTRODUCTION

Squatting, or the illegal occupancy of a house or building, is today the most extended informal housing modality in Buenos Aires. Due to the lack of affordable adequate housing in the city, people have opted for the practice of taking over and setting down in vacant residential buildings and abandoned warehouses scattered in different neighborhoods in the central area. According to our estimates, this phenomenon, initiated in the 1980s, involves around 150,000 inhabitants in a city with a population of about 3 million. This is why we have considered it appropriate to include squatting within the notion of "homelessness." This category encompasses a spectrum of vulnerable housing situations, meaning that they imply the risk of becoming homeless. Homelessness is not just defined by people living in the streets, squatting, or renting rooms in family hotels, *inquilinatos* (tenement houses), and *villas miseria* (shantytowns)—all constitute the possibilities low-income sectors use to solve their housing problems. Analytically speaking, they compose the critical housing deficit in Buenos Aires. In the last years, there has been an increase in the number of people in the city living in the streets. This situation, though, is limited and recent, and it has received some attention from local authorities who have developed programs involving shelters and social assistance. Squatting, however, is an older, far more extended and encompassing problem which has never really been seriously targeted as the object of public policies, and it receives little attention from the public in general, except for the stigmatization of the people involved and the occurrence of forced evictions that immediately attract the media and generate discourses about illegality. Nevertheless, the squatting in buildings in the city is a relevant social phenomenon which, due to its scattered nature, implies a deployment of poverty within the urban interstices.

During the 1990s, Buenos Aires has undergone a profound transformation of the built environment. Local effects of globalization trends that become inscribed in the urban landscape seem to generate a pattern of expulsion of low-income sectors from areas of the city that are currently required by corporate agents for development and investment. These trends enhance urban segregation and thus jeopardize the unfolding of conditions for the socio-spatial heterogeneity that is inherent to a really democratic city.

This chapter presents a brief history of housing deficit in Buenos Aires, and a more detailed description of the situation in the last two decades. Its focus is particularly on the development of urban squatting and a discussion of the inefficiency of the public policies applied by local authorities. As a conclusion, drawing from the experiences of a grassroots housing organization, we present systematized implications of the principle of self-management (*autogestion*) for the design of housing public policies elaborated on the basis of real needs and with the active participation of the beneficiaries involved.

ARGENTINA IN THE GLOBAL CONTEXT: THE NEOLIBERAL POLICIES OF THE LAST DECADES AND THEIR EFFECTS

Like most other countries in Latin America, Argentina is currently undergoing the process of opening its economy to a globalized world market. In general terms, this can be considered as the third economic wave the country has known throughout the twentieth century. In effect, after an extended epoch of economic outward expansion, which started at the turn of the century and was based on the export of cattle and agricultural products (mainly grains and beef), the country entered a period of internal readjustments. The first moment—characterized by a significant increase in the population as a result of an enormous mass of European immigrants who entered the country—ended in the 1930s. From then on, Argentina suffered decades of political and institutional instability, where military coup d'états interrupted every democratically elected government. Social mobility became stagnant when immigration decreased in the interwar period. The second epoch can be defined by a time of incipient industrialization, through the modality of "import substitution," which was encouraged during the 1940s and 1950s and aimed at developing the manufacture of consumer products and reinforcing the internal market. This trend accentuated the already dominant tendency toward urbanization in the country. Nevertheless, when the military took over the government yet once more in 1976–1983, an economic agenda that prioritized foreign interests and the opening of the markets was set in motion. It is not possible to describe here each of the phases of this transformation process, but it is relevant to remark that it was installed through violence. Actually, the first market opening measures were accompanied by a process of severe social disciplining in which terror was a structural feature.[1] Although the general economic trend has mainly been maintained since then, with the advent of democracy in the 1980s, there was an attempt to soften the regressive effects of this system. These efforts culminated with a peak of hyperinflation in 1989.[2]

The 1990s found the country applying globally acclaimed neoliberal reforms based principally on two generalized trends: the privatization of publicly owned companies and functions and the deregulation of state intervention in various markets, including the labor market. The "law of convertibility,"[3] which establishes an equity between the peso and the U.S. dollar, is one of the tools that has been applied to stabilize the economy as part of the all-encompassing adjustment policies. The strategies of free-market economic policies, regional economic alliances, rapprochement with neighboring countries, and disengagement of the state have attempted to globalize Argentina's economy and society. But, reportedly, the growth of the gross national product (GNP) does not necessarily entail positive effects on all sectors unless a benefit reallocation is redefined. Parallel to the flourishing of certain sectors of the economy, therefore, these trends have implied as their counterpart social polarization, rising unemployment, eroding middle-class lifestyles, deindustrialization, and declining health and social welfare (Keeling 1996). These features are the result of the same processes of concentration of capital and flexibility which involve reduction of the workforce, the lowering of labor costs, and pervasive deregulation to ensure competitive advantage with other countries and world regions in the struggle to attract transnational investments. Furthermore, the segmentation of the Argentinean productive structure, as well as the severe underutilization of the labor force implied, depicts the trend of capital toward the predominance of tendencies of exclusion over tendencies of economic integration of wide sectors of the population.

Some specifications on the evolution of capital concentration and the increase of poverty are necessary to illustrate these trends. In 1995 when, according to official data, 2 million people lacked a stable income, the largest 100 companies operating in the country reported altogether an annual turnover of $4,998 million. Moreover, the great concentration is evident within the corporate market itself. In effect, the first 10 of those firms obtained 56 percent of the mentioned profits. From this, it can be concluded that those companies were earning $500 a minute, or approximately the equivalent of three minimum monthly wages of $180 (Lozano 1998). Thus, while at the beginning of the "Convertibility" plan in 1992 the richest fifth of the population earned 10.8 times more than the poorest fifth; by 1999 that difference had grown to 13.5 times. A conclusive outcome of such high levels of concentration is an increase in poverty. Official data for 1998 show that 32.2 percent of the population is poor.[4] These figures imply that around 13 million people, or one out of every three adults and one out of every two children, are poor (Hicks 1999). One of the main causes of ever-increasing poverty has been the steady increment of unemployment, which in the last decade has reached levels unprecedented in Argentine history. Estimates by the National Ministry of Work show that around 7 million people (14.5 percent) are currently undergoing severe employment problems. This figure results from the combination of different situations, including unemployment, under-employment, people involved in government-administered temporary employment programs, and people working in the informal labor market with salaries below $400 per month. Privatizations, deregulation of the labor market, reduction of labor costs, and concentration of production in large corporations with the subsequent demise of medium and small companies all contribute to this situation. This structural change has generated an unprecedented increase in the incidence, intensity and heterogeneity of poverty (Torrado 1994).

Argentina has traditionally been considered a particular case in Latin America owing to the fairly high levels of its social standards, the dynamics of intense social mobility, and the extension of its middle class. These trends have been overturned as the middle- and low-income sectors have been the most affected by recent economic changes. Due to the absence of government protection through, for example, some kind of unemployment insurance, the situation becomes more worrisome and perspectives are not better. On the contrary, the adjustment plans applied have resulted in a dramatic spending reduction in public policies. These policies have been redefined according to neoliberal principles, thus assuming a subsidiary and compensatory character toward the low-income social sectors. Instead of reversing an increasingly structural situation of poverty, policies attempt to solve localized and immediate problems.

According to the national census of 1991, 3,039,000 households present some kind of housing deficit situation (30 percent of the households of the country). This figure is composed as follows: 510,000 families inhabit homes considered "irrecoverable" owing to the poor quality of the construction materials; 1,635,000 live in homes that could be recovered through repairs and improvements; 454,500 households inhabit homes that are in good condition but are overcrowded (more than two people per room); and 438,779 share a dwelling with at least one other household (family) (Martínez de Jimenez 1996).

The evolution of housing tenure status evidences the decline of living conditions through the decrease of formal occupancy (from 87.3 percent in 1980 to 82 percent in 1991). In these last measurements, over 1.5 million households presented some kind of informal occupancy (through borrowing or squatting in both buildings and plots of land). Finally, considering the distribution of the housing deficit among the different strata of the population as determined by income, 84 percent of the deficit situations are located among low- and middle-low income sectors—those who have been directly affected by the process of transformation and who inevitably require the action of the state to solve their problems.

The responses, however, have not been enough. The housing policy of the last decades basically has been financed by the National Fund for Housing (FONAVI), which was created in 1972 to be managed by the National Sub-Secretary of Housing. Between 1976 and 1996, these resources were used to build 515,247 homes by contractors to accommodate those in middle-low income sectors. The system never reached the lowest levels of the population, and thus it did not really have an effect on the worst deficit situations. In 1992 the federal government encouraged the decentralization of the FONAVI funds by transferring the responsibility to the provinces. This action has caused uneven results since the national agency was no longer able to regulate the utilization of resources. In some cases, the funds were assigned to different ends, such as maintaining the provinces' fiscal balance, as the stability policies and the commitments with transnational financial organisms required. As mentioned above, when referring to public policies in general, housing policies have been stripped of their aim at "social integration," and adequate housing is no longer considered a public good. Therefore, both the responsibility of the state and the role of public resources in solving the deficit are severely limited. The obvious result of these trends is that, contrary to other social rights such as health or education, housing is increasingly conceived and accepted as a private good attainable exclusively through individual means. In the current social and economic context, this constitutes an option which clearly excludes more and more extended sectors of the population. (See Table 9.1 for an overview of housing, poverty, and employment problems.) If we take into account that the total amount of the funds destined for the FONAVI program has been severely reduced in the last decade, from $1.4 million in 1990 to $0.7 in 1999, the forecast for the homeless who are increasingly poorer seems more than uncertain (Rodriguez 1997). The housing policy seems to run parallel to the general tendencies toward exclusion.

THE HOUSING SITUATION IN BUENOS AIRES

Historical Background

In view of its large population, Buenos Aires may be classified among the first 20 megacities of the world.[5] Although it constitutes less than 1 percent of the total area of the country, nearly one-third of Argentina's population resides in the city and its suburban metropolitan areas. In effect, the area occupied by the city proper is calculated at nearly 200 square kilometers in which 3 million people reside; the suburbs, accounting for 3,700 square kilometers, comprise 24 municipalities inhabited by around 8 million people.

Founded by the Spanish in the sixteenth century, long before the country came into existence, Buenos Aires soon became an important commercial and administrative center as a result of its most important asset: its location on the

Table 9.1
Argentine Population Data

Population	Number of People		Number of Households	
Total population[1]	34,180,171	100%	9,243,858	100%
Total population in a housing deficit situation[2]	12,782,279	37%	3,039,018	33%
Total population in a situation of poverty and extreme poverty[3]	13,000,000	38%	3,523,000	38%
Total population with employment problems[4]	6,800,000	14.5%		

[1] National Housing Census, INDEC 1991.
[2] Bases for an Integral Housing Policy, Document by the National Sub-Secretary of Housing, 1995.
[3] Permanent Household Survey, INDEC 1998.
[4] Calculations by the National Ministry of Work, October 1998. These estimates include the unemployed and underemployed, people registered in government-subsidized working programs, and informal workers earning up to $400 monthly.

shore of the Río de la Plata (de la Plata River), making the city a natural port. It was only in 1880, after the constitution of the nation-state, that the city was finally designated the capital of the country and turned into a federal district, thus detached from the province of Buenos Aires and directly administered by the federal government.

Even though for 300 hundred years after its foundation Buenos Aires grew and developed at a very slow pace, by 1910 it had become the largest city in Latin America, second only to New York City in the whole continent. This disproportionate growth was caused by massive immigration. What we have previously called the first moment of expansion of Argentinean economy brought important changes to the city. Buenos Aires, port and gate to the country, experienced the greatest increase in its growth rate between 1915 and 1945 (Lattes 1992). During those years, the city flourished as a center of culture, art, and stunning architecture. While Argentina was referred to as "the barn of the world" (mainly of Europe), Buenos Aires was called "the Paris of South America." The urban landscape of the city underwent its most profound transformation with the construction of luxurious theaters, wide avenues, impressive government premises, and petite hotels influenced by the Parisian style but also other European fashions, rendering the city architecture very eclectic indeed.[6] These great monuments, however, built by the emerging bourgeoisie, contrasted with the immigrant trends in housing, originally based on *inquilinatos*[7] and later developing the trend of the individually owned home, in two-story apartment buildings in the central area of the city and in detached houses in the suburbs, which became traditional working-class dwellings.

During the second period of expansion, that of industrialization, factories were mainly established around the metropolitan area generating a second wave of population movement, though this time migrants had their origins both in border countries and the provinces and consisted of former rural workers who arrived in Buenos Aires as a labor force seeking better job opportunities. From 1945 onward, however, the population of the city proper became stabilized, and it was the suburbs (Greater Buenos Aires) which incorporated the incoming population, achieving a growth rate of around 6 percent annually. Even though the city remained mainly an administrative and financial center, industrialization also left its imprints on the built environment with the spread of plants and warehouses and the extension of roads and communication arteries to facilitate economic activities. Due to prevalent political instability, there was an interruption in the industrialization process and the need for labor, but not of the internal migrations of people who moved to the "capital" fleeing from the economic crises that affected the provinces.

The city and the metropolitan area were not able to absorb much of this population, which formed *villas miseria* or *de emergencia* (shantytowns) around the city and in some cases—though limited by space—within the city itself. *Villas* are illegal occupations of public land, which are characterized by their lack of regular form or proper urban pattern.[8] Thus, the shape of the settlement is completely irregular, with narrow and sinuous corridors instead of streets. Two other features of *villas* directly related to this one are the prevailing deficit in urban infrastructure such as sewerage, running water, or pipelines and the serious overcrowding of the precarious houses built out of inappropriate materials, such as zinc panes and cardboard. Since their emergence in Buenos Aires, and despite alternative contractions or expansions, *villas de emergencia* have never completely vanished from the city thus definitively have become part of its urban landscape. In fact, since the 1940s, Buenos Aires has demonstrated a pervasive lack of sufficient and adequate housing for the population residing within its borders (Keeling 1996).

Between 1977 and 1981, under military dictatorship, the city government applied a repressive policy to remove *villas*. That particular population decreased dramatically from 280,000 in 1976 to 14,000 in 1981 (Yujnovsky 1984). Parallel to this, there was an extended process of expropriation of houses adjacent to the planned highways to be built throughout the city. The population involved was not able to solve the housing problem through the formal market. In addition, with the excuse of stimulating the real estate market, the government decreed rent deregulation allowing prices to rise unrestrictedly. This action resulted in a decrease in the number of tenants, from 19.1 percent in 1977 to 12.9 percent in 1981. At the same time, the Province of Buenos Aires, which rules over the suburbs of the metropolitan area, modified the law regulating territorial planning. In 1977 a provincial bill (Law 89/12) was passed which restricted divisions into urban lots, thus also provoking price increases and limiting access. Most of these lands were later destined to become country clubs and private neighborhoods, where part of the most affluent sectors moved, starting a process of "sub-urbanization" which was nevertheless not completed in Buenos Aires, as these sectors never completely abandoned the central areas of the city. Repressive expulsion (as in the case of the *villas*) added to decreases in real wages and in the economic capacity of wide middle-income sectors of the population, together with the unaffordable high prices and insurmountable restrictions, they have caused the decrease in demand in the housing market (Yujnovsky 1984). The population involved in these processes was therefore forced into informal housing modalities, which drastically expanded during the 1980s.

Informal Housing Modalities Since the 1980s: Squatting

The return to democracy in 1983 brought significant change to the political scenery and to government attitudes in general. Even if no comprehensive housing policies were developed to cope with the extended deficit, a certain level of "tolerance"[9] regarding informal settlements prevailed throughout the decade. The outcome of this situation was the deployment of a fairly wide range of alternatives devised by low-income sectors to solve the housing shortage. *Asentamientos*—organized land invasions—developed in the suburban areas; within the city, the spectrum can be divided into three general forms: *villas*, single-room renting in family hotels, *inquilinatos* (tenements), and squatting (occupied houses). Only *asentamientos* and squatting were relatively new phenomena in Buenos Aires. In the city proper, the number of people living with some kind of housing deficit reached 395,000 inhabitants,[10] or 13.7 percent of the population (see Table 9.2).

In fact, with the demise of the dictatorship and the loosening of restrictions, *villas* were eventually repopulated and, though they never reached the same figures of the 1970s, they are today estimated to have a population of around 100,000 inhabitants.[11] *Inquilinatos* and family hotels are presented here separately because of the significant difference in the legal constitution of the subjects and leases involved. Although in both cases the families usually rent one room and share facilities, such as kitchen and bathroom, with other families, *inquilinatos* are still under the ruling of a lease. As a result, renters are considered tenants and are actually protected by all the laws and civil rights concerning that legal figure. In hotels, on the contrary, people are considered passengers and thus are charged by the day and usually are subject to sudden evictions, price increases, and general abuse by the hotel owners or managers. Both forms of accommodation share the disadvantages of the lack of regular maintenance, overcrowding, safety hazards, and little privacy (Keeling 1996).

The two informal housing modalities that were actually introduced in the 1980s differed between themselves not only in the contrast between a suburban and an urban phenomenon but also in their implications. *Asentamientos* in Greater Buenos Aires entailed the construction of neighborhoods, the generation of city fragments, and new urban morphologies emerging in peripheral territories (sometimes even rural or vulnerable to floods) which involved low or even

Table 9.2
The Housing Deficit Situation in Buenos Aires

	Number of Households	Households (%)	Number of People	People (%)
Bueños Aires[1]	1,023,464	100	2,871,519	100
Total of housing deficit situations	122,000	11.9	395,000	13.7
Inquilinatos[2]	27,000	2.7	70,000	2.4
Room renting in family hotels[2]	25,000	2.4	75,000	2.7
Squatting[3]	45,000	4.4	150,000	5.2
Villas (shantytowns)[4]	25,000	2.4	100,000	3.4

[1]National Population Census 1991.
[2]Municipal Control, Annual Report 1992.
[3]Movement of Squatters and Tenants (MOI) 1995.
[4]Municipality of the City of Buenos Aires, Dept. of Statistics and Census, 1991.

neutral real estate value. Urban squatting, by contrast, developed in the interstices of the city proper, scattered and almost hidden in the central areas through "clutching" onto the city. They posed a distinctively inward attitude through the endogenous materialization of new morphologies within the squatter buildings under ambiguous governmental tolerance (Jeifetz 1997).

In effect, squatting is a fairly particular phenomenon, and its deployment and expansion were possible only because of the enormous proportion of vacant housing stock in the city.[12] Unoccupied land, empty residential buildings, abandoned small factories or warehouses, and any other available structure of private or public ownership have been used for accommodation. Though squatter buildings are scattered throughout the city, there is a higher concentration in neighborhoods that present certain regularities. Generally speaking, these are areas that combine environmental and physical decay (for example, vulnerability to floods or building obsolescence) with some urban function generating either a real or potential demand for labor (basically an informal service economy). As an example, a significant amount of squatter buildings are located in what is usually known as the "South Area," which comprises neighborhoods with sections that remained dilapidated and unkempt for a long time, presenting some level of deficient infrastructure, while at the same time granting accessibility to central areas of the city. Besides the availability of *changas* (very short-term jobs, usually informal and underpaid) and other possible work sources, the city offers other advantages over suburban areas. The amount and quality of health and social services, the level of public education, and security in general are far better in Buenos Aires than in the surrounding areas. Finally, another factor (maybe the most influential) for people to choose the city over the suburbs is the existing urban infrastructure. Usually, the peripheral areas where *asentamientos* are located lack the basic infrastructure (such as pavement, sewerage, and pipelines) which has to be developed together with the dwellings and must often be paid for by the inhabitants themselves.

Contrary to what could be supposed, the families inhabiting squatter buildings have frequently added market value to them. Because many of the buildings were previously warehouses or factories, or had been abandoned without maintenance, they needed repairs and improvements and the installation of services necessary for residence (sanitation and electricity). Squatters have generally fulfilled these tasks transforming inhospitable places into livable dwellings. Most of the buildings have been connected illegally to water and electricity, a typical situation of most self-help settlements in Buenos Aires (Keeling 1996). In the 1990s, with the privatization of service provision, this situation has become more tense because companies have threatened to cut off the supply to illegal users. Even though residents often express their interest in regularizing services, this aspiration is hampered by the unaffordable costs.

With some exceptions, occupations have not been sudden or organized. Rather, they happened in spontaneous and progressive ways, with families arriving once someone "opened" a building. This pattern has often resulted in an uneven distribution of space. It is common to find some families possessing extensive areas while others are crowded into a small room. Another feature of this process, and a consequence of the great need expressed in squatting itself, is the development of an informal real estate market parallel to the formal one. In effect, a good percentage of the families have actually bought the "apartment" they inhabit either from the people who were living there before or from those groups who initially entered the building and organized the "selling" of the space available. Thus, the addition of the cost of the rooms and the improvements made challenge the misconception that squatters have not dedicated their financial resources to the acquisition of their homes. Rather, they have actually made significant investments (albeit illegal and thus unprotected) in precarious conditions as a result of the absence of any other possibility of affordable housing.[13]

The squatter population is composed mostly of people coming from other Argentinean provinces and people originally from Buenos Aires; approximately 20 percent are immigrants from border countries.[14] Families are generally young (average adult age is below 30), and many households are headed by females. Most of the people are unemployed or underemployed; generally they work in the informal economy with independent activities (such as street vendors), cleaning and domestic service, and construction work. As squatting has mainly developed in sites with limited premises, most of the occupied buildings shelter an average of no more than 20 to 25 families who can be quite isolated from other people in similar situations. This feature, combined with the high dispersion of squatter buildings throughout the city, is one of the main obstacles to the emergence of a social organization among squatters that actually represents the scale of the phenomenon (Jeifetz 1997). In contrast to *villas*, which are clearly visible and obvious within the urban landscape, squatter buildings may be unnoticed or hidden within the environment. Behind the façade, an old house does not necessarily reveal the legal situation of its inhabitants. Furthermore, a decade of tacit approval on the part of local authorities has dissuaded squatters from publicly demanding adequate solutions to their housing situation. Rather, people tend to uphold the already existing invisibility in an attempt to avoid possible disadvantages such as eventual eviction orders. Even though squatting remained a pervasive phenomenon in Buenos Aires during the 1990s, most of the occupations actually occurred in the previous decade. Several factors have altered the government's overall benevolent approval of informal developments, and more restrictive and severe legislation against them has been passed. Even some "exemplary" repressive actions were taken, including a few forced evictions.[15] Though the threat did not spread, it did show a different general trend.

The City in the 1990s

If the 1980s can be characterized as the time of deployment and increase of informal modalities of housing for the poor, accompanied by general "tolerance" related to the return to democracy and the absence of real housing policies, the 1990s can be called the age of the "expansion" of capital. Liberalization of the economy and globalization trends have placed Buenos Aires in the position of one of the nodal points of transnational investment in the South Cone of Latin America. This situation has brought a profound transformation to the city through a wave of urban renewal, which consists of the redevelopment and functional alteration of rundown areas and urban infrastructure. Gigantic projects to renovate previously undervalued neighborhoods, the location of flourishing shopping centers in renewed old markets, the construction of a highway system facilitating the linkage between downtown (the financial district) and the surroundings, and improvements in communications are all expressions of the investment trends of the last decade.

The city, though, has not only become the location of transnational investment but also its object. In effect, the allocation of capital within the real estate market—particularly in the restoration and consequent revalorization of rundown areas—has become a substantial objective of transnational investment in the city owing to its extended possibilities and high profit perspectives. As it is, socio-spatial dynamics in renovated areas, in the last decade, have been determined by economic interests transcending those that previously defined the neighborhood structure. This can be illustrated by the takeover of real estate agencies of local capital by corporations whose profit-making logic is sustained

by the international value markets, which in turn operate directly over the whole
process of valorization of urban land.[16] These trends seem to draw a pattern of
"expulsion" from the city of the increasingly disadvantaged low-income sectors
who become displaced by redevelopment. In this context, squatting supposes a
deployment of poverty within the interstices of socially heterogeneous areas.
Thus it becomes emblematic of the exclusion implied by the economic conditions of the last two decades, as it depicts the intermixing of luxury and rudimentary forms of shelter lacking basic services within the same urban space.

The New Institutional Status of Buenos Aires and Housing Policies

The vanishing of tolerance toward informal housing practices demanded by
the expansion of capital was interrupted, however, by a very important change
in the institutional status of Buenos Aires. In effect, in 1994, the national constitution was reformed, and, among other things, it declared the city autonomous
from the federal government. As a result, local authorities were democratically
elected for the first time in history. The city government softened the drift
against rudimentary housing modalities and commenced a process of negotiation
with housing organizations which—despite few concrete results—is reflected in
the city constitution sanctioned in 1996.

The Municipal Housing Commission (CMV) is the agency in charge of housing policy and FONAVI funds in the city. Up to the present its impact has been
rather restrained, compared to the magnitude of the housing deficit and the main
modalities of informal housing for low-income sectors in the last decades. Original plans for the construction of low-rent apartments and affordable housing
have steadily deteriorated. Scarce production, little transparency regarding the
definition of criteria for construction and assignment of dwellings, and, basically,
the insistence on building only through contractors thus resulting in high construction costs are all features that have characterized the housing production of
the commission for a long time.

The commission, however, is not the only local government agency that addresses the housing deficit in the city. Scattered actions by other official organs
include the Secretary of Urban Planning which designs some infrastructure development programs for shantytowns, the Secretary of Social Promotion which
assists in emergency situations such as massive forced evictions or building
insecurity,[17] and the Secretary of Economy which administers government buildings for policies of *comodato* (public buildings conferred to groups of families,
both with or without rent).

The system of managing the housing crisis seems to be ruled by the reallocation of both responsibilities and costs through the implementation of atomized
interventions, the complete absence of an integral conception of the problem,
the lack of production of precise surveys and studies, and a budget assignment
which hardly reaches the population who severely requires improvements to

solve their critical situations. At the same time, it becomes quite obvious that public investment is directed at benefiting other sectors (contractors, hotel owners, and construction materials dealers). Sometimes, even funds earmarked for housing policy are reallocated for other functions within the city budget. The stubborn attitude of prioritizing only one modality of intervention (building through contractors), which has not furnished sufficient successful results in spite of the highly expanded housing deficit, strongly contrasts with the modalities established by the recently sanctioned constitution. In its Article 31, the Constitution of the Autonomous City of Buenos Aires declares that "the City recognizes the right to adequate housing and habitat." Thus, the article establishes that the city progressively attempts to solve the housing, infrastructure, and services deficit, prioritizing population involved in situations of critical poverty and special needs who possess scarce resources. Article 31 also advocates the incorporation of vacant buildings, supports self-managed projects, and the urban and social integration of the population in marginal situations, the recuperation of precarious dwellings, and the regularization of the situation in the site with the criterion of definitive residence. Finally, the article requires that city authorities regulate the establishments that provide temporary accommodation.

These general principles define the criteria with which to elaborate a housing law for the city. Housing policy, however, has not up to the present been a priority topic in the public agenda, and there is no explicit definition of how it could affect the perspectives for the low-income sectors of the population. On the contrary, the traditional approach—explicit or implicit in the current housing policies in the city—has been to transfer poverty to peripheral municipalities (suburban) and restrict the "right to the city" to social sectors with more economic resources.

THE EXPERIENCE OF ALTERNATIVE HOUSING POLICIES

This section explores some experiences of a grassroots housing organization which has attempted to reverse the traditional policy application by presenting alternatives. Through the conception of self-management (*autogestion*), these experiences aim at the design of socio-spatially integrative housing and habitat policies where the groups risking expulsion become the main participants. After an introduction and description of the organization and its practices, a systematic review of the concept of self-management in order to highlight how it challenges the premises and contents of the housing policies already presented.

Movimiento de Ocupantes e Inquilinos (MOI, or Movement of Squatters and Tenants) is a grassroots housing organization comprising several cooperatives. Founded in 1990 by a group of squatters and architects who had been working together in housing development activities, MOI is integrated by a technical advisory board formed by professionals from different fields[18] which grants the organization the capacity to elaborate thorough projects. The organization aims at finding alternatives for squatters and tenants while designing housing public policy proposals. It encourages the families to organize in cooperatives to generate a collective solution to their housing problems, departing from the issue of the right to the city or the defense of the entitlement of low-income sectors of the population to urban space. The central formulation of MOI is to develop social organization with the capacity to design proposals and negotiate with other agents an integral perspective on habitat, particularly through the rehabilitation of the existing built patrimony as an axis for housing policies in Buenos Aires. For this purpose, the main tool is self-management, understood as the direct administration of resources for public policies by the organized and trained beneficiaries, in order to generate more efficient alternatives both socially adequate to the characteristics of the demand and economically suitable at lower costs than traditional building through contractors.

What follows describes in general terms four lines of action MOI develops as part of its everyday struggle to achieve housing policies in Buenos Aires. The first two are the sections of what the organization calls the self-management program, the third is a more encompassing project that, nevertheless, still proposes self-management as its central feature, and the last one synthesizes the organization's proposal for housing policies in the city.

Construction without Bricks

In order to organize work and actions, MOI divides the process of self-management of housing into two stages or programs. The first one, called construction without bricks, begins with the organization of the population in situations of housing deficit and concludes in the collective purchase of a house or building. High prices in the urban real estate market prevent low-income families from buying property individually; however, collective purchases are a feasible alternative option. Therefore, the program implies the development of a self-managed capacity of the population in its organizational aspects as well as in its capacity to mobilize and reorient its scarce economic resources. In other words, the program aims at the construction of the cooperative as an organization (thus "without bricks") and at the establishment of its objectives and possessions. Despite how it may seem, this is not a simple endeavor. People are not necessarily used to collective work, and, when collaboration exists, it is usually understood as a personal attitude rather than as the rule and requirement of a formal structure. To ensure the functioning of the cooperative, members usually sign a strict agreement in which three criteria define belonging to the organization: participation, regularity in payments, and good cooperative behavior. Cooperatives are formed on two possible bases: those that include the families already living in a building, usually with the objective of purchasing that same building, and those that gather people coming from different housing situations (squatting, *inquilinatos*, hotels) who enter a cooperative once they join MOI. Construction without bricks, then, involves the construction of all the mechanisms to facilitate the functioning of a self-managed housing solution: the

gathering and organization of the group of families involved, the formal constitution of the cooperative as an institution (including formal training of the
members in different functions and tasks), and the purchase of the premises with
the previous acquirement of loans or financial assistance from government agencies. In this stage, MOI has been able to achieve results comprising a wide
spectrum of acquisition of collective housing in the city. Several cooperatives
have been formed, and a few have already obtained their living quarters through
purchases of publicly owned properties or directly in the real estate market.
Considering the economic investment, achieved through direct savings and public loans, the collective purchases throughout the history between the organization have mobilized approximately $530,000 in resources from the families.
This significant resource mobilization and payment capacity demonstrates that
a great part of the squatter population should become eligible for credit, assuming that their precarious and informal employment situation has not invalidated
this possibility.

Construction with Bricks

The second stage of the process, contained in the program called construction
with bricks, aims at developing the capacity to transform the buildings of cooperative property into clusters of livable dwellings. The aim of this phase is,
then, to endow the grassroots housing organization with the necessary strength
and capacity to administer public resources efficiently through self-managed
operations. Besides a wide-reaching transformation in the political realm,
through the participation of social organizations in the decision-making process
regarding the creation of public policies and the efficient solution of housing
needs, this program has several implications. On the one hand, it entails the
design of projects adequate to the scale and demands of the specific needs
emerging from the local context, through the collaboration between the intended
beneficiaries and government authorities. On the other, this program induces the
development of capabilities and training needed to implement the projects, on
the professional level as on the workforce level, through the generation and
recuperation of skills on the part of the population affected by the housing deficit
and targeted by the project.

For example, MOI has carried out the first experience of building rehabilitation through self-management in the central area of Buenos Aires. The cooperative *La Union* commenced, in 1997, the renovation of the old factory it
had purchased from the national government who was the legal proprietor of
the premises. Another government agency provided funds for construction,
which were granted in the form of noninterest loans to be reintegrated in several
payments. All the members of the families participated in the design of the
architectural project, collectively defining criteria for the equitable distribution
of space within the building and for distinctions between public and private
spaces. A relevant aspect is the way in which the cooperative has organized

work. Instead of hiring contractors, *La Union*, with support from the architects who direct the work, has undertaken the control of construction through, on the one hand, directly purchasing materials and, on the other, by hiring its own members (and members of other cooperatives organized by MOI) to work, thus generating employment. To save labor costs, the cooperative has applied the system of "mutual aid" (*ayuda mutua*), which relegates tasks that can be performed by unskilled workers (such as tearing down walls or cleaning the workplace) to be undertaken directly by the families themselves. Through avoiding profit-costs, the cooperative has been able to build at far lower prices than those of the market or even those of the publicly administered projects. Instead of the $750 per square meter spent by the CMV, MOI has built at $190 per square meter. The program involves, then, designing mechanisms for the efficient administration of public resources by the social organizations involved.

The Local Development Program

In 1997 MOI initiated another program which, including self-management as its development tool, aims at linking the housing solution for a cooperative of squatters to a more integrative project of local development. For this purpose, it has started working together with different agencies of the city government, other social organizations, and a confederation of trade unions located in the neighborhood of that cooperative to elaborate a unified program addressing various local needs, taking into account diverse interests. Departing from the idea that people, family, and community life should not be considered sectorially independent but rather as chains of complex relationships, this kind of program aims at defining mechanisms for the development of policies with an encompassing perspective. The project, designed through a participatory process, involves property belonging to the local government to be used for housing (low and middle income), schooling, and other communal activities. Its development and functioning will be regulated by an ad hoc agency composed of multiple and heterogeneous sectors. In short, the local development project entails the territorial grounding of a wider political alliance. Because it supposes direct participation of organizations in the decision-making process for intervention in the neighborhood, it seems to delineate a democratic mechanism for the construction of the city.

The Development of Housing Legislation

The fourth line MOI is currently working on is the consolidation of a permanent board, constituted by several grassroots housing organizations and different agencies from the city government, to discuss criteria for the definition of housing policies. The board started functioning from the beginning of the current municipal administration, which is the first democratically elected city government, and has since acquired new members as more organizations and local agencies have joined the initiators (MOI, CMV, and the Secretary of Social Promotion). Some specific experiences have developed, such as purchasing of buildings, monitoring projects, and also implementing some social programs as complementary to the "struggle" for housing in the city. The latter have mainly been articulated with already existing social programs aimed at supporting low-income families and deal particularly with the situation of women and children. These programs include child care, health services for women and children, provision of reinforced dietary supplies, and counseling for such situations as domestic violence and drug abuse. Since 1998 the Housing Commission of the Legislative Organ of the City has become involved in the board, and all efforts are currently focused on the elaboration of housing legislation based on the principle of self-management with the necessary assignment of funds for the actualization of a few initial experiences. From the perspective of MOI, this interaction aims at redefining housing policies in the city lacking an "expulsion" component that will acknowledge the "right to the city," for the low-income sectors, through self-managed processes involving the recuperation of the built patrimony in the city. Such results would fulfill the requirements stated by the city constitution regarding housing rights.

SELF-MANAGEMENT REVISITED

This chapter has tried to sketch the lines that draw a pattern of expulsion of low-income sectors of the population from the city, in times when the city appears as a center of and location for globalized markets and transnational investments. These trends jeopardize the prospects for socio-spatial heterogeneity, a feature we consider the basis for the constitution of a really democratic city. Finally, the public policies devised do not fully address the real needs provoked by ever-increasing poverty and the housing deficit, and this is not necessarily a problem related to the budget destined for such policies but to the assignment of those funds. An alternative option to these trends is a grassroots housing organization, MOI, which is exploring how more comprehensive and cooperative projects can be developed to cope with real needs in a far more efficient way while, at the same time, improving the social and personal conditions of participants in their everyday life.

In what follows, we will attempt to systematize some of the implications of the principle of self-management in the socio-cultural, economic and political aspects. Our discussion is based on the results obtained by the experiences mentioned and the possibilities they entail.

Self-managed cooperation implies, from a sociocultural perspective, a significant transformation based on two of its main requirements: participation and collective work. Because self-managed processes suppose the active commitment of the people involved, they enhance the development of organizational capacities and training to become engaged in the definition of the procedures of decision making, resource management, and planning. Through participation, then, people acquire the skills to achieve a comprehensive understanding and evaluation of the problems contemplated in order to take part in the design of possible solutions. Collective work, in addition, entails both the strengthening of cooperation potential and the ensuing shift of attitude in the perception of particular problems. In effect, when a need usually felt as individual (such as housing) is understood and addressed as collective, it engenders the possibility of expanding the same approach to other demands. People thus can assume organized ways to deal with such topics as education, health, and violence.

The implementation of rehabilitation projects through self-managed cooper-ativism in Buenos Aires, where there is a significant quantity of vacant or unused housing stock, entails meaningful economic implications. It effectively supposes the recuperation and utilization of the existing buildings and infrastructure in an inclusive procedure that involves low-income sectors of the population that re-side in the city and thus are part of its real, either formal or informal, economy. Self-management allows families to mobilize and optimize all their resources, particularly the economic ones, through cost reduction. The abolition of profit-oriented contractor costs, by means of direct administration of construction work, and the working time donated by members through the system of mutual aid to avoid labor costs of unskilled workers are examples of the ways in which this methodology supports resource mobilization. Furthermore, buildings and structures that are severely run down and deteriorated are usually sold at the price of the land. Thus, their physical rehabilitation partially adds value to the property, constituting a third factor of saving and capitalization on the part of the cooperative. Finally, self-managed construction generates employment op-portunities in construction work for the people involved in the process, and it encompasses the recuperation and training of skills for some sectors of the pop-ulation who, because the labor market had become more and more informal, were already losing them. On account of all these aspects, self-managed oper-ations, with grassroots organizations as administrators of public funds, propose a more efficient utilization of resources in terms of the results furnished and the quality of the habitat produced. This assertion is particularly true from the per-spective of low-income dwellers in critical situations who traditionally have been excluded from the design of housing policies based on building by contractors, and who received only "emergency" solutions such as subsidized temporary accommodation in hotels—responses that did not really transform their housing and everyday life conditions.

Regarding general political consequences, self-managed housing processes imply a significant shift in the relationship between social organizations and government agencies, which results in the transformation and democratization of public policies. This is so because the shift softens the apparently rigid divide between civil society and the state once the targeted population becomes actively involved in the identification of specific needs and the subsequent generation of political responses. This process develops through the progressive engagement of grassroots organizations which can impact the planning, enforcement, and monitoring of public policies using the experiences accumulated through the needs, features, and possibilities of the social sectors they represent.

These considerations lead to the conclusion that self-management as a tool facilitates the design of housing policies adequate to the needs and possibilities of the beneficiaries, independently from the level of their income, thus preventing the limitations caused by the situation in the labor market from becoming the central parameter for exclusion from the city. The system, however, privileges and requires the active engagement of the beneficiaries in the resolution of their needs through consistent community participation. These principles are diametrically opposed to the usual patronizing approach of public policies directed at attacking poverty in limited and narrowly focused ways. Thus, self-management entails a further development of citizenship and a redefinition of political culture.

REFERENCES

Beccaria, L., and A. Orsatti. 1989. *Precarización laboral y estructura productiva en la Argentina: 1974–1988.* Buenos Aires: Losada.

Cuenya, B., and A. Falú, eds. 1997. *Reestructuración del estado y política de vivienda en Argentina.* Buenos Aires: CEA-CBC.

Hardoy, J. E., and D. Satterthwaite. 1989. *Squatter Citizen: Life in the Urban Third World.* London: Earthscan Publications. This book seeks to describe the vast, rapid, and complex process of urban change in the Third World. Among several other topics concerning urbanization and urban housing for the poor, Hardoy and Satterhwaite discuss one feature that seems pervasive throughout urban settings: the gap that continues to grow between the "legal" and the "illegal" city. The inefficiency of government actions influences the formation of that gap instead of impeding it. Drawing from a myriad of case studies carried out by different researchers in various countries, the authors describe the ways in which poorer people find housing in the cities, usually through informal means, and the failure of public policies to improve housing conditions.

Herzer, H., M. Di Virgilio, M. Lanzetta, S. Lagos, A. Redondo, and C. Rodríguez. 1997. "Aqui, está todo mezclado: Percepciones de familias ocupantes de edificios sobre su situación habitacional. El caso de la Ex-AU3." *Revista Mexicana de sociología* 4:187–220. The article explores the apparently homogeneous world of the squatters of municipally owned dwellings (apartments, houses, and land) located on the former Highway 3 which crosses middle- and upper-middle class neighborhoods north of Buenos Aires. The case is placed within the context of the restricted housing options for the lowest income groups in the city. The authors analyze squatter families' perceptions of their housing situation and the way they relate to neighboring family groups living under the same circumstances. This analysis highlights significant internal differences which reflect the heterogeneity of the squatters.

Hicks, N. 1999. *Poverty and Income Distribution in Argentina: Patterns and Changes.* Washington, D.C.: World Bank.

Jeifetz, N. 1997. "Hacia la generación de políticas populares autogestionarias de rehabilitación: *E*dilicia en la ciudad de Buenos Aires. Dos casos (Cooperativas San
Telmo y La Unión) y una organización (el Movimiento de Ocupantes e Inquilinos)." *Ciudadanía. Primer Seminario Internacional Sobre Mejoramiento y Reor-
denamiento de Asentamientos Urbanos Precarios-MEJORHAB*. São Paulo:
CYTED. This article deals with organizational practices emerging in the context
of squatting in buildings in Buenos Aires. It compares this particular process to
that of organized land invasions (*asentamientos*) in the suburban area, and analyzes two paradigmatic cases in relation to the development of a wider and more
complex grassroots organization: MOI (Movement of Squatters and Tenants). The
concept of self-management (*autogestion*) proposed by this organization is discussed in terms of a passage from the "unidirectional" initiation in the organization's projects to the "bidirectional" perspective, which involves the active
commitment of governmental agencies to defining the allocation of public resources together with the participating grassroots organizations.

Keeling, D. 1996. *Buenos Aires: Global Dreams, Local Crises*. Chichester; England:
Wiley. This comprehensive study attempts to produce, according to its author, "a
detailed geographic examination of the city." In particular, it focuses on the spatial
changes that have occurred in Buenos Aires in the last two decades as a result
of the city's articulation with the global economy. After a thorough historical
account of the city's urban development, the author deals with a variety of aspects
such as environment, politics, planning, transportation, employment, and management of the city, always highlighting the contradictions emerging from the
constitution of Buenos Aires as a "world city" and local problems such as poverty
and obsolete urban infrastructure. The diversity of topics and the encompassing
framework constitute this work as a reference book for the study of the geographical aspects of the city.

Lattes, A. 1992. "Auge y declinación de las migraciones en Buenos Aires." In *Después
de Germani*, ed. J. Jorrat and R. Sautu. Buenos Aires: Paidos.

Lozano, C. 1998. "Crisis y agotamiento del sindicalismo tradicional." In *Una historia
silenciada. La discusión social y sindical en el fin de siglo*, ed. I. Rauber. Pen-
samiento Jurídico Editora.

Martínez de Jimenez, L. 1996. "La importancia del diagnóstico de la situación habita-
cional en el diseño de una política integral de vivienda." Paper presented in the
II International Seminar on Construction and Sustainable Development, Buenos
Aires.

Rodríguez, M. C. 1997. "Organizaciones de ocupantes de edificios en Capital Federal:
La trama poco visible de una ciudad negada." In *Postales Urbanas de final del
Milenio*, ed. H. Herzer. Buenos Aires: Ediciones CBC-Instituto Gino Germani.

Rodríguez, M. C., and V. Procupez, eds. 1998. *Autogestión, rehabilitación edilicia, con-
certación: Experiencias en políticas de vivienda popular*. Buenos Aires: CYTED-
BILANCE-Subsecretaríade Vivienda de la Nación-MOI. This book is a
compilation of papers presented at a seminar on alternative experiences in low-
income housing policies in Latin America held in Buenos Aires in 1997. The
articles were written by members of grassroots organizations, professionals, and
some government officials from different countries of the region. The experiences
presented aim at developing possibilities for access to the city and citizenship for
millions of people. With the corresponding differences according to local circum-

stances, these experiences promote social organization, capitalize on efforts already invested in survival, propose a rational utilization of the public resources available, and encourage alliances among those who strive to form democratic cities. In all the cases, there is an emphasis on the importance of the active engagement of grassroots organizations and the promotion and empowerment of the people involved in critical situations to project their future in the city.

Sassen, S. 1994. *Cities in a World Economy*. Thousand Oaks, Calif.: Pine Forge Press.

Torrado, S. 1994. "Notas sobre la estructura social argentina al comenzar los '90." Paper presented at the seminar New Challenges for Public Policies: Institutional and Economic Responses. Held by Fundación Konrad Adenauer and Universidad Austral, Buenos Aires.

Yujnovsky, O. 1984. *Claves políticas del problema habitacional argentino—1955, 1981*. Buenos Aires: GEL. This book delves into the extensive research carried out by the author with the aim of producing an interpretation of the housing problem pervasive in Argentina. Such interpretation is based on the idea that the theoretical framework of market self-regulation is not enough to explain the allocation of resources destined for housing policies and the level of the housing solutions achieved by different social sectors. The market is inserted within a specific society, ruled by particular power relations that need to be analyzed. This is the key to developing a thorough explanation to interpret the living conditions of the population.

NOTES

1. "Terror" here refers to general repression but specifically to the physical disappearance of 30,000 people considered by the military as "dangerous adversaries" which comprised a wide and heterogeneous range of political and social activists and thinkers of working and professional origin who were rooted in the social, institutional, and community life in Argentina in the early 1970s. Among these there were, as well, members of revolutionary organizations who promoted "armed resistance" against the military government.

2. Some economic and political analysts have depicted the hyperinflation process as an "economic coup" encouraged by powerful interest groups.

3. The law of convertibility aimed at controlling inflation and reducing the public deficit by establishing that all the money in circulation had to be backed by federal reserves in U.S. dollars, forcing the rate of convertibility of one peso equals one dollar. Therefore, the possibility of financing public deficit by fiscal credits or monetary emissions was forbidden. If the Central Bank needed U.S. dollars (to pay interests on the foreign debt, for example) it had to acquire them according to the rate established by law. These policies actually brought about a dramatic decrease of inflation.

4. Data have been obtained from a recently published survey by World Bank, which included the whole country. In that study, figures were calculated considering a "poverty line" of $460 of monthly income per household. This line is established according to the cost of a cluster of basic goods and services. A lower line to measure indigence (extreme poverty) is set at $288, and these figures should be compared to the average cost of what is usually called "family basket" or the group of goods and services normal for a nuclear

family, calculated to be around $1035 per household per month (*Fundacion de Investigaciones para el Desarrollo*).

5. The population of the whole metropolitan area, which encompasses "Greater Buenos Aires," amounts to around 13 million.

6. Many buildings such as small palaces were brought directly from France at the turn of the century.

7. An *inquilinato* is a tenement house which rented out rooms where a whole family lived, sharing a cooking area and sometimes even bathrooms with other immigrant families residing in the same building. Though it was a traditional modality at the turn of the century, *inquilinatos* still exist and are differentiated from family hotels in that their inhabitants are considered under the legal figure of "tenants" instead of "passengers."

8. Form constitutes the main difference between *villas* and *asentamientos*, the informal settlements located in suburban areas which expanded in the 1980s. The latter were organized and planned occupations of land where plots were divided formally into lots and parcels, thus establishing streets and public and private spaces and facilitating future provision of basic services. These settlements were eventually legalized, and many of them formed new neighborhoods. *Villas*, on the contrary, are characterized by the spontaneity in the settlement and the absence of any rational division of land and urban pattern, thus rendering it impossible to legalize the situation without intervention in the urban pattern.

9. It is important to highlight here that we consider the absence of specific policies, or the prevalence of tolerance particular kinds of policies in themselves.

10. These figures are approximate, as data have been obtained from different sources which, though they are highly trustworthy, do not constitute a homogeneous survey based on common criteria. Estimations done in 1995 with sources 1991–1995.

11. This figure is the result of recent surveys conducted by the CMV (Municipal Housing Commission), 1999.

12. Estimates show that a housing stock of over 100,000 homes or dwellings is currently vacant in Buenos Aires.

13. These investments sometimes represent good amounts of money. Some "apartments" in occupied buildings are known to cost around $5,000. People enter this informal market out of need and are thus trapped in the system, having spent considerable amounts without any kind of legal protection. Obviously the transactions they perform and contracts they sign have no legal validity and thus are no shield against eventual eviction by the legal owner. We believe this fact shows that, contrary to the conception usually implied in the patronizing public policies designed, low-income sectors do contribute significant amounts of money which could be directed—through precise policies—toward a definitive housing solution for the population involved.

14. Immigrants, both legal and illegal, come mainly from Peru, Bolivia, and Paraguay. It is important to note the low percentage of foreigners among squatters, because the claim that "all squatters are illegal immigrants" is one of the principal reasons produced by the authorities to justify the absence of particular policies and to advocate forced evictions. Beyond the xenophobic implications of this arbitrary assertion, it is actually false.

15. Such was the case of the eviction of *Bodegas Giol* in 1994. As an exception to the usual dimension of occupations we have described, almost 200 families inhabited the enormous premises of what had been the warehouse of a famous winery, located in a fairly upper-class neighborhood. The eviction was performed with an unprecedented (and

unnecessary) deployment of repressive force on the part of the police and the national secretary of security in what seemed to be a warning for squatters in general. However, with some exceptions, evictions did not proliferate in publicly owned premises. (Basically, governments did not have any better solutions for the housing deficit, and too many homeless people is a political cost nobody is willing to pay.)

16. Such is the case of IRSA, a real estate and urban development corporation owned by George Soros which owns most of the shopping centers in Buenos Aires as well as several of the recently renovated docks in the port and has invested great amounts of capital in the real estate market revalorizing complete neighborhoods.

17. The most outstanding actions are (1) a system of subsidies for room renting in family hotels through which the government actually transfers public funds to the private hotel system without effectively solving the housing problems of the people involved and thus legitimizing the inhuman living situations implied in the buildings, and (2) the donation of construction materials to the families for the self-help building of precarious homes in plots of land that the families have to obtain by themselves. Obviously both of these actions are performed from a government-patronizing attitude and, although they require the family to settle down in legal conditions, they also legitimize precariousness.

18. The technical advisory board includes architects, urban planners, sociologists, anthropologists, social workers, social psychologists, lawyers, an accountant, and communication specialists. It is necessary to remark here that the professionals are integrated into the grassroots organization instead of forming a separate nongovernmental organization.

10

Democracy and Homelessness in Brazil

RONALD E. AHNEN

INTRODUCTION

The return to democracy in Brazil has refocused attention on the massive numbers of socially and economically excluded members of the population in two important ways. First, politicians interested in achieving political office are forced to cater to the popular sector, since they are of great electoral consequence numerically. Second, democracy heightens awareness of citizenship rights, especially for socially or economically marginalized populations such as the homeless. The rights of homeless citizens are protected primarily in two specific clauses of the 1988 constitution: article 1, paragraph II postulates "the dignity of the human person" as one of the five foundations of the constitutional order, while article 203 states that social welfare assistance is secured for "whomever may be in need" (*Brazilian Constitution* 1988).

This chapter seeks to analyze the extent to which democratic governance has influenced the lives of homeless persons in Brazil's post-transition period through an examination of policies targeted toward them. Ten years after the full democratic transition in Brazil, this study seeks to adjudicate between two alternative conclusions regarding citizenship for the very poor. On the one hand, are the homeless in Brazil merely "paper citizens" whose rights are only perceptible on paper but not in reality?[1] Or, alternatively, have democratic institutions in Brazil become strong enough to protect effectively the right to a dignified life for all citizens—especially those who are summarily excluded from social and economic benefits?

Empirical data are presented from three cities: Rio de Janeiro, São Paulo, and

Guarapuava. The first two cities are the country's largest with homeless populations in the thousands; the third is a relatively small city (160,000) whose policies toward the homeless and the very poor differ sharply from the first two cases. The chapter is divided into six sections. The first section presents data on the size and important characteristics of homeless persons in each city, while the second addresses the relationship between salary levels in Brazil and homelessness. The consequences of homelessness are discussed in the third section, focusing specifically on violence against street children carried out by agents of the state. The fourth and fifth sections examine social welfare programs and housing policies designed to benefit the homeless. The final section offers policy recommendations based on the present analysis.

The analysis shows that the turn to democracy has not always been favorable for Brazil's homeless population. Social welfare programs that target persons living on the street were implemented or broadened in Rio de Janeiro and São Paulo, but in São Paulo only after state and municipal prosecutors brought class action suits on behalf of the homeless against the executive branch. Such legal measures are based on the protection of rights declared in the constitution, demonstrating that citizenship has moved—in at least some ways—away from its mere "paper" quality.

Mayors in each of these cities created new, multimillion dollar housing projects in the mid-1990s with international assistance. In two of the three cases, they successfully exploited the electoral payoff of these projects through the election of their party's candidate.[2] Propaganda aside, however, housing projects benefited only those individuals living in illegal or "irregular" housing (such as shanties) and did not benefit the truly homeless. Finally, democracy has led to only slight advances with respect to the safety of the homeless on the streets— especially for children and adolescents, who continue to suffer violence at the hands of the police at alarming rates.

HOMELESSNESS AND THE STREET: DEFINITIONS AND POPULATION

The literal translation of the word "homeless" in Portuguese is *sem-teto*. Although the truly homeless in Brazil are better captured by the term *população de rua*, or street people, *sem-teto* has been adopted by and is associated with organized social movements that struggle for affordable, decent housing. These groups, such as the Homeless Workers' Movement (Movimento de Trabalhadores de Sem-Teto, or MTST) in São Paulo and Rio de Janeiro, live in illegal housing or rented apartments, and only roughly 5 percent are literally without homes.[3] At the same time, many scholars and policy makers in Brazil differentiate between *população de rua* or population *of* the street and *população na rua* or population *in* the street. The former have taken up the street as a place of residence and survival in a more permanent manner. The latter signifies those whose problem of residence has temporarily reached a crisis level because of

Table 10.1
Homeless Population in São Paulo

Year	Population
1991	3,392
1994	4,549
1996	5,334
1998	6,453

Note: These figures are considered below actual levels since street population was only counted in areas where street people are known to congregate.

Source: SURBES-SP (1999) and Rosa (1999, 15).

the recent loss of employment, the removal from or destruction of the last place of residence, or because they are in transit from one city to the next. Anyone living on the street with no links to a permanent, private shelter is regarded as homeless, regardless of how long they have been in this condition, in this chapter.

No systemic national study of homeless individuals in Brazil has ever been undertaken; however, most experts agree that homelessness is a greater problem in the larger cities (Rosa 1999). A study conducted by a nonprofit child advocacy group of street children in four major cities of the state of Rio de Janeiro, in February 1989, counted 1,255 minors on the street at 11 P.M. and 797 minors sleeping in the streets at 4 A.M. (IBASE 1992). A more recent study of homelessness, conducted in June 1999, counted 3,535 people, not including roughly 2,000 persons housed in shelters (FAPERJ 1999). Studies conducted in São Paulo demonstrate a clear upward trend in which the homeless population nearly doubled between 1991 and 1998 (Table 10.1), though municipal officials admitted their estimate of nearly 6,500 is probably low.[4] Nongovernmental organizations and other scholars claim a more realistic figure lies in the range of from 7,000 to 10,000.[5] In the much smaller city of Guarapuava, on the other hand, a recent survey conducted by the municipal government in 1999 found 10 homeless people on the street, all of whom were adults.[6]

It is a common popular notion in Brazil that the homeless are northeasterners who have traveled to the industrialized southern regions in search of work or who simply are beggars, alcoholics, or mentally ill persons. While there is some truth to these generalizations, they are not wholly accurate. The migration influx from the northeast is well represented among the homeless of São Paulo (41.6 percent), but most of the street people are natives of the southeast region (46.7 percent). The great majority are unemployed (71.3 percent) and have not finished grade school (64.7 percent), and a large number have been on the street for less than six months (42.2 percent). In São Paulo, most homeless persons are unaccompanied adult males, though citywide differences are great, with children making up to 60 percent of homeless persons in the street in some regions of the city (SURBES-SP 1999).

In Rio de Janeiro, a substantial majority of homeless persons are male (76.6 percent), about an eighth are younger than 18 years old (12.4 percent), and the average amount of schooling completed is four and a half years. In contrast to São Paulo, however, nearly half (45.6 percent) of Rio's street population are employed in the formal sector.[7] A full one-third (33.9 percent)—mainly women—work in the sex industry,[8] a significant portion wash cars or carry out other minor services (17.6 percent), and others live primarily from begging (13.9 percent) or gathering recyclable products from the streets or garbage receptacles (10.9 percent). The greatest concentration of homeless people is found in the downtown area (33 percent), and about an equal percentage (32.5 percent) claim to have been victims of police violence (FAPERJ 1999).

The situation of the homeless population in Guarapuava is strikingly different. There the homeless fit into three categories: the mentally ill, alcoholics, and the unemployed. This small city counts only about eight to ten people who "permanently" live on the street. Other "homeless" persons most commonly make use of the city's overnight shelter for the homeless. The people who make use of the shelter are generally very poor and are traveling in search of work throughout the region.[9]

WAGES AND HOMELESSNESS

In recent years, the Brazilian government has adjusted the minimum wage only once a year, on May 1, Labor Day. In May 1999, the minimum wage was raised from 130 to 136 reais (about $70) per month. In 1996 government estimates show that family income (i.e., combined earnings of all family members) for the poorest 52.1 percent of Brazilian families was at or below five times the minimum salary ($350 per month). Nearly 23 percent of Brazilian families survive on two minimum salaries ($150 per month) or less. Only 8.4 percent of families have incomes greater than 20 minimum salaries ($1,400 per month). Brazil has one of the most inequitable distributions of income in the world with a Gini index of 0.59 in 1996 (PNAD 1996).[10] Expressed differently, the average GDP per capita from 1980 to 1994 of the richest 20 percent was $18,563 per year, while the poorest 20 percent averaged only $537 per year (United Nations 2000).

Such low income and brutal inequality have forced millions of poor and marginalized citizens to seek housing in a variety of illegal modes. By far the most common units are known as *barracos*, or shanties, in settlement areas known as *favelas*, or shantytowns. While the conditions of *favela* housing vary widely, *barracos* most often consist of wooden or clay block construction, have one or two rooms, and are supplied with makeshift and often an illegal electrical, water, and sewer infrastructure. The second most common illegal housing mode is *cortiços*. *Cortiços* are old, dilapidated apartment buildings that house entire families in what were originally multibedroom apartments. In one apartment of a *cortiço* building, each family occupies one room with all of their belongings including beds, closets, stove, refrigerator, and so on. Thus, five or six families (each with five or more members) frequently inhabit what used to be a single-family home—and all share the same bathroom.

According to São Paulo's municipal government, no less than 19 percent of that city's population lived in "subnormal" housing units in 1993, more than double the rate of 8.8 percent in 1987 (SMBDS-SP 1997). Moreover, population growth rates of this sector continue to outpace average population growth by nearly two to one, suggesting that the housing problem will continue well into the future. In Rio de Janeiro, the number of *favelas* grew from 376 with a population of 720,000 in 1980 to 573 with a population of over 950,000 in 1994, or roughly 17.2 percent of the population (SEHAB-RJ 1999). If one adds to that 583 clandestine (and illegal) settlements, 422 areas of shanty invasions, and 100 *cortiços*, the percentage of dwellers living in subnormal housing climbs to approximately 2 million.[11]

Without a doubt, a bifurcated economic and social structure lies at the root of the homeless problem in Brazil. Nevertheless, inequality per se, though continuing to grow, has been a constant trend in Brazilian history and alone cannot account for the recent explosion in the homeless population during the 1990s, especially in São Paulo. Part of the answer lies in Brazil's current economic conditions. After years of hyperinflation with rates as high as 50 percent a month, monetary stability was achieved with the introduction of the *real* currency in July 1994. Inflation was drastically reduced to annual rates of less than 10 percent by 1996. The poorest sectors of society benefited initially from this stability as their real buying power no longer eroded throughout the month as was the case under hyperinflation.

Most other neoliberal policies pursued by President Fernando Henrique Cardoso and his team were more detrimental to the lower socioeconomic classes, however. With trade barriers removed, the industrial sector of São Paulo moved toward international competitiveness and efficiency through a massive retooling of factories and a concomitant massive shedding of excessive labor. In just one decade, from July 1989 to July 1999, the number of workers formally employed in the industrial sector in Brazil was cut by 49.6 percent, representing hundreds of thousands of lost jobs (IBGE 1999). The most dramatic consequence of this effort was the move en masse from the formal to the informal sector for thousands of low-income workers. As formal employment declined, hundreds of thousands of individuals moved to *favela* or *cortiço* housing while many in the *favelas* were left to the street.

These trends are expected to continue in the near future. Brazil's finance minister, Pedro Malan, had admitted that the temporary upswing in real wages of the lowest socioeconomic classes caused by the ending of hyperinflation had worked its way through the economy by the end of 1996, leaving the poor with a shrinking share of national income. Brazil's economic restructuring may have led to returned growth throughout the mid-1990s, but the benefits have stubbornly refused to trickle down and for the most part have not reached the very needy.

STREET CHILDREN, POLICE VIOLENCE, AND HOMELESSNESS

The economic and social trends of the last two decades not only triggered an explosion in the number of poor, indigent, and homeless persons in Brazil, but also worsened one of Brazil's most pressing social problems: the growing population of street children. Though the phenomenon of street children in Brazil has a long history (Gomes 1994; Rizzini 1995), this topic began to command great attention only in the mid-1980s as the level of violence against them mushroomed. In response, international human rights organizations and foundations began funding programs specifically aimed toward assisting street children. Estimates of street children in Brazil vary from 7,000 to 7,000,000 depending on the source and the definition of the concept. Invariably, the government accused nonprofit organizations of exaggerating the numbers of street children in order to win international grants for their programs, while the organizations accused the government of refusing to recognize the real scope of the problem.

Consequently, these organizations and social scientists produced more careful and credible analyses that demonstrated clearly the extent to which street children were the victims of violence and death, often at the hands of the police. One of the first such works was *Vidas em Risco* ("Lives at Risk") published in 1991 by three organizations working with street children (MNMMR/IBASE/NEV-USP 1991). The report, which analyzed 457 homicides of street children in the cities of São Paulo, Rio de Janeiro, and Recife, confirmed that 16 percent of all known perpetrators were police officers (MNMMR/IBASE/NEV-USP 1991, 80). The contributions of Gilberto Dimenstein, a journalist in São Paulo, led to the publication of *A Guerra dos Meninos* (translated into English as *Brazil: The War on Children*) in 1990, and *Meninas da Noite (Girls of the Night*, about teenage prostitution) in 1992. Dimenstein reported that police officers, in cahoots with other criminal elements, murdered an average of one adolescent *per day* in 1989 as members of death squads in the state of Rio de Janeiro alone (1990, 33). Comparatively, this number is *three* times the annual average number of *all* citizens killed by police officers in fifty of the most populous cities in the United States (125 homicides) from 1985 to 1989 (Geller and Scott 1992, 512–13).[12]

Yara Bandeira, a social worker in the major city of Salvador in Brazil's northeast, published interviews with street children in *Decifra-me ou devoro-te (Understand me or I'll devour you)*. One 12-year-old street youth from Salvador exemplifies the relationship between street youth and the police:

If the police are suspicious of someone, they think the guy's a thief, and treat the person like a thief . . . beat them with their stick, shoot him and kill him . . . and shoot for no good reason, [and] the bullets kill those who are simply standing in the doors of their houses just watching what's happening.

I was arrested a bunch of times . . . I don't remember how many, but I know it was a lot . . . when the "pigs" arrest us, they punish us and beat us . . . they like to put our head in the toilet and flush it to wet our head . . . then they make fun of us, calling us vagabonds and shitheads.

The police abuse us . . . That is why I am afraid of the police. They shove their revolver in our mouths, in our ears, in our throats, they order us to run and threaten to shoot us. I am afraid of the future and of the police, because they could kill me. They already killed a friend of mine because he was stealing. (Bandeira 1993, 83–84, author's translation)

These and other studies of street children portray vividly and plainly the Hobbesian life patterns of many of Brazil's poorest and youngest citizens—nasty, brutish, and short. Imagining how six-, seven-, or eight-year olds come to the conclusion that he or she would be better off fending for themselves on the street—begging for food, sleeping under a cinema marquis, being hassled or beaten by the police, and exposing themselves to high levels of violence—is difficult at best. Poverty has dire consequences as hunger pangs lead children to beg for food not only for themselves, but for their family members. Generally speaking, however, street children have most often been victims of aggression and violence in their homes. The street offers some sense of security for them, away from parents or stepparents who might physically or sexually abuse them (Chalhub 1997).

Street children employ a variety of survival strategies depending on their age and the time they have spent on the street. Younger children are more successful at begging; preadolescents and adolescents try to find odd jobs such as washing windshields or shining shoes. Some become involved in petty theft or are attracted to the very high salaries offered in the drug trafficking industry, but this is less common than the conventional wisdom holds. Often street children become victims of violence carried out by police officers who, in conjunction with local business owners and frequently paid by them, take it upon themselves to "clean up" the streets by "getting rid" of these unwanted youth (Dimenstein 1990).

Capturing the essence of street life for children and adolescents is no easy task, though several themes run through the works cited above: fleeing from physical and sexual abuse at home; suffering violence in the street from other groups of street children, adults, and especially police officers; hunger; physical ailments including lethal diseases such as AIDS; drug use, including sniffing glue and fingernail polish, and smoking marijuana or crack cocaine; prostitution or other forms of sexual exploitation; drug trafficking; bullet or knife wounds; and early death. Amazingly, many children and adolescents are easily resigned to an early death, expecting not to live beyond 20 or 25 years. Unfortunately, many of them are correct in that assessment.

By the early 1990s, homicides were becoming the major cause of death among minors in Brazil, doubling between 1985 and 1995 (Ministry of Health 1999). The Brazilian Chamber of Deputies created a special committee in 1991 to investigate the problem of the extermination of minors. The committee found that 4,611 children and adolescents had been murdered in the three years previous to the report—4.2 assassinations per day (Brazilian Chamber of Deputies 1992, 32). The committee concluded,

The routine and continual participation of bad military and civil police officers in the massacres and individual assassinations of adolescents in the entire country is truly indubitable, as is police tolerance and omission in relation to known killers who have been seen publicly in offices, vehicles and in the company of agents of the law. (1992, 80, author's translation).

In Rio de Janeiro, where the problem of police violence against street children is well documented, a study of assassinations of children and adolescents from 1991 to 1993 concluded that police were responsible for the murder of 11 percent of children and 14 percent of adolescents (Milito, Santos, and Soares 1993). Reports produced by the Human Rights Watch (HRW 1997, 1994) revealed well-entrenched patterns of police involvement in the murders of minors in several major Brazilian states, especially of children and adolescents who live on the street. Finally, data from the National Human Rights Movement, located in Brasília, reveal that police officers constituted no less than 11.6 percent of known perpetrators of homicides against minors between 1993 and 1996 (Ahnen 1999, ch. 3).

Several dramatic occurrences of human rights violations reinforce the cruel reality described by these statistics. Indubitably, the most prominent violation of human rights against children in Brazil in the last decade was the Candelária massacre. On the night of July 25, 1993, between four and eight military police officers opened fire on approximately 20 youths at 4 A.M. while they were sleeping on the steps of the Candelária Church in downtown Rio de Janeiro, killing 8 of them. Apparently, some of these children had thrown rocks at a police car the previous day, breaking a car window and slightly injuring one of the officers. The killings were planned as an act of revenge. Three years later, on April 29, 1996, only one ex-police officer, Marcus Vinícius Borge Emanuel, was convicted and sent to prison for his participation in the massacre.[13] He remains the sole person punished for this act.

SOCIAL ASSISTANCE POLICIES FOR THE HOMELESS

State and local governments throughout the 1990s have generally been very slow to respond to the needs of the ever-increasing numbers of homeless persons. In the two largest cities, programs catering to the homeless are still woefully inadequate. Moreover, major state reforms aimed at decentralization and trimming the state budget have shifted the role of the executive branch from direct administration of social welfare programs toward manager-client relations with private, nonprofit organizations. The shift has been less than perfect and has resulted in thousands of social welfare clients who fall through the cracks and are left to fend for themselves with no real social protection.

Adults

Rio de Janeiro

State and municipal governments of Rio de Janeiro have only a few programs designed to benefit the homeless population. Furthermore, the capacity of these programs remains well below present demand levels. The state of Rio de Janeiro runs a farm shelter, called *Fazenda Modelo*, well outside the capital city with a capacity for 650 guests. The program is equipped with several vans that circulate throughout the city picking up homeless persons and transferring them out to the farm. There, they are registered and must remain for at least 48 hours, after which they obtain a pass and are free to come and go. One intention of this program is to introduce some of the guests to rural work in the hope that they might acquire a useful skill that would lead to gainful employment in the rural labor market.

This rarely happens. Most adult street persons have never had any rural experience, and rural life is completely alien to them. Moreover, the program does not have social workers or psychologists to work with these persons. The result is that few visitors to the farm find permanent solutions to their plight, and they often return to the streets in a few days or weeks after arriving at the farm.[14]

In addition to the evening shelter, a day program, Dispensário dos Pobres, or Care Center for the Poor, is located in the Botafogo neighborhood. This shelter provides a meal at noon to all who enter in the morning as well as a place for street people to shower, shave, write a letter or make other contacts, and receive limited medical assistance. Guests also have the opportunity to meet with a social worker and psychologist to assess their needs and seek out alternative avenues to life on the street. According to Edivaldo Roberto de Oliveira, director of the state's Leão XIII Foundation, the state government agency in charge of policies targeted toward the homeless, these programs were still being reviewed as of July 1999 by the new administration of Antonio Garotinho, which took over in January of that year. Oliveira claimed that a new, more comprehensive approach to social assistance for the homeless, emphasizing permanent solutions to individual cases rather than short-term geographical removal, is planned.[15]

São Paulo

The state government of São Paulo has six overnight shelters with a capacity of 1,610 beds (Rosa 1999, 111), and the municipal government supports 13 overnight shelters with a capacity of 2,700 beds (Governo Municipal de São Paulo 1999). This total covers less than half the estimated 10,000 homeless in the city. Most shelters house between 100 and 150 people, but the largest two centers house 600 and 900 persons each. Most homeless shelters are administered by private, nonprofit organizations who must raise funds for building maintenance, utilities, and incidental costs; the city or state pays for personnel, food, and some cleaning supplies. Homeless persons sign up to become a member at these shelters. They must leave during the day, but may return in the early evening and can maintain a private locker in the shelter. Guests are generally allowed to stay up to 90 days, but persons who demonstrate they are seeking alternative solutions to life on the street are often allowed to stay longer.

During the day, many homeless persons take advantage of one of the eight *Casas de Convivência*, or communal living houses. These centers generally open their doors at 7:30 or 8:00 A.M. and close their doors as soon as capacity has been reached—usually a half hour or so after they open. The door is then closed and no one is allowed to leave until after the noon meal. The great majority of guests are men, who take time to shower, shave, and make phone calls or other contacts in looking for work or housing. Communal living houses were designed to have a homelike atmosphere where homeless persons could visit with each other, establish friendships, and develop important social skills. A few social workers in each center are available to speak with individuals seeking help in finding work or housing, or to coordinate activities to keep the guests occupied, such as gardening or *capoeira*.[16]

Guarapuava

This medium-sized city has only one shelter for the homeless, called the Night Shelter Federico Ozanom, with a capacity to house 60 persons. According to the attendant on duty there, the shelter averages only 20 to 25 persons per night. Most guests at the shelter are travelers wandering the region looking for work and do not have the means to pay for food or lodging. The total number of visitors for 1998 was 11,935, but that number is expected to reach only approximately 8,500 in 1999 as the shelter recently instituted a rule of barring admittance to any persons under the influence of alcohol or other drugs.

The shelter allows guests to stay up to three days only, after which they must provide for themselves or simply move on. Exceptions to this rule are made for pregnant women and the sick. The shelter offers four meals a day to their guests: breakfast, lunch, afternoon snack, and supper. Food is donated by various businesses in town, while other operating expenses are paid by the local Saint Vincent de Paul Society. The shelter has eight employees whose salaries are paid by Guarapuava's municipal government.

The eight to ten adults who live more or less permanently on the street are generally alcoholic or mentally ill persons who have been treated at least once by psychologists provided through the city's outreach programs. In all cases, however, they have refused to leave the street. Thus, the municipal administration has concluded that homelessness does not constitute a social problem in Guarapuava, but rather reflects the personal problems of a small number of individuals.

Children and Adolescents

Brazil's 1988 constitution specifically guarantees the protection of child and adolescent[17] rights in article 227 (Brazilian Constitution 1988). In July 1990, President Collor signed the State of the Child and Adolescent (Estatuto da Criança e do Adolescente, or ECA), replacing the previous juvenile criminal code (Código de Menores) in both philosophy and approach. These two steps brought Brazilian children and adolescents something they had never had before: full citizenship. At least theoretically, they were no longer the *object* of state intervention in the process of social construction, but rather *subjects* of the state with the right to demand that their rights to a dignified life be upheld (Gomes da Costa 1994).

These legal changes reshaped the process of social welfare policy formation in areas attending to children and adolescents, including homeless minors who live on the street. According to the ECA, representatives from government agencies and nongovernmental organizations who work with youth must now form child and adolescent rights councils. The council members work together to design, adopt, and evaluate public policy regarding the social welfare of minors. While cooperation has been only slowly forthcoming in many places in Brazil and nonexistent in others, positive results are clearly perceptible in some cities.

Rio de Janeiro

The city of Rio de Janeiro's social assistance program for homeless youth is called Criança, vem para casa, or Child, Come Home. As the name suggests, the program has several projects designed to address the varied needs of street children with the ultimate goal of integrating them back into their families whenever possible. By March 1999, the program had expanded to include 62 centers assisting 2,208 children or adolescents. Approximately 15 percent of these projects are directly run by the municipal government; the rest are administered by nonprofit organizations with financial support from the city.

The most common project in the program is the creation of the Reception Houses, where minors are first received into the program. The project emphasizes the child's right to live with his or her family, whenever this is possible. After initial assessments, if circumstances do not allow for a successful reinsertion into the child's family, other solutions are investigated. In every case, the amount of time the child or adolescent spends in institutionalized settings is minimized. In no case, however, are children and adolescents allowed to remain living on the street. If need be, social workers are instructed to obtain the assistance of other social workers, the municipal guard, or a policeman from the special juvenile police precinct to remove youth from the street (SMDS-RJ

1999). In reality, however, these programs are grossly underfunded and inadequate in the face of real needs. Thus, hundreds of thousands of children still roam, live, and sleep on Brazilian streets.

São Paulo

The city of São Paulo has been much slower to develop projects designed to assist children and adolescents on the street. Mayor Celso Pitta approved the first major project in this regard in 1999 and created 22 *Casas de Convivência* for minors. This is a new experience in São Paulo where the right-wing Brazilian Progressive party (PPB) has stalled on cooperation with nonprofit organizations that work with street children, both under the previous municipal administration of Paulo Maluf (1993–1996) and the present administration of Celso Pita (1997–2000).[18] In the absence of strong action by the municipal government, the state has taken up some slack by providing funds to a wide variety of projects, including those that assist street children. Over $26 million were allocated for social welfare projects in the city of São Paulo in 1998 from the state, including shelters and *Casas de Convivência*.[19]

Guarapuava

The city has a program for up to 36 street children which occupies them in a variety of activities during the day. Social workers and psychologists work with this population to diagnose their home situation and seek out more permanent solutions to their problems. Nevertheless, no shelters exist for minors, and these children return to often precarious home situations at night, unless social workers judge the case worthy of foster home care.[20]

HOUSING AND HOUSING POLICIES

In 1993 recently elected mayors launched major housing projects in Guarapuava and Rio de Janeiro, and in 1995 in São Paulo. These projects aim to expand affordable housing for persons in the lowest economic income levels, especially those who earn two minimum salaries ($150/month) or less. The larger projects in Rio de Janeiro and São Paulo won significant funding support from the Inter-American Development Bank (IDB). Since providing subsidized housing units to the very poor pays electoral dividends, mayors in each case were criticized by their political opposition who claimed that "electioneering" was at the heart of the program. At any rate, these programs do not appear to have a direct impact on the homeless population since beneficiaries must be permanent residents of *favelas* or *cortiços*; in other words, they must have a fixed (albeit illegal) residence.

Rio de Janeiro

The largest housing project in Rio de Janeiro is the Favela-Bairro, or Slum to Neighborhood Project. As the name suggests, this project aims to convert the medium-sized *favela* areas in Rio de Janeiro into neighborhoods complete with basic infrastructure (including paved streets, and electrical, water, and sewer hookups), a school, a day care center, training programs, job-generation programs (including the construction of the project), and areas for sports, culture, and leisure activities. The first phase of the project aims to benefit 60 *favelas* and eight other areas with irregular housing units benefiting a total of 250,000 people (SEHAB-RJ 1999). The cost of the first phase was $230 million, of which 40 percent was funded by the city and 60 percent financed by the IDB. In July 1999, with 80 percent of the first phase complete, the IDB approved the second phase of the project, providing an additional $400 million in funding.[21]

Other major housing projects include a program designed specifically for smaller *favelas* and one for very large *favelas*, such as Rocinha, the largest slum area in Latin America with a population of 500,000 residents. The Morar sem Risco, or Live without Risk Project relocates persons living in precarious or dangerous areas, such as underneath viaducts, along highway entrance and exit ramps, or on hillsides prone to mud slides. The major thrust of Rio's housing policy, however, is to allow poor residents to maintain their current residence, whenever possible, while improving their structure and basic municipal infrastructure and services. Lower- to middle-income formal sector workers have also benefited from housing policy. The Morar Carioca or Live Carioca[22] project provides subsidized credit to low- to middle-income families wanting to own their own home. Total investments on housing projects coordinated by the municipal government in Rio de Janeiro came to over $250 million in 1998. In all, spending on housing from the inception of the Municipal Housing Secretary in 1993 to the end of 1999 was expected to reach over $600 million—quite an impressive figure given that the secretary began with a budget of only U.S. $5 million (SEHAB-RJ 1999).

São Paulo

The largest and most well-known housing project in São Paulo is called Cingapura, so named because the architecture of the housing units was copied from common designs found in Singapore. According to Attílio Piraíno Filho, the coordinator of development in the Housing and Urban Development Secretary of the Municipal Government of São Paulo, the initial idea for the project came in the early 1980s with a group of left-leaning common council members. Ironically, it was Paulo Maluf, leader of the right-wing Brazilian Progressive party (PPB) who, after many starts and stops, finally got the project off the ground in the mid-1990s. The objectives of the Cingapura project are similar to that of the Favela-Bairro project: to reform slum areas into neighborhoods with decent living standards. The fundamental difference lies in the method.

In the Cingapura project, existing residential units—usually *barracos*—are destroyed and replaced by four-story apartment buildings.[23] Construction is therefore much more disruptive than in the Favela-Bairro project, and has even caused the residents of some *favelas* to refuse the project when it was proposed for their area. The first phase of the project removes roughly half the residents from their current homes and places them in temporary, makeshift shelters built near the *favela* area. Their old homes are then destroyed, and apartment buildings are built where these once stood. The residents move into the apartment buildings, and the second half of the residents move to the temporary shelters, and the process repeats. Residents are required to pay $30 per month, plus utilities—a payment that many low-income families (earning $70 to $150 per month) with three or four children (or more) find difficult to make.

Critics of the program note several problems with the project. First, the amount of money spent on television and billboard ads to promote the Cingapura project, while linking it to a positive image of Mayor Paulo Maluf in the first six months of 1995, was $14 million. This represents enough resources to construct 2,000 apartments in the program, even though by that date the project had only delivered 1,221 apartments benefiting 6,000 persons (Rede Rua 1996). At the time, Maluf was in an intense political campaign to get his hand-picked successor, Celso Pitta, elected to the mayor's office, thereby setting Maluf up for a run for governor in 1997. According to Piraíno Filho, the criticisms about the political use of the program may be correct, but they should not distract from the program's merits. Yet even he conceded that the project was only 60 percent successful.[24]

Other problems are evident. Many former residents of *favelas* were unable to secure a unit in the apartment complex and were paid a sum of $1,200 to "go back home" or to "build a different shanty elsewhere" (Rede Rua 1996). In addition, a member of the SEHAB-RJ suggested that the apartment buildings of the Cingapura project do not take important sociological aspects of housing for the poor into account, such as the tendency of poor families to supplement their income by selling low-priced items out of their house including food items, candy, or cigarettes.[25] These sales are only feasible if one's house (or apartment) is at ground level. Finally, there are several reports that residents have sold their units (which is prohibited) or have stolen whatever they found useful from the apartment (sinks, toilets, windows) and disappeared with them.[26]

Guarapuava

The Núcleos Habitacionais, or Housing Nucleus Project began in 1993 with the arrival of the recently elected mayor. The project aspires to provide a long-term and ongoing solution to the acute shortage of basic housing in Guarapuava brought on by heavy waves of rural migration to the region's urban center. In addition, the city's population is growing at the alarming rate of 2.5 percent a year. Each nucleus contains between 100 and 250 homes. Residents make no down payment, and monthly payments are calculated at 10 percent of the minimum wage, or about $7.50 per month. After 20 years of payments, the city transfers the title to the occupant of the house.

The experience of a recently constructed housing nucleus reveals the strengths and weaknesses of the program. In 1997 the municipal government decided to relocate the residents of the infamous Toca da Onça, or Jaguar's Den *favela*, named for its far, out-of-the-way and hidden location. As with the Cingapura program, new prefabricated homes were constructed for residents of Toca da Onça and were then parceled out to them. Unfortunately, these houses brought many new expenses that residents of the Toca were not used to, including paying for propane tanks for cooking and electrical and water bills. Many residents continued to use firewood for cooking, since they are lifelong rural residents and were used to nothing else. Besides filling their chimneyless houses full of smoke, this brought a new problem: the housing nucleus was located far from any forest areas where they could forage for their daily supply of firewood.

In the end, many of these residents illegally sold their houses to other poor families and returned to the *Toca* area. Since municipal officials fenced off their original location to prevent rehabitation, some residents settled on the lot next to the old Toca, creating Toca II. These problems notwithstanding, some residents benefited from the plan and have been able to keep up their monthly payments in the Housing Nucleus area. The city has also allowed flexibility of payments when hardships arise, although the utility companies do not show the same flexibility, and services are cut off when payments are not paid on time.

In sum, municipal executives have implemented a variety of solutions to benefit the very poor with both positive and negative results. Significantly, however, these policies are aimed at persons who already have a fixed residence. Indeed, to be eligible for the Cingapura program in São Paulo, for example, residents must prove five years of residency in the city. Thus, a definite gap exists between providing for emergency or short-term shelter for the homeless, and seeking long-term housing solutions.

THE PRESENT CONJUNCTURE AND POLICY RECOMMENDATIONS

The return of democracy and its concomitant emphasis on citizenship brings about two new avenues for bringing changes in public policy toward the homeless. The first is political; that is, democracy allows for individuals and groups interested in guaranteeing minimal conditions of a dignified life for all citizens— especially the very poor—to have their views represented in government. Representation occurs in two fundamental ways. The most obvious is through the election of politicians from parties who prioritize the defense of rights for the disadvantaged. By and large, representatives of left-wing parties in the city's common council have pushed for legislation to provide protection for the homeless population, especially children and adolescents.[27] A second mode of interest representation occurs via direct contacts between members of nongovernmental organizations and representatives of the state or with policy makers. This has occurred via the Child and Adolescent Rights Councils in all three cities.

The other avenue is via the courts. When the executive branch of the state has failed in its responsibility to secure the basic rights of citizens, both private citizens as well as state institutions have the right and duty to take legal action against the executive branch in order to force compliance. This was the case in São Paulo where Alderman Aldaíza Sposati brought a civil public action suit against the city and state governments of São Paulo, forcing them to open more shelters for the homeless, especially during the winter months. Yet these types of judicial decisions are frequently bogged down in appeals and other legal maneuvers, or simply are ignored by stubborn executives counting on the weakness of enforcement mechanisms within the Brazilian judicial system.

Executive compliance does not generally result from enforcement mechanisms of the court, however, since these are indeed very weak. Rather, members of political and civil society exploit the political costs that a judicial ruling against the executive can have in the political arena. This strategy was successful against Mayor Pitta of São Paulo in 1999. After attracting a lot of attention to the issue in the media, the mayor was "forced" to rescind his veto and thus sign the so-called Street People Law (*Lei do Povo da Rua*), obliging the city to create and fund enough shelters and other programs for as many homeless people as are on the street.[28]

While this may have been good news for homeless people and for those struggling to defend their rights, the bad news is that this case clearly exposes the inherent weakness of mechanisms of accountability in Brazil's democracy. The defense of basic rights should not depend on the outcome of a power struggle, but should be guaranteed for all citizens no matter who holds the reins of power. Nevertheless, winning the political battle in favor of rights can, on a very practical level, be the foundation upon which the protection of basic rights becomes institutionalized—especially for the very poor and disadvantaged of society.

At least three policy recommendations can be made. First, actions by the Public Ministry (Ministério Público)[29] must be redoubled to strengthen enforcement mechanisms against the state. This requires renewed commitments by Public Ministry officials to prioritize such actions where necessary and follow up on executive compliance with judicial decisions. If the rule of law is to mean anything, its guardians must not be reticent to act both swiftly and boldly against those who transgress the law—even by omission.

Second, in terms of assisting street children, the World Bank has recently promoted the Bolsa-Escola (Scholarship-School) program originally put forth by then-governor Cristom Buarque of the Federal District. This project essentially pays a minimum salary to any family without a minimum level of income as long as they maintain their children in school. The results of this program in the Federal District have been drastic reductions in school evasion and significant improvements in literacy rates, raising them to levels comparable to some industrialized nations. The Bolsa-Escola program will go a long way to help prevent children from moving to the street and thereby lowering their chances of obtaining both a decent education and a decent job.

Finally, the housing policies implemented in the three cities generally do not benefit the homeless people. One exception to the rule is a new shelter for homeless persons in the city of São Paulo that was currently in the planning stages in July 1999.[30] This shelter will serve as a halfway house between the homeless shelters and the only viable but unattractive alternatives: building a *barraco* in a *favela* area, or renting from a boardinghouse that tends to be very expensive, filthy, and unsafe. Beneficiaries of the program are to be former homeless persons who have found jobs, but who are still living at a homeless shelter. The house will be owned by the city, but the residents will make payments over an extended period of time and eventually take over the title to the property. The city will use those funds to buy additional houses and continue the program. This is the only program of its kind in these three cities, and the only one that attends to the needs of homeless persons as they proceed from a life off the street to residence in a dignified dwelling.

CONCLUSION

The consolidation of political liberalization during the 1990s in Brazil had both positive and negative effects on basic rights of the very poor. First, institutions of horizontal accountability within the state designed to protect basic rights have been and continue to remain weak. In addition, the process of economic liberalization during this same time period has led to an explosion in the number of persons who are attempting to move up to the bottom rung of the ladder—that is, to become promoted to the social category of "exploitable" (Borón 1998). Democratic politics, on the other hand, has led to greater attention on the issue of poverty and, in some cases, has spawned housing and social welfare policies aimed at protecting the very poor against the strong undertow of neoliberalism's most recent wave. Nevertheless, the policies examined here are band-aid policies at best. Democracy may have had a positive impact on the plight of the homeless in some locales, but thus far it appears to have done nothing to alter the basic divided structure of Brazilian society or to attenuate the growth of poverty and misery.

REFERENCES

Ahnen, R. E. 1999. "Defending Human Rights Under Democracy: The Case of Minors in Brazil." Ph.D. diss., University of North Carolina at Chapel Hill.

Bandeira de Ataíde, Y. D. 1993. *Decifra-me ou devoro-te: História oral de vida dos meninos de Rua de Salvador*. São Paulo: Loyola. Bandeira interviewed 18 street children in the northeastern city of Salvador in the state of Bahia and brings their testimonies together in this work. The interviews are transcribed with great attention to accuracy, allowing the reader to grasp well the perception these youths have of themselves and their situations in life. In the final section, the author examines several topics of street life as seen by the youths she interviewed in-

cluding family life and home situations, poverty, survival strategies, theft, school,
sexual experiences, drugs, victimization, violence, police violence, and institutions for juvenile delinquents.

Borón, A. 1998. "Faulty Democracies? A Reflection on the Capitalist 'Fault Lines' in
Latin America." In *Fault Lines of Democracy in Post-Transition Latin America*,
eds. Felipe Agüero and Jeffrey Stark. Miami: North-South Center Press.

Brazilian Chamber of Deputies. 1992. *O Extermínio de crianças e adolescentes no Brasil.*
Brasília, DF: Brazilian Chamber of Deputies.

Brazilian Constitution. 1988. Brasília: Ediouro.

Chalhub de Oliveira, T. 1997. "Homeless Children in Rio de Janeiro: Exploring the
Meanings of Street Life." *Child and Youth Care Forum* 26, no. 3: 163–74.

Dimenstein, G. 1990. *A Guerra dos meninos.* São Paulo. Editora Ática.

———. 1992. *Meninas da noite: A prostituição de meninas-escravas no Brasil.* São
Paulo: Editora Ática.

———. 1993. *O Cidadão de papel: A infância, a adolescência e os direitos humanos
no Brasil.* São Paulo: Editora Ática.

FAPERJ (Fundação de Amparo à Pesquisa do Estado do Rio de Janeiro). 1999. Unpublished data on homeless population from research survey in June 1999.

Geller, W. A., and M. S. Scott. 1992. *Deadly Force: What We Know.* Washington, D.C.:
Police Executive Forum.

Gomes da Costa, A. C. 1994. "De Menor ao Cidadão." In *Das necessidades aos direitos*,
ed. Emílio Garcia Mendez and Antônio Carlos Gomes da Costa. São Paulo: Mal-
heiros Editores. Gomes, the former president of the Centro Brasileiro da Infância
e Adolescência (Brazilian Center for Childhood and Adolescence or CBIA), traces
in this work the trajectory of children and adolescent rights. Throughout the
1980s, academics and policy makers working both in Brazil and in the UN worked
on providing a new framework of rights for children and adolescents. The result
was the UN Convention on the Rights of the Child in 1989, and the Estatuto da
Criança e do Adolescente (Statute of the Child and Adolescent) in 1990. The
fundamental difference in the post-1989 era is that minors are viewed as subjects
of their countries (i.e., full citizens who have the legal right to make demands on
the state), instead of merely objects of state intervention. This watershed has
produced several public action lawsuits on behalf of children and adolescents in
Brazil which have effectively improved the protection of their rights in some
instances.

Governo Municipal de São Paulo (Secretaria da Criança, Familia e Bem-Estar Social/
SCFBES). 1999. Unpublished data on municipal shelters for the homeless.

HRW (Human Rights Watch). 1994. *Final Justice: Police and Death Squad Homicides
of Adolescents in Brazil.* New York: Human Rights Watch.

———. 1997. *Police Brutality in Brazil.* New York: Human Rights Watch. This HRW
report concentrates on police violence and death squad activities in three major
Brazilian cities: Rio de Janeiro, São Paulo, and Recife. Research revealed that
the great majority of underage victims of violence in Brazil are adolescent males.
Police involvement in extrajudicial executions and torture, as well as their links
to privately run death squads, was found. The report draws conclusions about the
dynamics of human rights violations by examining a few key cases in each city
rather than analyzing quantitative data. These events clearly reveal the insti-

tutional weaknesses of Brazil's democratic government. The report provides 17 recommendations to eliminate human rights violations against Brazilian youths.

IBASE (Instituto Brasileiro de Análises Sociais e Econômicas). 1992. *Levantamento de meninas e meninos nas ruas do Rio de Janeiro.* Unpublished mimeo.

IBGE (Instituto Brasileiro de Geografia e Estatística). 1999. *National Census.* Website version: www.sidra.ibge.gov.br. October 1, 1999.

Milito, C., Hélio Raimundo Santos Silva, and Luiz Eduardo Soares. 1993. *Homicídios dolosos contra menores no estado do Rio de Janeiro (1991 a julho de 1993).* Rio de Janeiro: ISER.

Ministry of Health (Brazil). 1999. *Mortality Database.* www.datasus.gov.br. October 1, 1999.

Municipality of Rio de Janeiro. 1998. "Programa vem pra casa!" Unpublished mimeo.

Municipality of São Paulo. 1995. *Diário Oficial.* January 5. Special Edition, "A Política setorial do governo municipal para a habitação."

MNMMR/IBASE/NEV-USP (Movimento Nacional de Meninos e Meninas de Rua/Instituto Brasileiro de Análises Sociais e Econômicas/Núcleo de Estudos sobre Violência-Universidade de São Paulo). 1991. *Vidas em risco.* Rio de Janeiro: MNMMR: IBASE: NEV-USP.

PNAD (Pesquisa Nacional de Amostras de Domicílio). 1996. Website version: www.ibge.org/informacões. October 2, 1999.

Rede Rua (Street Network). 1996. "Cingapura." Video. São Paulo: Rede Rua.

Rizzini, I. 1995. "Crianças e menores do pátrio poder ao pátrio dever: Um histórico da legislação para a infância no Brasil (1830–1990)." In *A arte de governar as Crianças: A história das políticas sociais, da legislação e da assistência no Brasil,* ed. Francisco Pilotti and Irene Rizzini. Rio de Janeiro: Amais.

Rosa, C. M. M., 1999. "Vidas de rua, destino de muitas." Master's thesis in Department of Social Service, Pontífica Universidade Católica, São Paulo.

Rosa, C. M. M., ed. 1995. *População de rua: Brasil e Canadá.* São Paulo: Editora Hucitec. This book represents the report of an international conference on homelessness that took place in São Paulo, June 3–5, 1992. The conference brought together experts and policy makers on homelessness in Brazil and Canada to exchange information and ideas about homelessness and public policy aimed toward homeless individuals. Among the topics discussed are the following: the profile of homeless persons in each city or state, existing programs and policies, specific questions such as housing and work, and commentaries about the future direction of public policy.

SEHAB-RJ (Secretário de Habitação-Rio de Janeiro). 1999. *Favela-Bairro.* CD-ROM. This CD-ROM, available from the Municipal Secretary of Housing in Rio de Janeiro, contains vital information for the understanding of both the housing challenges in that city as well as the various programs designed to address those challenges. Quantitatively, the CD-ROM combines maps of the city's shantytown areas with accurate and up-to-date statistics that provide the basis for the analysis of Rio de Janeiro's housing situation. Beyond informative statistics, the CD-ROM contains vital information on the major housing programs currently administered by the city.

SMBDS-SP (Secretário Municipal de Bem-estar e Desenvolvimento Social-São Paulo). 1997. "Habitação social: Tendências, problemas e alternativas." Unpublished pamphlet.

SMDS-RJ (Secretário Municipal de Desenvolvimento Social-Rio de Janeiro). 1999.
"Criança, vem para casa." Unpublished mimeo.
SURBES-SP (Superintendência Regional de Bem-Estar-São Paulo). 1999. "Street Pop-
ulation Survey." Unpublished mimeo.
United Nations. 2000. *Human Development Report for 2000.* November 24, <www.
undp.org/hdro>.

NOTES

1. This phrase borrows from Gilberto Dimenstein's (1995) work on the rights of children and adolescents in Brazil.

2. At the time of these elections in late 1995, immediate reelection was still proscribed.

3. Interview A, with homeless rights activist, June 1999.

4. Interview with Dora Maria de Campos Penteado, social worker, SURBES (Supervisão Regional de Bem-estar Social) Sé-Lapa, Municipal Government of São Paulo, July 1999.

5. Interview with representatives from Rede Rua, a nongovernmental organization dedicated to working with and for homeless persons.

6. Interview with Maria Magdalena Nerune, director, Department of Social Promotion, Guarapuava, July 1999.

7. Generally these are men who reside on the outlying communities of Duque de Caxias or Nova Iguaçu who can save themselves 4 hours and R$5 per day by sleeping on the street. They generally go home on weekends, though in the summer months may call their families to Rio's south zone to enjoy the wonderful beaches.

8. Work in the sex industry is illegal only for minors.

9. Interview with Maria Magdalena Nerune, director, Department of Social Promotion, Guarapuava, July 1999.

10. The Gini Index carries a value between 0 (perfect income equality) and 1 (perfect inequality). Nations generally range from 0.20 to 0.65.

11. "Um Rio de ilegalidade," *Jornal do Brasil,* September 14, 1997, p. 37.

12. Furthermore, the great majority of police killings in the United States were adults—not exclusively adolescents.

13. "PMs e serralheiro da Candelária são absolvidos," *Jornal do Brasil,* December 11, 1996, p. 24; U.S. Department of State, Country Report on Human Rights Practices, Brazil, 1997 and 1998.

14. Interview with Edivaldo de Oliveira, director, Leão XIII Foundation, Rio de Janeiro, June 1999.

15. Ibid.

16. *Capoeira* is a mixture of martial arts and dance.

17. Brazilian law has eliminated the category of "minors" because this term has become equivalent with "delinquent" in common usage. "Children" are persons ranging in age from birth to 11 years; adolescents, from 12 to 17 years.

18. Interview with Simone de Lemos, director and social worker, Casa de Paz, Embu Guaçu, São Paulo, July 1999.

19. Interview with Marila Vilela, secretaria de Assistência e Desenvolvimento Social, State Government of São Paulo, July 1999.

20. Interview with Maria Magdalena Nerune, director, Department of Social Promotion, Guarapuava, July 1999.

21. "Bid tira do papel Favela-Bairro 2," *Jornal do Brasil*, July 23, 1999, p. 19.

22. "Carioca" is a person who was born in or who lives in Rio de Janeiro.

23. The limit of four stories means that elevators are not needed, greatly reducing construction and maintenance costs.

24. Interview with Attílio Pariaíno Filho, Coordinator of Development in the Housing and Urban Development Secretary of the Municipal Government of São Paulo, June 1999.

25. Interview with Adriana de Araujo Larangeira, director of technical documentation, SEHAB-RJ, June 1999.

26. Interview with Simone de Lemos, director, Casa de Paz (home for abandoned girls), São Paulo, July 1999.

27. Right-wing legislators have proven to be just as interested in homeless issues as their leftist counterparts. São Paulo Councilman Mário Noda of the conservative PTB, for example, proposed that the city construct cardboard houses as a solution to the problem of homelessness! His proposal was ruled unconstitutional by the Justice Committee of the city's common council, and thus never made it to a floor vote. "Casas de Palelão," *Trecheiro*, September 1996, p. 3.

28. "Atitudes Demagógicas," *Trecheiro*, June 1999, pp. 1, 4.

29. Brazil's Public Ministry is similar to the U.S. Justice Department, though more autonomous.

30. Interview with Maria Isabel B. del Pozo, social worker, Arsenal da Esperança (homeless shelter in São Paulo), July 1999.

AFRICA

11

Mapping the Terrains of Homelessness in Postcolonial Kenya

BETH BLUE SWADENER AND KAGENDO N. MUTUA

INTRODUCTION

The phenomenon of homelessness in Kenya is complex, and it is entrenched in a myriad of social, political, economic, and cultural, including gender-related, factors. Some of the data used in this chapter come from a national study[1] of the impacts of rapid social, cultural, and economic change on child rearing based on interviews with nearly 500 parents, grandparents, children, teachers, and community leaders (Swadener, Kabiru, and Njenga 2000). Other sections of the chapter draw from a study of access to education of persons with disabilities in Kenya, who comprise a large portion of homeless persons in Kenya (Mutua 1999). Finally, the chapter draws from the first author's experiences working with street children in Nairobi since 1994 (Swadener, in press).

The chapter begins with brief background information about Kenya's history, diverse cultures, and notions of "home" within some of these cultures. It also provides a brief demographic overview and an analysis of the evolution of housing policies in Kenya, including the contrasts between policy and practice, particularly in urban contexts. The remainder of the chapter is divided into six sections that focus on different groups of people living in particularly difficult circumstances, who are either "at risk" for, or are experiencing "homelessness": (1) urban dwellers in informal or "squatter" settlements—street children, women, particularly single mothers, and persons with disabilities; (2) rural landless, including casual laborers on plantations or farming others' land; (3) Kenyans displaced by sponsored violence; (4) pastoralists who have experienced the loss of communal land and grazing corridors for their animals; (5) persons affected by HIV/AIDS; and (6) refugees from neighboring nations, fleeing warfare, famine, and oppression. The chapter concludes with recommendations for policy and practice, and offers actions which advocates for social justice in Kenya can take.

Kenya is located in Eastern Africa, near the equator, and has a landmass slightly smaller than Texas. Because Kenya is economically dependent on agriculture, rainfall is the most important climatic element in Kenya. Kenya comprises seven agro-ecological zones, and 18 percent of the arable land supports 80 percent of Kenya's total population. Human settlement, agriculture, and economic potential correlate with these agro-economic zones (GOK/UNICEF 1998). All these factors play significantly in the issues of land tenure, which plays directly into homelessness.

By 1990 Kenya had the fastest growing population in the world, with a projected 16-year doubling time. More recently, however, the population growth rate has leveled off at 2.6 (World Bank 1997a). The average life expectancy of Kenyans increased from 44 years at independence, in 1964, to 60 years in 1993. Tremendous gains have been made in child health since independence, with major reductions in infant and under-five death rates, estimated at 62 and 96 per thousand live births in 1998 (GOK/UNICEF 1998). Recently, however, many of these gains have been sharply eroded by AIDS/HIV, increased poverty combined with higher costs of living, and other related factors. Increases in child mortality rates have been observed nationally and in different regions, with the western, Nyanza, and coast regions persistently showing high levels of infant mortality (Kenya Demographic and Health Survey 1994). One of the highest correlates of child survival is the education of the mother; rural mothers tend to have lower rates of primary education. Children in rural areas face a 27 percent greater risk of dying before age five than children in urban settings (GOK/UNICEF 1998).

COLONIAL HISTORY

There are three broad tribal language groups in Kenya, with Bantu, Cushitic, and Nilotic origins, which form the ancestral roots of the 40 distinct ethnic groups found in Kenya today. Most of the traditional cultures that constitute Kenyan society contained strong elements of economic and political egalitarianism, in which all community members were expected to cooperate in a mutual sharing of benefits and to cooperate in a variety of contexts. From the struggle for independence until the present, these egalitarian ideals have been embodied in Kenya's principle of *Harambee*, a Kiswahili term meaning "to pull together." Within the *Harambee* ideal, people help each other, and no one is left behind or left out. Today, however, the core concepts underlying this principle have not been realized by a large majority of Kenyans, particularly the very poor, who continue "to pull" but reap few benefits of their labor.

When Kenya became a British colony in the 1880s, several legislative mandates were enacted to ensure a clear distinction between the white settlers and the "native" Africans. Such distinctions had strong economic underpinnings. For instance, a 1902 Crown Land Ordinance made provision for the sale and leasing of land to white settlers but gave only temporary occupation licenses (limited to one year and a maximum of five acres) to Africans (and other nonwhites) with rights only for occupancy, cultivation, and grazing. While such discriminatory laws did not survive after Kenya's independence, they did, however, leave a well-established infrastructure of land ownership and land tenure in which certain people could only occupy a piece of land but never have a title for it. Such a tenuous existence is evident in contemporary Kenya, in which certain people, or groups of people, cannot own land for a variety of reasons— financial inability, culturally based gender prohibitions, and displacement under the broad umbrella of restrictions from occupation of government-owned land— an infrastructure very similar to Crown Lands (U.S. Government 1984).

HOMELESSNESS IN KENYA: POLICY VERSUS PRACTICE

In discussing homelessness in Kenya, we are faced with the magnitude and complexity of a task in a country where the existence of homelessness is seldom acknowledged. It is proposed here that homelessness is a socially and culturally constructed phenomenon with many definitional dimensions. Traditionally, an African (more specifically, a Kenyan) could never be considered homeless, even if the person's family—both immediate and extended—were all deceased. In keeping with African traditions, such a person would be raised by the village and typically remain on collective, often ancestral, land. However, more recent economic, sociocultural, and sociopolitical conditions have led to the erosion of extended kinship, thereby robbing the village of its ability to carry out communal child rearing (c.f., Kilbride and Kilbride 1990; Kilbride, Suda, and Njeru 2000; Weisner, Bradley, and Kilbride 1997).

Despite this erosion of the cultural infrastructures that gave the village its ability to rear other people's children, it is not uncommon, even today, for Kenyans to consider their village to be their home. Kenyans often distinguish between "home" and "house." Home is considered one's ancestral village, specifically the *shamba*, or small farm, which is typically located in a rural area. On the other hand, "house" refers to a residence, usually rented in a city or a town, where the person currently resides and works. In either case, home or house is a place that provides shelter. In the case of a house, that shelter is real—a physical building. Within this definition, however, a home does not always offer a physical shelter, but offers a psychological one nevertheless. A person would always know that if things do not work out, there is somewhere to return to. The understanding of this distinction is important because it forms the cultural underpinnings upon which the meanings of homelessness in Kenya are constructed. Against this backdrop, this distinction might appear to infer erroneously that every Kenyan has a home.

For purposes of population and census, the United Nations (UN) recommends criteria for what constitutes a household and further recommends that individuals be listed within a household (United Nations 1980). The UN's definition of household recognizes homeless households, but the absence of census data on homeless persons in Kenya strongly suggests that such individuals are excluded in the census data because they are homeless. The actual census activity in Kenya[2] entails going door-to-door. However, persons without a physical door, or persons with a makeshift door, may not be counted at all. This absence of statistics on homelessness in Kenya is highly problematic given the extraordinary growth in population that Kenya has experienced in recent years, as well as the numbers of displaced persons and refugees it has absorbed.

One can argue that the policies governing zoning and housing in urban areas of Kenya exist in law books only. While there are policies that delineate industrial, residential, and commercial areas in cities, their enforcement is sporadic and often motivated by economic power and political clout. For instance, many residential estates are built in Nairobi every year. Often, they have a similar appearance based on the zoning laws. However, as soon as that house comes under individual ownership, the homeowner can make any alterations, including adding an extension to the house for use as kiosk (small store), or adding rooms to rent.

On the other hand, squatter settlements have sprung up in many areas of the city. Depending on their location, many such settlements become recognized communities. Such communities exist on the fringes of the law, making them susceptible to demolition without warning. In some cases, they are set on fire. The closer such illicit housing develops to a wealthy neighborhood, the higher the chances of demolition. Hence, the enforcement of housing policies is strongly mediated by economic power and political clout. Members of a wealthier community are more likely to demand the demolition of squatter shelters that spring up close to their residential areas than are less wealthy community members.

GROUPS VULNERABLE TO HOMELESSNESS IN KENYA

Different groups of people living in Kenya are particularly vulnerable to homelessness. Although these are not discrete, or mutually exclusive groups, unique and complex issues face members of each group. Much of contemporary homelessness is found in urban areas resulting from rapid urbanization in combination with high poverty. It is helpful to examine the situations of persons living in squatter settlements and slums, children living and working on the street, and the feminization of poverty in urban contexts.

Urbanization and Homelessness: The Growth of Squatter Settlements

> I thought I should go to the capital of Kenya to look for work. Why? Because when money is borrowed from foreign lands, it goes to build Nairobi and the big towns.
>
> —Ngugi wa Thiong'o, *Devil on the Cross* (1989)

A nation is considered overurbanized when it lacks the capacity to support its urban population. Overurbanization is one of the primary causes of Third World protest against austerity measures: "The urban poor and the working class are affected by a combination of subsidy cuts, real wage reductions, and price increases stemming from devaluations and the elimination of public services" (Walton and Ragin 1989, 877). Furthermore, "Externally imposed structural adjustment may be a key determinant of the growing over urbanization in many poor countries" (Bradshaw et al. 1993, 637). The World Bank estimates that

by 2010, most of the world's people will live in cities and more than two thirds of those urban dwellers will live in developing countries. In two more decades, developing countries will host 2.6 billion people and have more than two and a half times the size of urban populations as developed countries. (World Bank 1992, 5)

Between 1980 and 1990, the urban population in Kenya *doubled*, and most of the growth was concentrated in Nairobi, the capital, and Mombasa, the second largest city (Munyakho 1992). "Migration from rural areas to urban centers increased dramatically with poor families being driven from their homes by landlessness, drought and unemployment" (Human Rights Watch/Africa 1997a). The population of Nairobi is estimated at over 2.5 million, with 70 percent living in urban slums. Sprawling squatter settlements and informal housing schemes have spread over the outskirts of Nairobi.[3] The thousands of new urban slum dwellers include a rapidly growing number of single-parent households. Over one-third of Kenyan households are headed by women, and over 60 percent of urban households are headed by woman (GOK/UNICEF 1998; World Bank 1999).

The dramatic increase in the costs of housing, education, basic health care and medicine, food, and clothing in the last 15 to 20 years has contributed to the mounting pressures on single mothers raising children. There has been a large increase in the number of single parents in Kenya, particularly in the relative isolation of urban slums (Swadener, Kabiru, and Njenga 1997). In these settings, parents do not have the traditional community and extended family supports. Mothers are often forced to make very difficult choices, sometimes even neglect of their children, to enter the wage-based economy of the city or town. Traditional sources of child care, including a grandmother, are typically not available in urban settings, and impoverished mothers are unable to afford an *ayah* or housegirl. Mothers interviewed described leaving children unattended, including locking them in the house, or taking them to wherever they were working, if possible (Swadener, in press). Mothers must choose which, if any, of their children will attend primary school; they frequently leave children alone or in the care of only slightly older siblings or neighbors when going to work; and they cannot always provide enough food to meet the basic needs of growing children. Health care is either nonexistent or more expensive than it was in the early postcolonial years when the Ministry of Health subsidized primary health care and medications were free. This situation, combined with poor environmental sanitation and hygiene, makes children and their mothers vulnerable to a number of illnesses.

Many have argued that industrialization and urbanization have broken down traditional African family support systems, and have led directly to the high number of single-parent families (e.g., Kilbride and Kilbride 1990; Weisner, Bradley, and Kilbride 1997). These families are quite vulnerable to homelessness and displacement. Large-scale "slum clearance operations" undertaken by city authorities contribute significantly to homelessness and to the rise in the number of street children. The Kenyan government uses urban planning restrictions, which forbid the development of squatter settlements, to remove residents through eviction and the destruction of their homes, leaving already marginalized slum dwellers homeless (Human Rights Watch/Africa 1997a). Such operations are typically carried out without providing assistance, alternative arrangements, or notice to evicted residents. Families are frequently uprooted from their homes and left to fend for themselves on the streets.

During interviews held with urban parents, community leaders, and preschool teachers in Nairobi and Kisumu[4] slums, a number of issues related to housing were identified (Swadener, Kabiru, and Njenga 2000). A major theme was the scarcity of affordable housing and the vulnerability of families living in temporary, informal settlements. They were vulnerable to increasingly higher rents, paying for water from a communal tap, having few income-generating activities or work opportunities, and being under the frequent threat of the demolition of their housing—particularly if it was built from temporary or even semipermanent materials. In one group interview in Mukuru location (a large settlement near the industrial section of Naholi), several parents recalled a former chief who became upset when temporary homes made of cardboard, plastic, and perhaps some tin for a roof were destroyed on several occasions by city council bulldozers without much, if any, warning to residents. He declared, "I will not be the chief of cartons!" (Swadener, Kabiru, and Njenga 2000, 227) and worked hard to assist families to build at least semipermanent housing and to protect the community from further destruction and displacement.

Another constant threat to urban families' temporary housing is fire; a fire in one shack could engulf an entire community. This happened several times in recent years to temporary settlements in Nairobi, and each time families lost

everything, including valuable school uniforms and shoes for the children—
without which the children were not allowed to return to school. A number of
children who attended a street-based tutoring program had suffered burns that
had not been treated appropriately. Women's self-help groups provide some
informal support to single mothers and children affected by these threats to
housing, but they often lack the material resources for rebuilding houses or
replacing food, clothing, books for school, and other necessary items.

Flooding is another threat to slum housing during the rainy seasons, a factor
made far worse during recent years by the effects of El Niño. In 1998 many
people living in makeshift houses lost their homes in Nairobi as a result of the
flooding caused by El Niño. Other consequences of the flooding include restricted mobility within some of the slum areas, spread of disease, and general
loss of property. Flooding, open sewers, lack of refuse removal, lack of safe
drinking water, and the general lack of environmental sanitation all contribute
to the high incidence of waterborne illnesses[5] in the urban squatter settlements
and crowded slums.

The incidence of illness is high, especially among children in such settings,
reaching up to 76 percent (UNICEF 1994). About 75 percent of the illnesses in
slums are related to overcrowding and poor sanitary conditions (Naholi 1996).
In Nairobi, the amount of refuse generated ranges from about 800 to 1,000 tons
per day, of which only 25 tons are collected daily. Waste is not collected in
most slums and squatter settlements because they are regarded as illegal and
have no planned access roads. Children and women are most affected by the
resulting environmental health hazards. Children lose their playgrounds as they
become dumping grounds. In addition, some of the slums are located near industries, leading to exposure to a variety of hazardous effluents (GOK/UNICEF
1998, 174). The related lack of access to water for bathing and drinking is
another constant threat to those living in densely populated urban settings.

By the time children are old enough for primary school, only a minority of
families can afford to meet the expenses involved with "public" education in
Kenya, including buying school uniforms, shoes, textbooks, and paying fees for
examinations and other required contributions such as to the building fund.
Although there are public schools where no explicit tuition fee is required, the
cost of one year of primary education in Kenya has risen to over $250 per child
(Swadener, Kabiru, and Njenga 1997), while the average annual per capita income remains at approximately $350. Thus, dropout rates are high, in large part
due to the heavy expenses incurred by families to finance their child's education
(Human Rights Watch/Africa 1997a). Between 40 and 60 percent of children
living in the slum or "informal settlement" areas of Nairobi, Kisumu, and Mombasa do not attend primary schools, compared to enrollment rates of approximately 80 percent in the urban population as a whole (Munyakho 1992). A
growing number of nonformal or informal schools have begun to address this
huge need for affordable education, particularly in the urban slums. Such schools
do not require uniforms, often provide a meal during the day, sometimes provide

showers and primary health care, and typically rely on donations or church sponsorship to make an education available to children in extreme poverty.

Other issues compounding the challenges of high-poverty urban life in Kenya have included the growing problem of child neglect and abuse, including sexual abuse, particularly of young girls living in crowded slum settings (Kilbride and Kilbride 1990). A recent special supplement to the *East African Standard* (June 16, 1999) carried numerous articles describing the irony of the "Day of the African Child" for many urban children growing up without education, sufficient food, or housing. Several of the children, as young as five years of age, interviewed for this feature had been raped, beaten, arrested, and were living on the street.

Children Living and Working on the Street—A Growing Issue in Kenya

Among the most striking issues facing the growing number of street children in Kenya today is the fact that they are subject to frequent arrests for vagrancy, simply because they are homeless (Human Rights Watch/Africa 1997a). Since vagrancy is defined by Kenyan law as being "without a fixed abode," *being homeless is a criminal offense*. This vicious cycle of being homeless, characterized by victimization, frequent violence, exploitation, and arrests, is a growing tragedy in Nairobi and other Kenyan cities and towns. Street children are routinely dehumanized and are associated with being untouchable or defiled, inhabiting urban "geographies of exclusion" (Sibley 1995).

Estimates of the number of street children in Kenya vary greatly. The largest reported estimate appeared in an article published in the major Kenyan newspaper, the *Daily Nation*, which stated that "the number of street children in Nairobi grew from 3,600 in 1989 to 40,000 six years later in 1995. Today they number 60,000" (April 12, 1998, 1). The number of children "under care" or served by nongovernmental and governmental programs is also difficult to determine. Another newspaper article quoted Nairobi Provincial Commissioner Joseph Kaguthi, "27,278 street children are being rehabilitated in 39 centres in the city" (*Daily Nation*, July 7, 1998, 1). Street children are found in all major cities and in many rural areas. Estimates of the number of street children for other cities are the following: 5,000 in Mombasa, 4,000 in Kisumu, 2,500 in Malindi and Kilifi (along the coast of the Indian Ocean), and 2,000 each in Kitale and Nakuru (*Daily Nation*, July 7, 1998).

The data reported in the *Situation Analysis of Children and Women in Kenya 1998* (GOK/UNICEF 1998) were described as the "number of children in need of special protection (CNSP) by District."[6] The national estimate for CNSP was nearly 110,000 children, with the highest concentration in urban areas. Of that number, this report estimated that 26 percent live on the street. On a continent known for the proverb "It takes a village to raise a child," and in a nation that had few orphanages until fairly recently, these numbers are troubling, indeed.

In previous studies, children on the streets have been divided between those working for their families (children *in* the street) and those working for their own support (children *of* the street). The distinction between children *in* the street and children *of* the street is blurred in Kenya (Aptekar et al. 1995). Researchers caution against describing street children in melodramatic terms:

Unfortunately, this either understates or ignores the children's ability to cope in the face of difficult circumstances, or minimizes the children's problems, making them appear as heroic figures living the life of youthful adventurers (Aptekar 1989, 1993; Muraya 1993). Both scenarios are inaccurate, but the line between them is difficult to draw because it is so difficult to know to what degree the children are honest, to what degree one's own perception of them is accurate and to project how what is written about them will be perceived by readers. (Aptekar et al. 1995, 3)

Many theories exist about the large growth in the number of children in and of the streets of Kenya (Kilbride and Kilbride 1990; Weisner, Bradley, and Kilbride 1997). Several prevailing discourses resemble the U.S. "rhetoric of risk," which pathologizes children and families living in poverty (Swandener and Lubeck 1995). One such theory is that urban poverty leads to a breakdown of families and moral values. Another claims that street children are driven to the street by families who abandon, abuse, or neglect their children. Yet another theory blames the adverse effects of modernization, which is viewed as leading to the breakdown of traditional family values (Agnelli 1986; Dallape 1987; Kariuki 1989; Kilbride and Kilbride 1990; Nowrojee 1990; Onyango, Suda, and Orwa 1991; Weisner, Bradley, and Kilbride 1997). As several of these researchers point out, such analyses favor family dysfunction as the major causative factor for children living and working on the street.

According to L. Aptekar (1993, 1994), street boys are taught by their unmarried and impoverished mothers to cope with the economic necessity of having to become independent at a far earlier age than the dominant society deems appropriate. Aptekar attributes street boys' resilience and sense of survival, in part, to being able to leave home, and he even argues that boys staying at home in such circumstances may be worse off. Girls, in contrast, are taught to stay home and off the streets. Street girls tend here, as elsewhere in the world, to get involved in prostitution and addictive drugs and have fewer peer supports than street boys. Many have been raped and abused, were involved in prostitution, and bore one or more children at a young age. Girls are frequently detained by police and released only after being sexually abused (Kibride, Suda, and Njeru 2000).

Clearly there are multiple and complex causes of children being on the street. If anything, national economic policies required by the World Bank, the International Monetary Fund (IMF), and other donor agencies have led to austerity measures directly affecting many Kenyan families. Cost sharing for medical care, increased school fees, a high cost of living, and high unemployment are among the many changes described by the hundreds of parents interviewed in our study (Swadener, Kabiru, and Njenga 1997). A trickle down of austerity measures, which some have argued put "children in debt" (Bradshaw et al. 1993), have led to families no longer being able to send all—or any—of their children to school. This, in turn, could be seen as contributing to the growing number of both "compound children" and urban/peri-urban street children. The issue of corruption and mismanagement of public funds by the government of Kenya and other local municipalities is another likely contributing factor to the problem.

Working with the mothers' self-help group was particularly informative. In some cases, it was clear that urban migration, the breakup of families (all were single mothers raising fairly large families with meager resources and residing in very small, crowded housing in urban slums), and the lack of income sources have led to an inability to provide for their children. Although no mothers in the group stated that they had encouraged their sons to go to the street, some implied that things had gotten desperate and that their children were hungry and lacked even the basic needs. They were grateful when a program brought their children off the street and back home through sponsorship for school, buying books and school uniforms.

The self-help group also started a fund from which mothers could obtain small loans in emergencies or for micro-entrepreneurial projects (e.g., market activities, crafts, or kitchen gardens). They constantly struggled, but were also dignified, religious, and clearly loved their children. They did not appear to be "pathological" in any way. The group has continued to meet monthly since 1994 and has provided many types of support to each other. For example, the group helped several members who had lost everything in a fire to replace needed items and find temporary housing. Other groups, including the Single Mothers Association of Kenya and the Mwana Mwende Trust's young mothers' project (Kabiru and Njenga 1998), provide an array of support services and education for vulnerable mothers in a peri-urban area.

Whatever the complex causes are, the number of children living on the street is expected to continue to rise. Several highly visible campaigns to address the many unmet needs of these homeless children have begun in the past few years, with the largest funding to date coming through a new UNICEF initiative, providing assistance to groups working with street children in Kenya. Greater coordination and collaboration among the many charitable groups and nongovernmental organizations working with street children are also being encouraged with the formation of coalitions and coordinating bodies for their work. Finally, it is still hoped that the passage of the Kenya Children's Bill[7] will be helpful in protecting the rights of all children—particularly those most vulnerable, including the children and youth living and working on the street.

Women and Homelessness: The Feminization of Poverty

The high stakes of land ownership in Kenya form a critical factor in understanding the feminization of poverty and homelessness among impoverished

Kenyan women (GOK/UNICEF 1998; World Bank 1999). At least three factors account for the increased vulnerability of Kenyan women to homelessness. The first factor is the increase in single parenthood in Kenya, with the mother being the head of the household. Second, traditional cultural beliefs, attitudes, and practices among the majority of Kenya's ethnic groups have perpetuated the oppression of women by limiting their ability to inherit land. Third, Kenyan law, by upholding cultural practices in land inheritance, fails to protect a woman's right to own family land.

As in many other African countries, women in Kenya generally have had less access to education and paid employment opportunities, and they have suffered from a series of austerity measures associated with global debt restructuring policies. Whereas educated and professionally employed women might be able to take care of their children, many single mothers live with the possibility of homelessness looming over them. Stories of single mothers being thrown out onto the street by their fathers, former husbands, brothers, or other male relatives are not uncommon in rural areas in Kenya. Many such women find themselves moving to urban areas where the promise of a job is initially attractive, if short lived. Most such women participate in the informal sector in such activities as petty trade, hawking (street vending), small-skill production (*jua kali*), and personal service. However, like the fate of the makeshift housing in which the majority of street vendors live, the street markets are often raided by city council police who confiscate their wares and arrest whomever they catch. This reality dispels the myth of lucrative opportunities available to poor women in petty trade, which is not to say that the potential role of microenterprise loans and other income-generating strategies are doomed to fail. Rather, opportunities are far less than many rural women migrating to the cities have assumed.

Several recent newspaper articles have described homeless mothers with young children who are being taken off the street after over twenty years there. The advent of a *second generation of children being raised on the street* is troubling, indeed. The demographic face of Kenya has changed significantly, creating a unique situation, in which the workforce is exceeded by those thought to be dependent (World Bank 1999). Additionally, higher poverty rates among female-headed households in Kenya have been documented (Demerty, Grootaert, and Wong-Valle 1993; Sorensen 1990) compared to male-headed households. These statistics indicate that, in Kenya, homelessness is gendered and it has an age; *the majority of homeless persons in Kenya are female, and the fastest growing segment of the homeless are children.*

HOMELESSNESS AMONG PERSONS WITH DISABILITIES

Persons with disabilities constitute a special category of homeless Kenyans. Unlike any other sector of the homeless Kenyan population, persons with disabilities experience the highest interaction of risk factors that render Kenyans homeless. Culturally, among many tribes of Kenya, persons with disabilities

have been treated as significantly subhuman. As such, they have a higher likelihood of receiving no education or health care; they are not likely to inherit
land from their families; and, owing to their limitations in physical, cognitive,
or sensory functions, they are more likely to be unable to live independently.
Disproportionately large number of street beggars with disabilities greet a visitor
to Nairobi or any other urban center in Kenya today.

The 1989 census listed 251,000 people with disabilities, which constituted 2
percent of the population. Of these, 46 percent were children. While it is believed that the number of children with disabilities has increased, there are no
hard data to support this notion.[8] Children with disabilities are vulnerable to
mistreatment, neglect, abuse, and abandonment, and the UN has classified them
as "children in need of special protections" (GOK/UNICEF 1998).

Like other poor and homeless Kenyans, persons with disabilities perceive the
towns and cities as having the potential for offering them a chance for making
a better livelihood. Often the decision to move away from home is encouraged
by relatives. Thus, many persons with disabilities migrate to urban areas rather
than remain in rural areas where cultural beliefs about disabilities often preclude
independent functioning or, for that matter, prevent them from being viewed as
fully human. A 1982 national study of persons with disabilities in Kenya found
that about 94 percent of those surveyed said they resorted to begging after they
had failed to find a viable alternative for making a living (Nkinyangi and Mbindyo 1982). Many such people are homeless, and often they cannot remove themselves from a life on the streets because of their disabilities.

A common theme for those living in rural areas is the desire for independence,
which is often tempered by the reality that their disability precludes the achievement of total independence. Mr. K. K., who is paraplegic, captures this cycle of
poverty and homelessness:

You see, in the Kikuyu custom, one becomes mature after circumcision. Whether you
are a cripple like me or not, after circumcision you are considered to be ripe for self-
independence; indeed, to have your own ways, family and property. This is not difficult
for a person from a strong clan . . . but you see, I came from perhaps the poorest clan in
our area . . . shortly after circumcision, I learned that I was becoming a big burden to the
few relatives, friends, and neighbors. For a long time, I was worried about what to do.
Then friends advised me that if I came to Nairobi I would meet other cripples who
depended entirely on begging for their life . . . so I came to Nairobi in 1965 and started
a career of begging on the streets. It was hard to change, but soon I became happier than
I was at home. After begging for some time, I was able to save some little money to
open a vegetable kiosk. I gave up very soon as it was very difficult to get vegetables for
sale from the retail market . . . I went back to the streets very frustrated. (Nkinyangi and
Mbindyo 1982, 41)

The difficulties facing persons with disabilities are compounded and magni-
fied by their disabilities. The plight of Mr. K. K. mirrors that of many persons
with disabilities in Kenya who wind up in urban centers, homeless and often

helpless. Homeless women and girls with disabilities have also endured sexual abuses in the streets or in slums such as Kariobangi and Mukuru (Mutua 1999a).

INTERNALLY DISPLACED FAMILIES AND CHILDREN: A GROWING HOMELESS POPULATION

In recent years, state-sponsored ethnic violence in western Kenya and the Rift Valley has contributed to the internal displacement and migration of families, as well as to the breakup of families (Human Rights Watch/Africa 1993). In 1991, after the government was forced to concede to a multiparty system, the Moi government was responsible for instigating ethnic violence to punish those ethnic groups which supported the political opposition and to reward its own supporters with illegally obtained land. By 1993 Human Rights Watch/Africa estimated that 1,500 people had died in the clashes, and some 300,000 were internally displaced. It should be noted that there is very little public acknowledgement of the government's role in the "clashes," and, thus, few written sources are available which discuss its impacts on homelessness and other issues.

Although the large-scale attacks that characterized the violence have diminished since 1994, periodic incidents continue. Most of the displaced persons belong to the Kikuyu, Luo, and Luhya ethnic groups and were attacked by members of the Kalenjin ethnic group (President Moi's group), as well as the Maasai. Thousands of the displaced have still not returned to their land because of government inaction to provide adequate security, or because of forced or fraudulent sale of land at far below market prices. There is documentation of the government forcibly dispersing groups of displaced persons in order to avoid the attention of humanitarian and human rights groups and to evade its responsibility to return these citizens to their land and livelihood. Since most of those displaced were subsistence farmers with little formal education, they have been rendered destitute. Many members of the internally displaced ethnic groups have drifted to the slums of urban centers.

As a result, land continues to be fraudulently transferred, illegally occupied, and sold or exchanged unfairly, further disempowering the internally displaced and contributing to the removal of certain ethnic groups from the Rift Valley Province. (Human Rights Watch/Africa 1997b, 10)

The government has taken only the minimum steps to allay public criticism of its policies of ethnic persecution and discrimination, and it has not redressed the destruction and loss created by its sponsored violence. "As a result, a significant number of people are still not back on their land today, and will probably never be" (Human Rights Watch/Africa 1997b, 11).

The United Nations estimated that as much as 75 percent of the estimated 300,000 displaced were children. Many children witnessed the death or disappearance of close family members and suffered injuries themselves. Education was disrupted, with even makeshift, informal schools in the settlement camps sometimes closed down by local government officials. Human Rights Watch/ Africa interviewed a number of children who were forced to flee from their homes and were separated from their families during the so-called tribal clashes. Some had come to Nairobi in search of family members or because there was nowhere else to go. Quotes from these interviews from the Human Rights Watch/Africa source of 1997a, follow.

I had to flee in the middle of the night. I woke up and our house was on fire. There was no one left in the house, and I just ran. I stayed in a camp for about a year with a lot of other people who had to flee like me. After a while, people started talking about going back to their homes. I went back to my home [in Molo, Rift Valley], but our home was not there and my family was gone. The neighbors said they had heard nothing about my parents. So I came to Nairobi to look for my uncle and found him. He was surprised to see me—he said he thought we had all been killed. But he couldn't keep me with him. Sometimes I still see him when I can, but he can't take care of me. (Human Rights Watch interview with David, Nairobi, September 24, 1996)

According to another Kikuyu boy,

We're not real street boys, we were forced to leave our homes during the clashes. I had to run out of the house and hide at night—our house was burning. I came back the next day and my parents and brothers and sisters were gone. I don't know where they went. I came to Nairobi, and haven't been back [to Molo] since. (Human Rights Watch interview with Simon, September 26, 1996)

One study of displaced women in one camp found that women had suffered rape and other forms of sexual assault during the clashes (Gathirwa and Mpaka 1994). After becoming displaced, the study found that gender inequalities were exacerbated. Displaced women were victims of "rape, wife-beating by their husbands, sexually transmitted diseases, poverty, manipulations, hunger, fear, anger, anxiety, trauma, despondency, dehumanization, heavy workload and physical fatigue" (Gathirwa and Mpaka 1994). Women also tended to risk returning to farm on their land and suffered undernutrition, as they ate less in order to feed their husbands and children first.

Yet another contributing factor to homelessness and hunger made worse for the displaced Kenyans was the banning of nongovernmental organizations and church-sponsored feeding and other programs in the camps (e.g., at Maela camp) (National Christian Council of Kenya 1994). The lack of services provided to the "internal refugees," combined with fraudulent land transfers, illegal occupation, and pressured land sales and exchanges, contributed to increased homelessness through the permanent displacement on Kenyans.[9]

HOMELESSNESS IN RURAL AREAS

Although rapid urbanization and increased rural-urban migration in Kenya have contributed to the increase in poverty in urban areas, extreme poverty is still most prevalent in rural areas. The proportion of Kenyans living below poverty is 47 percent in rural areas compared to 30 percent in urban areas (World Bank 1997a). As previously discussed, the under-five mortality rate is much higher in rural areas, and several factors correlate with poverty levels in rural Kenya.

Many Kenyans in rural areas are small-scale farmers, and the amount and nature of commodities they produce account for a negligible portion of the market economy. Many rural subsistence farmers are mired in producing barely enough to live on and to feed their fairly large number of dependents. In a cash economy with a growing number of fees, copayments, and a rising cost of living, such subsistence farmers have very little that generates income. As one rural parent stated, "I go to the market only to look, not to buy. How can we afford school fees, clothing, kerosene for cooking, and food we do not grow?" Land subdivision among members of a family has left many rural Kenyans landless or homeless. As a result, there has been an increase in casual labor in which landless Kenyans work on others' farms for low wages and a place to have a kitchen garden. This trend[10] was correlated with early weaning practices and diminished child and maternal health, as young mothers walked far each day to work as casual farm laborers.

Polygamy as a cultural practice is prevalent among many rural tribes of Kenya. Economic realities have rendered polygamy impossible for many Kenyan urban dwellers, but among rural Kenyans, ironically, it is most rampant among the poorest and the least educated. Thus, in many rural homesteads, the proportion of dependent children is extremely high relative to the family's ability to provide adequate housing, health care, nutrition, or education. The size of families tends to be larger in rural Kenya compared to urban families (World Bank 1997a), and family size strongly correlates with poverty and conditions related to poverty (e.g., homelessness and higher infant mortality).

This increase in the number of children in a home correlates with the shrinkage of agricultural land in many rural communities in Kenya. With less available land, families are forced to think of creative ways to provide shelter and meet other basic needs. In rural Kenya, some poor families arrange for one of their children to live with a neighbor or someone with means who provides shelter, clothing, and sometimes education to a young person. In return, the young person performs housekeeping duties for the caregiver, serving as an *ayah*. Such in-kind arrangements are not an uncommon way for poor Kenyans to keep their children from becoming homeless.

In rural Kenya, owing to the existence of extremely large families with few to negligible assets, many young people who have no real shelter work on other people's farms, who, in turn, provide housing to such people. In communities where there are large plantations of tea or coffee, there are many homeless Kenyans who live their entire lives working on other people's farms, housed on those farms, and never knowing what would happen if they lost their jobs. A number of tea and coffee plantations provide shelter and health care only for "permanent" employees. The majority of workers in many cases are "casual laborers," who do not qualify for these "benefits" (Swadener, Kabiru, and Njenga 2000). For many such people, home is more a psychological state of mind than an actual shelter.

PASTORALISTS AFFECTED BY CHANGING LAND TENURE POLICIES

The discussion of homelessness among nomadic and pastoralist groups of Kenya presents some unique challenges. Traditionally, nomadic pastoralists have lived a life of homelessness (in terms of the definition of home provided earlier). Their traditional lifestyle has entailed moving from place to place in search of water and pastures for their herds. Changes in land tenure policies in Kenya have limited their access to pastures, forcing many of them to make lifestyle change (c.f., Fratkin 1998). Thus, among this group different notions underlie the construction of homelessness. The transient, or semipermanent, nature of the physical shelters used by this group and the restrictions that have been imposed by the prevailing land tenure policies must be considered.

During the colonial period, land tenure policies upheld customary land use, in which the land belonged to the entire clan and not to an individual person. The enactment of the Land Act of 1968 created group ranches which were headed by an elected representative, who was registered as the corporate owner of the ranch. More recently, among the seminomadic Maasai in Narok District, the tendency has been to subdivide ranches and seek individual ownership, especially in areas of greater agricultural productivity (U.S. Government 1984). This has accelerated the loss of grazing corridors and has led to the disruption of traditional clans which had previously held collective ownership, or use of land. Several of the Maasai parents interviewed, for example, were quite distressed about the subdivision and loss of land which previously had been communally held. The associated loss of traditional child care systems, including group care of young children by grandmothers, was a side effect of these changing land tenure policies (Swadener, Kabiru, and Njenga 1997). These factors have led to greater dislocation of pastoralist groups, including the Samburu, Maasai, Somali, and Turkana.

HIV/AIDS AND HOMELESSNESS

HIV-related deaths are increasing exponentially in Kenya. In 1997 NASCOP (the National AIDS and Sexually Transmitted Disease Control Program, cited in GOK/UNICEF 1998) reported that there are 110 adult deaths from AIDS every day in Kenya, but pointed out that this is likely an underestimate, since many deaths occur at home and are not reported through the health care system. It is also estimated that HIV alone has increased infant mortality by about 20 percent, since the majority of children infected with HIV die before their fifth birthday. These health issues intersect with an increase in homelessness in Kenya in several ways. First, the rise in the percentage of AIDS orphans in East Africa is dramatic and has greatly taxed the ability of traditional family and community resources to care for children losing parents to HIV/AIDS. The burden on grandparents and extended family members has exceeded many of their resources to care for additional children. Thus, the number of orphanages or children's homes has grown rapidly in the past decade, as has the number of children living and working on the street, many of whom have been directly affected by the virus.

The estimated national prevalence of HIV infection has risen from just over 3 percent in 1990 to 8 percent in 1996; the urban percent is estimated at 12.2 percent and the rural, 7.1 percent. The total population of individuals with HIV in Kenya in 1996 was estimated at 1,212,482 (GOK/UNICEF 1998). Another concern, affecting those living in urban slums or on the street, is the high incidence of tuberculosis. Because of its highly infectious nature, the resurgence of tuberculosis as a result of the AIDS epidemic is a major public health concern in Kenya. A study carried out in Nairobi, Mombasa, and Kisumu found a 29 percent, 40 percent, and 43 percent increase, respectively, in the incidence of tuberculosis from 1994 to 1995 (GOK/UNICEF 1998). HIV-infected individuals have a higher mortality from tuberculosis and frequently become reinfected after completing the course of tuberculosis therapy. Children born in high-poverty urban environments are more likely to be abandoned following the death of a parent infected with AIDS and/or tuberculosis. They, too, are vulnerable to acquiring the virus through sexual abuse, exploitation, and other forms of exposure. Women and children are the primary victims of the AIDS epidemic.

REFUGEE POPULATIONS IN KENYA

Although a comprehensive discussion of refugees in Kenya is beyond the scope and focus of this chapter, we want to conclude our summary of specific groups experiencing homelessness with an overview of their situation. There are approximately 6 million refugees in Africa at present, which is the largest number on any one continent in the world (Wilkes 1994). During the past 30 years, the Horn of Africa has experienced nearly constant refugee crises. In 1992 more than 400,000 people flooded into Kenya to escape from civil wars in Somalia and Sudan and from instability in southern Ethiopia. As a result of the civil war between rival clans in Somalia, 10 percent of the Somali population lives outside the country's borders (Wilkes 1994).

Several different waves of refugees have come to be at least temporary, homeless residents of Kenya, beginning in 1956 with southern Sudanese fleeing from civil war, many not returning until the early 1970s. In 1978 Somalis living in Ethiopia fled when war between Somalia and Ethiopia over the Ogaden region led to 500,000 people becoming refugees. Many Somalis remained in Kenya, which includes a Somali ethnic group in Northeastern Province. Later, beginning in 1988, thousands more Somalis fled when war broke out in northwest Somalia, and displaced Ethiopian refugees also fled to neighboring countries. By 1992 1 million refugees have fled to Kenya, Ethiopia, Djibouti, and Yemen.

Kenya's policies of dealing with such large numbers of refugees have varied. Often refugees are moved from one camp to another. Many of the refugee camps are located in arid or semiarid parts of northern and northeastern Kenya. Food is often scarce in the camps, health risks high, and little or no education provided for children. Children are frequently separated from their parents, and some end up in cities and towns, joining the ranks of street children. At Kakuma refugee camp in northwestern Kenya, there are 25,000 children in a camp of 40,000 people who have fled from Sudan. Almost all the children there are boys between the ages of 7 and 15, many of whom have already served as child soldiers. Although this camp provides better services for children than many others, including a foster care project and activities for children, many boys return to Sudan to fight as soon as they are old enough (Wilkes 1994, 24).

Other camps, in Mandera and Walda, near the Ethiopian and Somali borders in northeastern Kenya, serve mainly Somali refugees. Most refugees come on foot, but others have come to Kenya on crowded boats. Many children in these camps report seeing their parents and siblings killed or their fathers being taken away. Again, women and children enduring such extreme hardships and life-threatening circumstances constitute the majority in many Kenyan refugee camps. They are frequently moved from one camp to another and add to the number of displaced persons in Kenya today (Martin 1999). Somali and Sudanese refugees can be seen in most cities and towns of Kenya, where they attempt to live with relatives or in temporary shelters in the squatter settlements. In 1999 Somali families were camped outside the Nairobi headquarters of the UN High Commission on Refugees, where they were living on the street, alongside street children and other displaced persons.

The following narrative of a fifteen-year-old Somali refugee girl conveys the hardships of the journey and refugee camp experience for children:

I was the last person in my family to see my father. The fighting was horrible. The government was looking for people belonging to the rebel group . . . they were killing people, raping girls. Mama decided that we should leave Hargeisa and go to Kenya. I am the firstborn, so I am responsible. We are nine children, three from my aunt who died. My Mama cannot live without me. . . . By the second day we were walking only at night because during the day the enemy was fighting and there were roadblocks on the road. . . . I used to put my feet in water when we reached a village at the end of the day. I would just fall down. (Wilkes 1994, 19)

She further described her ill and pregnant mother and her fears about having to look after all the children, while not knowing where Kenya was,

We took a bus to Bula Nawa, on the border with Kenya. By this time my bones were aching. I thought I was going to die. After three years in Thika refugee camp, near

Nairobi, my family was transferred to Walda camp, in the north. We didn't like Walda, it was like a desert, but the people said we must go . . . so that we could be resettled. You see we cannot go back to Somalia. People hate us in Somalia, and we have no home, no family, no nothing. I am the firstborn and I feel very sad. Life here is very hard. The life in Somalia was very different. I will not get married or have a boyfriend because my Mama needs me. I don't think my Mama would survive without me. I have to look after my family first. I am without a father or brother to protect me. (Wilkes 1994, 19)

If this story is multiplied thousands of times, we can begin to imagine the lives of refugees in Kenya and see the clear links to chronic homelessness, hunger, and poverty that many will continue to experience. Like those displaced by ethnic clashes, refugees from neighboring nations add to the numbers of persons struggling to maintain a sense of home and family under extremely difficult circumstances.

CONCLUSIONS AND POLICY IMPLICATIONS

A number of themes are apparent in our examination of groups particularly vulnerable to homelessness in Kenya. Most striking is the feminization of poverty, with the fastest growing group of homeless in Kenya, *children*, often coming from single-parent families. The dramatic rise in the number of street children and the conditions of single mothers, particularly in urban areas, are interrelated and demand attention and appropriate intervention. Such conditions do not occur in isolation, but reflect the complex nested contexts of globalization; national austerity measures and other state policies, social, cultural, economic, and political factors; as well as dynamics of local communities and families in postcolonial contexts (Bhabha 1994; Gandhi 1998). The HIV/AIDS epidemic in East Africa has also affected many families in Kenya, creating large numbers of AIDS orphans and displacing families who have lost breadwinners to the virus. Many street children, for example, have lost parents to AIDS and may be HIV positive or vulnerable to contracting the disease through frequent sexual exploitation and abuse.

Other groups vulnerable to homelessness in Kenya include persons with disabilities and those displaced by government-sanctioned ethnic violence. These categories are sometimes blurred as well—a number of people became disabled as a result of the earlier clashes. Persons with disabilities face complex cultural stigmas and barriers to education and employment. They are frequently forced to leave rural homes as young adults for a life of living, working, and begging on the streets. An informal economy of begging has been documented in Kenya's major cities and towns (Nkinyangi and Mbindyo 1982), which includes whole families living on the street, as well as persons with disabilities. Many of those who lost their homes and property during the ethnic clashes in the early 1990s have yet to be resettled. They are moved from camp to camp, with limited services and little visibility. In fact, this group of homeless Kenyans is often rendered invisible to the public. In addition to displaced families, Kenya has absorbed over a million refugees in recent years, owing to civil wars, famine, and oppressive conditions in neighboring nations. Their plight and associated burden on the already taxed national infrastructure cannot be ignored in any discussion of homelessness in Kenya.

Some potential actions could be taken to address the causes of homelessness in Kenya. These are starting points for needed social and economic change to benefit the most vulnerable Kenyans and refugees in Kenya. A basic starting point for addressing homelessness would be to acknowledge fully its existence and the many forms it takes. Before any national or local strategies can be employed, an acceptance of the magnitude of the problem is necessary, and baseline data on the extent of homelessness would provide a measure for the progress made in attempting to alleviate it.

Given the feminization of poverty, measures must be taken to enhance the circumstances of girls and women in Kenya. These include the legally enforced right to inherit land and property, despite local and cultural custom, and providing access to credit or other community funds to assist women heads of households in starting small businesses. The high cost of public education must also be addressed, particularly given that an investment in education, particularly for girls, has direct correlations with child survival and other lifelong outcomes. We would also advocate a greater protection of the rights to housing and other basic needs for those living in semipermanent settlements or informal communities, particularly single mothers raising families in urban high-poverty areas. Better infrastructure—access to water, environmental sanitation, child care, improved safety measures, and transportation—as well as protection from displacement is clearly needed.

The need is also clear for more foster care and group homes for children orphaned by AIDS, as well as more direct support for families who have taken in extended family members or grandchildren. We would also advocate for more residential facilities and vocational training programs for children and youth forced to live on the street. We certainly do not advocate warehousing children in "remand homes" or other forms of legal detention, but would want nongovernmental organizations and the Kenya government to explore creative partnerships and support programs which meet children's basic physical, mental, and psychological needs. Such facilities or foster care arrangements should include paying for children's tuition to return to public school, or providing them with appropriate vocational training and job placement. Such transitional services are also obviously needed for persons with disabilities.

Turning to the rural majority of Kenyans, a number of recommendations can be made. We would advocate for strategies of rural development in cash-poor and agriculturally marginal areas, including providing better conditions for the growing number of casual laborers. Such improvements could include providing access to health care and housing in plantations and larger farms. Rural women's self-help groups, numbering in the hundreds in many districts, would also benefit from matching funds or small loans for their projects. We would also recommend taking legal action on behalf of farmers displaced by government-sanctioned violence so that they can either return to their land or be provided with equivalent land as restitution for their losses under illegal means. For pastoralists, we would recommend policies to protect grazing corridors and open land, as well as land tenure policies that respect and maintain, to the degree possible, collective land ownership by traditional clans.

Finally, turning to refugees, who constitute the largest single group of homeless in Kenya, we would advocate greater international support and national coordination of refugee programs. We would hope that a greater emphasis might be placed on education and skill building, as well as child and maternal health and empowerment for long-term resettlement.

In concluding, we would advocate maintaining a respectful awareness of the dignity, resilience, and creative acts of resistance of those who are experiencing or are vulnerable to homelessness in Kenya. They are not merely suffering at a distance (Boltanski 1999), nor should they be pathologized by their poverty; rather, they are members of dynamic and complex communities which are struggling to meet daily needs and build a life in Kenya.

REFERENCES

Agnelli, S. 1986. *Street Children: A Growing Urban Tragedy*. London: Weidenfeld and Nicholson.

Aptekar, L. 1993. "A Cross-cultural Comparison of Street Children." Paper presented at the annual meeting of the Society for Cross-Cultural Research, Washington, D.C., February 1993.

———. 1994. "Street Children in the Developing World: A Review of Their Condition." *Cross-Cultural Research* 28, no. 3: 195–224.

Aptekar, L., P. Cathey, L. Ciano, and G. Giardino. 1995. "Street Children in Nairobi, Kenya." *African Urban Quarterly* (February).

Banks, J. 1998. "The Lives and Values of Researchers: Implications for Educating Citizens in a Multicultural Society." *Educational Researcher* 27, no. 7: 4–17.

Bhabha, H. K. 1994. *The Location of Culture*. London: Routledge.

Boltanski, L. 1999. *Distant Suffering: Morality, Media and Politics*, trans. G. Burchell. Cambridge, England: Cambridge University Press.

Bradshaw, Y. W., R. Noonan, L, Gash, and C. B. Sershen. 1993. "Borrowing Against the Future: Children and Third World Indebtedness." *Social Forces* 71, no. 3: 629–56.

Dallape, F. 1987. *An Experience with Street Children*. Nairobi: Man Graphics.

Demetry, L., and C. Grootaert, with J. Wong-Valle, eds. 1993. *Understanding the Social Effects of Policy Reform*. Washington, D.C.: World Bank.

Fratkin, E. 1998. *Ariaal Pastoralists of Kenya: Surviving Drought and Development in Africa's Arid Lands*. Needham Heights, Mass.: Allyn and Bacon.

Gandhi, L. 1998. *Postcolonial Theory: A Critical Introduction*. New York: Columbia University Press.

Gathirwa, N.W., and C. Mpaka (1994, November). Reproductive and Psycho-social

Needs of Displaced Women in Kenya. The UN Development Fund for Women (UNIFEM) and UNICEF, Reproductive and Mental Health Issues of Women and Girls Under Situations of War and Conflict in Africa: Proceedings of an Expert Group Consultation. Nairobi: Regal Press.

Government of Kenya (GOK) and UNICEF. 1998. *Situation Analysis of Children and Women in Kenya 1998*. Nairobi: GOK and United Nations Children's Fund Kenya Country Office. This thorough report presents a broad portrait of the state of children and families in Kenya. Its thorough statistics provide readers with information on child and maternal health, demographic trends, nutritional factors, children in difficult circumstances (particularly street children), access to education, and an array of economic indicators. Data are framed in cultural and social contexts which bring the report to life. This readable report contains critical information.

Human Rights Watch/Africa. 1993. *Divide and Rule: State Sponsored Ethnic Violence in Kenya*. New York: Human Rights Watch/Africa.

———. 1997a. *Juvenile Injustice: Police Abuse and Detention of Street Children in Kenya*. New York: Human Rights Watch. This report highlights the issues of street children in three of Kenya's urban centers. Issues discussed include the brutalization of street children by police (including confinement without trial, beatings, and rape), the inability of the juvenile justice system to protect these children, and the growing presence of street children in Kenya. The report also addresses the criminalization of homelessness and recommends policy changes to protect children's rights.

———. 1997b. *Failing the Internally Displaced: The UNDP Displaced Persons Program in Kenya*. New York: Human Rights Watch. This report critiques the failures of the UNDP (United Nations Development Program) to address sufficiently the needs of Kenyans, 75 percent of whom were children, internally displaced as a result of government sponsored ethnic clashes in 1993. The report points out that the UNDP program missed opportunities to fully reintegrate displaced persons by not implementing human rights protection for the displaced individuals. It makes related recommendations.

Kabiru, M., and A. Njenga. 1998. *Teenage Motherhood: Children Raising Children. Report on the Mwana Mwende Young Mothers Project Baseline Survey in Machakos*. Nairobi: Mwana Mwende Child Development Trust.

Kariuki, P. 1989. "Some Educationally Valuable Aspects of African Traditional Approaches to Child Rearing." *Comparative Education* 23 no. 2:225–35.

Kayongo-Male, D. 1988. "Slum and Squatter Settlement in Kenya: Housing Problems and Planning Possibilities." In *Slum and Squatter Settlements in Sub-Saharan Africa: Toward a Planning Strategy*, ed. R. A. Obudho and C. C. Mhlanga. New York: Praeger Press.

Kenya Demographic and Health Survey. 1994. *Welfare Monitoring and Evaluation Survey*. Nairobi: Kenyan Ministry of Planning.

Keraro, J. 1994. "Brief Report for the Chairman on Street Children in Nairobi." Provincial Task Force, Nairobi, Kenya.

Kilbride, P., and J. Kilbride. 1990. *Changing Family Life in East Africa: Women and Children at Risk*: University Park: Pennsylvania State University Press.

Kilbride, P., C. Suda, and E. Njeru. (2000). *Street Children in Kenya: Voices of Children in Search of a Childhood*. Westport, Conn.: Bergin and Garvey.

Martin, J. 1999. *This Our Exile: A Spiritual Journey with the Refugees of East Africa.* Maryknoll, N.Y.: Orbis Books.

Munyakho, D. 1992. "Kenya: Child Newcomers in the Urban Jungle." UNICEF Innocenti Studies, p. 3.

Mutua, K. 1999a. "Macro- and Micro-level Factors That Predict Educational Access among Children with Disabilities in Kenya." Ph.D. diss. Kent State University.

———. 1999b. "Factors That Predict School Enrollment of Children with Disabilities in Kenya." Paper presented at the annual meeting of the American Educational Research Association, April, Montreal, Canada.

Naholi, M. 1996. *Community Management of Water and Sanitation Facilities in Peri-urban Areas of Mathare Area 4/B in Nairobi.* Nairobi: Development Alternatives Network.

National Christian Council of Kenya (NCCK). 1994. "NCCK Review Report on the Registered Land Clashes Affected Persons in Western Kenya." Nairobi: National Christian Council of Kenya.

Nkinyangi, J. A., and J. Mbindyo. 1982. *The Condition of Disabled Persons in Kenya: Results of a National Survey.* Nairobi: University of Nairobi, Institute of Development Studies.

Nowrojee, V. 1990. "Juvenile Delinquency and an Exploration of the Laws Governing Children in the Criminal Process in Kenya." Master's thesis, Bryn Mawr College.

Obudho, R. A., and C. C. Mhlanga. 1988. *Slum and Squatter Settlements in Sub-Saharan Africa: Toward a Planning Strategy.* New York: Praeger Press.

Onyango, P., C. Suda, and K. Orwa. 1991. *A Report on the Nairobi Case Study on Children in Especially Difficult Circumstances.* Florence, Italy: UNICEF.

Payne, G. K. 1984. *Low-income Housing in the Developing World: The Role of Sites and Services and Settlement Upgrading.* New York: John Wiley.

Polakow, V. 1993. *Lives on the Edge: Single Mothers and their Children in the Other America.* Chicago: University of Chicago Press.

Rogers, L. J., and B. B. Swadener. 1999. "Reflections on the Future Work of Anthropology and Education: Reframing the 'Field.' " *Anthropology and Education Quarterly* 30, no. 4:436–40.

Sibley, D. 1995. *Geographies of Exclusion: Society and Difference in the West.* London: Routledge.

Sorensen, A. 1990. "The Differential Effects on Women of Cash Crop Production: The Case of Smallholder Tea Production in Kenya." Danish Center for Development Research, CDR project paper no. 90.3.

Swadener, B. B. In Press. "Mapping Urban Places/Creating Expressive Spaces: Using Art to Enter the World of Street Children in Nairobi, Kenya." In *Semiotics of Third Space Across the Disciplines*, ed. L. J. Rogers. Madison, Wisc.: Atwood Press.

Swadener, B. B., and S. Lubeck. 1995. *Children and Families "at Promise": Deconstructing the Discourse of Risk.* Albany: State University of New York Press.

Swadener, B. B., M. Kabiru, and A. Njenga. 1997. "Does the Village Still Raise the Child? A Collaborative Study of Changing Childrearing in Kenya." *Early Education and Development* 8, no. 3:285–306.

———. 2000. *Does the Village Still Raise the Child? A Collaborative Study in Changing Child-rearing and Early Education in Kenya.* Albany: State University of New

York Press. This book presents findings from a national collaborative study which analyzed the impacts of rapid social and economic change on child rearing and early education in eight districts. The narratives of over 460 parents, grandparents, preschool teachers, children, and community leaders provide unique insights on the impacts of neocolonial policies, "development" practices, and national austerity measures on the everyday lives of families from contrasting settings.

Thiong'o, Ngugi wa. 1989. *Devil on the Cross*. Portsmouth, NH: Heinemann.

Tipple, A. G., and K. G. Willis. 1991. *Housing the Poor in the Developing World: Methods of Analysis, Case Studies and Policy*. London: Routledge.

"27,000 Nairobi Street Kids under Care," *Daily Nation*, July 7, 1998.

UNICEF. 1994. "Community-based Water Supply and Sanitation Projects, Baringo and Kisumu Districts." Nairobi: United Nations Children's Fund.

UNICEF/KCO. 1992. *Basic Needs Survey of the Urban Poor of Nairobi*. Nairobi: Kenya Consumers Organization.

United Nations. (1980). Principles and Recommendations for Population and Housing Censuses. Statistical Papers. Series M, No. 67. New York: United Nations Statistical Office.

U.S. Government. 1984. *Kenya: A Country Study*. Washington, D.C.: Department of the Army.

Walton, J., and C. Ragin. (1989). "Austerity and Dissent: Social Bases of Popular Struggle in Latin America." In W. Canak (ed.), *Lost Promises: Debt, Austerity and Development in Latin America*. Boulder: Westview Press.

Weisner, T. S., C. Bradley, and P. L. Kilbride, eds. 1997. *African Families and the Crisis of Social Change*. Westport, Conn.: Bergin and Garvey. This edited book brings together research done by anthropologists and other social scientists working in Kenya. A major theme of the book is a transcultural examination of the impacts of social change on the family. Specific issues addressed include health—particularly HIV/AIDS, food production, and nutrition—housing, gender—including women's property rights—issues facing the elderly, and the impacts of delocalization and urbanization on Kenyan women and children.

"What Does This Day Mean to the Child?," *East Africa Standard*, June 16, 1999.

Wilkes, S. 1994. *One Day We Had to Run! Refugee Children Tell Their Stories in Words and Paintings*. Brookfield, Conn.: Millbrook Press, in conjunction with UNHCR and Save the Children. This book, intended for children and youth, provides a moving account of a volunteer's experiences working with refugee children in Kenya. Powerful photographs and artwork made by children in refugee and settlement camps portray life for the 1 million refugees currently living in Kenya. Photographs and artwork are accompanied by the children's stories of how they came to be refugees and describe their hardships, losses, and their dreams for the future.

World Bank. 1980. "Poverty and Growth in Kenya," working paper no. 398. Washington, D.C.: World Bank.

———. 1995. *From Nairobi to Beijing: Second Review and Appraisal of the Implementation of the Nairobi Forward-looking Strategies for the Advancement of Women*. Washington, D.C.: World Bank.

———. 1997a. *Sector Strategy: Health, Nutrition and Population*. Washington, D.C.: World Bank.

——. 1997b. "Challenges and Opportunities for Sustainable Development," technical paper no. 331. Washington, D.C.: Africa Technical Department.

——. 1999. "Gender, Growth, and Poverty Reduction: Special Program for Assistance for Africa," 1998 status report on poverty in Sub-Saharan Africa. Washington, D.C.: World Bank.

NOTES

1. Supported partially by a Fulbright Senior Research fellowship and partially by the World Bank ECD Program.

2. The last national census to be conducted in Kenya was in 1989.

3. Such growing settlements or slums include Mathare Valley, Huruma, Dandora, Kariobangi, Mukuru, Dagorett, Kibera, Korogocho, Ngara, Uthiru, Kibete, and Kangemi.

4. Kisumu is a municipality in western Kenya, on the eastern shore of Lake Victoria.

5. Frequest illnesses include cholera, upper respiratory infections, malaria, and malabsorptive hunger due to parasites.

6. Statistics on the number of street children were reported as follows: Nairobi: 3,300 female, 6,700 male; Mombasa: 2,000 female, 6,000 male; Kisumu: 624 female, 4,800 male; and Nakuru: 775 female, 1,725 male.

7. The Kenya Children's Bill has been debated by the Parliament and supported by many child advocacy organizations for the past five years, but it has not yet passed. It is based, in part, on the UN Convention on the Rights of the Child, which Kenya has signed but not enforced.

8. The main disabilities, according to the 1989 census, were lower limb (31 percent), mental (23 percent), and hearing (19 percent). Other disabilities were upper limb, hunchback, and blindness.

9. While doing fieldwork in 1994–1995 in Kenya, the first author heard firsthand accounts of displaced Kenyans who had been told by local police or Kenyan soldiers to lock their families in their homes for safety, only to have their homes set on fire. In parts of the northern Rift Valley, the evidence of scores of abandoned, often burned out, farms was a chilling reminder of the ethnic clashes which had displaced so many Kenyans in previous years.

10. Particularly in Embu District, which had varied agricultural productivity and high population density.

12

Houses for All? Post-Apartheid Housing Policy and Shelter Needs in South Africa

ANDREW SPIEGEL, VANESSA WATSON, AND PETER WILKINSON

INTRODUCTION

"Give us houses not toilets" demands a graffito in a site-and-service area of Khayelitsha, a residential area planned for African people on the remote edge of the metropolitan area of Cape Town, South Africa. It conveys outrage that current public housing policy provides only small, serviced residential sites, each with just one toilet and one tap. The demand reflects a long-held position, expressed in the slogan of the African National Congress's 1955 Freedom Charter[1]—"houses for all"—which was the focus of much conflict during the "township revolt" of the late 1970s and the 1980s. The authors of the slogan and current policy makers can be seen to have failed to take account of the diversity of needs, means, and expectations of poor South Africans with regard to housing, the households they form, and what they understand as home.

Given its centrality in South African political history, housing provision inevitably became a key policy issue for the postapartheid government. The size of the national housing backlog inherited by the new government in 1994 was very large. It was estimated then that there was a shortage of 1.5 million units in the urban areas which included 720,000 shelters on serviced urban sites which needed upgrading and 450,000 people living in inadequate hostel[2] accommodations. There was also a very large number of rural dwellings which lacked basic services (Republic of South Africa 1994). The number of people who were literally homeless—in the sense that they were sleeping on the streets or in the open without any shelter at all—is unlikely to have been significant, and the Department of Housing saw its task as providing for a much wider cohort of people, including those living in overcrowded conditions, in shelters which provided inadequate protection, and on land which was unserviced and without secure tenure arrangements. Indeed, the new Department of Housing soon declared its aim to provide one million houses in five years (Republic of South Africa 1994) to accommodate the bulk of those whom it considered to be without "proper" housing.

Housing's political significance is unsurprising. First, housing is a basic human need. Without a shelter that can withstand the weather, which is affordable and secure, which is large enough to accommodate family needs, and which provides reasonably convenient access to facilities such as schools, clinics, and shops, a household's establishment and development—whether in urban or rural areas—is seriously impaired. In a situation where so many have been denied the resources to meet this basic need, it is inevitable that it should be a central political demand. Second, urban housing in South Africa was used as a political tool by previous governments to secure and control the labor force, and to control and direct the process of urbanization (Lupton and Murphy 1995). Inevitably, the cost and the location of public housing remain sensitive and contentious issues.

This chapter explores the extent to which current South African housing policy is able to meet diverse demands for housing, in a context in which complex processes of inter-regional and intra-urban movement fundamentally affect the nature of the demand. Using ethnographic evidence from greater Cape Town in the early 1990s, it begins by identifying some characteristics of the diversity of ways African[3] people construct households and social networks in order to create loci of domestic stability and reproduction. The focus is on how those are linked to experience of the interrelated processes of urbanization and incorporation into the wage-labor market.

With that as backdrop, the parameters of past and present South African public housing policy and the models and theories on which it is built are considered. The present policy's emphasis on incremental housing development, incorporating models of urbanization and household structure or composition which bear little relation to many people's on-the-ground experience, are examined in order to show how public housing policy fails to grasp the diversity of demand for housing. Consequently there is a serious lack of "fit" between the form in which housing is delivered and the housing needs of poorer families. The failure follows lack of recognition, in housing policy circles, of the diverse strategies people employ in their efforts to consolidate their domestic resource bases—to create households and homes—and the extent to which their strategies are constrained by their experiences of urbanization and incorporation into the wage-labor market.

CONSTRUCTING HOUSEHOLDS AND SOCIAL NETWORKS

This section presents four case histories of African households in Cape Town after a brief summary of the patterns and processes of settlement that occur in metropolitan Cape Town.

Settlement Patterns and Housing in Metropolitan Cape Town

Current patterns of settlement and housing of the African population of Cape Town need to be understood within the context of previous governments' efforts to contain and direct African people's urbanization patterns.[4] As early as 1923, legislation was passed to limit the growth of permanently settled African people in the urban areas. The provisions of this legislation were applied to Cape Town in 1926 with the effect that any Africans who were not registered property owners were required to live in a separate municipal "location," while Africans entering the municipal area had to obtain work seekers' or visitors' permits, valid for no more than a month. By the time the apartheid government came to power in 1948, there was already in place a set of legal controls for effectively controlling the movement of African people from the rural "homelands"[5] to the urban areas and their spatially segregated residence within the urban area.

In the era of "grand apartheid," initiated in 1948, the problems of removing existing freehold rights of Africans in "white" urban areas, and of controlling their influx from the homelands, were addressed inter alia through mass construction of public rental housing in "properly planned urban townships" where occupancy could be closely monitored and regulated. In Cape Town, the first African township of Langa had been developed in 1927, but in the 1950s and 1960s the much larger townships of Nyanga and Gugulethu were developed. During the 1960s, however, the logic of "separate development" increasingly emphasized accommodation of the growing African labor force within the homeland areas, from which, it was expected, they would commute to jobs in the towns and cities. To this end, housing resources were increasingly directed to homeland locations, and, in 1968, a state directive ordered the cessation of all provision of African family housing in townships in white urban areas. Inevitably these measures gave rise to severe housing shortages, high levels of overcrowding, and widespread illegal, informal settlement in the urban areas, as African people continued to attempt to gain or retain access (often illegally) to employment possibilities offered by the cities.

Increasing political resistance to apartheid rule from the mid-1970s threw the basic tenets of apartheid and separate development dramatically into question. Lack of clarity about the direction of necessary reform in the urban policy arena, coupled with the onset of severe economic recession, enabled nongovernmental agencies (particularly the big business–supported Urban Foundation) to establish a new approach to housing provision. From the end of the 1970s, therefore, state intervention in the housing process was effectively limited to the provision of serviced sites and "core" housing, a change in keeping with emerging international emphasis on self-help (World Bank 1974). At the same time, continuation of widespread and intense urban unrest throughout the country forced "reformist"[6] policy makers to recognize that African urbanization was inevitable and would have to be managed on a different basis from before. Consequently, in the light of their obvious inability to contain African people within the homelands, influx controls were finally abandoned in 1985.

In Cape Town, the late 1970s marked the start of a period of frequent battles by squatters to establish various informal settlements, some of which survive to the present. Divisions and conflicts within the African population, essentially over control of access to informally settled land, but encouraged in a number of instances by government agents in an attempt to cause political rifts (Cole 1987), resulted in the large-scale destruction of several informal settlements and the creation of sizable refugee populations within the metropolitan area (Fast 1995). In 1983, in an attempt to take control of the increasingly unstable situation in the city, the state opened up an extensive parcel of land for African settlement on the southeastern periphery of the metropolitan area. Known as Khayelitsha, it was intended to accommodate some 450,000 people, partly on serviced sites and partly in small, formal core houses, in both cases for eventual freehold ownership. Concerted efforts were made by the authorities to consolidate many of the scattered informal settlements around Cape Town into this area. But its distance some 35km from the central areas of Cape Town, its lack of work and service facilities, and its bleak and sandy, windswept nature have made it for many people a residential area of last resort.

The pattern of African settlement in Cape Town at the present time shows the strong imprint of the historical forces described above. There has been a very limited movement of African families into residential areas classified as white and colored under the apartheid regime, and the continuities between the housing policies of the apartheid government and the present government have meant that past patterns of public housing provision have been perpetuated. The development of serviced sites and core houses has continued in Khayelitsha and in pockets of land around the older formal townships, but at a slow rate. Most of the older informal settlements remain and have expanded, and many new informal settlements have emerged in and around Khayelitsha and the older townships. A significant number of people stay in "back-yard shacks," paying rental fees to the property holder (Watson and McCarthy 1998), and most of the old single-sex hostel accommodations, built originally for migrant workers, are now occupied by families living under highly overcrowded conditions (Jones 1993; Ramphele 1993).

A 1996 estimate made by the Provincial Department of Housing (Provincial Administration of the Western Cape 1996) puts the overall housing backlog within the metropolitan area at 109,300 units, and it can be assumed that a significant proportion of those needing housing are African. The figure excludes the 54,500 households living on serviced sites which will probably require public assistance to upgrade levels of shelter, and again it can be assumed that the majority of these are African. The central concern of poorer African households in the city has therefore continued to be how to gain access to land and shelter, under conditions in which the supply of both is highly constrained. The following cases indicate some of the ways in which particular individuals and households, each with different sets of needs and priorities, have, with greater or lesser degrees of success, managed to secure urban shelter for themselves.

Forms of Household Consolidation: Four Cases

The following cases indicate the diversity of domestic experience and expectations of people and identify various factors that constrain their domestic consolidation efforts. The term "consolidation" here means the strengthening of social bonds linking people who regard themselves as members of one domestic unit (household) even though they are not continuously co-resident or commensal (eating at the same table). It also reflects an investment of material resources in one or more residential structures and sometimes also in various small-scale production units. The units may be dispersed across the country, but they are tied together through social bonds and networks whereby people constitute "stretched" households (Spiegel, Watson, and Wilkinson 1996). These cases range along a continuum of consolidation trajectories from what, at one end, appears to be an example of successful urban consolidation, through examples of patently unsuccessful, or not yet achieved, consolidation in either the urban or rural context.

Case 1: Apparently Successful Urban Consolidation

GR and PR (file A2),[7] a couple in their thirties, purchased a small (two-bedroom) formal house in greater Khayelitsha in 1989. For many years they had shared accommodations with relatives in older formal townships. Their move to their own formal house in Khayelitsha revealed a clear intention to consolidate a distinct domestic unit around their own nuclear family.

> We stayed there [GR's parents' house] . . . but we could see that we had no future there because we had children, and we felt our kids should grow up in our own house. So we decided to buy this house. . . . We found that we could pay for [afford] it. There were other houses that we could find, and which were better than this one, but because of our standard and the money we earn we could see that we cannot afford those better houses. . . . I want to extend this house in the long run. So the savings clubs are the way to keep money.

Mr. GR's formal employment as a driver and Mrs. PR's part-time employment as a char had provided them with the income to support establishment of a separate home after they had accumulated funds through their membership in various local savings clubs.

The new unit's eight residents comprised the couple, their four young children, PR's 18-year-old-sister and GR's sister's toddler son. PR, describing the household as "packed" into the house, said they planned to extend the house in order to accommodate the residential unit's members and to provide space to entertain (and occasionally lodge) visitors, thereby maintaining their social networks, a practice which had involved accommodating six visitors, for varying periods, at times during the previous year. "This house . . . is small and since we have this large family we are 'packed.' We want to extend it. As you see, we do not have a dining room. We have only a lounge. . . . I want to build a new bedroom and extend the kids' bedroom. I will change our bedroom and make it into a dining room."

Both PR and GR had been raised in Cape Town, although both spent periods of their adolescence at Transkei schools. GR, born in the Transkei, had settled in Cape Town with his parents as a small child. PR was born in Cape Town to parents already resident there. When they married in 1982 they already had two children and had lived together some years, first in GR's parents' formal township house and then—because houses were in very short supply—in backyard shacks, sometimes rented from strangers, sometimes from relatives. On GR's father's death they decided to formalize their marriage and to move back to his house where they invested in improvements: they hoped to take it over from GR's widowed mother—an arrangement which, they said, had been bureaucratically blocked to await GR's mother's death when GR would be officially entitled to inherit. Their dependent status there, and pressures of space (the house also accommodated eight others), led them to buy and settle elsewhere.

As do many similar people's houses, GR and PR's house accommodated good quality furniture and appliances that reflected their commitment to consolidating a secure urban domestic space of their own.[8] While they disliked the remoteness of the house's location far from the city center, and the lack of nearby amenities, they understood that circumstances would improve with time, and they continued to invest their earnings, time and sentiments there.

GR and PR represent a category of township residents comprising younger people who are securely settled in urban areas, in the sense of having long personal histories of, and a commitment to, urban living, and who have regular employment which provides sufficient income to enter the emerging housing market in townships. Commonly such people attempt to reduce the intensity of their relationships with kin and establish separate households. Another respondent (file C1), an upwardly mobile young professional woman born in Cape Town, confirmed the tendency when she said that she planned to purchase the old formal township house her parents had long rented and where she had grown up, but not to live in it herself. Her aim was to secure their tenure over it and then leave it to her unemployed siblings while she and her husband and children established an autonomous household elsewhere, in another house they would purchase. She explained,

My brothers don't work. So it will simply mean that if I don't buy it [the old family house] they won't have a place to stay. . . . And the next thing, they will move straight to me and I won't be able to say to them "go back." So I'm just securing the house for them. Whether they make it a ghetto [slum-like] I don't care. Otherwise they'll be squatting there with me and upsetting my whole marriage.

Despite the expressed intention of such people to limit the intensity of their kinship links, most still need to maintain social networks stretching beyond their households. One result, as in GR and PR's case, is that their residential units continue to include persons who are not members of the nuclear family. Another is that they accommodate "visitors" in their households, for longer or shorter periods.

A second category of township residents comprises people who aspire to the same kinds of urban residential security and commitment as do those described above. But they differ in two important respects, namely, the reliability of their incomes, and therefore their ability to purchase or, in some cases, even to rent housing, and their experience of urban life.

Most of them are people who, having begun to settle in the city, have found employment but have yet to insert themselves securely in better-paying jobs. Despite their intentions to establish stable urban bases, most still struggle to do so as effectively as they might wish. Consequently, they find themselves still housed in one of the many shack areas on the edges of the city. Frequently they establish large residential units with multiple income earners so that incomes can be pooled, and the risks inherent in involvement in an oversupplied and unstable labor market can be spread.

By contrast with those already discussed who try to limit the intensity of their social networks, people in the second category invest time, energy, and resources in creating and maintaining social networks of mutual support, both within the urban area and beyond. Activation of the networks includes sporadic but quite common movement of individuals (particularly children) between domestic units so that advantage can be taken of fluctuating flows of income as circumstances in the labor market favor now one, now the other person and his or her dependent domestic unit. A consequence is fairly extensive "domestic fluidity," that is, households which frequently change their composition through the movement of members in and out of the unit, or between the various "bases" which make up the household.

Moreover, individual movement between domestic units also frequently involves long-distance travel between rural and urban settings. It thus helps to maintain long-established patterns of "oscillating migration," and simultaneously to reinforce reciprocities between individuals and groups needed to sustain networks linking urban and rural areas into one effective social field.

Case 2: Unsuccessful Urban Consolidation

MN, a Transkeian in his mid-fifties (file B2), headed a residential group of eleven people who, in 1993, lived in a shack in an area of invaded land on the margins of one of Cape Town's formal townships. They had only recently moved from another shack area where they had been paying a shacklord a monthly amount that they had understood would entitle them to a formal house: "He promised us houses, and we were paying him money to get us houses." When violence broke out destroying their shack, they moved to a new area, occupied a site there and erected another shack which they were slowly attempting to extend.

The residential group comprised MN, his wife, NTN, four of their six children and a grandchild plus MN's brother, BN—in his early fifties—his wife, NLN, and two of their children. Both couples had other children. Some lived in the Transkei, where MN had a small house and field. The children visited Cape Town occasionally when finances permitted. Others lived with relatives in various parts of Cape Town, and visited MN's shack on occasional weekends.

Most of the children in the co-resident group had first come to Cape Town on recent visits from the Transkei, and then just stayed on. Indeed, although the adult members of the group attempted to find the resources to visit their Transkei home every so often and take care of their ever diminishing resources and contacts there, their long-term intention was to settle permanently as families in Cape Town.

We have family there [Transkei], but we are planning to bring them here. I want to stay here for the rest of my life because my relatives and friends are here. The hospital is here. I want even to die here and I will, no matter we do not have houses. Tell me, who in their right mind would want to live in the Transkei? Life there is very difficult . . . everything is here, the schools, the doctors and everything . . . I want to be buried here [in Cape Town] because my family is here. No one could bury me there.

Although MN came to Cape Town in 1986, he and his brother, BN, had shared a shack since the latter's arrival in 1987. By that time MN's wife, NTN, was also in Cape Town. They shared because only MN had a reliable job—as a laborer at the nearby airport—while BN could find only poorly paid farmwork on a small holding some distance away. Pooling their incomes was one strategy to stretch them as far as possible in order to survive. Maintaining close relations with relatives was another survival strategy, although, as NTN pointed out when talking about relatives and visitors they entertained: "Not any of our visitors slept [here]. Which visitor can sleep in a shack, and a small one [at that]? . . . Our other relatives here are like us. They too do not have brick houses. Besides, who cares for visiting and sleeping [over] when we are so poor?"

People in the two categories of township residents discussed so far have a distinctly urban orientation in their perspectives on where they see their medium- and long-term futures. By contrast, other people are far less urban oriented, being very disinclined to commit themselves to urban living, and certainly antagonistic to the idea of urban settlement over the long term. For them, home is a rural place, often the place where they were born or, in their own terms, where their umbilical cord was buried at the time of their birth. That is where they believe they should retire and most certainly where they themselves should be buried. It is also where many such people think it would be proper to raise their children, away from the corrupting influence of urban life.

Just as this study disaggregates those who see the city as home in terms of their degree of insertion into the wage labor market and their experience of urban living, so, too, can one disaggregate the people who focus their attention and energies on rural homes: those who are rural-oriented. On the one hand, they include those with reliable jobs and long experience of living in town, but whose domestic life projects are focused on rural homes where they invest their earnings derived from urban jobs as well as most of their energies. Exemplified by BD whose circumstances we describe in case 3, they are people who create and maintain intense social networks that stretch across the urban-rural divide—effectively creating a single social field—and who regard themselves as temporary urban residents whose primary goal is to earn money to secure their rural resources.

On the other hand, some present township residents who would like to maintain rural homes are so weakly inserted into the urban labor market that they are, in a real sense, trapped in the city against their wishes and their own better judgment. Their rural orientation is more in the way of wishful thinking or nostalgia than a realizable project. Unemployed, in abject poverty and living in scantily provisioned shacks, they struggle on the city's very margins just to survive, all the while dreaming of using the city as a place to generate income to construct a rural base. We return to this, our fourth category of township people, after considering case 3.

Case 3: Apparently Successful Rural Consolidation

BD (file G1), an unschooled man in his mid-fifties, had spent the past 33 years working as a laborer in Cape Town. Although he had first arrived at a time when apartheid regulations were still such that he might have been able to settle in the city with his wife and children, only in recent years had his wife occasionally visited him and stayed in the hostel room he shared with six other people. For the most part, she and the children remained at their Transkei home in which BD invested as much as he could afford and which he visited annually: "What do you think I am doing here in Cape Town? . . . I have cows there [in the Transkei]. Fifteen of them. We also have sheep and goats and my wife has fowls. . . . I save money for them [my house and family]. I also save for my old age, and in order to buy cattle . . . and a plough."

For men such as BD, the city is a place just to earn money, even if it is in relatively poorly remunerated occupations—an attitude that, ironically, conforms closely with the separate development ideology of the apartheid period. Many such men seek accommodation in one or another of the hostels built, during the apartheid years, to house single migrant workers in spartan conditions (Jones 1993; Ramphele 1993). Some of them, including BD, had earlier sought jobs

that offered hostel accommodation because it allowed them to avoid the perceived evils of townships. As BD explained,

I like to live here because it keeps me away from the ills of the townships. . . . We have
come here to work, and not to complain. The place is not ideal, but I know deep down
that I do not belong here. I belong in the Transkei where my real home is. This place
is just temporary. . . . This is not our place. I have a big house there at home. This is
only a place to hide my head. I will not live here for the rest of my life.

Moreover, such men generally invest resources to sustain networks of reciprocity with other people from rural areas. Many, including BD, manage to
occupy hostel rooms with close male kin with a similar outlook to their own.
They do this in order to save as much as possible of their city earnings for
investment in their rural homesteads which they regard as their home.

Contrasting with the pictures above of determined and successful oscillating
migrants who have managed, over years of urban employment and spartan hostel
living, to accumulate resources in a rural area is a fourth category of people
who would wish to achieve a similar outcome but whose circumstances have
not enabled them to do so. They are currently township residents whose insertion
into both the wage-labor market and the mainstream urban nexus is extremely
fragile. Such people are often, although not invariably, relatively new and usually reluctant settlers in town, who wish to retain links with rural areas but are
too poor to do so. Frequently their rural orientation is reinforced by their experiences of internecine violence which has, over recent years, resulted in people
losing their shacks to fire as whole settlements have been razed. Yet the paradox
is that those experiences, in combination with their experience of chronic unemployment or underemployment, have rendered them so poor that they find
themselves trapped in the city with no source of wage or other income and no
resources on which to draw.

Case 4: Unsuccessful Urban or Rural Consolidation

PZ and his wife OZ (file B4) were Transkeians in their mid-thirties. Both
were unemployed and living with two of their four children in a plastic-sheet
shelter in a shack settlement on invaded land neighboring an old formal African
township. Like most residents there, they were refugees from violence that had
destroyed their previous shack and minimal resources.

PZ had been in the greater Cape Town area for ten years, having started out
as a laborer in a brick factory that offered hostel accommodation. OZ, meanwhile, remained in the Transkei, using remittances from PZ to care for their
family and begin developing a rural homestead including livestock. "I hated to
come to town. I felt more comfortable there at home."

Disaster struck, however, when PZ was retrenched, lost his hostel rights and
failed to find further employment. Then their few sheep died or were lost. When
OZ visited her husband, they found a site in a shack settlement from which PZ

began looking for work. But all he found were occasional piece-jobs, insufficient to support regular remittances, or to allow regular travel for either of them between Cape Town and their Transkei home. When two of their children fell ill, OZ managed, with financial help from her father's brother, to bring them to Cape Town for treatment. But then disaster struck again: the razing of their shack.

Now they were surely trapped. Their minimal resources were used to obtain a new site and build another wholly inadequate shack. But they did not stretch to allow even the purchase of bus tickets to return the two children to the Transkei where they preferred them to live because of the insecurity and threat of violence and fire in shack settlements, among other reasons: "We do not like the children to stay here . . . we are burning here . . . then if it [the violence] is bad again, we can easily move because we won't have children with us." Despite their wish for a stable domestic base in the Transkei, OZ was resigned to her urban entrapment:

I have no means to live there in the Transkei. . . . I cannot plan [even] to move away [from this shack area] when there is no way for me to move out. You can plan to move out of an area [only] when you have an option or means to achieve that. You cannot just move if you do not have money. . . . For this moment I am here because I am suffering. But my heart is there in the Transkei.

Our discussion has demonstrated something of the diversity of domestic unit construction among contemporary township residents. We have illustrated this diversity to indicate that there is a wide range of accommodation or shelter needs among South Africa's urban African population, primarily because of the varied nature of people's experiences of urbanization, their diverse incorporation into the wage labor market, and their differing orientations to urban life. The implication is that housing policy should take account of that diversity.

SOUTH AFRICAN HOUSING POLICY: WHAT IT OFFERS

In seeking to address the massive housing problem it has inherited—some 2 to 3 million poorer households in need of adequate shelter—the postapartheid government has indicated that, with a limited budget, it can contribute only one rand out of every four needed to house each family (Ministry of Housing 1997).[9] The balance must be contributed by households, through their own labor, from their savings, or from money they can borrow either informally or from a bank. A serviced site, possibly with a small core house, which is held in ownership by the recipient household, generally represents the maximum that can be built under the conditions of the present National Housing Subsidy Scheme.

The present policy framework for housing provision, known as the self-help or "incremental" approach, is not new in South Africa. In its current form, it is essentially a supply side approach, informed primarily by a concern to maximize the rate of housing delivery and streamline its administration—an approach which was promoted in the early 1980s by international aid agencies such as the World Bank. It was adopted by the reformist government of the late-apartheid period in an attempt to reduce its preeminent role in low-income housing provision and to promote political stability by encouraging a limited form of home ownership, the 99-year leasehold scheme, for legally resident urban Africans.[10] Simultaneously, the supply of serviced sites provided in urban areas was deliberately limited in order to reinforce the policy of influx control, before it was eventually abandoned as unsustainable in 1986. Both for this reason, and because people generally wanted more than just a serviced site, the policy was widely rejected by its intended recipients. However, as South Africa began to move toward its transition to a postapartheid order during the late 1980s, a clear consensus had emerged in policy circles that the appropriate approach to housing provision was a form of state-assisted self-help, based on full and unfettered "formal" home ownership.

In the years prior to, and immediately after, the first democratic elections held in 1994, the emerging housing policy framework was subject to extensive debate through the broadly based National Housing Forum (NHF). This body, which comprised representatives from a wide variety of "stakeholder" constituencies, was generally expected to provide a platform for the formulation of a viable and acceptable housing strategy for implementation under what was then emerging as the new political dispensation. Ultimately, however, the most important features of the policy framework formulated by the NHF (published as a White Paper policy discussion document in 1994) can be seen to bear a strong resemblance to earlier policy-making efforts and to reflect the interests of the private sector constituencies which had played a key role in its formation throughout the 1980s (Lupton and Murphy 1995).

The central component of the new policy framework is the National Housing Subsidy Scheme, initiated in March 1994. The scheme replaces all previously existing forms of state housing subsidy with a nationally uniform provision for a once-only capital grant of up to R16,000 ($2,631.40) to eligible applicants, graduated on a sliding scale according to household income. Eligibility is confined to South African citizens (or permanent residents) who are 21 or older, married or living with a long-term partner (or single with dependents), and earning a monthly household income of less than R3,500 ($575.40).

In principle, the subsidy is intended to be available in three forms: individual, institutional, and project-linked. The provision enables households to receive subsidies in their own right (the individual form), or collectively through the formation of housing cooperatives and nonprofit "social housing" agencies (the institutional form), as well as through participation in projects initiated by public or private sector development agencies (the project-linked form). In practice, given the conditions of instability and poverty under which many Africans currently live in urban areas, it is difficult to see how more than a relatively small minority would be able to take advantage of the individual and institutional options. For the great majority, therefore, access to the subsidy scheme will be obtained through the project-linked option.

A fundamental principle of the scheme is that the subsidy must be paid, not directly to households which qualify, but rather to the public, private or—where the necessary capacity exists—community-based developers who formulate appropriate project packages. Consequently, the choice of housing available to most poorer households will be constrained to what the market, the state, or community-based organizations are able, or willing, to offer within the limitations of the scheme.

While, at the level of rhetoric, a commitment has been made to provide a large number of units or sites—which are now termed "housing opportunities"— which are accessible to the poor, the central question which needs to be raised is: to what extent does the policy allow for housing provision that fits with the wide range of housing needs to be found among the poor?

HOUSING SUPPLY AND HOUSING NEED: POLICY FIT PROBLEMS

Household sizes, compositions, income, and domestic consolidation projects are diverse for a complex range of reasons, however, one factor—individual and household mobility—is particularly salient with regard to the issues of housing and housing policy.

A recent survey of Cape Town's African population revealed that 71 percent of all senior males and 62 percent of all senior females in the households surveyed were originally from rural areas (Mazur and Qangule 1995, Tables 4.1, 4.3). The survey also confirmed continuation of a long-established pattern of oscillating migration induced by apartheid legislation which had precluded permanent urban settlement by African people, particularly in the Western Cape. Given the present high levels of unemployment and job insecurity, particularly among Africans, this pattern seems to have become embedded in the risk-management strategies adopted, to greater or lesser effect, by many poor and working-class households.

One result is that many households are stretched in the sense of including, as members, individuals who live in different parts of the country for longer or shorter periods, and who contribute to, or draw from, a common resource pool. Such households constitute networks of domestic relations stretching across sometimes very considerable distances between urban centers and rural bases, which are held together by the shared perception of their members that they are, and ought to be, entailed in intensive reciprocity with one another. The aim of the reciprocity is twofold: to maintain the members of the household, and to develop a secure long-term resource base for them; in other words, to "consolidate" the household. Consequently, domestic groups are very fluid in both their composition and their size (Spiegel, Watson and Wilkinson 1996), and household fluidity and change have become common as people attempt in diverse ways to construct units that will offer them some long-term security. Moreover, such processes of change and recomposition are experienced not only by those households stretched between urban and rural areas, but also, frequently, by households which are essentially based within the city.

The dynamic nature of household formation has, however, gone largely unrecognized in current housing policy. The 1994 White Paper notes that many South Africans engage in a process of circulatory migration between urban and rural bases (Republic of South Africa 1994, 3.3.8), but it appears that the real complexities of household and individual mobility are either unacknowledged or misunderstood when it comes to policy formulation. Current housing policy, like its predecessors, implicitly assumes a model of urbanization known as the "urban transition model" (Zelinsky 1971). This model, now widely challenged in the literature (see Prothero and Chapman 1985; Standing 1985; Gugler 1991), assumes that households are stable in composition, and that members' ties with rural areas steadily diminish in intensity as they embed themselves in urban communities and secure reliable, income-generating employment; that is, as they steadily become more "modern." Continually changing household composition—a result of persistent movement both within cities and across regions—goes unrecognized because the model, based as it is on outmoded ideas about a unilinear process of modernization among people seeking permanent urban residence, cannot readily accommodate it.

The stretched and dynamic nature of many apparently urban households has fundamental implications for the nature of their housing needs. The focus of current housing policy on formal home ownership, and its incremental approach to housing provision, does not suit the needs of many people targeted by housing policy. One extreme is represented by people who might be described as successful rural consolidators and urban itinerants, such as the hostel dweller, BD (case 2). Their primary concern is to minimize expenditures on urban housing. They choose therefore to occupy whatever effectively free or cheap rental accommodations may be available—a hostel bed or informal rental of a backyard shack behind a formal township house. Yet, while both options are affordable, neither provides an adequate standard of shelter or sufficient space to allow the adequate development and maintenance of networks of reciprocity, which include accommodating family and friends. For such people, formal ownership of property in the city (with its recurrent property taxes and service charges), and necessary investment in extensions to the minimal core house which the current policy provides, would simply hinder realization of their domestic consolidation projects in rural areas. The failure within the present approach to consider support for appropriately sized yet inexpensive urban rental accommodations seriously constrains the housing options open to such rurally oriented urban residents.

The current policy focus on formal home ownership and incrementalism, together with its assumption that the private banking sector will provide credit to expand core units, also restricts the ability of certain kinds of households to obtain appropriate housing. Home ownership assumes that households can meet charges for infrastructure and service provision on a regular basis. In this regard, a recent policy document (Republic of South Africa 1995) suggests that households earning under R800 ($131.57) per month should be provided with sites and basic services (communal water standpipes, on-site sanitation, graded gravel roads, open stormwater drains and streetlights) and be charged for these at a rate of R35 to R50 ($5.76 to $8.22) per month. However, households such as those of PZ (case 4), who feed themselves by begging from neighbors and are unable to afford even the fare to reunite their families, are entirely unable to meet such financial demands. Nor are they a tiny minority. Many households are in precisely such situations: Mazur and Qangule (1995, 44) found that, in 1995, 41 percent of African households in Cape Town earned less than R800 ($131.57) a month, and more than a third were often unable to purchase their full food requirement. Moreover, the suggested levels of service and infrastructure charges would be difficult to meet even for households such as that of MN (case 2) with its two income earners (but nine dependents). Indeed, households such as GR's (case 1), despite having more than one formal-sector income earner, are also quite hard pressed to afford the costs associated with owning even an unsuitably small unit in a poor locality.

A further problem is that credit assistance from financial institutions is out of the question for all but those in GR's position (case 1), and even they must struggle. The kind of small loans they require are difficult to find and are subject to higher interest rates than those offered to middle-class South Africans. Moreover, many poorer townships have been redlined (designated as areas not worthy of loan support) by banks attempting to minimize their risks. It is no surprise, therefore, that only 6 percent of Cape Town's African households would consider approaching a formal financial institution for assistance (Mazur and Qangule 1995, Table 6.2).

Where households have no choice but to draw on their own resources to achieve adequate shelter, the maintenance of reciprocal networks becomes all important. However, the process is seriously constrained by the small size of both older formal township houses and newer units, which means that members of the household's social network can be accommodated only with great difficulty. MN's household (case 2), with its 11 residents, would certainly not have fitted into one of the completed houses currently on offer, and GR's family (case 1) had been forced by space considerations to move to a Khayelitsha house which nonetheless provided inadequate space, even for the eight permanently resident family members, let alone visitors. Significantly, the highest level of housing dissatisfaction in Mazur and Qangule's survey was recorded in the new formal township areas of Khayelitsha (1995, 34), and this corresponded closely with levels of overcrowding in the very small core houses provided there. The implicit assumption in both past and current housing policy—that families consist of stable nuclear households that grow only as children are born and then shrink again as they leave to establish their own units—which conform to the conventional notion of the household cycle, is clearly far from the realities of most African households.

Issues of housing tenure, cost, and size aside, a further and more general overall constraint to meeting household needs has been created by the very slow rate of delivery of serviced land and housing. Households such as that of MN (case 2) wish to gain access to better levels of service and shelter. Yet their relatively low incomes force them to wait in lengthy queues for state-subsidized sites that then turn out to be too small for their real needs—unless they can arrange adjacent sites and then incrementally expand their accommodations on the larger piece of land available to them.

Reasons for the slow delivery of housing are complex. They include lack of capacity on the part of implementing and delivery agencies and, until the requirements to establish "social compacts" with beneficiary communities were rescinded, difficulties in maintaining delivery program schedules. A particularly important stumbling block has been the assumption that project packaging and delivery can largely be left in the hands of private sector property developers and construction companies. While the approach has recently been modified to oblige local authorities to take increased responsibility for housing provision, they must still do so in partnership with the private sector. Yet the type of product that private sector–linked projects can deliver is inappropriate for households whose compositions are in flux and whose members' incomes are insecure and variable. The product cannot accommodate the high-risk and low-profit nature of low-income housing construction (Tomlinson 1995). One result is limited likelihood of large-scale private-sector housing delivery for the very poor, and houses of inappropriate form where they are offered.

CONCLUSION

There is clearly an inability on the part of housing policy makers to recognize, understand, and overcome the lack of fit between what is being provided and what is actually needed. One reason for this may be the administrative difficulties entailed by the delivery of many different housing products. In simpler words, it is possible to account for the expenditure of public funds within the limits of budget and subsidy policy when one can specify a number of core houses built and a further number of serviced sites prepared for settlement, particularly since easy inspection is feasible. To demonstrate success, there has to be a proven and appropriate number of households that will fit into the houses and sites provided. And so the households said to constitute the target population are normalized[11] as fixed in size and structure.

The tendency toward standardization may also be considered inherent in the incrementalist approach that currently prevails in South African public housing policy, influenced as it is by international privatization trends and a global, neoliberal, market-oriented ideology that emphasizes self-help and demands minimal involvement of the state in areas such as housing provision. Indeed, the language of current public housing policy in South Africa is that the aim is to provide "housing opportunities," rather than actual houses, and to leave the construction of dwellings to residents. The outcome is the provision of standard, small, serviced residential sites which take no cognizance of the survival strategies that result in domestic fluidity and are manifest in diverse household sizes and compositions. The further outcome for those households whose needs do not fit this model will, in some cases, be inadequate forms of shelter and, in other cases, actual homelessness.

People's housing needs and demands are extremely diverse. To attempt to meet them with any single-product delivery program will fail to achieve the intention of policy to provide adequate and appropriate shelter for all, through failing to cater to the diversity of housing demand that exists in the country. To succeed, policy makers must work against the structural tendency in bureaucratic institutions to demand normalization and standardization and to think innovatively to provide for diverse needs and changing or fluid circumstances.

REFERENCES

Cole, J. 1987. *Crossroads: The Politics of Reform and Repression*. Johannesburg: Raven Press.

Fast, H. 1995. "An overview of African Settlement in the Cape Metropolitan Area to 1990," working paper no. 53, Urban Problems Research Unit. Cape Town: University of Cape Town.

Gugler, J. 1991. "Life in a Dual System Revisited: Urban-Rural Ties in Enugu, Nigeria, 1961–1987." *World Development* 19, no. 5: 399–409.

Jones, S. 1993. *Assaulting Childhood: Children's Experiences of Migrancy and Hostel Life in South Africa*. Johannesburg: Witwatersrand University Press.

Lupton, M., and S. Murphy. 1995. "Housing Policy and Urban Reconstruction in South Africa." In *The Geography of Change in South Africa*, ed. Al Lemon, 143–67. New York: Wiley. This chapter provides an overview of the changing relationship between housing provision for blacks in South Africa and the wider geopolitical concerns of apartheid urban planners. It then examines competing contemporary housing policies and urban strategies within South Africa's establishment and alternative institutions. One set of local policy-formulating institutions shared a broad philosophy with the World Bank, based on a market-oriented approach to the resolution of the shelter crisis. Alternative approaches were forthcoming primarily from the nongovernmental-organization sector, focusing in some cases on housing credit cooperatives, and in other cases on state-directed public housing provision. The chapter concludes by noting the dominance of the market-oriented approach in post-1994 housing policy.

Mazur, R., and V. Qangule. 1995. *African Migration and Appropriate Housing Responses in Metropolitan Cape Town*. Cape Town: Report for the Western Cape Community-based Housing Trust.

Ministry of Housing. 1997. "Housing the Nation: Doing Justice to Delivery." Report. website http://www.polity.org.za/govdocs/reports/nation.html.

Prothero, R., and M. Chapman, eds. 1985. *Circulation in Third World Countries*. London:

Routledge and Keegan Paul. This is a collection of essays about circulatory movement in Third World countries, in which people move from their places of
residence for varying periods of time but ultimately return to them. Circulation
is defined as reciprocal flows of population, involving the interchange of individuals and small groups between places (origins and destinations) that frequently
are of differing size and function, such as villages and towns or regional centers
and primary cities. For people who circulate, the basic principle involved is territorial separation of obligations, activities, and goods. The two major influences
are security associated with the home or natal place (involving land, resources,
kin, presence of children, and shared values and beliefs) and more widespread
opportunities (employment, trade, services, entertainment, kin, and marriage partners). Authors claim that this is a grossly neglected aspect of population mobility.
Much of the literature on population mobility assumes a unidirectional transition
of population from rural to urban areas, otherwise termed migration.

Provincial Administration of the Western Cape. 1996. *Proposed Western Cape Housing
Strategy: Green Paper on Housing*. Provincial Administration of the Western
Cape: Department of Housing, Local Government and Planning.

Ramphele, M. 1993. *A Bed Called Home: Life in the Migrant Labor Hostels of Cape
Town*. Cape Town: David Philip. This book is the result of a study of social and
cultural life in Cape Town's migrant workers' hostels. Conducted in the later
1980s, the once all-male hostels had come to be inhabited by men, women, and
children. It exposes the dire effects of apartheid's legacy of constrained and hierarchically controlled use of space for domestic purposes. Such space was, however, still allocated only to men, and in the form of a bed space only, making
women and children critically dependent on men to "take them in." The book
explores the consequent gender dynamics, the multiple oppressions women-
migrants faced, and the strategies and tactics they used to deal with it.

Republic of South Africa. 1994. *White Paper on Housing*. Government Gazette no.
16178. Pretoria: Department of Housing.

———. 1995. *Urban Development Strategy of the Government of National Unity*. Ministry in the Office of the President, Government Notice no. 16679. Pretoria: Republic of South Africa.

Spiegel, A., V. Watson, and P. Wilkinson. 1996. "Domestic Diversity and Fluidity
Among Some African Households in Greater Cape Town." *Social Dynamics* 21,
no. 2:7–30.

———. 1999. "Speaking Truth to Power? Some Problems Using Ethnographic Methods
to Influence the Formulation of Housing Policy in South Africa." In *The Anthropology of Power: Empowerment and Disempowerment in Changing Structures*,
ed. A. Cheater, 175–91. London: Routledge. This chapter explores the problem
of using ethnographic methods to influence the making of policy. The aim of this
would be to engage with policy discourse to avoid the normalization or standardization of reality usually required by this mode of discourse. The chapter
takes, as its theoretical point of departure, Foucault's recognition of the ambiv-
alent, two-edged nature of the Enlightenment project, in which discourse and
practices of modernity inextricably couple questions of knowledge and power,
and Escobar's critique of development and social planning as key instruments of
governmentality. Housing policy (in the current context of South Africa) is part
of such a social planning effort, and the chapter considers the possibility that

ethnographically derived information on the diversity and complexity of housing need could influence housing policy formulation. The authors conclude that any attempt to "speak truth to power" is unlikely to be heard, given the present pre-occupation with the immediate practical tasks of housing project and program management.

Standing, G., ed. 1985. *Labor Circulation and the Labor Process*. London: Croom Helm.

Tomlinson, M. 1995. "From Principle to Practice: Implementor's View on the New Housing Subsidy Scheme." Research report no. 44, Social Policy Series. Johannesburg: Center for Policy Studies.

Watson, V., and M. McCarthy. 1998. "Rental Housing Policy and the Role of the Household Rental Sector: Evidence from South Africa." *Habitat International* 22, no. 1:49–56. A growing body of research on rental housing in developing countries has pointed to the fact that, while government and commercial investor provision of low-income rentals is at an all time low, the numbers of people in rented accommodations have increased steadily. In some cities this is now the dominant form of tenure. The bulk of this rental accommodation is in fact provided by the household sector, which tends to be unrecognized in policy terms. This paper examines attempts by both past and current South African governments to address housing problems and indicates how authorities have followed international trends in terms of attitudes to the provision of rental housing. The paper draws on a small-scale survey of households in South Africa to highlight the crucial role being played by the household rental sector and argues for its incorporation into current housing policy.

West, M. 1988. "Confusing Categories: Population Groups, National States and Citizenship." In *South African Keywords: The Uses and Abuses of Political Concepts*, ed. E. Boonzaier and J. Sharp, 100–10. Cape Town: David Philip.

Wilkinson, P. 1984. "The Sale of the Century? A Critical Review of Recent Developments in African Housing Policy in South Africa," paper no. 160 presented to Carnegie Conference. Cape Town.

World Bank. 1974. *Site and Services Project: A World Bank Report*. Washington D.C.: IBRD.

Zelinsky, W. 1971. "The Hypothesis of the Mobility Transition." *Geographical Review* 61:219–49.

NOTES

The material comes from a project conducted under the auspices of the Urban Problems Research Unit (UPRU), University of Cape Town. We acknowledge financial assistance from the Center for Science Development, but bear full responsibility for views expressed here. We also gratefully acknowledge the assistance of interviewers Anthony Mehlwana and Ayanda Canca.

1. The African National Congress is currently the ruling political party in South Africa. Founded in 1912, it spearheaded resistance to the previous apartheid government. The 1955 Freedom Charter committed the organization to a multiracial, social democratic future for South Africa. The Freedom Charter contained a set of demands relating to the meeting of basic needs (of which housing was one) and political and economic rights.

2. On the assumption that the majority of African men would be present in the

"white" urban areas only for the purposes of selling their labor, single-sex hostel, or dormitory, accommodation was built within the African townships, initially by the government and later by private sector companies as well.

3. "African" refers to a "population group" category, defined by the apartheid regime as comprising descendants of indigenous Bantu-speaking people, who were discriminated against most severely under that regime (West 1988). While the Population Registration Act—which introduced compulsory race classification in 1950—was repealed in 1991, the category remains in use in both official and popular discourse in order to recognize and address the legacy of its discriminatory effects.

4. Cape Town is currently a city of some 3 million people, of which the African population comprises approximately 850,000 people (although 1996 census information suggests that totals may be closer to 600,000). Of the balance of the population, the previously classified colored population totals some one and a half million people, and the white population 700,000 people. Under apartheid, the settlement patterns of the colored population were also fundamentally affected, but in rather different ways to that of the African population.

5. "Homelands" were labor reserves set aside for exclusive African occupation where, under the apartheid principle of "separate development," Africans should govern themselves according to their own traditions. Although all Africans (comprising over 80 percent of the population) were meant to be associated with one or another homeland, these areas constituted less than 13 percent of the whole of South Africa.

6. "Reformist" in this context refers to the efforts of the P.W. Botha government during the 1980s to introduce certain limited relaxations of the previously rigidly enforced system of controls on African urbanization—a series of reforms which were clearly intended to undermine widespread resistance to the apartheid regime within the urban African population.

7. Our interviews were coded A–G according to which of seven different types of housing area in the African areas of Cape Town they were conducted in. They were then numbered chronologically. We cite interview codes in the text to identify where the case material is located in the project files.

8. Indeed, recent evidence has indicated that people associate a move to a formal house with the purchase of new furniture and appliances.

9. 1 U.S. $ = R 7.6 at Nov. 20, 2000, rates of exchange.

10. Under apartheid, Africans were prohibited from owning land in what were deemed to be the white areas of South Africa, which included all the major cities. This prohibition was relaxed in 1978 when the Botha's government introduced the 99-year leasehold scheme at the urging of bodies like the Urban Foundation. The leasehold scheme was extended to Cape Town—where influx control was maintained more rigorously than elsewhere—in 1984, while full freehold property ownership for urban Africans was finally restored in 1986, after the abandonment of the influx control system.

11. Normalizing tendencies in state policy production are discussed in Spiegel, Watson, and Wilkinson (1999).

Index

less, 49–50; income ceiling, 10; number of homeless, 27; policies, viii, 43–47; providing adequate housing, 32–33; rent control, 16; reproducing homelessness, 54–57; rights to housing, 46; scope of problem, 47–50; secondary housing market, 51–53; social policy, 43–46; Social Service Act, 46; social-rented housing, 11; special housing, 53–54; student housing, 14; tenant rights, 47
Switzerland: gross national product, 85; owner-occupied dwellings, 85

Temporary Assistance to Needy Families (TANF), 201
Tenant rights, in Sweden, 47
Tertiary homelessness, in Australia, 167
Traditional homeless, in Denmark, 70

Unemployment: in Germany, 93, 98, 104; in Greece, 120; in relation to affordable housing, 18
United Kingdom. *See* England
United States: addiction, 204; Aid to Families with Dependent Children, 201; demographics, 204–5; domestic violence, 202–3; families, 205–8; Great Depression, 196–97; gross national product, 85; health care, 203; history, 196–97; housing supply, 198–99; McKinney Act, 207–9; mental illness, 203–4; policies, viii, 208–9; poverty, 197,

199–203, 206; public assistance, 200–203; rental housing, 197; Temporary Assistance to Needy Families, 201; Title I, 208–9
Urban consolidation, in South Africa, 293–97

Vagrants, 40–41; in Sweden, 54–55
Vandalism, 5

Welfare, ix; in Argentina, 217–19; in Australia, 190 n.8, 191–92 nn.21, 22; in Brazil, 240, 246–50; in Europe, 32, 33–34; in Germany, 90–91, 98–99; in Greece, 121; in Sweden, 42, 43–44; in the U.S., 197–99, 201–3
Welfare triangle, 135–36
Western Europe: overcrowding, 7; owner-occupied dwellings, 8; privatization of housing, 12; social-rented housing, 11
"Without defense," 40
Women, homeless: in Australia, 169, 172–73, 176; in England, 150; in Germany, 92–93, 101, 108; in Kenya, 272–73; in Sweden, 49–50, 52
Workers' Housing Association, 122–25, 129–31

Young adults: affordable housing for, 3, 18; in Australia, 170–71; housing needs, 6; impact of poor housing, 5; rental housing, 13, 19

About the Contributors

Ronald E. Ahnen is a Visiting Assistant Professor of Political Science at the University of the South, Sewanee, Tennessee.

Dragana Avramov is Director of the Population and Social Policy Consultants in Brussels, Belgium.

Volker Busch-Geertsema is a Senior Research Fellow for the Association for Social Planning and Social Research (Gesellschaft fuer Innovative Sozialforschung und Sozialplanung-GISS) in Bremen, Germany, and National Correspondent for Germany at the European Observatory on Homelessness.

Barbara Duffield is Director of Education at the National Coalition for the Homeless and serves on the board of the National Association for the Education of Homeless Children and Youth in the United States.

Katherine Duffy is a Principal Lecturer at De Montfort University in Leicester, England, and a member of the England Board of the European Anti-Poverty Network (EAPN).

Cindy Guillean is a Lecturer in English at Washtenaw Community College, Michigan.

Kagendo N. Mutua is an Assistant Professor of Special Education in the Department of Interdisciplinary Teacher Education at the University of Alabama.

Valerie Polakow is a Professor of Education at Eastern Michigan University.

Valeria Procupez is a graduate student of Anthropology at the Graduate Faculty of Political and Social Science at the New School for Social Research (New York City) in the United States and a Member of the Technical Advisory Board of MOI (Movimiento de Ocupantes e Inquilinos), a grassroots housing organization in Buenos Aires, Argentina.

Maria Carla Rodriguez is a Sociologist and Researcher at the Instituto Gino Germani, Facultad de Ciencias Socialies, Universidad de Buenos Aires and directs the area of Training, Research and Planning of MOI (Movimiento de Ocupantes e Inquilinos) in Argentina.

Anna Rubbo is an Associate Professor in the Department of Architecture, Planning and Allied Arts in Faculty of Architecture, University of Sydney in New South Wales, Australia.

Ingrid Sahlin is an Associate Professor in the Department of Sociology at Gothenburg University in Sweden and the Swedish Correspondent for the European Observatory on Homelessness.

Aristides Sapounakis is an Associate Professor in the Department of Regional Planning and Peripheral Development, University of Thesaly, Volos, and Director of the Research Institute "KIVOTOS" in Athens, Greece.

Andrew Spiegel is an Associate Professor and Head of the Department of Social Anthropology at the University of Cape Town in South Africa.

Tobias Børner Stax is a Researcher at The Danish National Institute of Social Research in Denmark.

Beth Blue Swadener is a Professor of Early Childhood Education at Arizona State University.

Vanessa Watson is an Associate Professor in the School of Architecture and Planning at the University of Cape Town in South Africa.

Peter Wilkinson is a Senior Lecturer in the School of Architecture and Planning at the University of Cape Town in South Africa.